Obligations *and* Omissions

MCGILL-QUEEN'S STUDIES IN GENDER, SEXUALITY, AND
SOCIAL JUSTICE IN THE GLOBAL SOUTH
Series editors: Marc Epprecht, Rebecca Tiessen, and Habiba Zaman

The twentieth century was a time of intense political, economic, social, and cultural change in the Global South. Continents were colonized, then decolonized. Millions of people relocated to cities, sought employment in new kinds of jobs, and experienced the effects of technological innovations and globalization. These changes have also reshaped the way that the people of Asia, Africa, and Latin America understand and experience gender and sexuality. In turn, gender roles and sexual ideologies have shaped political and economic changes.

The McGill-Queen's Studies in Gender, Sexuality, and Social Justice in the Global South series traces the changing conceptions of gender, sex, and sexuality in the developing world as well as the effects that these changes have had on politics, society, and social justice. Combining studies from a historical perspective with works focused on contemporary issues of social justice, this series welcomes publications from a variety of academic disciplines and backgrounds. At the heart of the series is a desire to raise awareness of forgotten histories and a range of topics including the intersections of gender, sexuality, and social justice in decolonization movements, sex work and questions about autonomy and agency, how gender constructs are shaped by economic, cultural, and religious conditions, and societies' responses to violence, activism, health, youth cultures, and global change. This series will also illuminate LGBTQ issues and transgender politics in different cultural contexts and the ways in which gender roles and sexual hierarchies are produced, reinforced, and challenged at the state and local level.

Obligations *and* Omissions

Canada's Ambiguous Actions on Gender Equality

Edited by Rebecca Tiessen and Stephen Baranyi

McGill-Queen's University Press
Montreal and Kingston • London • Chicago

© McGill-Queen's University Press 2017

ISBN 978-0-7735-5023-0 (cloth)
ISBN 978-0-7735-5024-7 (paper)
ISBN 978-0-7735-5025-4 (ePDF)
ISBN 978-0-7735-5026-1 (ePUB)

Legal deposit second quarter 2017
Bibliothèque nationale du Québec

Printed in Canada on acid-free paper that is 100% ancient forest free (100% post-consumer recycled), processed chlorine free

This book has been published with the help of a grant from the Canadian Federation for the Humanities and Social Sciences, through the Awards to Scholarly Publications Program, using funds provided by the Social Sciences and Humanities Research Council of Canada.

McGill-Queen's University Press acknowledges the support of the Canada Council for the Arts for our publishing program. We also acknowledge the financial support of the Government of Canada through the Canada Book Fund for our publishing activities.

LIBRARY AND ARCHIVES CANADA CATALOGUING IN PUBLICATION

Obligations and omissions : Canada's ambiguous actions on gender equality / edited by Rebecca Tiessen and Stephen Baranyi.

(McGill-Queen's studies in gender, sexuality, and social justice in the global south ; 1)
Includes bibliographical references and index.
Issued in print and electronic formats.

ISBN 978-0-7735-5023-0 (hardcover). – ISBN 978-0-7735-5024-7(softcover). – ISBN 978-0-7735-5025-4 (PDF). – ISBN 978-0-7735-5026-1 (EPUB)

1. Women's rights – Developing countries – Government policy – Canada. 2. Women's rights – Developing countries – International cooperation. 3. Sex discrimination against women – Developing countries – Government policy – Canada. 4. Sex discrimination against women – Developing countries. 5. Canada – Foreign relations – Developing countries. 6. Developing countries – Foreign relations – Canada. 7. Women – Legal status, laws, etc. – Developing countries. 8. Women – Government policy – Developing countries. I. Baranyi, Stephen, 1962–, editor II. Tiessen, Rebecca, 1970–, editor

HQ1237.5.D48O25 2017   305.4209172'4   C2017-900705-X
                                                       C2017-900706-8

This book was typeset by Sandra Friesen in 10.5/13 Minion.

Contents

Tables and Figures

Obligations *and* Omissions

Introduction

Canada's Ambiguous Actions on Gender Equality

Rebecca Tiessen and Stephen Baranyi

DISCOURSE, ACTION, AND OBLIGATIONS

On 15 April 2014, 276 girls were kidnapped from a secondary school in north-eastern Nigeria. The militant Islamist organization Boko Haram claimed responsibility for the kidnapping. In a video released after the kidnapping, the leader of the group, Abubakar Shekau, promised to sell the girls. When news of those events was picked up by global media, Western states offered assistance with intelligence, coordination, and negotiations to help the Nigerian government rescue the girls. On 6 May, John Baird, Canada's then minister of foreign affairs, announced that Canada had joined the United States and the United Kingdom in offering such assistance. Prime Minister Stephen Harper commented that the kidnapping was "truly a crime against innocent individuals" (as quoted by Payton 2014). Ottawa also supported the Brussels G7 Summit Declaration linking that incident to the global fight against terrorism (G7 2014).

Four months later, Prime Minister Harper used over a third of his speech to the United Nations General Assembly to highlight his government's contributions to the initiative on maternal, newborn, and child health (MNCH). "Saving the lives of the world's most vulnerable mothers, infants and children," he argued, "must remain a top global priority." Noting key actions taken since the 2010 G20 summit in Muskoka, he suggested that early childhood and maternal vaccination campaigns, nutrition programs, and other focused interventions have shown "remarkable progress," which we can "measure … in precious lives saved." Harper urged member states to increase their commitments to MNCH and announced that:

> Canada will financially support the World Bank's Global Financing Facility for Every Woman, Every Child. We urge other countries to do likewise because, to provide viable solutions to prevent the tragic death of women and children, we need to increase budget allocations on the part of both donors and the developing countries.

Those statements and others – such as then foreign minister Baird's speech to the UN in 2012 emphasizing the role that fighting homophobia should have in Canadian foreign policy – clearly positioned Canada as "a beacon of light" for the world. They offer revealing glimpses into Canada's official approach to girls, women, and gender at home and abroad under the Conservative governments led by Prime Minister Harper between 2006 and 2015. These commitments further speak to Canada's obligations under changing international development and security norms.

On the surface, the Conservative government's rhetoric and programmatic commitments to women's health and the protection of girls suggests a noteworthy path to the promotion of gender equality. Yet other actions taken between 2006 and 2015 point to a more ambiguous and even contradictory approach to gender equality. Among those is the discursive "erasure of gender equality" from Canada's official lexicon between 2010 and 2014 (Carrier and Tiessen 2013) and the instrumentalization of women for other foreign policy goals as the Conservatives increased spending on "hard" international measures like the military intervention in Afghanistan (Swiss 2012). Where Conservatives did engage – on MNCH, in the protection of women and girls in Afghanistan, or on forced child marriage – they pursued a paternalistic agenda framing women and girls in the Global South as victims needing "our help" – i.e., Western aid and security assistance. From a critical feminist standpoint, the Harper Conservatives missed opportunities to connect targeted interventions to the broader strategies required to challenge the patriarchal attitudes, unequal power relations, and economic structures that underpin gendered inequalities (Turenne-Sjolander and Trevenen 2010; Tiessen and Tuckey 2014; Tiessen and Carrier 2015).

To what extent was gender erased or instrumentalized in Canada's international practices under the Harper government? What factors (such as high-level political agency, bureaucratic resistance, and changing international norms) explain policy shifts under Conservative governments between 2006 and 2015? How do different strands of critical feminism help us make sense of those complex processes? Finally, what policy alternatives might the new Liberal-led government and future Canadian governments and other stakeholders consider in the promotion of gender equality, in addition to efforts to promote maternal and child health, and women's economic empowerment in contexts like the Democratic Republic of the Congo (DRC), or at the strategic level? These are the main questions explored in this collection.

In our introduction, we locate the volume in the literature characterizing Canada's approach to gender equality and on Othering within and outside of Canada since 2006, offering initial answers to the first two questions above. We then situate the book in the literature on Canada's international policies and national practices, offering initial responses to the question of why Canada's Conservatives have pursued their particular approach. We also begin reflecting on the diverse contributions that distinct critical feminist perspectives are making to scholarly debates on these issues.

Those issues are revisited in each chapter, focusing on key themes or on particular cases. In our conclusions, we summarize the policy recommendations set out in several chapters – such as pursuing more comprehensive approaches to MNCH or revitalizing institutional support for gender mainstreaming in Haiti. Drawing on influential work by Cornwall (2007) and Parpart (2014), the concluding chapter closes by exploring how theoretically informed analysis can shed light on more transformative possibilities beyond technical approaches to gender mainstreaming, including women's social agency, across the range of Canada's complex links to the Global South.

ERASING, INSTRUMENTALIZING, OR PRESERVING GENDER EQUALITY?

Prior to looking at different characterizations of approaches to women and gender under recent federal governments, it is important to recall major historical antecedents. Before the Conservatives took office in 2006, Canada had a fairly strong record of promoting women's rights and gender equality in the world. On the development side, the former Canadian International Development Agency (CIDA) adopted its first Women in Development (WID) guidelines in 1976; it established a WID directorate and adopted a WID policy in 1984. Ten years later that directorate became the WID and Gender Equity Division. In 1999, CIDA adopted its Policy on Gender Equality, committing itself to integrating gender equality as a cross-cutting priority in all its policies, programs, and projects (DFATD 2014a). In 2005, it adopted a Framework for Assessing Gender Equality Results to orient programming and evaluation. That document also laid the foundations for the evaluation of CIDA's Policy on Gender Equality in 2008.

A similar progression can be seen in the domain of international security, with Ottawa taking the lead in international campaigns against sexual and gender-based violence (SGBV) as part of its peacebuilding and human security agenda in the late 1990s, and playing a key role in the adoption of UN Security Council Resolution 1325 (UNSCR 1325) on Women, Peace and Security in 2000.

Those changes in Ottawa evolved in tandem with the evolution of international policy and practice in this domain, notably the shift from WID to gender and development (GAD) approaches and the gradual recognition of SGBV as a security issue in UN instruments. Foreign policy was also influenced by changing domestic norms and practices: by the adoption of the Canadian Charter of Rights and Freedoms in 1982, by the work of Status of Women Canada (SWC), and by the adoption of gender equality policies by other departments such as the former Department of Indian and Northern Affairs in the late 1990s. Yet even under Liberal governments during that era, analysts noted enduring gaps between policy commitments and actual practices on gender equality (Turenne-Sjolander, Smith and Stienstra 2003). After 9/11, they also noted a marked shift, in Ottawa as well as in other Western capitals, towards using the protection of women and girls to justify priorities like the consolidation of friendly governments in fragile and conflict-affected states (FCAS) like Afghanistan (Powell and Baranyi 2005).

Those concerns became more pronounced after Prime Minister Harper's first election in 2006. Within a few years, an ideological shift emerged as the government began removing references to "gender equality" in official correspondence and reports, reframing the issue as "equality between men and women" (Carrier and Tiessen 2013). CIDA's gender equality funds were being wound down in important partner countries and gender equality spending (by whatever name) was decreasing more than it had during the last years of Liberal rule (Swiss 2012). Critics argued that the instrumentalization of women and girls' vulnerabilities to justify other foreign policy priorities was becoming more pronounced in contexts like Afghanistan (Farhoumand-Simms 2008; Carrier and Tiessen 2013). Under the Conservatives, Canada pursued superficial approaches to protecting women and girls (for example on UNSCR 1325 or childhood marriage) instead of addressing the deeper attitudes and structures reproducing gender inequalities (Tiessen and Tuckey 2014). Successes such as those in the commitments leading up to UNSCR 1325 were marred by delays in the production of Canada's National Action Plan for the implementation of UN Security Council Resolutions on Women, Peace and Security. The Canadian National Action Plan was released five years later than other donor country plans, and the cause of the delay was blamed on editorial changes required to remove references in the document to "gender equality."

Between 2006 and 2015, Canadians witnessed a departure from previous commitments to gender equality. In addition to the challenges noted above, the Harper Conservatives cut $5 million to SWC funding upon entering office in 2006 and later shut twelve of the sixteen SWC regional offices. Additional funding cuts to SWC followed in 2010 when women's organizations were no longer able to fund advocacy or research work on women's issues. Rather, women's groups were now mandated to restrict their work to training and direct services to women. The introduction in 2014 of Bill C-36, titled *Protection of Communities and Exploited Persons Act,* by then justice minister Peter MacKay was widely criticized for its treatment of sex trade workers: the criminalization of sex trade acts and the precarious and increasingly dangerous situations sex trade workers would find themselves in as a result of this bill. Kate Grantham elaborates on the implications of Bill C-36 in her chapter in this volume.

Between 2006 and 2015, Canada's ranking on the Global Gender Gap Report, conducted by the World Economic Forum, slipped from fourteenth place in 2006 to thirtieth place in 2015 (WEF 2015). The data compiled for this ranking measures access to health care, economic inequality, limited political participation, and access to education. Advocates for women's rights and gender equality also criticized the Harper government's decision to vote down motion M-444: A National Action Plan to Address Violence Against Women, which recommended, among other things, an inquiry into missing and murdered Indigenous women as well as a national child care plan. Former prime minister Harper was very clear in his decision to not hold an inquiry into missing and murdered Indigenous women, noting that this issue was not "high on the radar" of the Conservative government, as Smith elaborates in chapter 11. Other evidence of limited support for the specific gender issues faced by Indigenous women in Canada includes the 2015 funding cuts to the Quebec Native Women's Association and the Native Women's Centre.

Although Canada suffered a number of setbacks on the gender equality front under the Harper Conservatives, there were also small signs of opportunity and evidence of ongoing commitments to promote gender equality at some levels of government. In fact, Liam Swiss and Jessica

Barry's chapter in this collection reminds us that all was not lost on the gender equality front in Canada. New commitments to program reporting on gender equality within Canada and among international donors in the Development Assistance Committee (DAC) point to a clear indication that measuring gender equality matters. Swiss and Barry's chapter shows that the reporting of funds spent on gender equality programming showed little deviation from previous government spending. Their chapter raises questions, however, about how gender equality is coded during reporting stages, particularly in light of the broader critiques addressed throughout this book around discursive challenges, reduced domestic funding, and other missed opportunities.

Furthermore, careful analysis of gender equality program efforts on the ground in Haiti (Baranyi and Binette, in this volume, chapter 10) point to examples of resilience and dedication to promoting women's rights and gender equality in spite of broader signals from the Harper Conservatives. For example, one could observe ongoing commitments to gender equality on the part of dedicated government staff. In CIDA, the evaluation of the Gender Equality Policy went ahead in 2008 and led to the adoption of a robust Gender Equality Action Plan (CIDA 2010). Following the merger of CIDA into the Department of Foreign Affairs, Trade and Development (DFATD) in 2013, references to gender equality began to make a comeback, with the new department's website stating that "gender equality or equality between women and men" remained a cross-cutting priority in the government's international practices (DFATD 2014b; Tiessen and Carrier 2015). Canada supported the Because I Am a Girl campaign and introduced the UN resolution that led to an annual International Day of the Girl being declared in 2012.

On the domestic front, despite substantial cuts to its programs and regional offices, SWC introduced the Gender-Based Analysis Plus (GBA+) framework in 2009 (Status of Women Canada 2013). The document aims to improve understanding among Canadian officials of the causes and consequences of gender inequality, combined with other factors (class, religion, race, etc.), which intersect with gender to perpetuate inequality. The GBA+ framework was adopted by some Canadian federal government departments. For example, the Department of Aboriginal Affairs and Northern Development Canada adopted a Gender-based Analysis Policy that required that gender equality be integrated into all of the department's work (AANDC 2013).

Replicating comparative research conducted in the post-9/11 era (Powell and Baranyi 2005), Paducel and Salahub (2011) observed that after the Harper Conservatives took office, Canada's gendered practices in FCAS remained average compared to that of other OECD donors: not exemplary but hardly the worst. Though CIDA had not officially adopted its own policy or budget lines to promote gender equality in FCAS, it maintained policy levers and creative gender programming in some countries. Based on the North-South Institute's earlier case studies, the authors observed that CIDA had developed substantial women-focused projects and integrated gender equality as a key objective of large projects in Afghanistan (Farhoumand-Sims 2008) and in Haiti (Salahub 2008). On that basis, the authors suggested that progress towards gender equality could happen in practice even when policy frames were ambiguous or weak. Yet they cautioned that without greater institutionalization, those gains could be reversed, especially in a whole-of-government environment where security or commercial interests could trump gender equality.[1]

Those ambiguous actions and enduring commitments speak to Canada's obligations to promote gender equality as one of its core priorities at home and abroad. Yet as suggested by the first generation of critical feminist scholarship on post-9/11 and post-2006 shifts, the full picture of policy and practice is much more complex, with evidence of systematic challenges and occasional – though highly limited – successes.

ORGANIZATION OF THE VOLUME

This volume adds much-needed data and analysis to our understanding of that messy picture. The book is divided into two parts, with part 1 focusing on themes and part 2 exploring specific cases. In so doing, the book invites the reader to move from broad trends in terms of data and thematic focus (spending trends, maternal health, lgbti, sex trade, and human trafficking, and disabilities) to more specific case studies in part 2, which provide more empirically based analyses of the problematic construction of gender in specific places. The case studies in this collection were selected to ensure representation across regions and to provide evidence of effects in the Conservative government-assigned priority countries, or "countries of focus." Afghanistan, Burkina Faso, the DRC, and Haiti were all identified as countries of focus, representing four out of the twenty-five development countries of focus where Canada would increase its proportion of bilateral assistance from 80 to 90 per cent (GAC 2016). Although Egypt was not deemed a country of focus, it is listed as one of DFATD's "development partners," and Egypt has served as an important economic and diplomatic partner country for Canada. The final case study provided in this volume represents an important North American example of gendered disadvantage, inequality of opportunity, and "Othering": Indigenous women in Canada. Canada's ambiguous efforts to promote gender equality and women's rights abroad came under increasing scrutiny as the 2015 UN Human Rights Committee slammed Canada for its involvement in mining projects around the world and the poor track record on gender pay gaps within the country, as well as high rates of violence against women, particularly among minority and Indigenous women. In these chapters we document some of the small gains and the broader challenges in the promotion of gender equality during the Harper Conservative era.

The first chapter in part 1, by Swiss and Barry, revisits Canadian spending on gender equality abroad. It reaches the conclusion that although spending had decreased under recent Conservative governments, the decrease was not as significant as the shifting discourse and funding cuts domestically may have signalled. Swiss and Barry attribute this to bureaucratic resistance, and also highlight unclear "gender" coding methods adopted both in Canada and by the broader DAC. The chapter by Julia Keast offers a more pointed, updated critique of the MNCH initiative as a missed opportunity for the promotion of gender equality and women's rights. Marc Epprecht and Stephen Brown's chapter sheds light on Ottawa's ambiguous approach to lesbian, gay, bisexual, transgender, and intersex rights (lgbti)[2] abroad. Kate Grantham documents the discursive challenges of Canada's efforts to address the sex trade and human trafficking under the Harper Conservatives. The chapter by Deborah Stienstra examines the rights of persons with disabilities, offering deep reflections on the significance of intersectionality.

In the second half of the book, Paula Butler deconstructs the Conservatives' support for the I Am a Girl campaign in relation to Canada's economic activities in mining operations in Burkina Faso. Julia Hartviksen and Rebecca Tiessen continue along the theme of gender inequality in mining communities by analyzing essentializing language and programmatic commitments in artisanal small-scale mining in the DRC. The chapter by Sarah Tuckey deepens our understanding of how the protection of women was instrumentalized by the Canadian Provincial Reconstruction Team in Kandahar, just as the chapter by Nadia Abu-Zahra, Ruby Dagher, Nicole Brandt, and Khalid Suliman reveals the contradictions of Canada's responses to women's rights under Egyptian governments/regimes since the Arab Spring. The chapter by Stephen Baranyi and Shantelle Binette shows how rich gender equality programming was maintained in Canada's large cooperation portfolio with Haiti, yet it provides nuance to that assessment by flagging the loss of instruments like the Kore Fanm women's fund and other missed opportunities.

Finally, Heather Smith's chapter provides a new look at the gaps between the Harper government's rhetoric against SGBV abroad and its responses to violence against Indigenous women in Canada.

THEORIZING THE POLITICS OF CHANGE AND CONTINUITY

These chapters add an important dimension to our understanding of gendered structural inequality and the need for transformation in policy and practice in a global world comprised of multiple forms of marginalization and inequalities. What emerges is a more nuanced reading of the Conservative government's ambiguous record in this domain, particularly in "othered" communities within and beyond Canada's borders. Piecing together that puzzle is also a starting point to explaining the social construction of Conservative governments' practices on gender, from different theoretical perspectives. As such it provides a snapshot of a particular approach shaped by the Harper Conservatives between 2006 and 2015, and reflected in discourse, aid spending, program commitments, and "development" priorities.

In Canada as in some other Western countries, there has been a "veritable renaissance" (Brown 2012, 3) of scholarship on aid, foreign policy, and global dynamics over the past thirty years. As observed by Black and Smith over two decades ago (1993), a feature of that renaissance has been the diversification of theoretical perspectives beyond the classical frames of realism, liberal internationalism, and Marxism. Neo-realists such as Dewitt and Kirton (1984) and Nossal (1985) drew on new institutional theories to rethink the relations between structure and agency – including the role of senior bureaucrats, domestic pressure groups, and international regimes in policy formation. Neo-Gramscians such as Neufeld (1995) drew on the work of Cox (1987) to re-examine Canada's foreign policies in light of changing international ideas, relations of power, and the globalization of production. Canadian feminists such as Keeble and Smith (1999), inspired by the global challenges to the "male-stream" study of international relations, shed new light on the gendered nature of Canada's global positioning.

Feminist scholarship expanded and converged with postcolonial studies of North-South relations. Drawing on Mohanty, Russo, and Torres's (1991) and Spivak's (1999) influential works on the othering of women from the Global South by institutions from the Global North (including by some women's rights activists), a new generation of feminist scholars is probing the intersection of neo-colonialism and patriarchy, and how these forces shape Canada's role in the world. In keeping with the central concerns of post-colonial studies, they are exploring how Canada's Liberal and Conservative governments have socially constructed women (and children) from the Global South as victims requiring Canada's charity and protection – rather than as the agents of rights-based social transformation (Turenne-Sjolander, Smith, and Stienstra 2003; Turenne-Sjolander and Trevenen 2010; Barnett 2012). Some argue that this framing harks back to the earlier era of WID (Clark-Kazak 2013). They analyze how portraying women and girls in an essentialist[3] and paternalistic manner sells to individual donors and appeals to conservative audiences, in Canada and in other countries in the Global North (Carpenter 2005; Dogra 2011). They situate such practices in the context of Northern countries' "civilizing mission," dating back to the colonial era (Valentin and Meinert 2009).

In Canada, that analysis resonates with critiques of internal colonialism, namely the domination of Indigenous peoples by settler institutions. As stated by Idle No More spokesperson Chief Spence: "The attitudes and treatment towards our Indigenous Peoples needs to change." In speaking specifically about the Harper Conservative government, Chief Spence went on to say, "We can no longer have a paternalistic relationship and be dictated to" (Spence, as quoted in the *National Post* 2013). It also converges with the growing activist and scholarly literature on "neo-colonial" (Grinspun and Shamsie 2010), "ugly" (Engler 2012), and "black" (Denault 2013) Canadian activities abroad – particularly in the extractive sector.

Those theoretical emphases on the discursive construction of helpless women and girls, and the instrumentalization[4] of that discourse, as well as the neo-colonial continuities that they reproduce, are reflected in many of the chapters in this volume. Keast's deconstruction of Ottawa's championing of the MNCH initiative and Butler's critique of the I Am a Girl campaign; Hartviksen and Tiessen's critique of the Harper government's gendered promotion of extractive capitalism in the DRC; and Smith's critique of Ottawa's record on SGBV against Indigenous women in Canada – are all informed by that strand of postcolonial feminism.

Epprecht and Brown stretch that frame by looking at lgbti rights and by peering inside parts of the state – at the tensions between different wings of the Conservative Party over this issue, and at how the "norm entrepreneurship" of politicians like Baird fits into a broader strategy to show Canadians the more compassionate face of Canadian conservatism. By looking at the social construction of Canada's approach to persons with disabilities abroad, Stienstra also challenges feminists to bring intersectional[5] and institutional analysis more fully into their work on Canada's international policies.

Others venture further beyond the theoretical and methodological comfort zone of much of Canadian postcolonial feminist scholarship. This introduction, the chapter by Swiss and Barry, and the piece by Baranyi and Binette all look beyond discourse, and at material practices such as gender equality spending and the gendered results of programming, overall and in significant cases like Haiti. Building on recent work by Tiessen (2015), they begin explaining the resistance that gender activists in the civil service have deployed in the face of Conservative Party agendas. They also draw our attention to the countervailing influence of international norms, notably the commitments to a gender and development (as opposed to a WID) approach codified in some UN and OECD DAC agreements to which Canada adheres (*de jure*). Such empirically rooted, dialectical analysis, informed by the critical international political economy of Cox in the case of Baranyi and Binette, leads them to perceive more room for agency by Canadian officials and their transnational allies – in resisting conservative policy shifts and even in extending spaces for the construction of emancipatory alternatives.

Instead of trying to resolve the debate between different strands of critical and postcolonial feminist theory, this book invites dialogue across perspectives. Some years ago, Beier and Wylie suggested that "one of the contributions of critical approaches in the broader discipline of IR [international relations] has been to show that the world is very much messier than the comparatively tidy and parsimonious theories of the mainstream might sometimes make it seem" (Beier and Wylie 2010, xiv). We encourage the extension of that idea to postcolonial perspectives, which offer a one-dimensional (as opposed to dialectical) reading of the world. We also embrace the call for methodological and theoretical hybridity expressed by some critical thinkers (Salter and Mutlu 2012; Balzacq 2010).

This openness to diversity and hybridity allows the authors to propose a variety of policy options for future Canadian governments and other stakeholders. It also brings the questions of more transformative possibilities, as well as the transnational agency that could socially construct those alternatives, back into the centre of the conversation in Canada and beyond.

This book was written at a pivotal moment: the end of nearly ten years of Conservative governments under the leadership of Stephen Harper and the start of a Liberal government under the leadership of Prime Minister Justin Trudeau. At the time of writing, the Liberals have been in power for a short time, yet there are clear signs of a distinct departure from the previous government in the actions and messages shared within and outside Canada. Among the first steps taken by the Liberal

Party was the nomination of a cabinet comprised of 50 per cent women, along with other diverse groups represented in this newly formed leadership. A promise to conduct an inquiry into the missing and murdered Indigenous women in the country came soon after, with the new leader of the Conservative Party and the Leader of the official opposition – Rona Ambrose – taking a distinctly different tack than did Harper by throwing her support behind the inquiry. Other gestures of a new approach to Canada's international commitments have been signalled through Prime Minister Trudeau's speeches to the international community, wherein he has declared that "Canada is back." This rhetoric offers a glimpse into the kind of path the Liberal Party may pursue in the years ahead – a path that may or may not signal a promise to (re)claim Canada's leadership role in the promotion of gender equality.

The critical analysis of gender equality discourse and programmatic commitments provided in this collection offer important insights into Canada's diminished role in the promotion of gender equality between 2006 and 2015. They also provide theoretical insights and policy recommendations that could inform the efforts of future Canadian governments to pursue a renewed gender equality strategy. Yet as underscored in the final chapter, this effort is too complex and important to be left to one government. All stakeholders, including academics and students, have a role to play in renewing Canada's policies and practices in this domain.

NOTES

1 Those findings are consistent with the study, by O'Connell and Harcourt (2011), of OECD donors' gender programming in FCAS. Looking at trends rather than comparing donors, they concluded that despite policy advances and solid programming in areas like women's electoral participation and small-scale enterprises, many Western donors missed opportunities to nurture comprehensive changes to gendered power relations – from the household to the economy and the state. Those authors also cautioned us against purist analyses of gender in international development cooperation that assumed a priori, for example, that support for women's participation in elections is inherently non-transformative.

2 Epprecht and Brown purposely opt for the lowercase acronym to reflect "discrete components of the struggle under a convenient, nonessentializing umbrella term" (chapter three, in this volume).

3 The term "gender essentialism" is used to describe the stereotypes and societal expectations of men and women and to analyze how they are reinforced through discourse, policy and practice. Charli Carpenter's (2005) examination

of gender essentialism, for example, claims that gender-stereotypical assumptions about women are used to create artificial divisions between women and men along the corresponding lines of peace-makers versus war-makers respectively. These simplistic divisions and artificial binaries (divisions that are artificially constructed and/or reinforced through simplistic associations) limit are ability to examine the multiple roles and contributions of both men and women to violence and security (Tiessen 2015).

4 Swiss (2012) used the term "instrumentalization" to refers to the way that women – or programs designed to meet women's needs – can become instruments for quite distinct development and/or security objectives. For example, he argues that in Afghanistan after 9/11, Canadian governments used women's vulnerability to violence discrimination to justify military and other programs aimed at protecting women from those threats. He also argues that the fundamental goals of such projects either subordinate or actually undermine human rights, gender equality and that project of redressing social injustices that affect women (and others).

5 Drawing on the work of Crenshaw (1991), McCall (2005), and Cho et al. (2013), Stienstra (in this volume) notes that intersectionality "suggests that the experiences of women, men, girls and boys are shaped not only by their identities or social locations, but also by their interactions with social structures including sexism, ableism, racism, colonization and capitalism." Intersectionality theory highlights "diversity and difference … privilege and oppression in differing experiences; highlights the ways that systems and structures over time and through space create and reinforce those inequalities; and (helps us) explore reflexively our own positions as researchers."

REFERENCES

Aboriginal Affairs and Northern Development Canada (AANDC). 2013. "Working Guide on Gender-Based Analysis." Accessed 16 October. https://www.aadnc-aandc.gc.ca/eng/1100100028541/1100100028545.

Balzacq, Thierry. 2010. *Securitization Theory: How Security Problems Emerge and Dissolve*. London: Taylor & Francis.

Barnett, Michael. 2012. "International Paternalism and Humanitarian Governance." *Global Constitutionalism* 1, no. 3: 485–521.

Beier, J. Marshall, and Lana Wylie. 2010. "Introduction: What's So Critical about Canadian Foreign Policy?" In *Canadian Foreign Policy in Critical Perspective*, edited by J. Marshall Beier and Lana Wylie, xi–xix. Don Mills, ON: Oxford University Press.

Beneria, Lourdes, Günseli Berik, and Maria Floro. 2003. *Gender, Development and Globalization: Economics as If All People Mattered*. New York: Routledge.

Black, David, and Heather Smith. 1993. "Notable Exceptions? New and Arrested Directions in Canadian Foreign Policy Literature." *Canadian Journal of Political Science* 26, no. 4: 745–74.

Brown, Stephen. 2012. "Introduction: Canadian Aid Enters the Twenty-First Century." In *Struggling for Effectiveness: CIDA and Canadian Foreign Aid*, edited by Stephen Brown, 3–24. Montreal and Kingston: McGill-Queen's University Press.

Canadian International Development Agency (CIDA). 2010. "Gender Equality Action Plan." Accessed 1 October 2014. http://www.acdi-cida.gc.ca/acdi-cida/ acdi-cida.nsf/eng/nad-101311435-kpf.

Carpenter, Charli. 2005. "Women, Children and Other Vulnerable Groups." *International Studies Quarterly* 49, no. 2: 295–334.

Carrier, Krystal, and Rebecca Tiessen. 2013. "Women and Children First: Maternal Health and the Silence of Gender in Canadian Foreign Policy." In *Canada in the World: Perspectives on Canadian Foreign Policy*, edited by H. Smith, and C. Turenne-Sjolander, 183–200. Oxford: Oxford University Press.

Cho, Sumi, Kimberlé Williams Crenshaw, and Leslie McCall. 2013. "Toward a Field of Intersectionality Studies: Theory, Applications, and Praxis." *Signs: Journal of Women in Culture and Society* 38, no. 4: 785–810.

Clark-Kazak, Christina. 2013. "From 'Children-in-Development' to Social Age Mainstreaming in Canada's Development Policy and Programming? Practice, Prospects and Proposals." Paper presented at the Canadian Foreign Aid workshop, Halifax, Nova Scotia, 22–23 September.

Cornwall, Andrea. 2007. "Introduction: Repositioning Feminisms in Gender and Development." *IDS Bulletin* 35, no. 4: 1–10.

Cox, Robert. 1987. *Production, Power and World Order: Social Forces in the Making of World History*. New York: Columbia University Press.

Crenshaw, Kimberlé Williams. 1991. "Mapping the Margins: Intersectionality, Identity Politics, and Violence against Women of Color." *Stanford Law Review* 43, no. 6: 1241–99.

Denault, Alain. 2013. *Noir Canada: Pillage, corruption et criminalité en Afrique*. Montréal: Les éditions ecosociete.

Dewitt, David, and John Kirton. 1984. *Canada as a Principal Power: A Study in Foreign Policy and International Relations*. Toronto and New York: John Wiley & Sons.

Department of Foreign Affairs and International Trade (DFAIT). 2010. *Building Peace and Security for All: Canada's Action Plan for the Implementation of United Nations Security Council Resolutions on Women, Peace and Security*. Department of Foreign Affairs and International Trade.

Department of Foreign Affairs, Trade and Development (DFATD). 2014a. "Gender Equality: Chronology, Selected Key Dates." Department of Foreign Affairs, Trade and Development.

– 2014b. "Gender Equality." Department of Foreign Affairs, Trade and Development. Accessed 1 October 2014. http://www.international.gc.ca/development-developpement/priorities-priorites/ge-es/index.aspx?lang=eng.

– 2014c. *2012–2013 Progress Report: Canada's Action Plan for the Implementation of United Nations Security Council Resolutions on Women, Peace and Security*. Department of Foreign Affairs, Trade and Development. Accessed 10 July 2014. http://www.international.gc.ca/START-GTSR/women_report_2012-2013_rapport_femmes.aspx.

Dogra, Nandita. 2011. "The Mixed Metaphor of 'Third World Woman': Gendered Representations by International Development NGOs." *Third World Quarterly* 32, no. 2: 333–48.

– 2012. *Representations of Global Poverty: Aid, Development and International NGOs*. London: L.B. Tauris.

Dunn, Máiréad, Sara Humphreys, and Fiona Leach. 2006. "Gender Violence in Schools in the Developing World." *Gender and Education* 18, no. 1: 75–98.

Engler, Yves. 2012. *The Ugly Canadian: Stephen Harper's Foreign Policy*. Halifax: Fernwood Publishing.

Farhoumand-Sims, Cheshmak. 2008. *Canada's Contribution to Gender Equity in Afghanistan: Canadian Development Report 2008 – Fragile States or Failing Development?* Ottawa: North-South Institute, 25–48.

Global Affairs Canada (GAC). 2016. "Where We Work in International Development." Accessed 18 November 2016. http://www.international.gc.ca/development-developpement/countries-pays/index.aspx?lang=eng.

Grinspun, Ricardo, and Yasmine Shamsie. 2010. "Empire's Apprentice: Canada in Latin America." *NACLA Report on the Americas*. May/June.

Group of Seven (G7) Secretariat. 2014. *G7 Leaders' Communiqué, June 2014 – Foreign Policy*. Brussels, Belgium: Group of Seven, 5 June. Accessed 1 October 2014. http://www.international.gc.ca/g8/g7_brussels_communique-g7_bruxelles_communique.aspx?lang=eng.

Kabir, Naila. 2003. *Gender Mainstreaming in Poverty Eradication and the Millennium Development Goals: A Handbook for Policy-Makers and Other Stakeholders*. Commonwealth Secretariat, International Development Research Centre, Canadian International Development Agency.

Keeble, Edna, and Heather Smith. 1999. *(Re)defining Traditions: Gender and Canadian Foreign Policy*. Halifax: Fernwood Publishing.

Leach, Fiona, and Sara Humphreys. 2007. "Gender Violence in Schools: Taking the 'Girls as Victims' Discourse Forward." *Gender and Development* 15, no. 1: 51–65.

McCall, Leslie. 2005. "The Complexity of Intersectionality." *Signs: Journal of Women in Culture and Society* 30, no. 3: 1771–800.

Mohanty, Chandra Talpade, Ann Russo, and Lourdes Torres. 1991. *Third World Women and the Politics of Feminism*. Indiana: Indiana University Press.

National Post. 2013. "Fresh Road and Rail Blockade Threats as Chaos and Confusion Mar First Nations Meeting." *National Post*, 11 January.

Neufeld, Mark. 1995. "Hegemony and Foreign Policy Analysis: The Case of Canada as a Middle Power." *Studies in Political Economy* 48: 7–49.

Nossal, Kim Richard. 1985. *The Politics of Canadian Foreign Policy*. 1st ed. Scarborough: Prentice Hall.

O'Connell, Helen, and Wendy Harcourt. 2011. *Conflict-Affected and Fragile States: Opportunities to Promote Gender Equality and Equity?* UK DFID. Accessed 17 October 2014. http://www.gsdrc.org/docs/open/CAFS_gender_study2011.pdf.

Paducel, Anca, and Jennifer Salahub. 2011. *Gender Equality and Fragile States Policies and Programming: A Comparative Study of the OECD/DAC and Six OECD Donors*. Ottawa: North-South Institute. Accessed 11 September 2014. http://dl.dropbox.com/u/41702390/PaducelandSalahubGEinFS.pdf.

Parpart, Jane. 2014. "Exploring the Transformative Potential of Gender Mainstreaming in International Development Institutions." *Journal of International Development* 26, no. 3: 382–95.

Payton, Laura. 2014. "Nigeria Offered Canadian Gear to Help Search for Kidnapped Girls." *CBC News*. 7 May.

Porter, Ann. 2012. "Neo-Conservatism, Neo-liberalism and Canadian Social Policy: Challenges for Feminism." *Canadian Woman Studies* 29, no. 3: 19–31.

Powell, Kristiana, and Stephen Baranyi. 2005. *Fragile States, Gender Equality and Aid Effectiveness: A Review of Donor Perspectives*. Report for the Gender Equality Division of the Canadian International Development Agency. Ottawa: North-South Institute. Accessed 11 September 2014. http://www.nsi-ins.ca/wp-content/uploads/2012/10/2005-Fragile-States-Gender-Equality-and-Aid-Effectiveness-A-Review-of-Donor-Perspectives.pdf.

Prinsloo, Sakkie. 2006. "Sexual Harassment and Violence in South African Schools." *South African Journal of Education* 26, no. 2: 305–18.

Salahub, Jennifer. 2008. "Canada, Haiti, and Gender Equality in a 'Fragile State.'" In *Fragile States or Failing Development? Canadian Development Report 2008*, edited by Stephen Baranyi and Roy Culpepper, 49–68. Ottawa: The North-South Institute.

Salter, Mark, and Can Mutlu, eds. 2012. *Research Methods in Critical Security Studies*. London/New York: Routledge.

Smith, Heather, and Claire Turenne-Sjolander. 2013. "Conversations without Consenus: Internationalism under the Harper Government." In *Canada in the World: Internationalism in Canadian Foreign Policy*, edited by Heather Smith and Claire Turenne-Sjolander. Don Mills, ON: Oxford University Press, xiii–xxvii.

Spivak, Gayatri. 1999. *A Critique of Postcolonial Reason: Toward a Critique of the Vanishing Present*, Cambridge, MA: Harvard University Press.

Status of Women Canada. 2013. *An Overview of GBA+ in the Federal Government*. Status of Women Canada.

Swiss, Liam. 2012. "Gender, Security, and Instrumentalism: Canada's Foreign Aid in Support of National Interest?" In *Struggling for Effectiveness: CIDA and Canadian Foreign Aid*, edited by Stephen Brown, 135–58. Montreal and Kingston: McGill-Queen's University Press.

Tiessen, Rebecca. 2015. "Gender Essentialism in Canadian Foreign Aid Commitments to Women, Peace and Security." *International Journal* 70, no. 1: 84–100.

Tiessen, Rebecca, and Sarah Tuckey. 2014. "Loose Promises and Vague Reporting: Analysing Canada's National Action Plan and Reports on Women, Peace and Security." In *Worth the Wait?: Reflections on Canada's National Action Plan & Reports on Women, Peace and Security*, edited by Beth Woroniuk and Amber Minnings. Women, Peace and Security Network-Canada, 14–18. Accessed 18 November 2016. https://wpsncanada.files.wordpress.com/2012/05/worth-the-wait-report.pdf.

Tiessen, Rebecca, and Krystel Carrier. 2015. "The Erasure of 'Gender' in Canadian Foreign Policy under the Harper Conservatives: The Significance of the Discursive Shift from 'Gender Equality' to 'Equality between Women and Men.'" *Canadian Foreign Policy Journal* 21, no. 1: 95–111.

Turenne-Sjolander, Claire, Heather Smith, and Deborah Steinstra, eds. 2003. *Feminist Perspectives on Canadian Foreign Policy*. Oxford: Oxford University Press.

Turenne-Sjolander, Claire, and Kathryn Trevenen. 2010. "Constructing Canadian Foreign Policy: Myths of Good International Citizens, Protectors, and the War in Afghanistan." In *Canadian Foreign Policy in Critical Perspective*, edited by J. Marshall Beier, and Lana Wylie. Don Mills, ON: Oxford University Press, 44–58.

United Nations. 2015. Human Rights Committee Report, Office of the High Commissioner. "Consideration of State Reports: Canada." Accessed 2 December 2015. http://tbinternet.ohchr.org/_layouts/treatybodyexternal/SessionDetails1.aspx?SessionID=899&Lang=en#sthash.XzzyC1Bz.dpuf.

United Nations Population Fund (UNFPA). 2014. *Motherhood in Childhood: Facing the Challenge of Adolescent Pregnancy*. State of the World Population 2013. United Nations Population Fund. Accessed 15 May 2014. http://www.unfpa.org/webdav/site/global/shared/swp2013/EN-SWOP2013-final.pdf.

Valentin, Karen, and Lotte Meinert. 2009. "The Adult North and the Young South." *Anthropology Today* 25, no. 3: 23–8.

PART ONE

Themes

Chapter 1

Did Changes in Official Language Lead to Spending Shifts?

Liam Swiss and Jessica Barry

INTRODUCTION

Canada has long been considered a leader in the promotion of gender equality in the international context (Baranyi and Powell 2005; McGill 2012; Stienstra 1995; Sjolander 2005; Riddell-Dixon 2001). Despite this reputation, it had become increasingly evident that the Canadian International Development Agency (CIDA) had "reduced [its] over- all commitment to gender equality despite strong rhetoric and policy guidelines" ("Members of Informal," 1). Since the early 2000s, Canada's commitments to gender equality have been on the decline (Swiss 2012b), a trend mirrored in much of the international community (Alpízar et al. 2010; Alpízar Durán 2015). In 2009, government staff responsible for international aid policy through the Department of Foreign Affairs and International Trade (DFAIT) and CIDA – which changed to the Depart- ment of Foreign Affairs, Trade and Development (DFATD) under the Harper Conservatives and then to Global Affairs Canada (GAC) under the Liberal party in 2015 – were instructed to replace the term "gender equality" with "equality between women and men" (Collins 2009). The move surprised many, and has been interpreted by some as a challenge to Canada's longstanding history of promoting the concept of gender equal- ity globally. Tiessen and Carrier (2015) have thoroughly documented the politics and perceptions of this discursive shift, as the change in language was met with much criticism by many in the development sector. The rationale for the change is unclear, although one possibility is that elected officials may have considered the term "gender equality" as being too "liberal" for a conservative constituency, or being equated with the promotion of gender diversity, homosexuality, or the sexual and reproductive rights of women, including the right to an abortion. Another possibility is that a limited understanding of the term "gender equality" among officials may have made the expression "equality between men and women" a desirable variation, being easier to understand from a communications standpoint.

Whatever the government's rationale, Tiessen and Carrier outline the important theoretical and programmatic implications of such a departure from Canada's traditionally robust commitment to the concept of gender equality. Despite the controversy surrounding the discursive shift, the question of whether the change in language corresponds to a significant change in spending on gender equality at the former CIDA has yet to be investigated. This chapter analyzes CIDA's own Open Data Historical Project Data Set and International Aid Transparency Initiative Data Set to examine the trends in spending on gender equality by Canada in the period from 2005 to 2014 – the period in which the shift away from the language of gender equality occurred. Using a sample of over 240,000 project transactions during this period and comparing CIDA's gender equality marker coding to Development Assistance Committee (DAC) gender coding sources, this chapter examines whether the discursive shift away from gender equality was associated with any notable shift in spending on gender equality at CIDA. Surprisingly, the study concludes that Canada's aid spending on gender equality did not decrease significantly during the Harper years, due partly to bureaucratic resistance.

BACKGROUND

Gender Equality and Canadian Development Assistance

Over the past several decades, the rights of women have gained prominence in global international development discourse. The adoption of women and gender as development priorities can be observe through the increased engagement of major donors with these issues over the past four decades (Moser 2005; Moser and Moser 2005; Rathgeber 1990; Swiss 2012a; Smyth 2007). Donors have subsequently developed specialized units and policies addressing women's rights and gender equality concerns in their programs, and as Smyth (2007) notes, "gender talk" has become pervasive across a wide range of development issues, from economic policy to human rights to political participation. The increase in support for women's rights globally has coincided with the expansion of the global women's movement and increased visibility of gender equality issues at international conferences, such as the high profile United Nations (UN) World Conferences on Women and the UN Decade for Women between 1976 and 1985. As a result, many countries began to emphasize the rights of women in a broad spectrum of policy areas, including development assistance (Swiss 2012a).

Canada, as a relatively large provider of development aid, has long been considered a leader in the promotion of gender equality on the global stage (McGill 2012; Stienstra 1995; Sjolander 2005; Riddell-Dixon 2001; Baranyi and Powell 2005; Hendriks 2005; Angeles 2003). Canada was considered ahead of the pack on gender equality policy on the global stage, ratifying the UN Convention on the Elimination of All Forms of Discrimination Against Women (CEDAW) in 1981, endorsing gender mainstreaming through the UN's 1995 Beijing Declaration at the UN's Fourth World Conference on Women, and endorsing the UN's Security Council Resolution 1325, as well as adopting the Organisation for Economic Co-operation and Development (OECD) DAC's Guidelines for Gender Equality (Baranyi and Powell 2005). Some argue that these policy commitments contribute to an image of the Canadian state as a leader on gender equality issues. Howell (2005) argues that Canadian foreign policy discourses produce narratives of Canada as "peaceful, tolerant, and orderly," and Richey (2001) points to Canada as portraying a "feminist state identity" in international relations.

The former CIDA's policies on gender equality were long considered to be on the "leading edge" of international practice (Brown 2012). The McLeod Group, a Canadian foreign policy advocacy group, has noted Canada's consistent work since the mid-1970s on the work they have done internally, with their Canadian partners and with international institutions, in the promotion of women's "full participation" in the development process. They state that for many years, CIDA "worked to promote a deeper understanding within CIDA and globally of the systemic causes of women's subordination and the social construction of gender relations, and translated that understanding into policies and programming" (McLeod Group 2013). Throughout the 1970s and 1980s CIDA adopted a number of gender equality-related policies, including its first policy guidelines on Women in Development (WID) in 1976 and the creation of a WID directorate in 1984. Policy commitments to gender equality continued throughout the 1990s, through the establishment of a Women in Development and Gender Equity Division in CIDA's Policy Branch in 1994, the adoption of gender mainstreaming principles through Canada's participating in the Beijing Platform for Action in 1995, and the introduction of CIDA's Policy on Gender Equality in 1999 (CIDA 2012).

The rationale for the 1999 policy asserted that "gender inequalities intensify poverty, perpetuate it from one generation to the next and weaken women's and girls' ability to overcome it. ... For poverty reduction to be achieved, the constraints that women and girls face must be eliminated" (CIDA 1999, ii). In 1999 the policy was well received by civil society organizations (CSOs) because "it concretely required gender equality and the realization of women's rights as an overall goal, consideration and methodology for all of the Agency's programs. In fact, many other donor agencies have referenced CIDA's Policy on Gender Equality as a basis for developing their own" ("Members of the Informal" 2009, 2). It remains highly relevant to Canada's engagement internationally, considered by the government, scholars, and civil society organizations alike as a progressive, long-term commitment to promoting gender equality (McGill 2012; Baranyi and Powell 2005).

In the 1999 policy, CIDA was committed to promoting gender equality in all its development policy and programming, stating that "gender equality must be considered as an integral part of all CIDA policies, programs and projects" (CIDA 1999). Furthermore, CIDA's 2005 Framework for Assessing Gender Equality Results clearly outlined how CIDA quantified the three "corporate objectives" of the 1999 policy: decision making (equal participation between women and men in contributing to sustainable development in their communities), rights (the ability for women and girls to realize their full human rights), and development resources and benefits (reduced inequalities between women and men in terms of access to and control over "benefits of development" (CIDA 2005). It also provided an overview of CIDA's attempts to integrate gender equality as a "cross-cutting theme" in its policies and programs. In 2008 the agency completed an evaluation of its implementation of its 1999 Policy on Gender Equality and a plan of action to address recommendations, which included the need for further progress on gender mainstreaming within the agency.

Politicization of Aid

Despite its reputation as a leader on gender equality in the aid sector, Canada's focus on gender has been questioned in the wake of a recent trend toward increased politicization of its aid programs. In June of 2013, CIDA and DFAIT were amalgamated into a new "mega-department" known at first as DFATD and renamed again to GAC in late 2015. In a statement following the budget release, former CIDA minister Julian Fantino stated that the amalgamation would "put development on equal footing with trade and diplomacy" (CCIC 2013, 1), justified by the need for "policy coherence" or the alignment of three spheres of Canadian foreign policy: diplomacy, trade, and development. This announcement did not come as a surprise to those following the "quest for policy coherence" that had been prominent on the global donor agenda for over a decade (Brown 2012, 93) and the increasing alignment between Canadian international development priorities and domestic trade and economic interests over the several years prior (OECD 2012). This raised concerns for some that national interests, or ensuring that aid spending would result in concrete benefits for Canadians, would overpower more "altruistic" rationale for aid-giving (Black and Tiessen 2007).

Several scholars advance the argument that Canadian aid has been "politicized" for domestic political purposes. For example, Hales (2007) argues that gender equality goals are undermined by the Canadian government's desire to advance a neoliberal economic agenda through its aid program. Black and Tiessen (2007) point to the desire on behalf of some in government to ensure that Canadian aid priorities are aligned with the pursuit of such national interests as increasing competitiveness, advancing prosperity, and international security. Swiss (2012b) argues that Canadian foreign aid directed at women in Afghanistan has been "instrumentalized" to advance domestic security and military goals. Likewise, Canada has been shown to have done only limited work in integrating a gender equality approach in its security-related aid (Swiss 2015). Brown and Raddatz (2012) attribute the decline of Canada's international strength in gender equality more generally to the election of the Conservative government in 2006 and the "politicization" of foreign aid for domestic political purposes.

Politicization of Gender Equality

Although most scholars and development practitioners point to CIDA's 1999 Policy on Gender Equality as a progressive policy framework, demonstrating CIDA's strong commitment to gender equality, in the past several years civil society actors and several scholars have expressed concern regarding Canada's performance on gender equality in its aid program (Swiss 2012b; Tiessen 2014; McLeod Group 2013; McGill 2012). Plewes and Kerr (2010) argue that "The gender equality and women's rights focus of our international co-operation and foreign policy is slipping away. It's been happening slowly and quietly, but with devastating impact." Although Canada was once considered a leader in international cooperation regarding women's rights and gender equality, some have argued that recently the space for this kind of work has been "shrinking."

This change in approach is further illustrated by a shift in language in Canadian development policy. Michelle Collins, a writer for *Embassy Magazine*, pointed out that since 2009 government staff responsible for international aid policy have been instructed to replace the term "gender equality" with "equality between men and women." This shift may be interpreted as a challenge to Canada's tradition of a strong rhetorical commitment to the promotion of the concept of gender equality in the international context (Tiessen and Carrier 2015). It may also be interpreted as a "step back" from a focus on systemic inequalities and power imbalances between men and women, reducing the "gender focus" to the point where women are regarded as no more than instruments of economic development or military support.

Despite this, the Canadian government has attempted to retain an image of global leadership on gender equality issues by championing two high profile issues on the international stage: maternal and child health, and the early and forced marriage of young girls in countries in the Global South. On International Women's Day in 2014, Prime Minister Harper released a statement stating:

> Internationally, Canada is a recognized global leader in promoting the health of women and children in developing countries and in reducing the unacceptable mortality rates faced each year by these vulnerable populations. We are also taking a leadership role in supporting women who continue to struggle for equality. This includes increasing girls' access to quality education and working to protect women and children from violence and abuse by prioritizing the elimination of child, early and forced marriage.

The Muskoka Initiative on Maternal, Newborn and Child Health (MNCH) was introduced in June of 2010 at the Group of Eight (G8) leaders meeting in Huntsville, Ontario. It included a commitment on behalf of the Canadian government of $1.2 billion in new funding and $1.75 billion in ongoing spending dedicated to improving child and maternal health in countries in the Global South. The MNCH initiative was extremely controversial among Canadian development NGOs and the wider Canadian public because it excluded funding for safe abortions, a procedure legal in Canada and a significant barrier to improving maternal health globally (Carrier and Tiessen 2012; Delacourt 2010; Plewes and Kerr 2010; Swiss 2012b). After significant pressure from within and outside the government, the prime minister agreed to provide some funds for "access to modern methods of family planning for 12 million couples," but maintained his stance against including funding for safe abortions (DFATD 2012a).

The controversy surrounding the Muskoka Initiative created significant tensions between several civil society organizations and the Canadian government. In one instance, a group of international development advocates who had gathered on Parliament Hill to protest the government's stance on abortion in foreign aid were told to "shut the fuck up" on this issue by Conservative senator Nancy Ruth (Delacourt 2010). The senator warned that more advocacy efforts on the part of development NGOs on this issue would result in more pushback from the government. The senator said that the issue had become a "political football" and that linking the issue to women's health in Canada could risk re-opening a debate on abortion in Canada. The resulting controversies are one example of how "gender equality" is being "politicized" in Canada's aid program. In a 2010 *Embassy Magazine* article entitled "Politicizing, Undermining Gender Equality," Plewes and Kerr describe how the Muskoka Initiative demonstrates how a "socially conservative agenda is being imposed on development priorities without any public discussion or accountability. This is what happened in the discussions about the G8 mother and child health initiative. It is also happening in all of Canada's support for women's rights internationally."

Despite past leadership on gender equality, it has been argued that in both policy and practice, Canada's leadership has decreased substantially in recent years. Stuart (2011, 2) states that "Funding for gender equality has slipped, and there has been a steady marginalization of women's rights in our international aid program." In 2000 under a Liberal government, CIDA's funding for gender equality–specific programming consisted of 1.85 per cent of its spending. By 2006 this had fallen to only 1.01 per cent (Stuart 2011, 2).

The most visible of these gender-specific projects, bilateral funds for initiatives on women or gender managed locally in recipient countries, has been one seeming casualty of this reduction. Lauded in the 2009 evaluation of CIDA's gender policy and programming, these locally responsive funds supported small initiatives (typically less than C$50,000) implemented by women's groups and NGOs in recipient countries that targeted women's rights or issues and gender equality. Such projects were common in the pre-Conservative era, with a review of the DFATD project browser data set (confirmed by the International Aid Transparency Initiative [IATI] data set) suggesting that at least ten operated in the 2001–2007 period, totalling more than C$34 million. The same data suggests no similar bilateral, responsive funds for women's or gender initiatives have been approved by CIDA or DFATD since at least 2007, indicating an end to the use of this aid modality under the Conservative government.

Gender Coding

Coding aid programs for the extent to which they integrate gender equality goals is one way in which donors attempt to implement gender-mainstreaming strategies. The OECD DAC has implemented a policy marker for gender equality with which members of the committee are asked to categorize their bilateral aid commitments. The marker system has three levels, each corresponding with a degree of integration of gender equality goals. Level 0 is considered not targeted at gender equality; level 1 is significant, in which gender equality is an important but secondary objective of the program; and level 2 is principal, in which gender equality is "an explicit objective of the activity and fundamental in its design" (as cited in Tomlinson 2013, 1). Though they seem to naturalize the measure of gender equality in aid programming, indicators of this sort have been critiqued as being inherently political processes rife with debate and contestation that is often obscured by the indicators or markers themselves (Merry and Coutin 2014).

Not surprisingly, then, there has been some controversy over the way in which Canada's commitment to gender equality in its bilateral aid program has been measured using the marker system. Tomlinson (2013) describes how CIDA's bilateral commitments to projects where "gender equality was an explicit objective of the activity and fundamental in its design" under the DAC guidelines increased significantly from 2008/2009 to 2010/2011. The results in the later time period showed that Canada had by far surpassed every other donor, with 43 per cent of all marked projects corresponding with the highest DAC gender equality marker value. The Association for Women's Rights in Development (AWID) noted this as a remarkable achievement and an indication that Canada was a major supporter of women's rights globally (Arutyunova and Clark 2013). As Tomlinson argues, the reason for this increase has less to do with the substantive increase in the integration of gender equality goals into projects, and more to do with a change in how CIDA coded for gender equality in its projects. In 2011, CIDA began publishing an historical data set that included four possible values: no results coded as 0, results at the immediate outcome level as 1, results at the intermediate outcome level as 2, and gender equality as the principal objective and result of the initiative as 3. An inquiry by DFATD officials responsible for official development assistance (ODA) statistics noted that CIDA had begun equating the DAC marker 2 (principal) with the CIDA marker 3 (principal) in addition to the

CIDA marker 2 (intermediate outcome). The inclusion of intermediate outcomes into the DAC system, with gender equality as the principal purpose, may have exaggerated the 2010/2011 CIDA outcomes, and thus raises questions about whether or not these results demonstrate a real increase in Canada's commitment to gender equality. The fact that this shift in coding is occurring nearly simultaneously with the discursive shift in gender language is a complicating factor in our analysis.

ANALYSIS

The discursive shift from gender equality to equality between women and men in the context of increased politicization of Canadian aid not surprisingly raised significant concerns within the Canadian development community (Plewes and Kerr 2010). Did this shift in language entail a shift in aid spending or program planning? Acknowledging the misgivings around the quality and validity of available gender coding data for Canadian aid (Tomlinson 2013) and more general concerns about such measurement systems (Merry and Coutin 2014), we examined the available data to assess the effect of the shift to equality between women and men on Canada's aid programs.

Drawing upon two separate Government of Canada data sets, we examined Canada's aid programming pre- and post-2009 to assess how the discursive shift to equality between women and men influenced:

1　the proportion of Canadian aid programs targeting gender equality;
2　the amount of aid funds dedicated to programs targeting gender equality; and
3　the nature of the language used in project titles, descriptions, and results statements for new aid programming.

Data Sets
Tomlinson (2013) identifies the discrepancies between the gender equality marker coding used by CIDA and that used by the OECD DAC. Regrettably, no single Government of Canada data set exists that incorporates both forms of coding. As a result, we examined two separate data sources on Canadian aid: DFATD's Historical Project Data Set (HPDS)[1] and the DFATD IATI data set.[2] Regrettably, each data set yields a slightly different sample of Canadian aid projects over a similar window of time.

The HPDS includes all project transactions active in a given fiscal year, and when all available years are combined and duplicate entries for multiple project transactions are eliminated yields a sample of 15,085 project years and a total of 6,930 unique project numbers over the period 2005 to 2012.[3] The gender equality marker data included in the HPDS is the CIDA gender marker. It is not clear in the HPDS documentation whether the HPDS reflects the gender equality marker coding because it happened in the year the project was created, or if these codes have been retroactively revised with the introduction of the new CIDA gender equality marker in 2009.

In contrast, the IATI data set contains information on 2,817 projects with start dates ranging from 1996 onwards, but with the majority concentrated in year 2007 onwards (this number drops to 2,170 once duplicate project-level activities are eliminated). Using end dates included in the data set, we were able to project the initiatives out across the fiscal years in which they were active and create a project-by-fiscal-year data set comparable to the HPDS. This resulted in a total sample of 7,054 project years. The IATI data set, in contrast to the HPDS, does not include the CIDA gender equality marker; instead, it includes the DAC gender equality policy marker – a standard measure in IATI data across many donors.

Using these two complementary but not overlapping samples of Canadian aid programs, we were able to examine the trends in how gender eqality has been funded, coded, and referred to in CIDA's aid projects both before and after the discursive shift from "gender equality" to "equality between women and men."

Gender Equality Coding
We examined how CIDA's programs have been coded for gender equality over time and whether a change could be seen between the pre- and post-2009 periods, when the discursive shift occurred. Tables 1.1 and 1.2 show the breakdown of the CIDA and DAC gender equality marker coding by per cent of active projects in both data sets. The same results are depicted in figures 1.1 and 1.2 to better assess the trends over time. The CIDA and DAC markers do not align entirely, owing to our complementary but not identical samples; however, some similar trends are seen in both data sets.[4]

First, the proportion of projects coded as having no gender equality results or as not targeting gender equality has declined over time. In the HPDS we see it decline from a height of more than 66 per cent in 2005/2006 to just over 38 per cent in 2011/2012. Likewise, the IATI data shows a similar, though less stark, decline in the category in which gender equality was not targeted, from a height of 48 per cent in 2008/2009 to just below 32 per cent in 2013/2014. Both these trends ahead of the 2009 discursive shift and continue through it, though the reductions in the category in which there are no results or gender equality was not targeted are sharpest in the most recent years in each table. Taken at face value, this

TABLE 1.1 Per cent active projects by CIDA GE policy marker, 2005–2012 (HPD dataset)

FISCAL YEAR

CIDA GENDER MARKER	2005–06	2006–07	2007–08	2008–09	2009–10	2010–11	2011–12	TOTAL
No GE results	66.38	63.24	59.79	52.90	47.10	40.32	38.34	54.81
GE results at immediate outcome level	7.00	7.13	8.47	11.59	15.88	17.46	20.94	11.52
GE results at intermediate outcome level	23.88	26.23	28.52	31.75	32.68	38.36	37.24	30.19
GE is principal objective/result	2.75	3.40	3.22	3.77	4.34	3.86	3.48	3.48
TOTAL	100.00	100.00	100.00	100.00	100.00	100.00	100.00	100.00

Chi-square statistic: 701.79; p<0.001

TABLE 1.2 Per cent active projects by DAC GE policy marker, 2007–2014 (IATI dataset)

FISCAL YEAR

DAC GENDER MARKER	2007–08	2008–09	2009–10	2010–11	2011–12	2012–13	2013–14	TOTAL
GE not targeted	41.27	48.21	46.47	43.83	41.14	33.84	31.96	40.27
GE significant objective	14.29	12.99	15.23	16.21	20.41	23.03	25.00	19.11
GE principal objective	44.44	38.80	38.30	39.96	38.45	43.14	43.04	40.63
TOTAL	100.00	100.00	100.00	100.00	100.00	100.00	100.00	100.00

Chi-square statistic: 116; p<0.001

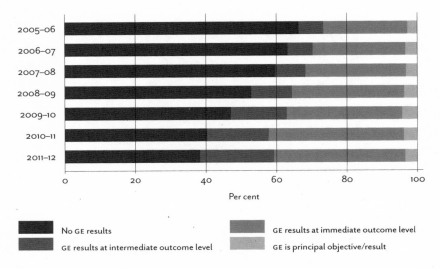

FIGURE 1.1 Per cent of active projects by CIDA GE marker category, 2005–2012 (HPD dataset)

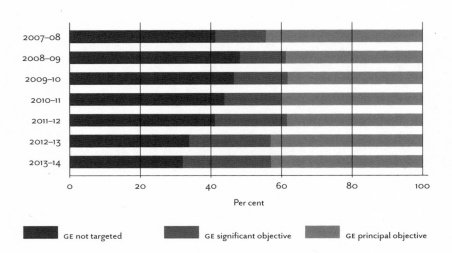

FIGURE 1.2 Per cent of active projects by DAC GE marker category, 2007–2013 (IATI dataset)

finding suggests that a larger proportion of Canada's aid programs have some sort of gender equality result, or are at least being coded as such.

If a significant proportion of projects are now incorporating gender results, which category is growing as the "no result" and "not targeted" categories shrink? This is the second similar pattern seen in both data sets. In each case it appears that these projects are shifting into the immediate and intermediate, and the significant objective marker categories. Gender equality as a principal objective is relatively consistent over time in each data set, though it fluctuates more in the IATI data. If we look at the uppermost categories in figures 1.1 and 1.2, we see that they remain relatively consistent, while the middle marker categories expand over time as the "no results" category shrinks. Independent of changes to the coding system that would lead to an over-reporting at the DAC of projects with gender equality as a principal objective, we do see a growth post-2009 in the immediate and intermediate categories of gender equality results. In the HPDS, the near tripling of the gender equality results at the immediate outcome level is notable, while the intermediate outcome level increases by more than half between 2005 and 2012. In the IATI data, the growth of the "significant objective" DAC category is also appreciable, increasing by more than 10 percentage points from 2007 through 2014, thus absorbing much of the reduction in the "not targeted" category over this time.

Tomlinson's concern that the DAC marker over-reports Canada's focus on gender equality results is given weight by comparing the two figures, as there is a significant difference between 3.5 per cent of projects having gender equality as a principal objective/result in 2011/2012 in the HPDS data and 38.5 per cent being reported as having the same by the IATI data's DAC marker in the same year. Interestingly, however, this data reveals no major shift as a result of a change in CIDA coding practices and how they are forwarded to the DAC. This is likely a result of the nature of the IATI data presently, in which projects are likely coded with their current gender equality marker result rather than the one they received when they were first established.

Overall, it appears that the discursive shift (and the change in coding practices) at CIDA in 2009 had no negative effect on the proportion of projects being coded as having gender equality results. Indeed, the trends from both data sets suggest that CIDA/DFATD are reporting more gender results in all their programming now than at any point since 2005. This finding would seem to run counter to the expectations suggested by critics of the discursive shift and of the abandoning of locally managed gender funds as an aid modality. In the next section we examine whether similar patterns emerge when comparing the amount of aid funding dedi-cated to gender equality results.

Gender Equality Spending

The HPDS allows us to track annual spending by projects and aggregate that spending at the fiscal year level by gender equality marker category. Figure 1.3 shows total annual spending by gender equality marker cate-gory from 2005 to 2012 for all projects in the HPDS. While we see a slight decline in the amount spent in the "no results" category over time, both the "intermediate results" and "principal objective" category remain more or less consistent. In contrast, we see a sharp uptick in the amount of funds disbursed to projects with gender equality results at the immediate outcome level, growing from under $250 million in 2005/2006 to more than $1.7 billion in 2011/2012. It is not possible using the current HPDS data to determine if this shift is a result of revised coding approaches – however, if we assume it is not, then the sharp increase in spending on projects with gender equality results at the immediate level seems to sup-port the trends in the proportion of projects with gender equality results examined in the previous section. When considering the post-2009 period, we see that this growth is actually strongest between the 2010/2011 and 2011/2012 fiscal years, lending little support to the idea that the dis-cursive shift from gender equality to equality between women and men might be effecting spending on gender at CIDA/DFATD.

The content of the IATI data set does not enable an annual aggregation of spending by DAC gender equality marker category, but similar data is available directly from the DAC and its Creditor Reporting Service data set. Figure 1.4 shows a similar annual aggregate (based on calendar years) of aid spending in terms of total commitments in US dollars by gender equality marker category. Here we see several interesting trends that all coincide with the shift in how CIDA practised gender equality coding in 2009. First, all Canadian projects were screened from this point forward, with the category of "not screened" dropping to zero from 2009 on. Sec-ond, we see a massive jump in the gender equality as a principal objective category in the same period. This corresponds to the decision reported by Tomlinson (2013) to equate both the intermediate and principal catego-ries of the CIDA gender equality marker with the principal category of the DAC marker. Regardless, there is an overall increase in spending coded with significant or principal objectives in this period, largely as a result of increased screening of programs.

Looking at the average annual project disbursement in the HPDS (fig-ure 1.4) or the average annual new project commitment in the IATI data

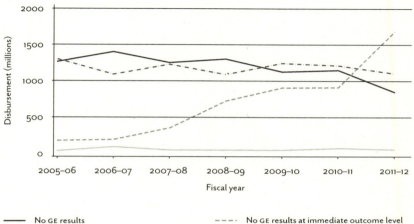

FIGURE 1.3 Total annual disbursements by CIDA GE marker, 2005–2012 (HPD dataset)

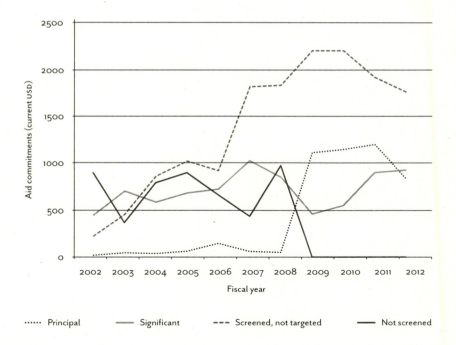

FIGURE 1.4 Total annual commitments by DAC GE marker, 2002–2012 (DAC CRS)

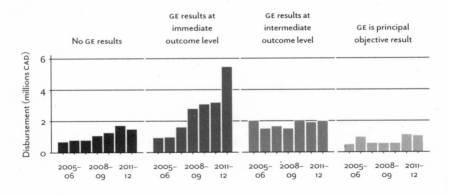

FIGURE 1.5 Average annual dispersements by CIDA GE marker, 2005–2012, (HDP dataset)

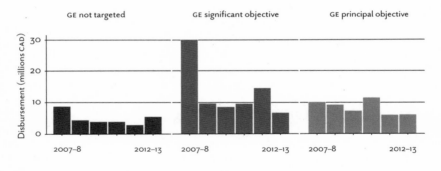

FIGURE 1.6 Average annual new project commitment by DAC GE marker, 2007–2013 (IATI dataset)

(figure 1.5), we see similar trends in the immediate outcome category and – to a lesser degree – in the significant objective category. In both cases, we see increased spending in these areas after 2009, although there is a significant drop-off between 2011/2012 and 2012/2013 in the IATI data for new project commitments in this category.[5]

In terms of spending, the most striking finding is the trend toward larger amounts of CIDA/DFATD funding devoted annually to those projects with immediate gender equality outcomes. Both at the aggregate

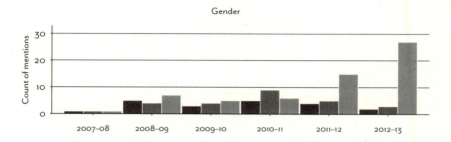

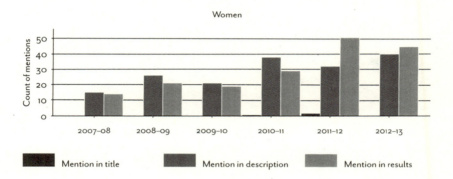

FIGURE 1.7 Mentions of "gender" or "women" in project titles, descriptions, and results statements, 2007–2013 (IATI dataset)

and at the project average level, this category of gender equality spending has grown both in proportion of total projects and in terms of dollars dedicated to those projects. This growth has been sharpest after 2009, suggesting again that the discursive shift from gender equality to equality between women and men had little influence on spending.

Gender Equality Mentions

If there was no decline in proportion of projects or spending dedicated to gender equality, what are we to make of the shift in discourse as it manifests at the project level? The best way to get at such a question would tend to be through document content analysis of project documentation, but we can also start to look at this through a simple accounting of the mentions of key terminology in project titles, descriptions, and results statements available in the IATI data set.[6] Figure 1.6 shows the results of such an accounting, plotting the absolute number of new projects begun in a given fiscal year that include either the term "gender" or "women" in these fields. As a crude barometer of how the gender equality efforts of CIDA programs reflect the way these initiatives are described and reported on, figure 1.6 shows a sharp increase in the mention of the word "women" in project descriptions and results post-2009, while use of the word "gender" drops in both project titles and descriptions from 2010 onwards. These contrasting trends would seem to be in keeping with the shift in language, except that the upper plot in figure 1.6 shows a steady increase in the use of the word "gender" in the results statements of projects begun in 2010 onwards. In contrast, only two projects actually use the term "equality between women and men" in their title, four use the term in their description, and one uses the term in its results statement (not shown in figure 1.6).

With the use of the words "women" and "gender" in results statements increasing in the post-2009 period, but limited uptake of the language of "equality between women and men," we have found an interesting potential disconnect between the top-down prescription of this discursive shift and the continuing and increasing use of the term "gender" in the same period. Even though the language of gender equality may not be reflected in project titles and descriptions at the time of project creation, it may appear in the results statements for the projects once they have begun operation. Such a disconnect would suggest that CIDA/DFATD project planners and managers might be tacitly adopting the discursive shift to equality between women and men at the planning stage for the sake of compliance with ministerial directives, but then maintaining a discourse of gender equality as projects unfold.

Perhaps the effects of the shift from gender equality to equality between women and men is most evident in this accounting of the use of the terms "gender" and "women" in new projects, but at the same time, we see evidence of a surge in the use of gender terminology when it comes to the reporting of project results. Further examination of the content of project titles, descriptions, and results statements using alternate data sources and/or project documentation and reports would add greater clarity to this trend.

DISCUSSION

Though we started our analysis with no formal hypothesis about how the discursive shift from gender equality to equality between women and men might have shaped the work of CIDA/DFATD on gender equality post-2009, the prevailing notion from critics of the shift and others in the development community at the time was that it was likely to negatively affect work on gender equality at CIDA. Our analysis paints a contrary picture, one in which – assuming its employees are effectively and accurately coding aid programs – CIDA/DFATD's work on gender equality has been resilient to the politicized discursive shift, and in which work on gender equality has intensified in terms of the proportion of projects with gender equality results, the amount spent on gender equality programming, and even in terms of the frequency of mentioning gender in project results statements (though this remains limited). Moreover, in the same post-2009 period, CIDA/DFATD has introduced new coding for gender equality results and begun reporting the gender equality coding of *all* programs to the DAC. Regardless of whether this new reporting to the DAC exaggerates Canada's commitments to gender equality, the fact that Canada is screening all programs against the gender equality coding system is a positive development.

On the surface, at least, it would appear that the discursive shift from gender equality to equality between women and men had little or no effect on the everyday practices of gender equality at CIDA in terms of spending or programming. What can account for this seemingly counterintuitive finding? Three explanations warrant consideration:

1 "Equality between women and men" had no effect: Perhaps the simplest possible explanation is that the discursive shift from gender equality to equality between women and men was nothing more than a tempest in a teapot and had no effect. Critics and development practitioners were alarmed by the politicized shift in language, but it did little to alter the substantial organizational inertia that Canada possessed on promoting gender equality. Such an explanation might explain the outward shifts in the language used to describe or title projects, but little reduction in resources or programming coded as being dedicated toward gender equality results.

2 "Equality between women and men" had a negative effect that is obscured by other countervailing factors: This explanation would be plausible if we are simply missing the effects of the discursive shift because of other more pro-gender equality developments at CIDA that were already in motion or happened coincidentally with the change in language. For instance, if the gender equality coding system had not been revised and the way in which CIDA/DFATD reported gender equality results to the DAC had not been altered, perhaps we would see a declining commitment to gender equality or the ending of the use of local gender funds in other metrics. If the gender equality coding changes and the seeming intensified inclusion of gender equality results were done purposefully to hide a declining space for gender

equality within the donor agency, this might be a plausible explanation, but on the surface no evidence points at a broader politicized conspiracy of this nature.

3   "Equality between women and men" had an unintended positive effect on the conduct of gender equality programming: The final explanation to consider is that by politicizing a shift in language away from gender equality to equality between women and men, the government instead motivated additional action from bureaucrats to intensify the work of gender equality within Canada's aid program. In this way, the politicization of the language used to describe Canada's gender efforts may have led to a form of bureaucratic entrepreneurialism or activism that has been employed previously at CIDA to further gender equality goals (Swiss 2009). Could the intensification of gender results reporting, revision of the gender equality coding scheme, or increases in aid to gender equality programs be a response to the politicization by the minister and the Harper government? This explanation is worth investigating further through ethnographic methods, which our current data set unfortunately does not enable.

CONCLUSION

As an exploratory analysis to assess the effect of the discursive shift from gender equality to equality between women and men, this study has made use of CIDA/DFATD data to find that – at least at face value – Canada appears to be devoting a larger proportion of its programming and more funds than ever toward aid in support of gender equality, despite the elimination of gender-specific programs like local gender funds. The simplest conclusion is that there appear to be few negative effects of the shift using the heuristics available to us. In this respect, the first explanation explored above appears most appealing. Despite the well-documented politics surrounding the discursive shift and potential problems that could have arisen from it, Canada's gender equality programming remained resilient – and indeed grew (Plewes and Kerr 2010; Tiessen and Carrier 2015). Some of this might have been enabled by key players within CIDA and DFATD, who helped to further the gender equality agenda in the face of a retrograde, top-down approach received with disdain, but it is beyond the scope of this chapter to confirm that possibility. The gender equality coding figures do not tell the entire story. Future research with access to GAC officials involved in the work of gender equality within the aid program would be valuable to shed light on how the shift from gender equality to equality between women and men was received and/or resisted within CIDA/DFATD itself.

More than six years on from the discursive shift, it seems clear that the controversy it inspired has not resulted in significant shifts in Canada's gender equality-related aid programming. This finding should not be seen to diminish the political damage such a shift has inflicted on Canada's international reputation as a leader in the gender equality field or the troubles faced by an increasingly politicized aid program within the gender equality context and beyond (Howell 2005; Richey 2001). Such concerns about Canada's reputation may be well founded. There is no denying that outwardly the discursive shift away from gender equality is highly politicized and appears to send contradictory signals about Canada's approach to gender. Despite this red flag, we argue that the fact that Canada's gender programming – at least in terms of spending and relative share of programming – has remained resilient to this naked politicization is encouraging. The coding controversy aside, the expansion of Canada's gender equality programming and spending in this period and the screening of all programs against the gender equality markers both internally and for reporting to the DAC are signs of an institutional momentum on gender equality at CIDA and DFATD that effectively resisted the potentially negative effects of a shameless political ploy aimed at diminishing the gender equality agenda.

NOTES

1 Available at http://www.international.gc.ca/department-ministere/open_data
-donnees_ouvertes/dev/historical_project-historiques_projets.aspx?lang=eng.

2 Available at http://www.international.gc.ca/department-ministere/open_
data-donnees_ouvertes/dev/iati-iita.aspx?lang=eng.

3 These are top-level seven character project numbers taking the format
X000000, where X is a letter indicating the former CIDA branch delivering
the project and 000000 is the six-digit project ID number. Projects might have
lower-level sub-projects, but for the purposes of this analysis we aggregate data
at this top-level ID. The same process was carried out on the IATI data, leaving
one project observation per fiscal year while a project is active.

4 Chi-square statistics reported for both tables indicate that the reported differences between categories are statistically significant in each data set.

5 This may be owing to the reported lapse of funds and low levels of project
approvals witnessed at CIDA in the 2012/2013 fiscal year. See: http://
ottawacitizen.com/opinion/project-approval-paralysis-and-canadas
-declining-aid-spending.

6 The exclusion of these fields from the HPDS did not permit comparing results
from that data set.

REFERENCES

Alpízar, Lydia. 2015. "20 Years of Shamefully Scarce Funding for Feminists and Women's Rights Movements." United Nations Research Institute for Social Development, 13 May. http://www.unrisd.org/beijing+20-alpizar.

Alpízar, Lydia, Cindy Clark, Sarah Rosenhek, and Verónica Vidal. 2010. *Context and Trends Influencing the Funding Landscape for Gender Equality and Women's Organizations and Movements*. Mexico City: Association for Women's Rights in Development.

Angeles, Leonora. 2003. "Creating Social Spaces for Transnational Feminist Advocacy: The Canadian International Development Agency, the National Commission on the Role of Filipino Women and Philippine Women's NGOS." *Canadian Geographer* 47, no. 3: 283–302.

Arutyunova, Angelika, and Cindy Clark. 2013. "Watering the Leaves, Starving the Roots: The Status of Financing for Women's Rights Organizing and Gender Equality." Toronto: Association for Women's Rights in Development. https://www.awid.org/publications/watering-leaves-starving-roots.

Baranyi, Stephen, and Kristiana Powell. 2005. "Bringing Gender Back into Canada's Engagement in Fragile States." Ottawa: North-South Institute. http://www.nsi-ins.ca/publications/bringing-gender-back-into-canadas-engagement-in-fragile-states.

Black, David, and Rebecca Tiessen. 2007. "The Canadian International Development Agency: New Policies, Old Problems." *Canadian Journal of Development Studies/Revue Canadienne d'études du développement* 28, no. 2: 191–212.

Brown, Stephen. 2012. "CIDA's New Partnership with Canadian NGOs." In *Struggling for Effectiveness: CIDA and Canadian Foreign Aid*, edited by Stephen Brown, 287–304. Montreal and Kingston: McGill-Queen's University Press.

Brown, Stephen, and Rosalind Raddatz. 2012. "Conclusion: Taking Stock, Looking Ahead." In *Struggling for Effectiveness: CIDA and Canadian Foreign Aid*, edited by Stephen Brown, 327–44. Montreal and Kingston: McGill-Queen's University Press.

Bytown Consulting and CAC International. 2008. *Evaluation of CIDA's Implementation of Its Policy on Gender Equality: Executive Report*. Gatineau, QC: Canadian International Development Agency.

Canadian Council for International Cooperation. 2013. *Creating the Department of Foreign Affairs, Trade and Development: Benchmarks for More Effective and Coherent International Development and Humanitarian Assistance*. Ottawa: Canadian Council for International Cooperation. http://www.ccic.ca/_files/en/what_we_do/2013-04-29_Benchmarks_for_development_and_HA.pdf.

Canadian International Development Agency. 1989. *Women in Development: A Sectoral Perspective*. Canadian International Development Agency, Public Affairs Branch.

- 1999. CIDA's Policy on Gender Equality. Canadian International Development Agency, Public Affairs Branch.
- 2005. CIDA's Framework for Assessing Gender Equality Results. Canadian International Development Agency.
Carrier, Krystel, and Rebecca Tiessen. 2013. "Women and Children First: Maternal Health and the Silence of Gender in Canadian Foreign Policy." In Canada in the World: Perspectives on Canadian Foreign Policy, edited by Heather Smith and Claire Turenne-Sjolander, 183–200. Toronto: Oxford University Press.
Collins, Michelle. 2009. "'Gender Equality,' 'Child Soldiers' and 'Humanitarian Law' Are Axed from Foreign Policy Language." Embassy Magazine, 29 July.
CSO Working Group on Women's Rights. 2009. Strengthening Canada's International Leadership in the Promotion of Gender Equality: A Civil Society Response to the Evaluation of the Implementation of CIDA's 1999 Policy on Gender Equality. Canadian Council for International Cooperation. http://www.ccic.ca/_files/en/what_we_do/002_gender_cida_analysis_cso_response.pdf.
Delacourt, Susan. 2010. "Aid Groups Advised to 'Shut the F--- up' on Abortion." Toronto Star, 3 May.
Department of Foreign Affairs, Trade and Development (DFATD). 2012a. The Muskoka Initiative: Background. Department of Foreign Affairs, Trade and Development. http://mnch.international.gc.ca/en/topics/leadership-muskoka_background.html.
- 2012b. Gender Equality: Chronology, Selected Key Dates. Department of Foreign Affairs, Trade and Development.
Hales, Jennifer. 2007. "Rhetoric and Reality: World Bank and CIDA Gender Policies." Convergence 40, nos. 1–2: 147–69.
Hendriks, Sarah. 2005. "Advocates, Adversaries, and Anomalies: The Politics of Feminist Spaces in Gender and Development." Canadian Journal of Development Studies 26, special issue: 619–32.
Howell, Alison. 2005. "Peaceful, Tolerant and Orderly? A Feminist Analysis of Discourses of 'Canadian Values' in Canadian Foreign Policy." Canadian Foreign Policy Journal 12, no. 1: 49–69.
McGill, Hunter. 2012. "Canada among Donors: How Does Canadian Aid Compare?" In Struggling for Effectiveness: CIDA and Canadian Foreign Aid, edited by Stephen Brown, 24–52. Montreal and Kingston: McGill-Queen's University Press.
McLeod Group. 2013. Gender Equality. McLeod Group. http://www.mcleodgroup.ca/topics-3/a-place-for-women-gender-equality-and-canadian-development-policy.
Merry, Sally, and Susan Coutin. 2014. "Technologies of Truth in the Anthropology of Conflict: AES/APLA Presidential Address 2013." American Ethnologist 41, no. 1: 1–16.
Moser, Caroline. 2005. "Has Gender Mainstreaming Failed?" International Feminist Journal of Police 7, no. 4: 576–90.

Moser, Caroline, and Annalise Moser. 2005. "Gender Mainstreaming since
    Beijing: A Review of Success and Limitations in International Institutions."
    Gender and Development 13, no. 2: 11–22.
Organisation for Economic Co-operation and Development (OECD). 2012.
    Canada: Development Assistance Committee (DAC) Peer Review 2012. Paris:
    Organisation for Economic Co-operation and Development.
Plewes, Betty, and Joanna Kerr. 2010. "Politicizing, Undermining Gender Equal-
    ity." *Embassy News,* 5 May.
Rathgeber, Eva. 1990. "WID, WAD, GAD: Trends in Research and Practice." *Journal
    of Developing Areas* 24: 489–502.
Richey, Lisa. 2001. "In Search of Feminist Foreign Policy: Gender, Development,
    and Danish State Identity." *Cooperation and Conflict* 36, no. 2: 177–212.
Riddell-Dixon, Elizabeth. 2001. *Canada and the Beijing Conference on Women:
    Governmental Politics and NGO Participation.* Vancouver: University of British
    Columbia Press.
Rivington, Diana. 2014. "What's So Hard about Gender Equality?" Panel discus-
    sion at the CCIC-CAIDP Conference, May 2014. http://www.mcleodgroup.
    ca/2014/05/18/mcleod-group-at-the-ccic-ciadp-conference-may-2014.
Ruben, Ruerd, and Lau Schulpen. 2009. "How to Allocate Public Funding to Non-
    governmental Development Organizations." *Nonprofit and Voluntary Sector
    Quarterly* 38, no. 2: 287–306.
Smyth, Ines. 2007. "Talking of Gender: Words and Meanings in Development
    Organisations." *Development in Practice* 17, nos. 4–5: 582–8.
Stienstra, Deborah. 1995. "Can the Silence Be Broken? Gender and Canadian
    Foreign Policy." *International Journal* 50, no. 1: 103–27.
Stuart, Rieky. 2011. "Women, Canada, and the World: Is Canada Failing?" McLeod
    Group. http://www.mcleodgroup.ca/wp-content/uploads/2013/02/Women-
    Canada-and-the-World.pdf.
Swiss, Liam. 2009. "Developing Consensus: The Globalisation of Development
    Assistance Policies." PhD diss., McGill University.
– 2012a. "The Adoption of Women and Gender as Development Assistance
    Priorities: An Event History Analysis of World Polity Effects." *International
    Sociology* 27, no. 1: 96–119.
– 2012b. "Gender, Security and Instrumentalism: Canada's Foreign Aid in Support
    of National Interest?" In *Struggling for Aid Effectiveness: CIDA and Canadian
    Foreign Aid,* edited by Stephen Brown, 135–58. Montreal and Kingston: McGill-
    Queen's University Press.
– 2015. "Space for Gender Equality in the Security and Development Agenda?
    Insights from Three Donors." In *The Securitization of Foreign Aid,* edited by
    Stephen Brown and Jörn Grävingholt, 188–211. Basingstoke, UK: Palgrave
    Macmillan.

Tiessen, Rebecca. 2014. "Gender Equality and the 'Two CIDAs': Successes and
    Setbacks, 1976–2013." In *Rethinking Canadian Aid*, edited by Stephen Brown,
    David Black, and Molly Den Heyer, 195–209. Ottawa: University of Ottawa
    Press.

Tiessen, Rebecca, and Krystel Carrier. 2015. "The Erasure of 'Gender' in Canadian
    Foreign Policy under the Harper Conservatives: The Significance of the Shift
    from 'Gender Equality' to 'Equality between Women and Men.'" *Canadian
    Foreign Policy Journal* 21, no. 2: 95–111.

Tomlinson, Brian. 2013. *Briefing Note on Canada's Aid Marker for Gender Equality*.
    AidWatch Canada.

Turenne-Sjolander, Claire. 2005. "Canadian Foreign Policy: Does Gender Mat-
    ter?" *Canadian Foreign Policy Journal* 12, no. 1: 19–31.

Chapter 2

Missed Opportunity: A Discursive Analysis of Canada's Commitments to Maternal Health under the Muskoka Initiative

Julia Keast

INTRODUCTION

The 2010 Canadian-hosted G8 summit provided the Canadian government with an opportunity to lead discussions about existing global priorities and to establish new ones. Setting the agenda for the G8 summit is not only about establishing global priorities; it is also an act of self-definition by the host country on the world stage. The issues that a country chooses to focus on send a message to the world about what that country deems important. In 2010, Canada chose to focus on maternal, newborn, and child health (MNCH), and the summit culminated in the creation of the Muskoka Initiative (MI) – a major commitment that aims to address MNCH in the Global South.

Paradoxically, the announcement that Canada would be spearheading an initiative targeting MNCH came at a time when the Canadian government seemed to be in the process of shifting focus away from gender equality issues in its development discourse (Carrier and Tiessen 2013). These events are puzzling because improving maternal health is arguably closely linked to advancing gender equality (Paruzzolo et al. 2010). The puzzle surrounding Canada's commitments to gender equality has been explored in both the introduction and the previous chapter. As the introduction points out, there has been on one level a discursive erasure of gender equality – a decreased emphasis under the Harper Conservatives. Yet, as Swiss and Barry (in this volume) note in an examination of how development projects are coded, there has not been a meaningful shift away from gender equality issues over the past several years. In this chapter, I offer insights into this puzzle, and give context to and analysis of what it means to make a discursive commitment to promoting maternal and newborn health. I also examine how this discourse can inform us about Canada's gender equality commitments, and even how gender inequality can be (inadvertently) perpetuated through the use of particular discourses. I present the discursive analysis of maternal health as a missed opportunity to (1) recognize the importance of gender equality in maternal health initiatives and (2) advance women's rights and gender equality in a progressive and sustainable way, and more specifically at the discursive level a missed opportunity to engage Canadians and the international community in a discussion about the deeper issues perpetuating maternal health-related challenges.

Addressing maternal and newborn health can significantly advance gender equality (Paruzzolo et al. 2010). However, it does not necessarily do so unless efforts are also made to tackle root problems. For example, building a maternal health clinic can allow women access to safer births, important information about childhood nutrition, and sexual and reproductive health information and services that can help them gain greater control over decisions affecting their bodies. However, if entrenched forms of inequality, including gender inequality, prevent women from accessing these services, then the clinics offer little more than partial and temporary solutions to bigger challenges. This chapter examines the way in which MNCH is discussed in terms of gender equality, if at all. The study involves a discourse analysis of several key government documents to better understand the effect of maternal health programming. It does not solve the puzzle noted above, but it does offer glimpses into the limitations and missed opportunities in how MNCH is promoted.

The core argument presented in this chapter is that despite critical connections between gender inequality and maternal health outcomes, as well as ongoing commitments to women's health through the MI, gender equality and women's rights have not been considered relevant to the achievement of the MI goals. Evidence of this missed opportunity can be found in how a particular discourse is used to frame MNCH policies.

THE IMPORTANCE OF A DISCOURSE ANALYSIS TO UNDER-
STANDING CANADIAN COMMITMENTS AND THE PORTRAYAL OF
CANADIAN VALUES

Language is fundamental to understanding the way that we order, understand, and act in the world. It is through discourse that the social world is
made meaningful, and the importance of discourse should not be under-
estimated. The discursive shift away from gender equality examined in
chapter one, for example, provides the entry point for my examination of
language use in the MI – specifically how the Canadian government uses
language to portray certain ideas (about maternal health and women)
and to promote particular policies (in response to identified problems
like maternal mortality). I interrogate how the Canadian government,
through the MI, not only represents women and maternal mortality, but
itself as well (its own identity and role in combatting maternal mortality).
Using critical discourse analysis guided by intersectional, postcolonial
perspectives, I explore how Canada has promoted MNCH through official
government communications. This analysis can inform our understanding of how the Canadian government presents information about women,
itself, and maternal health in the context of the MI. Ultimately, this
understanding brings into focus the principles and priorities that guide
Canada's international development policy.

The findings articulated in this chapter draw on a content analysis of
fifteen publicly available documents produced by the Harper Conservatives on the MI between January 2010 and November 2013. I examined
a combination of press releases, backgrounders, and key policy documents from the former Canadian International Development Agency's
(CIDA) website and the prime minister of Canada's website. The analysis
also includes official speech transcripts available on the MI through the
websites of former prime minister Stephen Harper and the ministers for
both international development and cooperation. The most prominent
finding is the failure to address gender (or even use the language of gender or gender equality), which I argue is a glaring omission in efforts to
promote programming to reduce maternal mortality. Rather, the rhetorical approach is one of victims (pregnant women and mothers) requiring
saviours (Canada as a "champion" of women's health), a juxtaposition
or dichotomy that perpetuates a process of othering. Furthermore, the
emphasis on accountability and results leads to a policy centred narrowly
on the technical aspects of maternal and child mortality, which allows
Canada to appear to remain committed to gender equality through the
coding of maternal health programs as addressing gender equality (to

build on some of Swiss and Barry's findings and analysis). In the section that follows I provide some context to the MI and return to the above analyses in subsequent sections.

THE MUSKOKA INITIATIVE AND CANADA'S MATERNAL HEALTH COMMITMENTS

One of the UN's Millennium Development Goals (MDGs), established in 2000, was the promotion of improved maternal and newborn health. The launching of the MI, carefully timed to coincide with the G8 meetings in Canada in 2010, capitalized on this MDG priority. The purpose of the MI is to improve the health of mothers, newborns, and children in the Global South through three related areas of focus: (1) strengthening health systems, (2) improving nutrition, and (3) reducing the burden of disease affecting mothers and children (CIDA n.d.). The Canadian government committed a total of $2.85 billion in funding between 2010 and 2015. The MI is implemented through three different channels: bilateral aid focused on ten priority countries, multilateral and global institutions, and partnerships with twenty-eight Canadian civil society organizations as part of the Muskoka Initiative Partnership Program (MIPP). Assistance provided through each channel is focused on at least one of the three priority areas. Canada renewed its commitment to maternal health in 2014 at the Saving Every Woman, Every Child summit in Toronto where Canada pledged to continue to support maternal and newborn health programming through the Saving Women, Saving Lives commitment. Here again, the Harper Conservatives promised a large sum of funds – $3.5 billion – to continue to advance maternal health programming in developing countries between 2015 and 2020 (DFATD 2014).

Critics of the MI were quick to point out a range of problems with the earliest iterations of the maternal health strategy. Actors ranging from scholars to women's groups have, among other things, emphasized the MI's failure to include abortion (Auld and MacDonald 2010; Campbell 2010; Haussman and Mills 2012) or to adequately address gender and other socio-economic determinants of maternal and child health (Black 2011; Caplan 2010; Carrier and Tiessen 2013).

There was much confusion and controversy surrounding the question of whether or not funding for family planning and/or abortion would be included in the Initiative. This confusion was fuelled by inconsistency in the comments made by government representatives. First, in March 2010, foreign minister Lawrence Cannon claimed that the Initiative would not include funding for contraceptives, saying that maternal health "does not deal in any way, shape or form with family planning. Indeed, the purpose of this is to be able to save lives" (Campbell 2010). A few days later, Prime Minister Harper stated that "we are not closing the doors to any options, and that includes contraception, but we do not want a debate, here or elsewhere, on abortion" (Harper, cited in Haussman and Mills 2012). This was followed by high profile criticism from Hillary Clinton in April 2010, condemning the decision to exclude family planning and abortion. She insisted that maternal health must include access to contraception, family planning, and safe, legal abortion (cited by Clark 2010). In spite of some of these early criticisms, the Harper Conservatives continued on its particular course in its efforts to promote maternal health strategies. Although the MI and maternal health commitments were a highly important response to a real development challenge, the official rhetoric that followed reflected a particularly narrow vision of saving vulnerable victims – an argument advanced by Tiessen (2015a) – with highly targeted but limited strategies for maternal health outcomes. An analysis of what the organizations working in maternal health did with the funds is beyond the scope of this analysis. Rather, this piece begins to explore the context in which these practices take place on the ground – the rhetorical commitments. I turn now to the analysis of the documents and how the identities of Canadian actors and beneficiaries of the MI have been constructed within them.

IDENTITY CONSTRUCTION: CANADIAN CHAMPIONS AND VULNERABLE MOTHERS

Canadian Government's Portrayal of Itself/Stephen Harper (Champions)

Many lexical choices have been made in the texts to portray Prime Minister Harper and the Canadian government as possessing authority, power, and legitimacy vis-à-vis maternal and child health. The consistent use of words such as "champion" and "leadership," particularly in the context of "saving the lives" of mothers and children, connotes the sense that Canada is leading the international community's efforts to improve maternal and child health. These words appear in all of the fifteen documents examined. The word "champion" was used seven times to describe Canada, while on nineteen occasions Canada was depicted as a "leader" or displaying "leadership" and/or accountability on maternal and child health. A representative press release from 12 August 2010 states: "Canada led the way in mobilizing support among G8 and non-G8 leaders, key donors and private foundations for this initiative to reduce the mortality rates of mothers and their children. We have been successful." Some documents even allude to Canada's leadership role at the G8 summit as the reason for renewed attention being paid to maternal and child health, such as this press release from 26 January 2011: "Canada was a catalyst in 2010 for the renewed effort to save the lives of mothers, children and newborns in developing countries." The frequent use of words such as "champion" and "leader" puts the focus on Canada rather than on those who are in need of improved maternal health care. This is perhaps not surprising, as it is common for governments to engage in this form of bullhorn diplomacy.

Canada is portrayed not simply as a leader in promoting women and children's health, but as a legitimate leader with authority and knowledge about the best ways to address maternal and child health. This portrayal is formed in the texts through the use of specific linguistic techniques – including "quoting verbs" and the use of "material processes" – that work to solidify Canada's position of authority on the issue of maternal and child health.

The type of verb used in a text to describe actions influences the reader's interpretation of those actions. For instance, in every headline discussing the MI, the prime minister "announces" decisions. For example: "On September 25th 2013, Prime Minister Stephen Harper announced Canadian support in the amount of $203.55 million for nine projects with a global reach." The verb "announce" is a metapropositional verb, a type of quoting verb. These verbs are assertive and directive, making the subject appear to be in control. The MI-related statements would not exude the same confidence and authority if the verb "announced" was replaced with the verb "said," which sounds more neutral. Here, the verb "announce" suggests to the reader that Prime Minister Harper, the announcer, has power and legitimacy.

Another technique for conveying authority, power, and legitimacy in texts is to describe people as active agents – making decisions and performing actions – through the use of material processes. In the texts, I discovered multiple references to Canada as an active agent. For instance, from a 20 September 2011 press release: "Since the launch of the Muskoka Initiative in June 2010, Canada has taken decisive actions with its maternal, newborn and child health partners to achieve sustainable and meaningful results for mothers and children in developing countries." Material processes must include two participants: the actor, who performs the action, and the goal or the participant to whom the process is directed (Machin and Mayr 2012, 106). As such, material processes reinforce the idea that only the actor – the active agent – possesses agency. In this case, Canada's action to address maternal and child health is juxtaposed with the lack of agency of the women, who are presented as the beneficiaries of the Canadian government's actions.

The examples drawn from the texts demonstrate the manner in which Canada portrays itself as a knowledgeable leader on maternal and child health. They also demonstrate how, through the use of language, the Canadian government presents itself as an authority figure on these issues, giving its ideas on how to understand and respond to maternal mortality considerable weight, legitimacy, and credibility.

Canadian Government's Portrayal of the "Other" (Vulnerable Mothers)
Identity cannot stand alone; it must be shaped in opposition to something or someone else. In this case, a category of "vulnerable women" is created in opposition to Canada's position of authority and power. There is a long history of women being represented as powerless, passive recipients of development assistance in discourses of international development (Klenk 2004; Mohanty 1988; Parpart 1995). The way women are depicted in the documents analyzed is similar to the way they are depicted under the women in development (WID) approach: as a homogenous group of voiceless victims. They represent the passive, agency-less "other" to a Canada that sees itself as powerful and authoritative.

Women are also depicted as highly – and nearly exclusively – vulnerable and in need of saving. Throughout the texts, the words used most frequently in relation to women include "mothers," "vulnerable," and "saving lives." There were 134 references to "women" and 75 references to women as "mothers." These references appear in press releases – "Canada champions accountability in global efforts to save mothers and children in developing countries" (from 20 September 2011) – and in Harper's speeches on the topic of maternal and child health – "one of the world's great tragedies ... is the shocking mortality of mothers and their young children in developing countries" (from a speech to the United Nations in 2013). Moreover, women were referred to as "vulnerable" twenty-four times in fifteen documents. The criticism here is not necessarily the depiction of women and children as vulnerable per se. The problem is that consistently linking "mothers" and "women" to vulnerability creates the sense that all women throughout the Global South are mothers, and that all mothers are vulnerable simply because they are women and mothers.

While it may seem obvious that women would be referred to as mothers in the context of an initiative that addresses maternal health, there are times when it is unnecessary. In the following example, it would make just as much sense to substitute "women" for "mothers": "Canada's contribution to the Muskoka Initiative supports comprehensive and integrated approaches that provide the necessary health services for mothers and children" (CIDA 2011, 1). The decision to describe women as "mothers" may very well be deliberate, given that motherhood evokes a particular image and role both for the recipient and for the donor. Using the language of "motherhood," however, has implications. It emphasizes women's reproductive roles while moving other elements of a woman's identity to the background. In so doing, women (or "mothers") are relegated to specific roles by virtue of biology. They are denied their agency as productive members of the family and contributors to community-based work.

As the examples and discussion above illustrate, the Canadian government uses language to create an image of itself as a champion of MNCH, and positions itself as an authority on what should and should not be included in a policy addressing MNCH. At the same time, women are constructed as vulnerable victims in need of saving. Combining these two ideas creates an overarching narrative that places Canada as the saviour and protector of women and children's health in the Global South.

In international development, representations are often framed in an us/them dichotomy (Kapoor 2004) or the language of Othering (Spivak 1988). In this case, the Canadian government is working to save the lives of women in the Global South ("others"). Inherent in this kind of framing is a power relationship between those who are doing the representing and those who are being represented; those whose voices are heard and those whose voices are excluded (Spivak 1988). Moreover, as Kapoor (2004) points out, we construct the "Third World" – or in this case, women in the Global South – through discourse to satisfy our own idea of what it should look like. Those doing the representing are often acting in line with personal, professional, institutional, or organizational interests. As a result, "representations say more about those doing the representing than those represented" (Kapoor 2004, 636).

A DISCOURSE ANALYSIS OF WHAT IS NOT SAID: WHERE IS GENDER EQUALITY IN THE MUSKOKA INITIATIVE?

A review of the fifteen Canadian government documents turned up very few references to broader socioeconomic or cultural factors such as pervasive gender inequality. These broader socioeconomic and cultural factors provide an intersectional lens through which to better understand inequality in access to health care. As Stienstra (in this volume) explains, engaging in a "rich analysis with complex policy responses requires that we ask what power relations or inequalities are at work, and examine ways in which these diverse relations are mutually constituted or mutually shaped, and their various effects" (119). Incorporating intersectionality into the discussion is important because it sheds light on the ways in which interlocking systems of oppression, including sexism, racism, classism, ableism, and colonialism, are all entwined in complex ways that contribute to the perpetuation of maternal and child mortality.

To say that systems of oppression are interlocking means that "systems of oppression come into existence in and through one another so that class exploitation could not be accomplished without gender and racial hierarchies; imperialism could not function without class exploitation, sexism, heterosexism, and so on" (Fellows and Razack 1998, 335). This way of thinking challenges the idea that "each discrimination has a single, direct, and independent effect on status, wherein the relative contribution of each is readily apparent" (King 1997, 222). In turn, oppression cannot be categorized simply in terms of gender, race, or class; rather, these categories are all linked (Fellows and Razack 1998, 335). Intersectionality helps us understand the complex issue of maternal mortality – which is affected by a mix of factors, including but not limited to cultural practices, ethnicity, racism, age, ability, and gender – as well as how access to maternal and child health services can vary greatly within societies. For example, even if health clinics are built and staffed by qualified people, broader social forces may prevent some women and girls, or men and boys, from using these services. This can be seen in a study in Ghana (Ganle et al. 2015), which suggested that family members (including husbands and mothers-in-law) and other community members heavily influenced the decisions women were making regarding access to and use of maternal health services. The study concludes that interconnected processes of gender inequality, economic marginalization, and social power dynamics undercut women's autonomy in decision making, thus complicating efforts to improve access to maternal health services. Provision of services, therefore, does not ensure that people will be able to access them. Rather, comprehensive development strategies require careful attention to gender relations and social processes that may inhibit the full use of services. They also require educational campaigns that promote a change in attitudes and behaviours that addresses social inequalities, thereby encouraging equitable access to reproductive health care for everyone.

Just as overusing certain words helps reinforce a particular message (such as the overuse of the term "mother"), not using certain words sends a powerful message as well. My textual analysis revealed that references to or discussion about gender, race, ability, or sexuality are either scarce or missing in the texts examined. The absence of gender is particularly glaring in the Muskoka Declaration, which outlines the purpose and scope of the Initiative. This document indicates that the MI will focus on the fourth MDG (reducing child mortality) and the fifth MDG (reducing maternal mortality), while also touching on parts of the first MDG (nutrition) and the sixth MDG (preventing HIV/AIDS and malaria). Although this document connects MDGs one and six with maternal and child mortality, it fails to acknowledge the critical connections with the third MDG – promoting gender equality and empowering women. Although the document acknowledges the importance of adopting a comprehensive approach to address maternal and child mortality, no reference is made to underlying causes of maternal and child mortality.

Although gender is mostly absent in the texts examined, it was mentioned in one of the MI's guiding documents, titled "The G8 Muskoka Flagship Initiative: Maternal, Newborn and Under-Five Child Health." The document connects the importance of addressing root causes of maternal and child mortality with sustainability of results: "Major improvements in the health and well-being of women and children will not be sustainable without parallel acceleration of donor and developing country commitments to gender equality, human rights of women and girls, women's economic empowerment and political engagement, to education for all children, particularly for girls, and to protection of women and children in situations of conflict" (G8 2010b, 2).

Although this statement clearly indicates the importance of addressing gender inequality as well as other underlying causes of maternal and child mortality, the document goes on to explain that the MI will not actively work on these issues. There is no justification provided in this document as to why issues surrounding gender inequality will not be addressed through the MI. Moreover, despite a brief acknowledgement of some factors that influence maternal health outcomes, the document fails to understand the way in which multiple forms of inequality interact and influence one another to contribute to poor maternal health outcomes. This exclusion helps to position maternal and child mortality as technical development issues, void of the social, economic, cultural, and legal contexts within which they occur. Although maternal and child mortality have been framed in technical terms, this strategy could be construed as highly political – pandering to conservative values by avoiding an approach that might not fall in line with traditional family values.

MEASURING SUCCESS: AID EFFECTIVENESS,
ACCOUNTABILITY, AND RESULTS

The way in which development problems are framed through language is important because language also serves to frame the range of acceptable solutions for dealing with a problem (Crush 1995). The emphasis in the texts on accountability and results provides the Canadian public with a lens through which to interpret the Canadian government's MI-related activities. I argue that in using the discourses of aid effectiveness and accountability for results, the Canadian government frames the issue of maternal mortality as a technical problem, which works to emphasize the elements of maternal mortality that can be addressed through technical solutions while concealing the range of social, cultural, political, and legal dimensions that contribute to the perpetuation of maternal and child mortality. Incorporating this type of language also serves to position maternal mortality as a problem that can be solved through Western or Canadian interventions, when it is largely the result of a number of complex factors including deeply embedded social norms. The specific discursive silence on rights and the failure to acknowledge and promote advancements in gender relations can be seen as a political move, as mentioned above.

Aid effectiveness has become an important buzzword in aid circles (Brown 2012). It has taken on specific meanings in current aid discourse, representing a new ideal of how aid can be better managed according to a certain set of criteria (Hayman 2009, 582). The emphasis on aid effectiveness has materialized in the Canadian aid context with respect to the MI. Several scholars have suggested that development assistance in Canada has undergone major transformations since 2000, including a new focus on aid effectiveness and accountability in government spending and a focus on results and increased policy coherence (Brown 2012; Haussman and Mills 2012; Huish and Spiegel 2012). Brown suggests that Canada has developed an unhealthy preoccupation with results, a "fixation bordering on obsession" (Brown 2012, 87). This fixation favours development assistance that leads to tangible and immediate results, which Brown (2012) claims is epitomized by Canada's development projects in Afghanistan. As many critics note, this preoccupation with results can negatively affect programming relating to gender equality and women's rights, as these types of programs do not always yield tangible or quick results (Hendriks 2005; McGill 2012, 44; Plewes and Kerr 2010). Nor can substantial progress towards transforming unequal gender and power relations be achieved in a short period of time. By emphasizing results, the Canadian government is prioritizing measurable results at the expense of fostering meaningful, sustainable change through a more nuanced, multi-dimensional approach to development work. The Canadian government appears to be returning to a WID approach, and moving away from the more progressive gender and development approach (Tiessen 2015b). This can be seen through a rise in programming that defines women as victims as opposed to agents who can be actively involved in the development process.

A focus on accountability, results, and measuring success is a major theme in the texts I examined. There are thirty-nine references made to accountability in the texts I reviewed. These references pertain to ensuring accountability for results related to maternal and child health, and often highlight Canada's leadership role in this regard. Canada's leadership role is emphasized in this quote, pulled from CIDA's 2011–2012 Departmental Performance Report: "At the Forum, Canada emphasized the need to re-centre the development dialogue on results and accountability and highlighted its leadership in enhancing accountability in the health sector through the G8 Muskoka Initiative on Maternal, Newborn and Child Health and the UN Commission on Information and Accountability for Women's and Children's Health" (CIDA 2012a, 31).

This quote clearly positions Canada as a leader in accountability, and confirms that the Canadian government wishes to centre its development initiatives for maternal and child health on results and accountability. As well as ensuring accountability for results, the texts I reviewed also include multiple references to ensuring the sustainability of results, such as this press release from 20 September 2011: "Canada places accountability at the core of its international development efforts and has worked closely with its partners to develop a framework to measure progress, track results and ensure that funding helps partner countries achieve a sustainable reduction in maternal and child mortality rates."

These ideas are also referenced in both of the MI's guiding policy documents. From the multiple references to sustainability of results, this seems to be an important goal attached to the MI. Moreover, the Canadian government has used this discourse to frame maternal mortality as a problem that can be solved through interventions that are both measurable and "technical." Several scholars highlight the technical framing of international development (Escobar 1995; Ferguson 1990). Ferguson advances the argument that agencies involved in development work are interested in locating the right kind of problem, one that requires a solution that the agency is then able to provide. Part of Escobar's (1995) critique of international development concerns the process of professionalization, which allows development problems (such as poverty) to be removed from political and cultural realms and reframed in more neutral, scientific terms. As Harcourt (2009) argues, removing issues from their political or cultural context and reframing them in more scientific terms shifts the policy focus from long-term transformative change to delivering short-term solutions that yield immediate results.

Focusing on the professional intervention and management of childbirth fits into the long historical trend towards the medicalization of childbirth, in which pregnancy and childbirth need to be managed and monitored by specialists (Pigg 1995). This medicalization, combined with a preference for biomedical approaches over local knowledge and abilities, highlights a clear continuity from the colonial period: in the same way that the health of colonized people needed to be managed by colonizers, the health of people living in the Global South today still needs to be managed by development experts (Packard 2000).

The examples presented above clearly illustrate that the Canadian government is sympathetic towards development initiatives that can be easily measured, and that success will be determined based on what can be counted. The focus on tangible and measurable results is not surprising, particularly since politicians are not usually interested in tackling problems that are complicated and require long-term efforts (Wendland 2012). The heavy emphasis on accountability and results, therefore, fits very well with the chosen areas of focus in the MI. Each of the Initiative's goals (strengthening health systems, improving nutrition, and reducing the burden of disease) can easily have corresponding interventions that can be measured without too much difficulty.

There are two major implications of the Harper government's decision to focus on service delivery and the technical side of maternal mortality. First, the government is able to portray itself as promoting an "unqualified normative good" (Robinson 2014, 89). As Robinson points out, it is difficult to argue with the promotion of maternal health, particularly when it is constructed outside the realm of politics. After all, who would disagree with supporting the health of mothers and children? By de-politicizing maternal health, the Canadian government is able to shift the focus away from the different economic, political, social, and legal structures that contribute to the marginalization of women around the world. Second, in framing MNCH as an apolitical and technical issue, the Canadian government is able to speak confidently about how they will be ensuring accountability and achieving results.

In sum, the language used to frame and discuss development problems is important, especially because it can establish the range of solutions deemed acceptable or available to deal with the problems. As has been discussed here, the focus on accountability and results in the official discourse surrounding the MI works to de-politicize the issue of maternal and child mortality. This framing helps to create the idea that maternal and child mortality are simply technical problems, while pushing the more complex issues surrounding maternal and child mortality out of the frame. As a result, the acceptable solutions promoted are also mostly technical in nature. These types of solutions are more easily measured, and as a result it is easier for the government of Canada to demonstrate progress and accountability. As Black (2011) argues, by failing to incorporate the underlying causes of maternal and child mortality, the MI is in effect accepting the conditions that contribute to maternal and child mortality, which in turn jeopardizes the sustainability of the Initiative itself.

CONCLUSION

The Canadian government has invested a significant amount of resources to advancing maternal health care through the MI, an initiative that was endorsed through ongoing commitments in 2014 through the Saving Every Woman, Every Child conference. These are impressive commitments that have yielded important results, and have the potential to produce positive change in the lives of women and girls, as well as men and boys. Yet, so far it has been a largely missed opportunity in the sense that it has focused narrowly on women's victimhood rather than rights, and on measurable results in terms of clinics built without equal consideration for whether or not they can be accessed. Canada's approach has looked like a return to WID programming, without sufficient regard for how entrenched social inequalities may prevent people from accessing the services that are being delivered.

However, with the advent of a new government comes a fresh opportunity to build upon the commitments and advancements in maternal and child health that have been made thus far. During their campaign, the Liberal Party of Canada pledged to maintain the positive momentum Canada has made on improving maternal and child health. They have also acknowledged the importance of advancing a more comprehensive approach to maternal and child health. This is an important first step, but it will need to be followed up with concrete action that supports a more holistic and inclusive approach to MNCH issues. More specifically, the new government could adopt a more multi-sectoral approach, as well as focus more on demand-side factors in its MNCH activities.

A multi-sectoral approach would involve addressing MNCH concerns that cut across various sections, including education and employment

(Tolhurst, Raven, and Theobald 2009). It would involve striving towards transformational change, by targeting root causes that contribute to maternal and child mortality. Moreover, additional interventions to increase the demand for MNCH services should accompany the MI's heavy focus on supply-side projects. A number of studies and scholars support addressing both supply- and demand-side barriers to improved MNCH, in suggesting that not all women (particularly the poorest and most marginalized) will necessarily benefit from improved maternal health through an expansion of service delivery (Freedman 2001; Grown et al. 2005; Paruzolo et al. 2010; Tolhurst, Raven, and Theobald 2009). To be sure, the MI does include *some* projects that focus on demand, but these are heavily outweighed by the myriad supply-side projects that focus on such things as training birth attendants, preventing mother-to-child transmission of HIV/AIDS, and providing education on perinatal and infant nutrition. There is thus a need to strike a more judicious balance between supply- and demand-side factors if women are to more fully benefit from the work of the MI. If women are unable to use the essential health services that are being provided, the MI will have missed a critical opportunity to improve MNCH.

REFERENCES

Auld, Alison, and Michael Macdonald. 2010. "Canada Wants Flexible Approach to G8 Plan on Maternal and Child Health." Canadian Press, 28 April. Accessed 14 October 2013. http://www.cigionline.org/articles/2010/04/canada-wants-flexible-approach-g8-plan-maternal-and-child-health.

Black, David. 2009. "Canada, the G8, and Africa: The Rise and Decline of a Hegemonic Project?" Paper presented at Africa International: Agency and Interdependency in a Changing World, London, UK, 9 October 2009. Accessed 5 February 2014. http://www.open.ac.uk/socialsciences/bisa-africa/confpapers/Black%20D%20Canada%20G8%20Africa.pdf.

Brown, Stephen. 2012. "Aid Effectiveness and the Framing of New Canadian Aid Initiatives." In *Struggling for Effectiveness: CIDA and Canadian Foreign Aid*, edited by Stephen Brown, 79–107. Montreal and Kingston: McGill-Queen's University Press.

Campbell, Clark. 2010. "G8 Pledges Fall Short of What's Needed." *Globe and Mail*, 25 June.

Canadian International Development Agency (CIDA). 2011. *Departmental Performance Report: 2010–11*. Canadian International Development Agency.

– 2012a. *Departmental Performance Report: 2011–12*. Canadian International Development Agency.

– 2012b. *Report to Parliament on the Government of Canada's Official Development Assistance: 2011–2012*. Canadian International Development Agency.

– n.d. *Maternal, Newborn and Child Health*. Canadian International Development Agency.

Caplan, Gerald. 2010. "The Sad Truth about Harper and Maternal Health." *Globe and Mail*, 26 March.

Carrier, Krystel, and Rebecca Tiessen. 2013. "Women and Children First: Maternal Health and the Silence of Gender in Canadian Foreign Policy." In *Canada in the World: Feminist Perspectives on Canadian Foreign Policy*, edited by Heather Smith and Claire Turenne-Sjolander, 183–200. Oxford: Oxford University Press.

Clark, Campbell. 2010. "Birth Control Won't Be in G8 Plan to Protect Mothers, Tories Say." *Globe and Mail*, 17 March.

Collins, Michelle. 2009. "'Gender Equality,' 'Child Soldiers' and 'Humanitarian Law' Are Axed from Foreign Policy Language." *Embassy Magazine*, 29 July.

Crush, Jonathan. 1995. Introduction to *Power of Development*, edited by Jonathan Crush, 1–27. New York: Routledge.

Department of Foreign Affairs, Trade and Development (DFATD). 2014. *Canadian Leadership Saving the Lives of Women and Children across the Developing World*. Department of Foreign Affairs, Trade and Development.

Escobar, Arturo. 1995. *Encountering Development: The Making and Unmaking of the Third World*. Oxfordshire: Princeton University Press.

Fellows, Mary Louise, and Sherene Razack. 1998. "The Race to Innocence: Confronting Hierarchical Relations among Women." *Journal of Gender, Race and Justice* 1, no. 2: 335–52.

Ferguson, James. 1990. *The Anti-Politics Machine: 'Development,' Depoliticization, and Bureaucratic Power in Lesotho*. Cambridge: Cambridge University Press.

Foucault, Michel. 1980. "Truth and Power." In *The Foucault Reader*, edited by Paul Rabinow, 51–75. London: Penguin.

Freedman, Lynn. 2001. "Using Human Rights in Maternal Mortality Programs: From Analysis to Strategy." *International Journal of Gynecology and Obstetrics* 75: 51–60.

Ganle, John Kuumuori, Bernard Obeng, Alexander Yao Segbefia, Vitalis Mwinyuir, Joseph Yaw Yeboah, and Leonard Baatiema. 2015. "How Intra-Familial Decision-Making Affects Women's Access to, and Use of Maternal Healthcare Services in Ghana: A Qualitative Study." *BMC Pregnancy and Childbirth* 173: 1–17.

Group of Eight (G8). 2010a. *Muskoka Declaration: Recovery and New Beginnings. Annex 1: Muskoka Initiative on Maternal, Newborn and Under-Five Child Health*. Group of Eight. Accessed 1 October 2013. http://www.g8.utoronto.ca/summit/2010muskoka/communique.html.

– 2010b. *The G8 Muskoka Flagship Initiative: Maternal, Newborn and Under-Five Child Health*. Group of Eight. Accessed 1 October 2013. http://can-mnch.ca/wp-content/uploads/2011/10/Muskoka_G8_MNCH_Recommendations.pdf.

Grown, Caren, Geeta Rao Gupta, and Rohini Pande. 2005. "Taking Action to Improve Women's Health through Gender and Women's Empowerment." *Lancet* 365: 541–3.

Harcourt, Wendy. 2009. *Body Politics in Development: Critical Debates in Gender and Development*. London: Zed Books.

Haussman, Melissa, and Lisa Mills. 2012. "Doing the North American Two-Step on a Global Stage: Canada, the G8 Muskoka Initiative and Safe Abortion Funding." In *How Ottawa Spends: 2012–2013*, edited by Christopher Stoney and Bruce Doern. Montreal and Kingston: McGill-Queen's University Press.

Hayman, Rachel. 2009. "From Rome to Accra via Kigali: 'Aid Effectiveness' in Rwanda." *Development Policy Review* 27, no. 5: 581–99.

Hendriks, Sarah. 2005. "Advocates, Adversaries, and Anomalies: The Politics of Feminist Spaces in Gender and Development." *Canadian Journal of Development Studies* 26, special issue: 619–32.

Horton, Richard. 2010. "Gender Equity Is the Key to Maternal and Child Health." *Lancet* 375: 1939.

Huish, Robert, and Jerry Spiegel. 2012. "First as Tragedy and Then on to Farce: Canadian Foreign Aid for Global Health." *Canadian Foreign Policy Journal* 18, no. 2: 244–6.

Kapoor, Ilan. 2004. "Hyper-Self-Reflexive Development? Spivak on Representing the Third World 'Other.'" *Third World Quarterly* 25, no. 4: 627–47.

King, Deborah. 1997. "Multiple Jeopardy, Multiple Consciousness: The Context of a Black Feminist Ideology." In *Feminist Social Thought*, edited by Diana Meyers, 219–44. New York: Routledge.

Klenk, Rebecca. 2004. "Who Is the Developed Woman? Women as a Category of Development Discourse, Kumaon, India." *Development and Change* 35, no. 1: 57–78.

Machin, David, and Andrea Mayr. 2012. *How to Do Critical Discourse Analysis: A Multimodal Introduction*. London: Sage Publications.

McEwan, Cheryl. 2009. *Postcolonialism and Development*. New York: Routledge.

McGill, Hunter. 2012. "Canada among Donors: How Does Canadian Aid Compare?" In *Struggling for Effectiveness: CIDA and Canadian Foreign Aid*, edited by Stephen Brown, 24–52. Montreal and Kingston: McGill-Queen's University Press.

Mohanty, Chandra. 1988. "Under Western Eyes: Feminist Scholarship and Colonial Discourses." *Feminist Review* 30: 61–88.

Packard, Randall. 2000. "Post-Colonial Medicine." In *Medicine in the 20th Century*, edited by Roger Cooter and John Pickstone, 97–112. Amsterdam: Overseas Publishers Association.

Paruzzolo, Silvia, Mehra Rekha, Aslihan Kes, and Charles Ashbaugh. 2010. *Targeting Poverty and Gender Inequality to Improve Maternal Health*. Washington: Women Deliver.

Parpart, Jane. 1995. "Deconstructing the Development 'Expert': Gender, Development and the 'Vulnerable Groups.'" In *Feminism/Postmodernism/Development*, edited by Marianne Marchand and Jane Parpart, 221–43. New York: Routledge.

Percival, Valerie. 2010. "Women's Health Initiative Fails to Inspire." *Ottawa Citizen*, 28 June.

Pigg, Stacy. 1995. "Acronyms and Effacement: Traditional Medical Practitioners (TMP) in International Health Development." *Social Science Medicine* 41: 47–68.

Plewes, Betty, and Joanna Kerr. 2010. "Politicizing, Undermining Gender Equality." *Embassy*, 5 May.

Robinson, Fiona. 2014. "Discourses of Motherhood and Women's Health: Maternal Thinking as Feminist Politics." *Journal of International Political Theory* 10, no. 1: 94–108.

Rosenfield, Allan, and Caroline Min. 2009. "A History of International Cooperation in Maternal and Child Health." In *Maternal and Child Health: Global Challenges, Programs, and Policies*, edited by John Ehiri, 3–17. New York: Springer Science and Business Media.

Sjolander, Claire, Heather Smith, and Deborah Stienstra. 2003. *Feminist Perspectives on Canadian Foreign Policy*. Toronto: Oxford University Press 2003.

Sjolander, Claire, and Kathryn Trevenen. 2010. "Constructing Canadian Foreign Policy: Myths of Good International Citizens, Protectors and the War in Afghanistan." In *Canadian Foreign Policy in Critical Perspective*, edited by Marshall Beier and Lana Wylie, 44–57. Toronto: Oxford University Press.

Spivak, Gayatri. 1988. "Can the Subaltern Speak?" In *Marxism and Interpretation of Culture*, edited by Cary Nelson and Lawrence Grossberg, 271–313. Chicago: University of Illinois Press.

Tiessen, Rebecca. 2015a. "'Walking Wombs': Making Sense of the Muskoka Initiative and the Emphasis on Motherhood in Canadian Foreign Policy." *Global Justice: Theory Practice Rhetoric* 8, no. 1: 74–93.

– 2015b. "Gender Equality and the 'Two CIDAs': Successes and Setbacks, 1976–2013." In *Rethinking Canadian Aid*, edited by Stephen Brown, Molly den Heyer, and David Black, 195–210. Toronto: University of Ottawa Press.

Tolhurst, Rachel, Jo Raven, and Sally Theobald. 2009. "Gender Equity: Perspectives on Maternal and Child Health." In *Maternal and Child Health: Global*

Challenges, Programs, and Policies, edited by John Ehiri, 151–66. New York: Springer Science and Business Media.

Wendland, Claire. 2012. "New Approaches to Maternal Mortality in Africa." An interdisciplinary workshop sponsored by King's College, Cambridge.

Chapter 3

Queer Canada? The Harper Government and International Lesbian, Gay, Bisexual, Transgender, and Intersex Rights

Marc Epprecht and Stephen Brown

Canadian foreign policy took an unprecedented turn in 2009 when Prime Minister Stephen Harper "privately" lobbied Ugandan president Yoweri Museveni not to allow the passage of a private member's bill by his country's parliament. The Anti-Homosexuality Act would have created a slew of new crimes including "aggravated homosexuality" (which carried a potential death sentence) and called for Uganda to have its citizens living abroad extradited back home to face "justice." We put "privately" in scare quotes because Harper was widely quoted in the media for his strong public rebuke of the sentiments behind the proposed bill: "We deplore these kinds of measures. We find them inconsistent with, frankly, I think any reasonable understanding of human rights" (quoted in Chase 2009).

In one sense this perspective was not new. The Canadian government decriminalized consenting adult same-sex sexual activity in 1969, under the Liberal government of Pierre Trudeau. In the late 1990s, under Jean Chrétien, it began to outlaw discrimination, including in the military. In the 2000s, provincial and federal courts gradually pressed the government to recognize same-sex partnerships, culminating in the full recognition of same-sex marriage in 2005. Internationally, since the late 1980s Canada supported multilateral institutions such as the World Health Organization and the United Nations Programme on HIV/AIDS (UNAIDS), which have promoted sexual rights and targeted homophobia as part of their broad approach to combatting HIV. Canada backed the so-called Brazilian resolution, which introduced concern over human rights violations on the basis of sexual orientation into the United Nations in 2003. It also supported the Yogyakarta Principles, which developed guidelines in 2006 for international law with respect to sexual orientation and gender identity. In short, Canada has unquestionably been among the leaders in the world in establishing lesbian, gay, bisexual, transgender, and intersex (lgbti) rights as an important component of an overarching human rights and global public health framework.[1]

Still, to directly criticize a friendly country over a highly sensitive issue currently before its parliament was a different matter. Harper's strong language on Uganda thus signalled a turn that drew unusual praise for his government from sexual rights activists, and pointed criticism from its conservative base (MacKinnon 2013). It was speculated to have contributed to the disinvitation of Nigerian president Goodluck Jonathan from a planned 2014 official state visit to protest his signing of an odiously homophobic bill into Nigerian law (Pink News 2014; York 2014). There is no evidence that it did, but had that been true, it would have been an act of remarkable diplomatic principle against Canada's largest and rapidly growing trading partner in Africa.

Critics of the Harper government from the political left had good reason to be sceptical that principles were really in play behind the anti-homophobia turn in Canada's foreign policy. The Harper government had its roots in the Reform Party and in Christian "family values," which historically had opposed sexual rights in Canada in often highly inflammatory terms. Only three Conservative members of parliament (MPs) (out of ninety-six present) voted in favour of same-sex marriage in 2005 – and Harper was prominent among the opponents (Parliament of Canada 2005). As late as May 2013, the large majority of Tory MPs opposed a bill that would prohibit hate crimes against transgender people (Canadian Press 2013a). Harper was also notorious for exploiting emotive "wedge" issues in order to court votes in highly targeted constituencies. There certainly seemed to be an element of cynicism involved when Minister of Immigration Jason Kenney sent out a targeted mass email that boasted of his facilitating refugee asylum for Iranian lgbti claimants (CBC News 2012). Kenney's voting record in parliament on related issues of gender equality and sexual rights did not suggest an easy affinity with this sudden concern about discrimination against lgbti Iranians. Not only had he voted against same-sex marriage in Canada in 2005, but according to the anti-abortion, anti–sexual rights lobby group Campaign Life Coalition (n.d.), "Jason also has a perfect voting record on life & family."

A number of scholars – including the editors of and contributors to this book – offer a broad critique of countries such as Canada that pose as defenders of human rights yet at the same time work assiduously to defend economic or strategic interests that in many cases undermine the very rights they loudly proclaim. The concepts of homonormativity (Duggan 2002), homonationalism (Puar 2008), and homocolonialism (Rahmin 2014) all highlight ways in which ahistorical sexual rights discourses have recently emerged in the West to define, celebrate, project, and police narrowly normative identity categories. Far from being queer in a liberatory sense, these discourses perpetuate inherited colonial privileges and facilitate ongoing neoliberal assaults on local cultures and autonomies. The United States, notably, has only recently and only partially extended human rights protections to its own citizens on the basis of sexual orientation and gender identity, and yet it now holds select other countries up for condemnation. This, in the context of US militarism, trade unilateralism, aggressive promotion of intellectual property rights, "gag rules," and "loyalty oaths" in its development assistance, raises some eyebrows. From a Nigerian point of view, it certainly looks deeply hypocritical that the same country that criticizes Nigeria's Same Sex Marriage (Prohibition) Act had its own Defense of Marriage Act (DOMA) from 1996 until 2013 that explicitly enabled discrimination against same-sex couples. The president of Senegal gently pointed out another inconsistency when US president Barack Obama visited Senegal in 2013 and trumpeted the demise of DOMA as proof of American democratic values. Maybe Senegal should follow the shining American example and decriminalize homosexual acts? "It is just like the capital punishment," President Macky Sall responded drolly, "In our country, we have abolished it for many years. In other countries, it is still the order of the day, because the situation in the country requires it." In short, the gap between the recent concern in the US for lgbti rights abroad and its own deeply entrenched domestic practices raises a question to many people outside the bubble of Western triumphalism: Is there another, hidden agenda at play?

Jasbir Puar's term *homonationalism* captures the instrumentalist use of lgbti rights to create an aura of moral superiority and developmental sophistication (Puar 2008). Nations or parties that fail to meet the new yardstick can in this vein legitimately have their bona fides questioned on any number of unrelated issues. The term "pinkwashing" has also been coined to describe using praise for lgbti rights as a ploy to distract from other forms of discrimination or violence conducted by us or our friends (Schulman 2011). In the case of Israel, for example, the lack of sexual minority rights in the Islamic world could ostensibly offset criticism of the Israeli occupation of most of Palestine.

We aim in this chapter to assess just how queer Canada has become on the international stage in light of the above critiques. Our underlying assumption is that promoting lgbti rights is indeed a good and necessary step in promoting human rights for the whole population, for global public health, and for broad development objectives, including poverty mitigation and maternal health (Beyrer et al. 2011; UN, n.d.). However, we start from the position that a chauvinistic, instrumentalist, selective, or culturally colonializing approach to promoting such rights cannot succeed, and indeed could potentially abet human rights abuses against not just scapegoated sexual minorities but other people suffering from "normal" discriminations and abuses as well. Outside narrowly partisan interests, nobody benefits from pinkwashing, so it is important to identify if, how, and why such instrumentalism is in play.[2]

CANADA'S RECORD

Let us start by simply noting that in the first three years of Harper's minority government, sexual rights were not an issue of diplomatic concern, notwithstanding serious violations or threats to those rights such as Nigeria's Same Sex Marriage (Prohibition) Act (tabled in 2007), proposed discriminatory laws and political homophobia in Poland, and the reported rise of extrajudicial homophobic or transphobic killings in US-occupied Iraq (for example, Tatchell 2007).

Public interventions only began with Harper's criticism of the Anti-Homosexuality Act in Uganda in 2009 – and they were not very common or consistent. John Baird first leapt into the debate even before he became minister of foreign affairs by denouncing the Ugandan bill in the House of Commons as "vile, abhorrent, offensive and it offends Canadian values and decency" (Parliament of Canada 2009). Similar sentiments were expressed by MPs from all parties through 2010 and 2011 (Parliament of Canada 2010, 2011). In June 2011, Canada co-sponsored (with forty other countries) the UN Human Rights Council resolution that explicitly demanded the protection of sexual minorities and the appointment of a rapporteur to monitor human rights abuses against lgbti individuals and their allies globally. Three months later, Baird made his inaugural address as minister of foreign affairs to the UN General Assembly. Out of roughly 2,300 words extolling the importance of human rights in general terms – and specifically denouncing North Korea, Libya, Iran, China, Egypt, and Burma – he mentioned gays and lesbians once, with reference to Uganda only. This was to demonstrate Canada's "solemn duty to defend the vulnerable" (Baird 2011a). Baird also brought up sexual orientation at the Organization for Security and Co-operation in Europe (OSCE) ministerial conference in Vilnius, Lithuania, that December, calling it "unacceptable" that people were still attacked and imprisoned on that basis in the region – implicitly meaning the former Eastern Bloc countries. The following year he mentioned the issue twice in his address to the General Assembly. He first included Iran's repression of gays and lesbians in his list of why Iran was the world's "most significant threat to global peace and security." Second, in an elaboration of the meaning of modern slavery, Baird noted that "[a]nother, despicable type of enslavement is the criminalization of sexuality: jailing, torturing and killing people for who they are, and whom they love." Canada urged fellow members to target all forms of modern slavery for eradication.

Baird's 2012 speech to the UN was followed soon after by a more extensive domestic discussion of the role that fighting homophobia should have in Canadian foreign policy. In a speech to the Montreal Council on Foreign Relations, Baird focused on Canada as being "a beacon of light" in a world where repression, injustice, extremism, and indignity were commonplace. Among the many "tough conversations" Canada would henceforth be "aggressively pursuing" on the global scene was the issue of the criminalization of homosexuality as an affront to human dignity, no matter how unpopular doing so would be with certain audiences. Baird spoke at length about the "unspeakable violence" taking place in Uganda and claimed to have played a lead role in promoting sexual minority rights worldwide with allies in the European Union and the US. In remarkably undiplomatic terms, he in effect referred to Ugandan parliamentarians as "violent mobs." Baird repeated the criticism the next day at the Inter-Parliamentary Union conference in Quebec City, with the Speaker of the Ugandan Parliament in the audience. She responded in kind by accusing Baird of "arrogance" and having a "colonial attitude" that only made her and her fellow citizens more determined to resist the bullying (Ling 2012).

Baird was by far the most outspoken minister on this file, with press releases over the years praising Malawi and Myanmar/Burma (for moving to repeal repressive laws), denouncing Russia, Uganda, and Nigeria (for invoking new ones), and generally promoting the benefits of freedom and human rights for all, including through a spirited defence of moral certainty against his critics from the political right. In 2013 he went as far as to claim that no country in the world had spoken as loudly as Canada in promoting the rights of "women and gays" (Parliament of Canada 2013). Successive ministers of immigration (Kenney and Chris Alexander) also pledged their support to the cause by making it easier for lgbti people to flee repression in their countries for asylum in Canada. Another strong voice was Conservative senator Hugh Segal, tasked with monitoring how

Commonwealth countries followed up the commitments to strengthen human rights that they made at the 2011 Commonwealth Heads of Government Meeting in Perth, Australia. That conference featured British prime minister David Cameron's threat to withdraw development aid from countries that violate lgbti rights, and Ghanaian president John Atta Mills's angry rejection of such conditionalities. Although Canada did not engage in the imbroglio at the time, Segal subsequently made the case for lgbti rights on the grounds of both natural justice and public health (Segal 2012). During the 2015 federal election campaign it was reported (albeit without evidence) that the Conservatives had included gays and lesbians who faced discrimination because of their sexuality among the asylum-seeking groups that Canada was specifically prioritizing for acceptance (Friesen 2015).

Compared to past silence or vague and euphemistic commitments, these statements were unquestionably remarkable. However, before accepting that the promotion of lgbti rights was an important component of Conservative foreign policy or that Canada was in fact a world leader, we should take careful note of continuing silences. Harper's low profile was perhaps the most striking, given his dominating role in defining so many other aspects of his government's agenda. Indeed, after Harper's early intervention with President Museveni, he almost always allowed others to speak on his government's behalf – a Boolean search of the *Hansard* from 2006 to 2015 does not turn up a single clear statement by Harper on the issue, including in response to direct questions. Harper also pointedly did not support the more assertive position of some of Canada's closest allies. When Harper walked out of the 2011 Perth Commonwealth summit and boycotted the following meeting in Colombo in 2013, he did not do so because of homophobia in many member states (which British parliamentarians had pointed out) but because of crimes committed by the government of Sri Lanka against the Tamil minority (*Pink News* 2013). When he did not attend the Sochi Olympics, it was not because of Russia's new law against "homosexual propaganda" (which Obama denounced), but because he normally did not attend such events (Koring 2013). One looks in vain for an expression of disapproval by Harper against any number of setbacks in other countries, or of praise for victories in the global movement for sexual rights.

The selectivity of the public discourse is also suggestive. Whereas the Ugandan parliament was talking about putting a patently unenforceable and likely unconstitutional law in place, Saudi Arabia actually carried out executions and other brutal punishments. Why did the one earn condemnation but not the other? Why was there no Canadian government objection to the enactment of shari'a law in Brunei, under which homosexuality would be punishable by stoning to death (Plecash 2014)? Why pursue a free trade agreement with Honduras, a country that has "the highest per capita transgender murder rate in the world," as noted in the House of Commons by NDP MP Randall Garrison (Parliament of Canada 2014). Baird praised Malawi, but progress in the United States such as the overturning of DOMA was apparently not a matter for Canada to judge. Russia's law banning homosexual propaganda was an offence against "decency," in Harper's words (quoted in Canadian Press 2013b), but the censorship of lgbti-oriented social media in China (Jiang 2011) and the recriminalization of sodomy in India passed without comment (Ghosh 2013). Meanwhile, no country was actually sanctioned for introducing new discriminatory laws – on the contrary, the Department of Foreign Affairs, Trade and Development (DFATD) continued to promote trade and investment with both Nigeria and Uganda, including through a Foreign Investment Promotion and Protection Agreement (FIPA) and alongside high praise for Nigeria's leadership in the region (Canada's International Gateway 2014). Other than the selective granting of refugee asylum, our search for evidence of specific actions against homophobia in the developing world turned up just one ambiguous instance. This was the case of a Canadian nongovernment organization that received government funds to support a development project in Uganda. Crossroads Christian Communications appears to have been quietly pressured or shamed into taking homophobic statements off its website, although the minister responsible strongly denied anything untoward in the project (Canadian Press 2013c; Dib and Olivier 2013).

It may be that rarity of expressions of public concern about human rights violations based on sexual orientation was a reflection of the Harper government's stated aversion to "bullhorn diplomacy." Baird explained this in his approach to the military government of Egypt. Again, however, the inconsistency is troubling. It is not just that loud bullhorn diplomacy remained the order of the day elsewhere (against Russian actions in Ukraine and against Egypt's previous, elected government, for example). The soft approach to the unconstitutional regime that replaced the Muslim Brotherhood in Egypt was troubling, given that the regime fundamentally contradicted so many ostensibly Canadian values, amid a general climate of vicious and deteriorating human rights abuses (see Abu-Zahra et al., this volume) – including a severe police crackdown on the country's nascent lgbti movement. An ironic aspect of Baird's quiet diplomacy here was that space for lgbti organizing had reportedly been improving under the previous government (Chapnick 2014; Trew 2014).

Discretion towards the putschists in Egypt is disquietingly reminiscent of Canada's response to the 2009 coup in Honduras, in which the military also replaced a democratically elected government, and which was followed by massive repression, including dozens of brazen assassinations of "faggots" (in the language reportedly used by the killers). Not only did Canada not protest, it maintained its military aid to Honduras and continued pursuing "free trade" (Ditchburn 2009, Parliament of Canada 2014).

Issues of sexual orientation have very little prominence in official government documents, and gender identity even less. Under the Harper government, DFATD (now Global Affairs Canada) included an extensive discussion on its website of human rights and the promotion of gender equality as foreign policy priorities, but did so without mentioning sexual orientation and gender identity. At the time of this research, sexual orientation was merely included in the long list of discriminations under the topic "development challenges and priorities" (sub-heading "governance"). Such discrimination was similarly mentioned in passing as an issue that would disqualify the minister from providing development assistance to a country or NGO under the Official Development Assistance Accountability Act. The department meanwhile publicized a small number of press releases to draw attention to events sponsored by Canadian embassies where the issue had been discussed, such as a screening of the film *Fire* in Vietnam in 2013 (DFATD 2014a, 2014b). The government also listed "membership in a particular social group, such as women or people of a particular sexual orientation" as legitimate grounds for applying for refugee status (CIC 2014), republishing detailed reports by the US State Department and independent rights watchdogs on the state of lgbti and other human rights in various countries. Yet the study guide for immigrants applying for Canadian citizenship made virtually no mention of lgbti rights in its information on Canadian culture and history, and indeed Minister Kenney was accused of specifically editing the issue out from an earlier draft of the guide (Beeby 2010). Government travel advisories contained no specific warnings for lgbti Canadians heading to places with even the most "vile and abhorrent" policies, to use Baird's language.

Two other absences need to be noted. First, where did the new political homophobia that so selectively appalled certain cabinet ministers come from? Baird and other ministers' public pronouncements lead us to assume it was rooted in political systems or traditional cultures that simply do not understand the importance of lgbti rights, and that if decency (or rationality, or compassion, or modernity) could be restored or introduced, then the homophobia would, presumably, just wither away. Yet powerful evidence links the new political homophobia in many places

such as Uganda and Russia to the economic, social, and political crises attending the neoliberal, dog-eat-dog forms of capitalism in those
countries. Canada has been a strong proponent of neoliberal nostrums
and structures since at least the mid-1980s, but became especially active
in its aggressive defence of economic advantage over all other considerations after the advent of the Conservative majority government in 2011
(Brown 2016; Dubinsky and Epprecht 2016). These policies have created
a great deal of misery across wide swathes of the world (through unemployment, austerity, declining public infrastructure, and so on), as well
as a vast pool of alienation that local politicians can exploit by proffering
up easy scapegoats like "the West," and sexual or other minorities. Even
in countries that have performed relatively well under this economic
model – Saudi Arabia and China, for example – yawning inequalities and
social unrest provide renewed impetus to cultural or religious justifica-
tions for homophobia. They also provide fertile ground for opportunistic
missionaries from the West, including politically well-connected American evangelists on the Christian right. Uganda's Anti-Homosexuality
Act thus did not simply emerge from traditional Ugandan culture; it has
been demonstrably linked to proselytization by evangelical Americans of
their capitalism-friendly, homophobic faith (Kaoma 2009, for example).
An umbrella association of lgbti activists in Uganda is actually suing an
American evangelist in a US federal court for his role in promoting hate in
their country (CCR 2013).

Failure to explain this context, let alone accept some responsibility to
address it, made much of the Conservative rhetoric ring hollow. Indeed,
when Baird characterized the issue as the freedom to love, and Harper
portrayed it as a question of decency, they obscured many painful aspects
of the broader picture, including that much of the sex in same-sex relationships in the Global South is not particularly about love at all. It is often
about survival, and it sometimes takes the form of rape, especially in the
context of difficult socio-economic conditions, which have often starkly
worsened under the advice of countries like Canada and institutions like
the World Bank. Many countries, and even the largest multilateral donors,
now recognize the deleterious effect that structural adjustment has had
over the decades, including the deterioration of prison conditions and the
rise of a transactional sexual economy. Some governments in the Global
South would prefer to approach issues like condoms in prisons and sexuality education as public health or harm reduction issues, tackling them
in ways that might also foster a pragmatic acceptance or tolerance of lgbti
identity. Claims about romantic love do not help these efforts in the short
term, particularly when it comes from countries like Canada that have

done so much over so many decades to undermine the ability of states to counteract the effects of market fundamentalism.

Finally, where are the voices of lgbti activists and scholars that could inform us on how Canada could best assist them in their struggles? In Canadian political discourse, they are notable both for their rarity and the way their major insights are ignored. An important example of this is the appearance of witnesses before a parliamentary subcommittee in 2010–2011. Two Ugandans described the plight of lgbti people in their country and appealed for Canada to help in a number of specific ways, in particular through facilitating refugee asylum claims. The problem was that claimants from Uganda had to travel hundreds of kilometres to lodge their application for asylum in Nairobi, Kenya. There the High Commission was so overburdened with other applications that it had a waiting list of up to a year to process. According to the testimony of Nicole LaViolette, a professor at the University of Ottawa and an advocate for lgbti asylum law reforms, "we have been told by credible refugee organizations working in Uganda and Kenya that they will not, under any circumstance, refer an LGBT individual for resettlement in Canada because of the unacceptable delay in processing private sponsorship at the Nairobi mission" (quoted in Parliament of Canada 2011). Rather, they were being referred to the embassies of the United States and some European countries. Moreover, Canadian and local African staff at the mission were not necessarily sensitive to the issue of homophobic persecution. According to a witness from Pride Uganda International, "these [Canadian] missions are scary. With all that security around, you're going through one, two, three roadblocks. They will ask you what you are there for, for visa, for whatever; you're already disclosing information about what you wanted of the mission. They will intimidate. I would be scared to disclose to an officer at the visa mission that I wanted to apply for asylum. I'd be stopped there" (quoted in Parliament of Canada 2010).

Since that time, cuts to the federal budget have significantly compromised the potential for reform at almost all steps in the process. The cuts have given rise to a pervasive sense of vulnerability among lgbti refugees and claimants both outside and within Canada. Health care for claimants already in Canada, for example, was cut in 2012 against almost all scientific and humanitarian arguments (this funding has since been restored). Mexico, hitherto a major source of refugee claimants for many reasons including homophobic and transphobic violence, became in 2103 a "designated country of origin," that is, presumed safe – virtually precluding new claims. In a climate of heightened vigilance against fraud, claimants awaiting appeals within Canada face enormous pressure to conform to bureaucratized, homonationalist identities and discourses (Massaquoi 2013, Murray 2014, Gamble et al. 2015, for example). As successful claimant Val Kalende put it, "They wanted the names of my girlfriends and all of my previous relationships and their support letters to prove that. It made me feel horrible. They just focused on these private, intimate things about my partners, sex life and breakups, instead of the way I was persecuted back home. There's something about the process that breaks you down, that breaks your emotions down" (quoted in Keung 2015).

Meanwhile, visas remain difficult to obtain even for short-term visitors. In 2014, nine Ugandan activists were denied permission to attend the Toronto World Pride Conference in 2014, until press attention brought a rare reversal (see Keeling 2014). As for working with Ugandan activists in that country, "Canada did not do much when the [Anti-Homosexuality] bill was being debated. One reason given was that Canada's presence in Uganda is very small and that most of what they do is out of the Nairobi office. Compared to the US and particularly the Nordic countries, Canada did very little to support Ugandan activists, to privately lobby government, or to expedite refugee asylum seekers" (Emma Paszat, personal communication, 14 October 2015).

The overall picture thus does not appear to be consistent with the Harper government's claims to be leading the world in promoting lgbti rights, health, and security.

EXPLANATIONS

Four interrelated factors can explain the Conservatives' occasional strong focus and yet overall mixed record on international lgbti issues: (1) growing international recognition of lgbti rights; (2) tensions between two wings of the Conservative party, i.e., the socially progressive and the socially conservative; (3) the "norm entrepreneurship" of individual Conservative politicians; and (4) the instrumentalization of lgbti-friendly policies for domestic electoral advantage.

The "international moment," in which the Harper government found itself to a significant extent, hemmed it in. When the Conservatives were first elected in 2006, same-sex marriage was legal in a few countries, including Canada, the Netherlands, Norway, and Spain. The list has continued to grow since then, with the addition of most of the European Union, the US, and a few in the Global South (Argentina, Brazil, Uruguay, and South Africa), as well as an increasing number of Mexican states. Several other countries have legislation proposed or pending, including Australia, Chile, Taiwan, and Venezuela. UN secretary-general Ban

Ki-moon spoke out strongly for lgbti rights (Ban 2012), and the Office of the UN High Commissioner on Human Rights has an ongoing campaign in favour of lgbti equality (UN n.d.). The World Bank has begun to engage with lgbti rights and assess the "economic cost of homophobia" (Tyson 2014b; World Bank 2014), while one of the world's most successful corporate leaders, the CEO of Apple, has come out as proudly gay.

The Conservatives were thus in power at a time when most industrialized democracies – and even historically conservative international organizations and historically Catholic countries – were promoting lgbti rights. Recognizing such rights at home and, by extension, abroad has become a hallmark of modern, tolerant, pluralistic, democratic systems. To deny them is to not only appear retrograde and put oneself in the company of distasteful authoritarian regimes, it is to align oneself against "best practices" for public health and economic growth. The Harper government was thus subject to a certain amount of peer pressure to reject discrimination against lgbti people, and to be seen as proactively promoting lgbti rights abroad. When other aspects of Canada's reputation as a peacekeeper or honest broker were in retreat if not in tatters (see the introduction to this volume or Dubinsky et al. 2016), promoting lgbti rights allowed the Harper government to shore up Canada's progressive image among its international friends at very low cost.

One wing of the Conservative Party supports such a position, but many members oppose it. The attempt to balance this historical divide between social and fiscal conservatives is a second factor that could explain the party's ambivalence on several foreign policy issues, including this one. Social conservatives generally embrace "traditional family values," centred around a nuclear family based on a married heterosexual couple. Often linked to evangelical Christianity, they generally reject homosexuality on moral grounds and oppose lgbti rights at home. Although they may begrudgingly accept such rights as an irreversible fait accompli in Canada, they decry the promotion of lgbti rights abroad as culturally or religiously inappropriate, and an imposition that betrays Canada's historically respectful attitude towards its friends (Berthiaume 2013). Fiscal conservatives, on the other hand, support the Conservatives' policies on taxation and regulation, but are not necessarily concerned about what goes on in the bedroom. They range from social progressives, a subset that was prominent in the Progressive Conservative Party in the days of Joe Clark and Brian Mulroney, to libertarians. From the latter perspective, one may strongly disapprove of homosexuality but not sanction discrimination. Tory MP Maurice Vellacott put it this way in an interview with the *National Post*: "They should not be hunted or hounded in those kind[s] of ways ... There should be basic protections for all. And as much as I would disagree with the homosexual lifestyle, there should be basic protections for them" (quoted in Berthiaume 2013).

Adding to the complexity is an increasingly unapologetic and organized gay caucus within the conservative movement. This is made visible through its "Fabulous Blue Tent" events featuring prominent Tory figures on the socially progressive side, such as Laureen Harper and Chris Alexander (Payton 2013). The Conservative caucus certainly contained some homophobic members who opposed such events, but Harper kept them in check – as he did with other social conservative bugbears such as abortion – in large part to maintain centrist appeal and not alienate socially progressive or libertarian fiscal conservatives, who were needed to maintain or extend the party's appeal in vote-rich urban constituencies.

A third factor was the "norm entrepreneurship" of the two cabinet ministers most responsible for promoting "gay friendly" conservatism – Baird and Kenney. Neither politician is openly gay or straight.[3] Yet whatever their sexual orientation and despite Kenney's mixed political record at home, both men deployed international lgbti rights to promote themselves and to rebrand the party in a politically adept manner. Sharp limits remained, however, with regard to what they were advocating, and marketing such controversial ideas demonstrated considerable rhetorical and leadership skills. Notably, they pointedly did not speak in favour of equal rights, but instead advocated a minimum level of protection. In Baird's words, "What we've talked about are three things: the criminalization of sexuality; violence against sexual minorities and the death penalty against sexual minorities. I don't know any conservative in Canada who supports any of those three things" (quoted in Chase 2013; see also Shane 2012, 11). Tellingly, with Baird's departure from political life in early 2015, even that level of talk virtually disappeared.

A pro-gay position on such limited terms could be seen as instrumentally useful for the party – a final factor that could help explain why the Conservative government was more outspoken than its predecessors. Because Canadians increasingly support lgbti rights, it would be counterproductive from an electoral perspective to be seen as the party of unreformed homophobia. Occasionally criticizing countries that are strategically unimportant to Canada without reference to the wider context (and without budget commitments) was a politically easy gambit to mollify both wings within the party. It also allowed the party to court votes from those sitting on the fence on the right wing of the Liberals and NDP who could see themselves voting for a "kinder, gentler" Conservative Party. We have mentioned the big cities as important electoral battlegrounds. Worth considering as well is whether or not international lgbti rights were politically useful in selling the Harper government in the otherwise inhospitable territory of Quebec. The government of Quebec, which controls its own immigration and refugee asylum process, is significantly more welcoming to claimants based on sexual orientation, and proactively promotes the values that Baird and others proclaimed for the Conservative Party (Quebec n.d.).

CONCLUSION: QUEER INDEED!

The Harper government's discovery of lgbti rights after 2009 was unquestionably queer in the old sense of the word – counterintuitive, odd, and out of step both with historical norms and contemporary voting patterns of the majority of Conservative MPs. But was it queer in the way in which global lgbti activists themselves define the word? That is, did it effectively challenge oppressive and unhealthy norms in heteropatriarchal cultures, or the structural – and often physical – violence against sexual and other minorities that is underpinned by the global political economy? Clearly no, far from it. Baird may have been sincere in his desire to protect "women and gays" globally, and a clear, principled rhetorical position was, generally speaking, an improvement over apathetic silence. However – and this is our first major conclusion – the topic appeared and disappeared in Canadian foreign policy as a matter of convenience, rather than according to principle. In practice, Canada's interventions were limited to a small number of countries where new forms of state-backed homophobia had been picked up by the Canadian media. Countries where such homophobia remained in keeping with inherited laws and attitudes (including the vast majority former British colonies in Africa and the Caribbean), or escaped media attention (such as Honduras or Saudi Arabia) were not the recipients of helpful suggestions from Canada. Compared to its allies, Canada under Harper was not particularly outspoken and did not put its money where its mouth was by withdrawing from aid, trade, or military cooperation deals.

A strong case can be made that such restraint is actually a good thing compared to loud, "homocolonialist" lectures or aid cut-offs. As Obama likely learned on his visit to Senegal and as was seen in the passing of Uganda's Anti-Homosexuality Act into law shortly after Baird personally humiliated the speaker of the Ugandan parliament, such lectures have a way of backfiring. Indeed, many African lgbti activists have strongly urged Western governments not to openly pressure their governments because it can invite a populist backlash and thus hurt the very people the

West claims it wants to help (Aken'Ova et al. 2007; AMSHeR 2011). It can also invite attention to our sometimes glaring hypocrisies around human rights on other issues (such as Canada's treatment of Indigenous peoples) and even alienate African lgbti refugees in Canada from the project (Massaquoi 2013; Murray 2014).

Quiet diplomacy, if it is to be effective, thus needs to be guided by more than largely empty and self-serving rhetorical gestures, as was the case under the Harper government. This leads to our second conclusion: Rather than blaming barbarous attitudes or cultural traits, and thereby potentially exposing lgbti people to greater harm, the Canadian government should ground its understanding of rising state homophobia in certain parts of the world in the context of nationalist responses to Western economic domination and "value imperialism" (see Bosia 2014; Weiss and Bosia 2013). It should also develop a policy on responding to the abuse of lgbti rights that is applied consistently, rather than in an ad hoc and highly selective manner. This will require a willingness to criticize Canada's friends and allies if and when their policies impede the attainment of such rights.

The Canadian government also needs to take concrete action beyond simple statements of approval and disapproval; in that regard, the policy recommendations developed by Egale (n.d.), Larcher (2012), and Jackson et al. (2013) are most helpful. To elaborate, our final conclusion is that Canada should work in partnership with governments rather than lecturing them, at times engaging at the subnational or ministerial levels to avoid undue negative attention. It should actively seek and respect strategic advice from lgbti groups within those countries to adapt its approach to the specific, changing local conditions. It should work in close partnership with multilateral institutions and relatively "homo-friendly" countries in the Global South, such as Cuba, Brazil, and South Africa, to promote lgbti rights at the regional and international level, and outside the crude construct of "Western cultural imperialism."

On the domestic front, the Canadian government should set up an Office of LGBTI Rights within Global Affairs Canada (GAC), similar to its former Office of Religious Freedom, led by an appointee at the level of ambassador. This should be backed by a well-endowed special fund to discreetly support local lgbti groups in developing countries, as well as international lgbti rights programs, such as the LGBT Global Development Partnership and the UN-sponsored Being LGBT in Asia initiative (as is done by Sweden and the US – see Tyson 2014a; White 2014).[4] Canada should also "mainstream" lgbti rights in its international development program and improve access to asylum in Canada for lgbti people at risk.

It should enact measures to ensure that all organizations whose activities are funded by GAC and other Canadian government bodies respect the full range of nondiscrimination provisions in the Canadian Charter of Rights and Freedoms, including lgbti rights. In all of the above, Canada should both ensure that transgender and intersex rights are explicitly included in any discussion of lgbti rights and consider lgbti rights within the broad range of human rights, especially women's rights, rather than in isolation.

ACKNOWLEDGMENTS

Special thanks to Dana Hayward for research assistance and to Emma Paszat for sharing insights from her own doctoral research with activists in Uganda and Rwanda.

NOTES

1 See O'Flaherty and Fisher (2008), Smith (2012), and Lennox and Waites (2013) for a small window into that history. For the purposes of this article we acknowledge disputes in the scholarship over appropriate terminology (concisely discussed in Wilkinson and Langlois 2014) but respectfully opt for the lowercase acronym, which draws together the main discrete components of the struggle under a convenient, nonessentializing umbrella term – lgbti ("q" for queer remains somewhat controversial in the Global South as a signifier of Western identity politics, hence we eschew it here; "a" for allies is assumed as a normal part of any social movement). We also note that Canada has done much more, both domestically and internationally, on sexual orientation issues (lesbian, gay, and bisexual) than on gender identity and gender expression issues (transgender and intersexual), and that our research from public documents necessarily, if regretfully, tends to adhere to that bias.

2 A rich literature supports this argument, including Massad (2007), Epprecht (2013), and Nyeck and Epprecht (2013).

3 Baird, however, was "outed" by a Conservative candidate in 2010 (McCann 2010).

4 As of 14 November 2014, not a single project in the online DFATD International Development Project Browser contained the terms gay, lesbian, LGBT, homosexual, homosexuality, intersex, or transgender.

REFERENCES

African Men for Sexual Health and Rights (AMSHeR). 2011. "Statement of African Social Justice Activists on the Threats of the British Government to 'Cut Aid' to African Countries That Violate the Rights of LGBTI People in Africa." African Men for Sexual Health and Rights, 27 October. Accessed 28 October 2011. http://www.amsher.net/news/ViewArticle.aspx?id=1200

Aken'Ova, Dorothy et al. 2007. "African LGBTI Human Rights Defenders Warn Public against Participation in Campaigns Concerning LGBTI Issues in Africa Led by Peter Tatchell and Outrage!" MRzine, 31 January. Accessed 5 November 2014. http://mrzine.monthlyreview.org/2007/increse310107.html.

Ban Ki-moon. 2012. "Remarks to Special Event on 'Leadership in the Fight against Homophobia.'" Speech presented to the Office of the United Nations High Commissioner for Human Rights, New York, 11 December. Accessed 9 November 2014. http://www.ohchr.org/Documents/Issues/Discrimination/LGBT/SGSpeech11122012LGBT.doc.

Beeby, Dean. 2010. "Immigration Minister Pulled Gay Rights from Citizenship Guide, Documents Show." *Globe and Mail*, 2 March.

Berthiaume, Lee. 2013. "Canadian Conservatives Divided over Harper Government's Defence of Gay Rights." *National Post*, 10 August.

Beyrer, Chris, Andrea Wirtz, Damian Walker, Benjamin Johns, Frangiscos Sifakis, and Stephan D. Baral. 2011. *The Global HIV Epidemics among Men Who Have Sex with Men*. Washington: World Bank. Accessed 26 December 2014. http://siteresources.worldbank.org/INTHIVAIDS/Resources/375798-1103037153392/MSMReport.pdf.

Bosia, Michael J. 2014. "Strange Fruit: Homophobia, the State, and the Politics of LGBT Rights and Capabilities." *Journal of Human Rights* 13, no. 3: 256–73.

Brown, Stephen. 2016. "Undermining Foreign Aid: The Extractive Sector and the Recommercialization of Canadian Development Assistance." In *Rethinking Canadian Aid*, 2nd ed., edited by Stephen Brown, Molly den Heyer, and David R. Black, 273–94. Ottawa: University of Ottawa Press.

Campaign Life Coalition. n.d. "Federal Voting Records: Candidate Jason Kenney, Conservative Party, Calgary Midnapore, AB." Campaign Life Coalition. Accessed 9 November 2014. http://www.campaignlifecoalition.com/index.php?p=Federal_Voting_Records&id=155.

Canada's International Gateway. 2014. "Canada-Nigeria Relations." Canada's International Gateway. 15 May. Accessed 9 November 2014. http://www.canadainternational.gc.ca/nigeria/bilateral_relations_bilaterales/canada_nigeria.aspx?lang=eng.

Canadian Press. 2013a. "Commons Approves Transgender Rights Bill: 18 Tories Voted in Support of Bill." *CBC News*, 20 March.

– 2013b. "Harper Joins Controversy over Russia's Anti-Gay Law." *Globe and Mail*, 9 August.

– 2013c. "Fantino Defends Uganda Grant Decision against Anti-Gay Claims." CBC *News*, 11 February.

CBC News. 2012. "Minister's Email to Gay Community Sparks Privacy Complaints." CBC *News*, 25 September .

Center for Constitutional Rights (CCR). 2013. "LGBTI Uganda Fights Back! Synopsis, Sexual Minorities Uganda v. Scott Lively." New York: Center for Constitutional Rights. Accessed November 12 2014. http://ccrjustice.org/home/what-we-do/our-cases/sexual-minorities-uganda-v-scott-lively.

Chapnick, Adam. 2014. "John Baird's Conversion to Quiet Diplomacy." *Ottawa Citizen*, 25 June.

Chase, Steven. 2009. "Harper Lobbies Uganda on Anti-Gay Bill." *Globe and Mail*, 29 November.

– 2013. "Baird Belies Conservative Image Through Defence of Gay Rights Abroad." *Globe and Mail*, 8 August.

Citizenship and Immigration Canada (CIC). 2014. "Resettlement from Outside Canada." Citizenship and Immigration Canada, May 2. Accessed 13 November 2014. http://www.cic.gc.ca/english/refugees/outside/index.asp.

Department of Foreign Affairs, Trade and Development (DFATD). 2014a. "Key Development Challenges: Governance." Department of Foreign Affairs, Trade and Development. 23 September.

– 2014b. "Official Development Assistance Accountability Act: Consistency with International Human Rights Standards." Department of Foreign Affairs, Trade and Development. 10 February.

Dib, Lina, and Fannie Olivier. 2013. "Anti-Gay Religious Group Gets Funding from Ottawa to Work in Uganda." *Toronto Star*, 10 February.

Ditchburn, Jennifer. 2009. "Military Aid Flows to Honduras Despite Coup." *Globe and Mail*, 30 July.

Dubinsky, Karen, and Marc Epprecht. 2016. "Business, Development and the State." In *Canada and the Third World: Overlapping Histories*, edited by Karen Dubinsky, Sean Mills, and Scott Rutherford, 60–87. Toronto: University of Toronto Press.

Dubinsky, Karen, Sean Mills, and Scott Rutherford, eds. 2016. *Canada and the Third World: Overlapping Histories*. Toronto: University of Toronto Press.

Duggan, Lisa. 2002. "The New Homonormativity: The Sexual Politics of Neoliberalism." In *Materializing Democracy: Toward a Revitalized Cultural Politics*, edited by Russ Castronovo and Dana D. Nelson, 175–94. Durham, NC: Duke University Press.

Egale. N.d. "Advancing Equality, Diversity, Education, and Justice." Egale. Accessed 9 November 2014. http://egale.ca.

Epprecht, Marc. 2013. *Sexuality and Human Rights in Africa*. London: Zed Books, 2013.

Friesen, Joe. "Tories Apply Specific Criteria for Refugees." *Globe and Mail*, 9 October.

Gamble, Kathleen, Nick J. Mulé, Nancy Nicol, Phyllis Waugh, Sharalyn Jordan, and Ontario Council of Agencies Serving Immigrants. 2015. "Envisioning Global LGBT Rights." Toronto: York University, Centre for Feminist Research.

Ghosh, Deepshikha. 2013. "Supreme Court Says Gay Sex Is a Criminal Offence, Activists to Seek Review." *NDTV*, 11 December. Accessed 9 November 2014. http://www.ndtv.com/article/india/supreme-court-says-gay-sex-is-a-criminal -offence-activists-to-seek-review-457216.

Jackson, Edward, Ian Smillie, and Stephen Brown. 2013. *Lesbian, Gay, Bisexual and Transgender Rights: A Call for Canadian Leadership*. Ottawa: McLeod Group. Accessed 9 November 2014. http://www.mcleodgroup.ca/wp-content/ uploads/2013/02/LGBT-March.pdf.

Jiang, Jessie. 2011. "Beijing's Gay Community Fights Censorship." *Time*, 1 July.

Kaoma, Kapya. 2009. *Globalizing the Culture Wars: US Conservatives, African Churches, and Homophobia*. Somerville, MA: Political Research Associates.

Keeling, James. 2014. "Denouncing Double Standards: Canada's Two-Faced Stance on LGBTQ Rights in Uganda." NATO Association of Canada. Accessed 14 November 2014. http://natoassociation.ca/denouncing-double-standards- canadas-two-faced-stance-on-lgbtq-rights-in-uganda.

Keung, Nicholas. 2015. "Canada's Asylum System Re-Victimizes LGBTQ Refu- gees." *Toronto Star*, 29 September.

Koring, Paul. 2013. "Obama Sending Gay Athletes to Sochi as Harper Says He'll Skip Olympics." *Globe and Mail*, 18 December.

Larcher, Akim Adé. 2012. "Canada's Gay Rights Defence Is All Hot Air." *Embassy*, 1 February.

Lennox, Corinne, and Matthew Waites, eds. 2013. *Human Rights, Sexual Orienta- tion and Gender Identity in the Commonwealth: Struggles for Decriminalization and Change*. London: Institute of Commonwealth Studies.

Ling, Justin. 2012. "Baird Battles Ugandan Politician over Gay Rights." *Daily Xtra*, 25 October. Accessed 9 November 2014. http://dailyxtra.com/canada/news/ baird-battles-ugandan-politician-gay-rights.

MacKinnon, Leslie. 2013. "Women's Group Slams Baird over Anti-Gay Laws Stance: REAL Women Accuses Foreign Affairs Minister of Abuse of Office for Comments on Foreign Countries." *CBC News*, 7 August.

Massad, Joseph. 2007. *Desiring Arabs*. Chicago: University of Chicago Press.

Massaquoi, Notisha. 2013. "No Place Like Home: African Refugees and the Emergence of a New Queer Frame of Reference." In *Sexual Diversity in Africa*, edited by S.N. Nyeck and Marc Epprecht, 37–53. Montreal and Kingston: McGill-Queen's University Press.

McCann, Marcus. 2010. "OPEN SECRET: Conservative Cabinet Minister John Baird Outed," *Daily Xtra*, 1 February. Accessed 9 November 2014. http://dailyxtra.com/canada/news/open-secret-conservative-cabinet-minister-john-baird-outed.

Murray, David A.B. 2014. "Real Queer: 'Authentic' LGBT Refugee Claimants and Homonationalism in the Canadian Refugee System." *Anthropologica* 56, no. 2: 21–32.

Nyeck, S.N., and Marc Epprecht, eds. 2013. *Sexual Diversity in Africa*. Montreal and Kingston: McGill-Queen's University Press.

O'Flaherty, Michael, and John Fisher. 2008. "Sexual Orientation, Gender Identity and Human Rights Law: Contextualizing the Yogyakarta Principles." *Human Rights Law Review* 8, no. 2: 207–48.

Parliament of Canada, House of Commons. 2005. Vote no. 156. 38th Parliament, 1st Session, Sitting no. 124, 28 June. Accessed 11 November 2014. http://www.parl.gc.ca/HouseChamberBusiness/ChamberVoteDetail.aspx?Language=E&Mode=1&Parl=41&Ses=2&Vote=156&GroupBy=party&FltrParl=38&FltrSes=1.

– 2009. *Hansard*, no. 118 of the 40th Parliament, 2nd Session, 26 November. Accessed 13 November 2014. http://openparliament.ca/debates/2009/11/26/john-baird-9.

– 2010. Subcommittee on International Human Rights of the Standing Committee on Foreign Affairs and International Development, *Minutes of Proceedings*, no. 30, 4 November. Accessed 5 November 2014. http://www.parl.gc.ca/HousePublications/Publication.aspx?DocId=4764881&Language=E&Mode=1.

– 2011. Subcommittee on International Human Rights of the Standing Committee on Foreign Affairs and International Development, *Minutes of Proceedings*, no. 46, 17 February. Accessed 5 November 2014. http://www.parl.gc.ca/HousePublications/Publication.aspx?DocId=4984029&Mode=2&Parl=40&Ses=3&Language=E.

– 2013. *Edited Hansard*, no. 214 of the 41st Parliament, 1st session, 26 February. Accessed 12 November 2014. http://www.parl.gc.ca/HousePublications/Publication.aspx?Language=E&Mode=1&Parl=41&Ses=1&DocId=6002844.

– 2014. *Edited Hansard*, no. 58 of the 41st Parliament, 2nd session, 6 March. Accessed 13 November 2014. http://www.parl.gc.ca/HousePublications/Publication.aspx?DocId=6449373.

Payton, Laura. 2013. "'Fabulous Blue Tent' Showcases Gay Conservatives' Power." *CBC News*, 30 December.

Pink News. 2013. "Shadow Foreign Secretary: Sri Lanka Is 'Heading in the Wrong Direction' on LGBT Rights." 11 November. Accessed 9 November 2014. http://

www.pinknews.co.uk/2013/11/11/shadow-foreign-secretary-sri-lanka-is-head-ing-in-the-wrong-direction-on-lgbt-rights.

– 2014. "Canada Punishes Nigerian President for Signing Anti-Gay Law by Cancelling State Visit." *Pink News*, 20 January. Accessed 25 September 2014. http://www.pinknews.co.uk/2014/01/20/canada-punishes-nigerian-presi-dent-for-signing-anti-gay-law-by-cancelling-state-visit.

Plecash, Chris. 2014. "Canada Quiet on Shariah Law in Brunei." *Embassy*, 10 September.

Puar, Jasbir K. 2008. "Homonationalism and Biopower." In *Out of Place: Interro-gating Silences in Queerness/Raciality*, edited by Adi Kuntsman and Esperanza Miyake, 13–70. London: Raw Nerve Books.

Quebec. N.d. "Immigrating to Québec. A Society Based on the Rule of Law." Immigration, Diversité et Inclusion Québec. Accessed 13 November 2014. http://www.immigration-quebec.gouv.qc.ca/en/choose-quebec/common-va-lues/society-law.html.

Rahmin, Momin. 2014. "Queer Rights and the Triangulation of Western Exception-alism." *Journal of Human Rights* 13, no. 3: 274–89.

Schulman, Sarah. 2011. "Israel and 'Pinkwashing.'" *New York Times*, 22 November.

Segal, Hugh. 2012. "CJA Malta: Senator Hugh Segal's Speech in Full." *Common-wealth Journalists Association*, 1 February. Accessed 9 November 2014. http://www.cja-uk.org/2012/02/cja-2012-senator-hugh-segals-speech-in-full.

Shane, Kristen. 2012. "Why Is Canada Speaking Out More for Gay Rights Abroad?" *Embassy*, 18 January.

Smith, Miriam. 2012. "Identity and Opportunity: The Lesbian and Gay Rights Movement." In *Queerly Canadian: An Introductory Reader in Sexuality Studies*, edited by Maureen Fitzgerald and Scott Rayter, 121–39. Toronto: Canadian Scholars' Press and Women's Press.

Tatchell, Peter. 2007. "Iraq's Homophobic Terror," *Red Pepper*, December. Accessed 6 January 2015. http://www.redpepper.org.uk/Iraq-s-homophobic-terror.

Trew, Bel. 2014. "Al-Sisi's Egypt Is Worse for Gays Than the Muslim Brotherhood." *Daily Beast*, 28 June.

Tyson, Jeff. 2014a. "USAID, Top Donors to Mainstream LGBTI Rights in Develop-ment Programs." *Devex*, 17 November. Accessed 28 December 2014. https://www.devex.com/news/usaid-top-donors-to-mainstream-lgbti-rights-in-development-programs-84857.

– 2014b. "The World Bank's Uneasy Relationship with LGBTI Rights." *Devex*, 21 November. Accessed 28 December 2014. https://www.devex.com/news/the-world-bank-s-uneasy-relationship-with-lgbti-rights-84896.

Weiss, Meredith L., and Michael J. Bosia, eds. 2013. *Global Homophobia: States, Movements, and the Politics of Oppression*. Urbana: University of Illinois Press.

White, Thomas. 2014. "'Being LGBT' in Asia." *USAID blog*, 13 November. Accessed 28 December 2014. http://blog.usaid.gov/2014/11/implementing-usaids-being-lgbt-in-asia-initiative.

Wilkinson, Cai, and Anthony J. Langlois. 2014. "Special Issue: Not Such an International Human Rights Norm? Local Resistance to Lesbian, Gay, Bisexual, and Transgender Rights – Preliminary Comments." *Journal of Human Rights* 13, no. 3: 249–55.

World Bank. 2014. "The Economic Cost of Homophobia: How LGBT Exclusion Impacts Development." 12 March. Accessed 9 November 2014. http://www.worldbank.org/en/events/2014/02/26/the-economic-cost-of-homophobia-how-lgbt-exclusion-impacts-development.

York, Geoffrey. 2014. "Friction over Anti-Gay Law Sapping Harper's Overtures to Nigeria." *Globe and Mail*, 21 January.

Chapter 4

Criminals or Victims? An Analysis of the Harper Conservatives' Efforts on the Sex Trade and Human Trafficking

Kate Grantham

INTRODUCTION

On 17 September 2015 – just weeks before the Conservative Party of Canada lost power to the Liberals in the 19 October 2015 election – then prime minister Stephen Harper announced additional actions to combat human trafficking. As part of their election platform, the Harper Conservatives announced steps to support victims of human trafficking and to end criminal activities in human trafficking, noting that the "Conservative Party will make it a priority to stand up for victims and crack down on the scourge of human trafficking" (Conservative Party 2015). As part of these commitments, the party highlighted the international leadership that Canada has taken to address human trafficking, pointing to the Conservative government's launching of the National Action Plan to Combat Human Trafficking.

In this chapter I assess Canada's efforts to address human trafficking and the sex trade, in particular by highlighting the Harper Conservatives' strategic deployment of certain trafficking narratives and policies in order to prop up a reductive and paternalistic anti-prostitution agenda. I use a critical discourse analysis to explore how the Harper Conservatives have (or have not) promoted the rights of women in their official commitments through thirteen official government communications, reports, policy documents, and promotional materials pertaining to human trafficking and the sex trade from 2012 to 2015. This analysis helps to shed light on how the Conservative majority government framed discussions about the global sex trade for the purpose of public awareness, as well as for state regulation and foreign intervention. Ultimately, it serves to elucidate the principles and priorities that guided Canadian domestic and foreign policy on this issue under the direction of the Harper Conservatives.

Although important developments such as the National Action Plan to Combat Human Trafficking are noteworthy, Canada's efforts to address human trafficking – particularly as it pertains to the sex trade – were insufficient and often counterproductive. Three major findings emerge from my analysis of thirteen documents produced by the Harper Conservatives and members of the Human Trafficking Task Force from 2012 to 2015.

First, the underlying ideology of the Action Plan is paternalistic, framing all women in the sex trade as victims in need of saving. This essentializing language fails to adequately represent women's diverse experiences and rationales for participating in prostitution.

Second, despite the fact that the victimization of women and girls features prominently in public discourse and promotional material for the Action Plan, the actual implementation of the plan focuses on law enforcement, with almost no resources being allocated to prevention or to victim services. In fact, the "criminalization" of women who engage in sex trade work through the Harper Conservatives' introduction of the Protection of Communities and Exploited Persons Act put women in even greater danger, forcing them to work in increasingly unsafe conditions and in more hidden contexts, leaving sex trade workers with reduced protection from police and fewer opportunities to ensure their safety.

Third, the reductive and depoliticized mandate of the Action Plan fails to connect law enforcement tactics to strategies for addressing the broader structural issues underlying the growth of the global sex trade. Instead, the plan draws direct links between prostitution and immigration, cracking down aggressively on both in an approach that I argue will only exacerbate the problem and the scope of human trafficking.

After providing an introduction to the issues underlying the growth of the global sex trade under neoliberalism and the Action Plan itself, I detail the three main findings of my discourse analysis. In closing, I advocate for the adoption of human rights–based approaches for addressing women's complex and diverse experiences within the global sex trade. Human rights–based approaches deal directly with changing the structural conditions that allow for the growing prevalence of the sex trade itself, including, increasingly, the effect of neoliberal policies. They further endeavour to eradicate the abuses faced by women prior to, during, and after their involvement in the sex trade – abuses that most often occur as a result of social stigma and criminalization. Such an approach is entirely precluded within a simplistic narrative of human trafficking that conceptualizes the sex trade as inherently violent, and assumes a passivity or lack of agency for the women who choose this profession.

AN INTRODUCTION TO THE GLOBAL SEX TRADE

In the last twenty years the global sex trade has been growing rapidly, generating profits amounting to tens of billions of dollars annually (Poulin 2004). The "sex trade" is an umbrella term that encompasses both legal and illegal transactions through which sexual acts are exchanged for money or other goods. This includes prostitution, but also escort services, erotic dancing, pornography, and sensual massage. The sex trade is also increasingly transnational, with a growing number of women migrating in order to work in the adult sex industry (Agustin 2007; Weitzer 2011), putting those most vulnerable at risk of being trafficked for the purpose of sexual exploitation (United Nations Office on Drugs and Crime 2014).[1] The growth of the global sex trade has been precipitated by a confluence of factors, including the international presence of military forces engaged in wars or territorial occupation that provide new local markets for commercial sex (Kofman and Raghuram 2015, 30), the growth and normalization of pornography via the internet (Jeffreys 2009), and the unprecedented expansion of sex tourism industries to attract foreign currency and investment (Poulin 2004). Increasingly, poor women in developing countries are also turning to sex trade work as a survival strategy in response to deteriorating living conditions resulting from neoliberal policies.

Neoliberalism is an approach to economic development that holds that international economic growth is only possible by opening up borders and national economies in pursuit of pro-market and anti-state policies. These policies, imposed by international financial institutions like the World Bank and the International Monetary Fund (IMF), demand the withdrawal of the state from providing essential social services and economic resources to the poor in order to focus on generating national economic growth. This is typically achieved through the enactment of free trade agreements to bolster trading relationships, the establishment of export processing zones to encourage foreign direct investment, and, perhaps most disastrously, the implementation of structural adjustment programs designed to reduce government debt.

Economic reforms enacted under neoliberalism are widely known to have had devastating consequences for the economies and populations of developing countries. These consequences include reductions in government subsidies and the introduction of user fees for health care and education services, growing unemployment rates, a general fall in living standards, the promotion of export-oriented cash crops (which have increasingly replaced subsistence agriculture and food production for local or national markets), and finally an ongoing and sometimes increased burden of government debt (Sassen 2000, 504–5). It is now clear that for most countries involved, neoliberal policies have precipitated a decline in living conditions, employment, local industry, agricultural diversity, and health and education levels. Other authors in this volume make a similar case regarding neoliberalism and its discontents (see, for example, Butler, Tuckey, and Abu-Zahra et al.).

The effects of neoliberal policies are also deeply uneven, with poor women and children most negatively affected. Particularly widely documented are the gender-specific repercussions of structural adjustment programs, which are a series of economic reforms implemented by the IMF and the World Bank since the 1980s as stipulations for providing debt relief to poor countries. Conditions for the use of loaned money are designed to complement macroeconomic policies and increase program success. They require, among other things, the withdrawal of the state from subsidizing social services and local industry, the privatization of state assets such as water and transportation systems, devaluing the national currency to promote the sale of exports, and supporting commercial and enterprise development through free trade agreements. Global women's rights organization MADRE explains why the elimination of free education, free health care and free water, for instance, poses a particular burden for women:

> When services become unaffordable, peoples' needs do not disappear; instead the job of providing necessities shifts to women, who must intensify their work in social reproduction – hauling water, collecting wood, processing food, building community support networks, and providing their families with health care, day care, and the basic nutrition once guaranteed by public funding ... [The net result is that] the needs of women and girls are sacrificed first. In fact, women in poor countries have shown drastic drops in school enrolments, food intake, hospital admittance and life expectancy since SAPS [structural adjustment programs] have taken hold. (MADRE, in Eisenstein 2009, 148)

Households and entire communities become increasingly dependent on women for their survival under structural adjustment. It is noteworthy that governments also rely on women to compensate for the reduction in social services and economic resources resulting from structural adjustment. Some commenters have argued that an unspoken conditionality of structural adjustment programs is the increased reliance on poor and working class women's labour, both paid and unpaid (Enriquez 2006, 4; Tsikata 1995).

In many developing countries, neoliberal policies have led to an increase in the number of women seeking employment opportunities in the informal labour sector (Lascamana and Aguilar 2004; Sassen 2000). The main types of employment available to women in developing countries include factory work in export processing zones, contract or piecemeal work for multinational corporations, service work in the tourism industry, and, increasingly, sex trade work (Eisenstein 2009). Due to a lack of regulations, this work tends to be highly exploitative and dangerous, as well as insecure.

A growing body of research indicates that in many areas of the world the number of women entering the sex trade as a survival strategy is rising as a result of deteriorating living conditions resulting from neoliberal policies (Jeffreys 2009; Sanders 2008; Weitzer 2010). In developing countries hard hit by structural adjustment programs, for instance, the privatization of essential services like health care and education, combined with the dismantling of local industries, has led to an increase in unemployment, poverty, and all types of "black market" survival strategies, including prostitution (Lascamana and Aguilar 2004). Factors such as environmental degradation, natural disasters, postconflict dislocation, and restrictive immigration policies also seem to influence the number of women entering into the sex trade, as a response to increased economic insecurity (Brock 2009; Ditmore 2005).

The rise in sex trade work in some regions can also be linked to the development of tourism, as part of neoliberal strategies to attract foreign currency and encourage foreign investment (Poulin 2004). In developing countries with high levels of poverty and unemployment, and where governments are desperate for revenue and foreign currency, the sex trade itself can become a development strategy in so far as it is linked with the development of the tourism and entertainment industries (Sassen 2000, 519). Sex tourism is incredibly profitable for governments that unofficially accept or legalize prostitution (Weiss 2002, 2). International financial institutions also play a role, by viewing tourism as a solution to challenges of growth in developing countries, and routinely providing loans to help indebted governments strengthen this sector of their economy. Governments in developing countries build beaches, hotels, conference centres, and retail outlets, all financed with World Bank and IMF loans, with the aim of attracting foreigners and foreign currency into their country. In this way, the sex trade itself becomes an attraction alongside other investments funded by government revenues under neoliberal globalization.

Advances in telecommunications technology have further bolstered the global sex tourism industry. Henderson and Jeydel (2014) contend that "the Internet has been a crucial force in facilitating foreign travel with the express purpose of purchasing sex," and, further, that the internet is "teeming with websites that provide potential sex tourists with accounts written by other tourists and that supply information on destinations, process and procurement" (267). Places such as Thailand, Indonesia, Malaysia, and the Philippines have become hubs of the sex tourism industry, and the profits represent 2 to 14 per cent of the gross domestic product of these countries (Henderson and Jeydel 2014, 267). Other popular locations for sex tourism include Cambodia, Brazil, the Dominican Republic, the Netherlands, and Kenya (Kofman and Raghuram 2015, 30).

INSUFFICIENT ANALYSES OF SEX TRADE WORK

A substantial body of literature exists on the issue of women's involvement in the global sex trade. Feminist scholars in particular have attempted to grapple with the complex conditions and constraints under which some women decide to engage in sex trade work in different parts of the world. Their analyses have produced remarkable strife and disagreement. Mainstream analyses also tend to lack sufficient examination of neoliberalism and its effect on the growing number of women entering the sex trade internationally, particularly in developing countries.

In their 2001 text, *Sex Work Reassessed*, Wendy Rickard and Meryl Storr convey their dissatisfaction with the classic binaries through which sex trade work has come to be understood. They critique feminist discourses that "either posit that commercialized sexuality indicates victimhood or vulnerability *or* that it is valid work and meaningful sexual expression for seller and buyer alike" (1–2). "In reality," Rickard and Storr contend, "these positions are rarely absolute either for sex trade workers or for those who undertake research, provide services or set policies" (2). Sex trade work is a more socially and personally complex phenomenon than mainstream feminist accounts appreciate. Nonetheless, these fixed ideologies continue to provide the predominant frameworks for thinking about sex trade work.

Furthermore, feminist debates pertaining to sex trade work can be narrow in scope and unproductive if they take place within a social and

political vacuum, divorced from wider discussions about the growing influence of neoliberal economic policies, which have precipitated
the growth of the sex trade internationally. As Lascamana (2004) notes,
those defending the rights of sex trade workers from either the liberal
regulationist or radical abolitionist perspective have not come up with a
"tangible strategy for collectively organizing against the structural mechanisms that have led to the increase in the global sex trade. Instead, we are
encouraged to negotiate prostitution/sex work within the existing social
order" (400). Lascamana goes on to argue that the debate over sex trade
work cannot stay within the framework of an assumed capitalist system,
otherwise a feminist argument for women's sexual and economic freedom
can wind up reinforcing the free market doctrines of neoliberalism (400–
1). On the other hand, feminist arguments advocating the abolition of
the sex industry on the basis that it is inherently exploitative can wind up
reinforcing global anti-prostitution agendas that predominantly result in
the alienation, criminalization, and endangerment of sex trade workers.

The twenty-first century has witnessed an international growth in
anti-prostitution programs and policies that are designed to protect
women from the assumed inherent dangers of the sex trade, and are
characterized by punitive law enforcement practices, intimidation, entrap-
ment, the confiscation of condoms and personal property as evidence
of illegal conduct, compulsory or coerced HIV and STI testing, and the
denial of government services and certain legal rights to sex trade workers (United Nations Development Programme 2012). These interventions
have the effect of alienating sex trade workers and criminalizing their clientele. In doing so, they make women more vulnerable to violence and
other health risks by driving the sex trade further underground, reducing women's ability to communicate with one another, to screen potential
clients, to negotiate prices or condom use, and to scan a vehicle for possible threats (Mulvenna 2014). Criminalization also fuels social stigma
and discrimination, and reduces sex trade workers' willingness to report
cases of assault and theft by clients to law enforcement. Anti-prostitution
programs further suffer from a number of ideological flaws, including an
uneven focus on the victimization of women, a tendency to conflate sex
trade work with human trafficking, and a failure to recognize how the sex
trade is influenced by broader global economic trends and processes that
are deeply gendered. In their attempt to address women's experiences in
the sex trade, anti-prostitution programs and policies treat sex trade workers exclusively as victims. Meanwhile, anti-prostitution interventions
address the symptoms of poverty and gender inequality as opposed to
their underlying causes, leaving the needs of sex trade workers unmet.

Under Harper's leadership, Canada's commitments to address human trafficking and the sex trade were constrained by an ingrained and problematic anti-prostitution agenda. The imposition of this agenda was sometimes subtle but often overt, and it can be seen in examples of programs and policies enacted by the Conservative majority government both within Canada and abroad.

CANADA'S COMMITMENTS TO ADDRESSING HUMAN TRAFFICKING AND THE SEX TRADE

While in government, the Harper Conservatives introduced several legal instruments and policy papers guiding their efforts to address the sex trade and human trafficking. On the domestic front, in June 2014, the Conservative government introduced Bill C-36, the Protection of Communities and Exploited Persons Act, intended to crack down on individuals who purchase commercial sex – or "obtain for consideration ... the sexual services of a person" (Bill C-36, section 268.1). More precisely, Bill C-36, which formally passed into law in December 2014, criminalizes the purchase of sex (Bill C-36, section 268.1), communicating for the purpose of selling sex (Bill C-36, section 213(1.1)), gaining material benefit from sex work (Bill C-36, section 286.2), and advertising sexual services (Bill C-36, section 286.4), making each offence punishable by fines and a possible prison sentence. To this end, the new legislation bears remarkable similarity to Canada's previous Criminal Code provisions criminalizing sex trade work, which were deemed unconstitutional and struck down by the Supreme Court of Canada in 2013; the laws have simply been repackaged as a response aimed at protecting sex trade workers from exploitation. The underlying ideology of Bill C-36 is that prostitution is inherently coercive and harmful for women, framing all sex trade workers as victims in need of saving.

In terms of foreign policy and programming, the Canadian federal government has concentrated its efforts and resources on combatting human trafficking for the purposes of sexual exploitation, citing a direct link between the prevalence of trafficking and organized prostitution (Public Safety Canada 2012a, 1). In 2002, Canada was among the first countries to ratify the United Nations Protocol to Prevent, Suppress and Punish Trafficking in Persons, especially Women and Children ("Trafficking Protocol"). In the years since, the Canadian government has participated in a number of multilateral fora to support global anti-trafficking efforts, including, most recently, the 2015 UN General Assembly high-level meeting to assess the implementation of the Global Plan of Action to Combat Trafficking in Persons.

The Department of Foreign Affairs, Trade and Development (DFATD) also provides funding to a number of international organizations and NGOs that work with governments to address human trafficking for the purposes of sexual exploitation or forced labour (Public Safety Canada 2012a, 31; Public Safety Canada 2015, 5). Two initiatives that currently receive funding from DFATD are the Children and Youth Human Rights Empowerment Project in Haiti and the Tripartite Action for the Protection and Promotion of the Rights of Migrant Workers in the ASEAN region (DFATD 2015). Both projects include strategies to enhance the capacity of governments to identify and protect victims of human trafficking (DFATD 2015). According to a recent Public Safety Canada report documenting key DFATD achievements in the fight to combat human trafficking, "official humanitarian assistance in response to Typhoon Haiyan or the Syria crisis have [also], for example, included activities to address the increased risks of human trafficking of women and girls" (2015, 6). The report goes on to state that even "in the context of Canada's international leadership around maternal, newborn and child health, significant new programming is underway to support effective civil registration and vital statistics, including birth registration, which contributes to providing new trafficking prevention tools to national authorities" (6). These commitments reflect a recent surge in attention and funding in order to combat the growth of the global sex trade.

The Harper Conservatives' flagship program promoting women's rights in the context of the global sex trade was the National Action Plan to Combat Human Trafficking ("Action Plan"), which has guided Canada's international efforts and funding since 2012. To oversee more than C$25 million in funding, a Human Trafficking Taskforce replaced the Interdepartmental Working Group on Trafficking in Persons, which had previously administered Canada's anti-trafficking efforts (Public Safety Canada 2012a, 9). The Human Trafficking Taskforce is comprised of eighteen federal government departments[2] and is chaired by Public Safety Canada. Guided by the efforts and findings of the taskforce, the Action Plan aims to "consolidate the ongoing efforts of the Canadian federal government to combat human trafficking and introduce aggressive new initiatives to prevent human trafficking, identify victims, protect the most vulnerable and prosecute perpetrators" (Public Safety Canada 2012a, 9). It follows international best practices for combatting trafficking, as set out in the United Nations Trafficking Protocol, focusing on four core areas, known as the "four pillars": the *prevention* of human trafficking, the *protection* of victims, the *prosecution* of offenders, and working in *partnership* with domestic and international groups (9, emphasis added). Crime fighting and a criminal justice approach feature prominently.

The Action Plan formalizes Canada's financial and political obligations to protect women, girls, and other vulnerable populations against the growing threat of organized crime, sexual exploitation, and forced labour as they occur in the context of the global sex trade. Compared to the previous Interdepartmental Working Group on Trafficking in Persons, the Action Plan more than doubles the federal government's annual financial commitments, as well as the number of government departments involved in implementing Canada's anti-trafficking efforts (DFATD 2015). This level of commitment to combatting trafficking, domestically or abroad, is unprecedented for Canada. As such, the plan has been received positively by the majority of Canadians, as well as many Canadian NGOs and law enforcement officials. For this same reason, the Action Plan and its supporting documents provide an important and timely opportunity for analyzing Canada's work in this area.

The remainder of this chapter outlines the findings from my analysis of thirteen documents produced by the Harper Conservatives and members of the Human Trafficking Task Force over a three-year period, beginning in July 2012. Included in this investigation was the Action Plan itself, two annual progress reports produced by Public Safety Canada, all six existing issues of *Canada's Anti-Trafficking Newsletter* (published semi-annually by the federal government since the enactment of the Action Plan), various partner and stakeholder publications, and a recent overview of Canada's international programs and partnerships combatting human trafficking, produced by DFATD. I further engaged with literature and research produced by scholars who are likewise critical of the dominant narratives and policies promoted by the Harper Conservatives with regard to the global sex trade.

A CRITICAL DISCOURSE ANALYSIS OF CANADA'S NATIONAL ACTION PLAN TO COMBAT HUMAN TRAFFICKING

Myths and Figures

Research has shown that conceptions of human trafficking in Canada are less often informed by concrete evidence than by highly emotive and vague or contradictory rhetoric (Roots and De Shalit 2015). The speculative nature of claims regarding the prevalence of human trafficking is evident within Canada's Action Plan. Interestingly, the Action Plan reminds us on several occasions of the difficulty of collecting reliable data. Therein it is acknowledged that "the extent of human trafficking, either in Canada or internationally is difficult to assess due to the hidden nature of these offences, the reluctance of victims and witnesses to come forward to law enforcement, and the difficulty of identifying victims in practice" (Public Safety Canada 2012a, 5). Yet, what follows is a series of staggering statistics about the international scope of human trafficking activities, which encourage Canadians to get on board with the goals of the Action Plan. For instance, it is reported that "at any given time, it is believed that worldwide at least 2.45 million people are forced to perform degrading, dehumanizing and dangerous work in conditions akin to slavery" (4), that "the numbers of individuals who are trafficked annually continues to increase" (4), and that "human trafficking is amongst the most lucrative of criminal activities, rivaled only by drug and firearms trafficking, generating billions of dollars annually for sophisticated criminal organizations" (4). The exact amount generated annually by perpetrators of human trafficking is later stated to be US$32 billion (6). Although this context is important for raising public awareness and understanding about the problem of human trafficking, the accuracy of these figures is suspect.

The highly regulated approach to information management implemented by the Harper Conservatives has made it even more difficult to access reliable information on human trafficking. In 2012, Statistics Canada reported that information on human trafficking required additional research and data collection (Ogrodnik 2012). Under the Harper Conservatives, however, there was a marked shift away from data collection, epitomized by – but by no means limited to – the elimination of the long-form census. According to De Shalit et al. (2014), "one result of this tightening of government control over information has been a tendency to shift from evidence-based approaches to policy in favour of more ideologically driven policies, which is particularly evident in relation to human trafficking" (393). In this context, dominant narratives produced through laws, policies, and official government communications provide the basis for public understanding about both the underlying causes and the contemporary scope of human trafficking. It is for this reason that an examination of the Action Plan is so important.

Reductive and Paternalistic Ideologies

The dominant human trafficking narrative promoted throughout the Action Plan is rooted in a victim/saviour dichotomy, wherein the Harper Conservatives depict themselves as defenders of women's rights, an image they juxtapose with the image of sexually exploited women and girls.[3]

The victimization of women and girls features overwhelmingly in public discourse and promotional material for the Action Plan. In the thirteen documents included in the study, the term "victim" is virtually always used to refer to women and children who are trafficked for the purpose of sexual exploitation, and far less often to men who are trafficked for the purpose of forced labour. The introduction to the plan makes the focus on women and children explicit, stating, "this crime is taking place in Canada, where human trafficking for the purpose of sexual exploitation is, to date, the most common manifestation of this crime and where the vast majority of the victims are Canadian women and children" (Public Safety Canada 2012a, 5). Through this uneven focus, women and girls become the objects of state intervention, and are essentialized as passive victims in need of rescuing by the Canadian government.

The victim/saviour dichotomy deployed in public discourse and promotional material for the Action Plan is reinforced through the repeated conflation of trafficking with sex trade work. The underlying ideology of the plan is reductive and paternalistic, framing all women in the sex trade as victims in need of saving, regardless of whether they are engaged in adult, consensual sex trade work or have been trafficked for the purposes of sexual exploitation. In addressing the issue of prostitution, the Action Plan explicitly states that "the Government's view is that prostitution victimizes the vulnerable and that the demand for sexual services can be a contributing cause of human trafficking," and thus concludes that "prevention [of prostitution] is a critical component in responding to human trafficking" (Public Safety Canada 2012a, 11). Harper made similar remarks linking sex work to trafficking as recently as the weeks leading up to the 2015 federal election. In a Conservative press release promising to expand the mandate of the Action Plan until 2021 if re-elected, Harper initiated a discussion about domestic policy regulating prostitution. Specifically, he criticized Liberal leader Justin Trudeau for rejecting Bill C-36, declaring, "Justin voted against our legislation to criminalize the activities of pimps and johns ... He doesn't understand that prostitution is not a lifestyle choice, but is in almost all cases the result of human trafficking and sexual exploitation" (Conservative Party of Canada 2015). Repeated statements such as this reinforce the idea of a direct link and a comparison between women who are trafficked and women who engage in adult, consensual sex trade work. This lack of nuance is problematic, both ideologically and practically.

Research in Canada has shown that public discourse conflating trafficking with sex trade work serves mainly to disenfranchise sex trade workers and stigmatize their clientele (Brock 2009). Such a framework also ignores the complex conditions and constraints under which some women decide to engage in sex trade work in different parts of the world. Contrary to abiding myths, violence – whether sexual or physical – is not an inherent or tolerated part of sex trade work (Campbell 2014). Some women may enter prostitution as an economic choice, while others are compelled to do so in response to significant economic constraints and vulnerability. The growing number of women turning to sex trade work as a survival strategy under neoliberalism, for instance, was discussed at length in the previous section. However, as Csete and Saraswathi Seshu (2004) explain, "to reduce prostitution to victimization, to something involving no choice or agency on the part of the women practicing it, is as demeaning and as much a human rights violation as the violence and stigma that sex workers regularly face" (28). In this framework, sex trade workers are not only robbed of their agency, they are also deprived the benefit of a more grounded and nuanced legal framework, one capable of addressing their actual needs and experiences. Recent research produced by Canadian researchers and organizations critical of Bill C-36 provides evidence of this (see, for example, Canadian HIV/AIDS Legal Network 2014, Mulvenna 2014, Pivot Legal Society 2014, and Sex Professionals of Canada 2014).

Some critics have speculated about whether the establishment of the Action Plan in the months leading up the Conservative government's proposal of Bill C-36 had any effect on the latter being passed into law. Speaking about the uneven focus on sex trafficking in the Action Plan, former Royal Canadian Mounted Police (RCMP) superintendent John Ferguson remarked:

> This is a moral crusade, dressed up as concern for women … If we look at Canada's attention to trafficking over the past ten years, it's telling that our total focus has been on *sex* trafficking … In comparison, there is little discussion of the people who are trafficked into the fisheries, farms, and factories that are sites for forced labour across North America. (as cited in Kimball 2014, emphasis added)

Others have pointed out that inflated and unsubstantiated trafficking statistics are often disseminated by supporters of Bill C-36 (Loreto 2015). For instance, Kimball (2014) writes that, "in railing against sex trafficking, they [supporters of Bill C-36] can argue against the inherent evils of the sex trade without relying on explicitly moral or religious rhetoric – a useful digression when the public is less inclined than ever to condemn prostitution on moral grounds." Inflating statistics by conflating the number of trafficking victims with sex trade workers is an effective strategy for misleading the public into believing that the trafficking problem is more pervasive than it actually is.

Despite staggering claims regarding the prevalence of trafficking and the vast resources that have been poured into policing and prosecution in Canada, criminal charges for trafficking are relatively rare, suggesting that the figures may be smaller than is often claimed. According to Public Safety Canada's 2015 annual report on progress for the Action Plan, between 2005 and 2014, eighty-five convictions of human trafficking offences were secured in Canada, and approximately eighty-seven additional cases were before the courts at the time that the report was released (3). A closer examination of these figures reveals that over 90 per cent of convicted and pending cases of human trafficking in Canada were comprised of domestic human trafficking, with a majority involving offences only indirectly related to trafficking, such as assault, kidnapping, uttering threats, extortion, conspiracy, and, overwhelmingly, prostitution-related offenses (RCMP 2013; Roots and De Shalit 2015). This indicates that anti-trafficking legislation is frequently being applied in order to prosecute individuals participating in prostitution. The relatively low number of specific human trafficking convictions in Canada since 2005 also contradicts the emphasis placed on enhancing prosecution and policing measures within the Action Plan.

Uneven Focus on Law Enforcement

Although the victimization of women and girls features prominently in the public discourse and the promotional material for the Action Plan, the actual implementation of the plan focuses predominantly on law enforcement, with almost no resources being allocated to prevention or to victim services. Even the most generous estimates indicate that only 8 per cent of funds (or C$500,000) allocated under the Action Plan will go toward actually helping victims (Public Safety Canada 2015, 1). Of that 8 per cent, it is likely that at least some money is going back to police, including one grant valued at C$75,000, given by the Department of Justice to the Calgary Police in order to increase awareness among police officers about the realities of prostitution and to assist women wishing to exit prostitution (Department of Justice 2015). It is ironic given the pervasive emphasis on "victimhood" and "prevention" within the Action Plan itself that the vast amount of resources being provided by the federal government is going towards enhanced policing, law enforcement, and prosecution rates.

Of particular concern is the significant amount of resources being devoted to increasing government control over immigration. The Action Plan does not outright state the Conservative government's agenda to restrict immigration. It does, however, include financial support and provisions to amend the Immigration and Refugee Protection Act, providing government departments with greater authority over Canadian employers who want to hire foreign workers (Public Safety Canada 2012a, 15). As a result of their increased power to regulate employers, one month after the Action Plan took effect the Canadian government announced that the country's sex industry would no longer be allowed to employ foreign workers because of the risks of exploitation, abuse, and trafficking in that environment. As part of this policy, the Department of Citizenship and Immigration stopped issuing temporary work permits for foreigners seeking work with escort agencies, massage parlours, and strip clubs (Moran 2012). In a press release announcing the ban, Jason Kenney, then minister of citizenship and immigration, said that he hoped the Action Plan would be strengthened by this new policy, and that its purpose was "to protect foreigners from what they might not know will happen to them when they get to Canada" (Moran 2012). This is a clear example of what Swiss (2012) has termed "instrumentalization," wherein programs designed to meet women's needs can become instruments for quite distinct development and security objectives on the part of the Canadian government, in this case restricting immigration. This tendency on the part of the Harper Conservatives is noted elsewhere in this volume, including in the introduction by Tiessen and Baranyi.

The ability to combine concern for women's rights with greater control over immigration encouraged the Harper government's interest in anti-trafficking measures (De Shalit et al. 2014, 393; Dobrowolsky 2008). As Cheng (2008) contends, the strengthening of law enforcement and border control, as well as the fortifying of anti-immigrant policies and anti-prostitution agendas, serves to enhance the powers of the state and divert attention from problems of unsafe migration and the larger-scale exploitation of migrant labour (16). Indeed, the Harper Conservatives' reductive and depoliticized approach failed to connect law enforcement tactics to strategies for addressing the broader structural issues underlying the growth of the global sex trade. In particular, nowhere in the Action Plan are the gendered impacts of global economic policies acknowledged or addressed. Instead, the plan misattributes the problem of human trafficking to prostitution and illegal immigration.

Research has found that anti-trafficking interventions are weakened by an uneven focus on prostitution and immigration, because it drains attention and funding from identifying and assisting actual trafficking victims (Agustin 2007; Di Nicola et al. 2007; Sanghera 2005). The Action Plan is guilty of this. It also fails to address the real drivers behind international trafficking, namely, restrictive and criminalizing immigration policies that require the poorest populations to seek employment abroad without the benefit of adequate social and legal protections (Ditmore 2005; Weitzer 2011, 1,344). In order to combat trafficking for the purpose of sexual exploitation, the global community should eliminate punitive immigration policies that create conditions that are ripe for an illicit sex trade (O'Brien 2009, 9). Trafficking must be distinguished from sex trade work in Canadian domestic and foreign policy in order to accurately identify their distinct root causes, and to develop appropriate safeguards and interventions. This is the only way to protect the rights of both women who are sex trade workers and women who are trafficked, and in ways that are not to the detriment of one another.

CONCLUSION AND RECOMMENDATIONS

The growth of the global sex trade has not been matched by an international response that adequately protects and promotes human rights for women and girls. Instead, there has been an international growth in anti-prostitution programs and policies that are designed to protect women but have the adverse effect of alienating sex trade workers and criminalizing their clientele. Anti-prostitution programs further suffer from a number of ideological flaws, including an uneven focus on the victimization of women, a tendency to conflate sex trade work with trafficking, and a failure to recognize how the sex trade is influenced by broader global trends and processes that are deeply gendered. Anti-prostitution programs and policies treat sex trade workers exclusively as victims, while the needs of these workers go unmet by interventions that seek to address the symptoms of poverty and gender inequality as opposed to their underlying causes.

Although concern over the growth of the global sex trade has swelled in recent years, Canada's work in this area has been constrained by an anti-prostitution agenda. Public discourse and promotional material pertaining to the Action Plan is illustrative of this trend. As I have shown, the underlying ideology of the Action Plan is problematic for three main reasons: first, it essentializes all women in the sex trade as victims in need of saving; second, it prioritizes law enforcement and prosecution over victim services; and third, it fails to address the structural issues underlying the contemporary growth of the global sex trade. Instead, the plan misattributes the problem of human trafficking to prostitution and illegal immigration, with punitive effects for both sex trade workers and immigrant populations.

In place of reductive and paternalistic approaches, I advocate that alternative narratives and strategies be developed to promote the rights of women and girls in the global sex trade – strategies that adopt more nuanced, complex, and authentic conceptions of sex trade work, but also of human trafficking, labour, and migration. In particular, I recommend the adoption of human rights–based approaches for addressing women's complex and diverse experiences within the global sex trade. Human rights–based approaches are capable of addressing the structural conditions that make for the growing prevalence of the sex trade itself, and of eradicating the abuses that sex trade workers face due to gender inequality, social stigma, and criminalization.

At least twenty years have passed since the sex workers' rights movement first advocated the adoption of human rights–based approaches. In 1985, the International Committee for Prostitutes' Rights (ICPR) drafted the World Charter for Prostitutes' Rights (WCPR), demanding that sex trade workers be guaranteed human rights, including freedom of speech, travel, immigration, work, marriage, motherhood, health, and housing (Saunders 2000, 7). In terms of legal frameworks, the WCPR advocates the decriminalization of all aspects of adult sex trade work resulting from individual choice. As for advocacy and policy approaches, the WCPR advocates safer working environments; improved access to social services including health care, affordable legal counselling, and optional alternative skills training; and support for educational programs to change social attitudes that criminalize, stigmatize, and discriminate against sex trade workers and ex–sex trade workers (International Committee for Prostitutes' Rights 1989, 40). Along with working to advance these goals, the ICPR engages in discussions about the role of clients and the demand for sex trade work, aspects that are routinely overlooked within prevailing analyses, including those produced by feminists. The WCPR stipulates that the customer should not be criminalized or condemned on a moral basis, but strictly penalized if they commit a crime such as assault or theft against a sex trade worker (40). This distinction is important. A human rights-based approach does not perceive commercial sex transactions as criminal behaviour; such a view merely reinforces social stigma against sex trade workers on the basis of normative sexual morality.

Human rights–based approaches further emphasize the importance of moving beyond anti-prostitution analyses that conflate sex work and human trafficking, thus refocusing attention on identifying and assisting victims and/or those seeking alternative economic and employment options. The best way to support women who are trafficked is to work holistically and address the underlying gender, economic, social, and political inequalities that perpetuate the violence and exploitation that they face. Doing so will require more nuanced analyses, and undoubtedly more time and effort on the part of governments and global develop-- ment organizations. Yet, it is the only way to ensure equal protection for the rights of sex trade workers and women who are trafficked. Such an approach is made impossible by a trafficking framework that views the sex trade as inherently violent and women as exclusively victims.

Several policy recommendations emerge from this analysis of the Harper governments' treatment of the sex trade and human trafficking, and these recommendations may offer some entry points for the Liberal government as it begins to enact some much-anticipated changes to domestic and international policy. In particular, these recommendations build on the gaps identified above, including increased support and resources for a broader range of services that will allow women participating in the sex trade to receive victim support services when needed. The provision of victim services is already emphasized in the Action Plan; the Liberal government need only remove the focus on law enforcement and prosecution, and fulfill the obligations set out therein. The decriminalization of the sex trade is also essential for ensuring that sex trade workers are not further marginalized and/or forced into difficult situations that will reduce their security. Additionally, improved data collection and research is needed to better understand the number of people involved in the sex trade and human trafficking, and in what particular contexts. Reinvesting in good data collection and support for research will enable a more sound basis from which to create evidence-based policies aimed at protecting sex trade workers, preventing entry into human trafficking rings, and providing alternatives for those who engage in sex trade work as a survival strategy.

NOTES

1 This chapter clearly distinguishes between adult, consensual sex trade work (which is sometimes referred to as "prostitution") and trafficking for the purposes of sexual exploitation, though both are on the rise internationally (ILO 2012).

2 The key federal departments are Public Safety Canada; the Canadian Border Service Agency; the Royal Canadian Mounted Police; Citizenship and Immigration Canada (now Immigration, Refugees and Citizenship Canada); Aboriginal Affairs and Northern Development Canada; the Department of Foreign Affairs, Trade and Development (now Global Affairs Canada); Status of Women

Canada; the Department of Justice; and Employment and Social Development Canada. Additional departments that participate on an ad hoc basis include the Department of National Defence, the Financial Transactions and Reports Analysis Centre of Canada, Passport Canada, the Public Health Agency of Canada, the Public Prosecution Service of Canada, and Statistics Canada.

3 Keast (in this volume) analyzes a similarly problematic victim/saviour dichotomy in relation to the Muskoka Initiative.

REFERENCES

Agustín, Laura. 2007. *Sex at the Margins: Migration, Labour Markets and the Rescue Industry*. London: Zed Books.

Brock, Deborah. 2009. *Making Work, Making Trouble: The Social Regulation of Sexual Labour*. 2nd ed. Toronto: University of Toronto Press.

Campbell, Angela. 2014. "We Condemn Attacks on Women at Work, Unless It's Sex Work." *Globe and Mail*, 11 November.

Canadian HIV/AIDS Legal Network. 2014. "Brief to the Senate Standing Committee on Legal and Constitutional Affairs regarding Bill C-36, the *Protection of Communities and Exploited Persons Act*." Canadian HIV/AIDS Legal Network. Accessed 28 October 2014. http://www.aidslaw.ca/site/brief-to-the-senate-standing-committee-on-legal-and-constitutional-affairs-regarding-bill-c-36-the-protection-of-communities-and-exploited-persons-act/?lang=en.

Cheng, Sealing. 2008. "Muckraking and Stories Untold: Ethnography Meets Journalism on Trafficked Women and the U.S. Military." *Sexuality Research and Social Policy* 5, no. 4: 6–18.

Conservative Party of Canada. 2015. "Harper Announces Further Action to Combat Human Trafficking." Conservative Party of Canada. Accessed 1 October 2015. http://www.conservative.ca/harper-announces-further-actions-to-combat-human-trafficking-2.

Cseste, Joanne, and Sarawswathi Seshu, Meena. 2004. "Still Underground: Searching for Progress in Realizing the Human Rights of Women in Prostitution." *HIV/AIDS Policy and Law Review* 9, no. 2: 7–13.

De Shalit, Ann, Robert Heynen, and Emily van der Meulen. 2014. "Human Trafficking and Media Myths: Federal Funding, Communication Strategies, and Canadian Anti-Trafficking Programs." *Canadian Journal of Communication* 39: 385–412.

Department of Foreign Affairs, Trade and Development (DFATD). 2015. "Human Trafficking and Migrant Smuggling." Department of Foreign Affairs, Trade and Development. Accessed 1 October 2015. http://www.international.gc.ca/crime/human-traf-personne.aspx?lang=eng.

Department of Justice. 2015. "Disclosure of Grant and Contribution Awards over $25,000." Department of Justice. Accessed 1 October 2015. http://www.justice. gc.ca/eng/trans/pd-dp/gc-sc/details.asp?yr=20152016&q=Q1&id=21611.

Di Nicola, Andrea, Andrea Cauduro, Marco Lombardi, and Paolo Ruspini. 2007. *Prostitution and Human Trafficking: Focus on Clients*. New York: Springer.

Ditmore, Melissa. 2005. "Trafficking in Lives: How Ideology Shapes Policy." In *Trafficking and Prostitution Reconsidered*, edited by Kamala Kempadoo, 107–26. London: Paradigm Publishers.

Dobrowolsky, Alexandra. 2008. "Interrogating 'Invisibilization' and 'Instrumentalization': Women and Current Citizenship Trends in Canada." *Citizenship Studies* 12, no. 5: 465–79.

Eisenstein, Hester. 2009. *Feminism Seduced: How Global Elites Use Women's Labor and Ideas to Exploit the World*. London: Paradigm.

Enriquez, Jean. 2006. "Globalization, Militarism and Sex Trafficking." *Sisyphe*, 10 November.

Ferguson, Ann. 1984. "Sex Wars: The Debate between Radical and Libertarian Feminists." *Signs: Journal of Women in Culture and Society* 10, no. 1: 106–12.

Henderson, Sarah, and Alana Jeydel. 2014. *Women and Politics in a Global World*. Oxford: Oxford University Press.

International Committee for Prostitutes' Rights (ICPR). 1989. "World Charter for Prostitutes' Rights." In *A Vindication of the Rights of Whores*, edited by Gail Pheterson, 40. Seattle: Seal Press.

International Labor Organization (ILO). 2012. *ILO Global Estimate of Forced Labor*. International Labor Organization. Accessed 22 November 2015. http:// www.ilo.org/wcmsp5/groups/public/---ed_norm/---declaration/documents/ publication/wcms_182004.pdf.

Jeffreys, Sheila. 2009. *The Industrial Vagina: The Political Economy of the Global Sex Trade*. New York: Routledge.

Kimball, Alexandra. 2014. "Dirty Tricks: Is the Anti-Prostitution Lobby Inflating Sex-Trafficking Stats?" *Walrus*, 18 November.

Kofman, Eleonore, and Parvati Raghuram. 2015. *Gendered Migration and Global Social Reproduction*. London: Palgrave.

Lacsamana, Anne. 2004. "Sex Worker or Prostituted Woman? An Examination of the Sex Work Debates in Western Feminist Theory." In *Women and Globalization*, edited by Anne Lacsamana and Delia Aguilar, 387–403. New York: Humanity Books.

Lacsamana, Anne, and Delia Aguilar. 2004. *Women and Globalization*. New York: Humanity Books.

Loreto, Nora. 2015. "Fact Check: Harper's 'Human Trafficking' Plan Will Do Nothing to Curb Violence against Women." *Rabble.ca*, 28 September.

Moran, Andrew. 2012. *"Foreign Workers Can't Be Hired in Sex Trade Industry."*
    Digital Journal, 5 July. Accessed 1 October 2015. http://www.digitaljournal.
    com/article/327984.

Mulvenna, Alexis. 2014. "Selling Sex: Bill C-36, Prostitution, and the Canadian
    Constitution." *Public Policy and Governance Review*, 7 October. Accessed 28
    October 2015. http://ppgreview.ca/2014/10/07/selling-sex-bill-c-36
    -prostitution-and-the-canadian-constitution.

O'Brien, Cheryl. 2008/09. "An Analysis of Global Sex Trafficking." *Indiana Jour-
    nal of Political Science* (Winter): 7–19.

Ogrodnik, Lucie. 2012. "Towards the Development of a National Data Collection
    Framework to Measure Trafficking in Persons." Crime and Justice Research
    Paper Series. Statistics Canada. Accessed 28 November 2015. http://www.
    statcan.gc.ca/pub/85-561-m/85-561-m2010021-eng.htm.

Pivot Legal Society. 2014. "Reckless Endangerment: Q&A on Bill C-36: Protection
    of Communities and Exploited Persons Act." Pivot Legal Society. Accessed 28
    October 2014. https://d3n8a8pro7vhmx.cloudfront.net/pivotlegal/pages/737/
    attachments/original/1415296321/BILLC36_info_english-Amendments.
    pdf?14152963211.

Poulin, Richard. 2004. "Globalization and the Sex Trade: Trafficking and the
    Commodification of Women and Children." *Canadian Women's Studies* 22,
    nos. 3–4: 38–43.

Public Safety Canada. 2012a. *National Action Plan to Combat Human Trafficking.*
    Public Safety Canada. Accessed 3 January 2015. http://www.publicsafety.gc.ca/
    cnt/rsrcs/pblctns/ntnl-ctn-pln-cmbt/index-eng.aspx.

– 2012b. *Canada's Anti-Human Trafficking Newsletter, Issue 1.* Public Safety Can-
    ada, October. Accessed 2 October 2015. http://www.publicsafety.gc.ca/cnt/
    rsrcs/pblctns/hmn-trffckng-nwslttr-2012/index-eng.aspx.

– 2013a. *Canada's Anti-Human Trafficking Newsletter, Issue 2.* Public Safety Can-
    ada, February. Accessed 2 October 2015. http://www.publicsafety.gc.ca/cnt/
    rsrcs/pblctns/hmn-trffckng-nwslttr-2013/index-eng.aspx.

– 2013b. *Canada's Anti-Human Trafficking Newsletter, Issue 3.* Public Safety Can-
    ada, July. Accessed 2 October 2015. http://www.publicsafety.gc.ca/cnt/rsrcs/
    pblctns/hmn-trffckng-nwslttr-2013-03/index-eng.aspx.

– 2013c. *Local Safety Audit Guide: To Prevent Trafficking in Persons and Related
    Exploitation.* Public Safety Canada. Accessed 2 October 2015. http://www.
    publicsafety.gc.ca/cnt/rsrcs/pblctns/lcl-sfty-dtgd/index-eng.aspx.

– 2013d. *Canada's Anti-Human Trafficking Newsletter, Special Edition.* Public
    Safety Canada, February. Accessed 2 October 2015. https://www.publicsafety.
    gc.ca/cnt/rsrcs/pblctns/hmn-trffckng-nwslttr-2013-10/index-en.aspx.

– 2013e. *2012–2013 Human Trafficking Stakeholder Consultations: National Summary Report*. Public Safety Canada. Accessed 2 October 2015. http://www.publicsafety.gc.ca/cnt/rsrcs/pblctns/2013-hmn-trffckng-stkhldr/index-eng.aspx.

– 2014a. *National Forum on Human Trafficking: January 2014; Summary Report*. Public Safety Canada. Accessed 2 October 2015. http://www.publicsafety.gc.ca/cnt/rsrcs/pblctns/2014-ntnl-frm-hmn-trffckng-smmry/2014-ntnl-frm-hmn-trffckng-smmry-en.pdf.

– 2014b. *Canada's Anti-Human Trafficking Newsletter, Issue 5*. Public Safety Canada, February. Accessed 2 October 2015. http://www.publicsafety.gc.ca/cnt/rsrcs/pblctns/hmn-trffckng-nwslttr-2014-02/index-eng.aspx.

– 2014c. *Canada's Anti-Human Trafficking Newsletter, Issue 6*. Public Safety Canada, July. Accessed 2 October 2015. http://www.publicsafety.gc.ca/cnt/rsrcs/pblctns/hmn-trffckng-nwslttr-2014-07/index-eng.aspx.

– 2014d. *National Action Plan to Combat Human Trafficking: 2012–2013; Annual Report on Progress*. Public Safety Canada. Accessed 2 October 2015. https://www.publicsafety.gc.ca/cnt/rsrcs/pblctns/ntnl-ctn-pln-cmbt-prgrss-2013/index-en.aspx.

– 2015. *National Action Plan to Combat Human Trafficking: 2013–2014 Annual Report on Progress*. Public Safety Canada. Accessed 2 October 2015. https://www.publicsafety.gc.ca/cnt/rsrcs/pblctns/ntnl-ctn-pln-cmbt-prgrss-2014/index-en.aspx.

Rickard, Wendy, and Merl Storr. 2001. "Sex Work Reassessed." *Feminist Review* 67: 1–4.

Roots, Katrin, and Ann De Shalit. 2015. "Evidence That Evidence Doesn't Matter: Human Trafficking Cases in Canada." *Atlantis: Critical Studies in Gender, Culture & Social Justice* 37, no. 2: 65–80.

Royal Canadian Mounted Police (RCMP). 2013. "Project Safekeeping: Domestic Human Trafficking for Sexual Exploitation in Canada." Ottawa: The Human Trafficking National Coordination Centre.

Sanders, Teela. 2008. *Paying for Pleasure: Men Who Buy Sex*. Devon: Willan Publishing.

Sanghera, Jyoti. 2005. "Unpacking the Trafficking Discourse." In *Trafficking and Prostitution Reconsidered*, edited by Kamala Kempadoo, 3–24. London: Paradigm Publishers.

Sassen, Saskia. 2000. "Women's Burden: Counter-Geographies of Globalization and the Feminization of Survival." *Journal of International Affairs* 53, no. 2: 503–24.

Saunders, Penelope. 2000. "Fifteen Years after the World Charter for Prostitutes' Rights." *Human Rights Dialogue* 2, no. 3: 7–14.

Sex Professionals of Canada. 2014. "Sex Workers' Mourn the Lives Bill C36 Will
Cost Us." Sex Professionals of Canada, 6 November.

Swiss, Liam. 2012. "Gender, Security, and Instrumentalism: Canada's Foreign
Aid in Support of National Interest?" In *Struggling for Effectiveness: CIDA and
Canadian Foreign Aid*, edited by Stephen Brown, 135–58. Montreal and Kingston: McGill-Queen's University Press.

Tsikata, Dzodzi. 1995. "Effects of Structural Adjustment on Women and the Poor."
Third World Network 61/62.

United Nations Development Programme (UNDP). 2012. *Sex Work and the Law
in Asia and the Pacific*. New York: United Nations Development Programme.
Accessed 1 October 2015. http://www.undp.org/content/dam/undp/library/
hivaids/English/HIV-2012-SexWorkAndLaw.pdf.

United Nations General Assembly. 2000. "Protocol to Prevent, Suppress and Punish Trafficking in Persons Especially Women and Children." New York: United
Nations General Assembly.

United Nations Office on Drugs and Crime. *Global Report on Trafficking in Persons*. United Nations Office on Drugs and Crime, 2014. Accessed 28 November
2015. https://www.unodc.org/documents/data-and-analysis/glotip/GLO-
TIP_2014_full_report.pdf.

Weiss, Michael. 2002. "Women for Sale." *Ladies' Home Journal* 1–4.

Weitzer, Ronald. 2010. "Paradigms and Policies." In *Sex for Sale: Prostitution,
Pornography, and the Sex Industry*, edited by Ronald Weitzer, 1–44. New York:
Routledge.

– 2011. "Sex Trafficking and the Sex Industry: The Need for Evidence-Based
Theory and Legislation." *Journal of Criminal Law and Criminology* 101, no. 4:
1337–70.

Legislation Cited

Criminal Code, RSC 1985, c C-46, ss 210, 212(1), 213.

Chapter 5

Lost without Way-Finders?
Disability, Gender, and Canadian
Foreign and Development Policy

Deborah Stienstra

INTRODUCTION

Since the so-called golden era of the late 1980s and early 1990s when Canada was recognized internationally for its leadership in the area of disability, there has been a waning in attention paid to disability in Canada's foreign and development policies. This decline happened despite Canada's ratification of the United Nations Convention on the Rights of Persons with Disabilities (CRPD) in 2010 and the development of the 1999 policy on gender equality within the Canadian International Development Agency (CIDA). What has caused this seeming tension between Canada's commitment to disability rights and gender, and a diminishing implementation of disability related initiatives?

Using the metaphor of way-finding – or, methods for navigation – this chapter suggests that the Canadian government has lost its way because it is not using the "way-finders" of disability rights and intersectionality necessary to navigate to more inclusive and accessible policies and programs. Good way-finding requires clear signage and directions in multiple formats so that many people – blind or sighted, from here or from elsewhere, confident in the language or not, and multiple variations in between – may find their way from one place to another. Using way-finding as a metaphor can challenge us to think about how international and national norms, policies, and practices, as well as civil society organizations, provide indicators of how to engage in particular areas.

Way-finders address and are understood by a wide audience, reflect diverse values, and articulate common standards. Way-finders in public policy help us find common ground for action between policy makers, practitioners, activists, and researchers. This chapter examines how the CRPD and Canada's gender equality policy act as way-finders in Canadian foreign and development policies.

More specifically, this chapter argues that the Canadian government's global development practices in relation to disability fail to promote both disability rights and inclusion as identified in the CRPD. Canada's gender equality policy, on the other hand, uses an asymmetrical and gender-first intersectional approach that inadequately addresses inequalities that result from both disability and the intersections of gender and disability.

HOW DO WE UNDERSTAND DISABILITY?

More than one billion people around the world live with disability, and many more live in families in which disabilities shape their lives (WHO 2011). More than half are women and over one hundred million are children. The majority of disabled people live in the Global South. Why do we label some bodies or ways of being as normal or able, while others are disabled and by extension abnormal?

For disabled women and men, girls and boys, disability is part of the rich diversity of life. This diversity includes blindness; sightedness; hearing; deafness; amputations; living with chronic or episodic illness or conditions; walking with legs, prosthetics, walkers, or wheelchairs; diverse ways of learning, communicating and comprehending; neuro-diversity; and many more. Yet these diverse ways of being have not been valued equally, with some labelled as normal and others as abnormal (Davis 2006).

This devaluing of so-called abnormal ways of being has led to the exclusion, imprisonment, institutionalization, and impoverishment of women and men, girls and boys with disabilities. The field of critical disability studies engages in understanding these differences, recognizing that they are socially constructed – as is evident in discourses, ideas, environments, and the material realities of those who *fit* and those who *misfit*, using the terms of Rosemarie Garland-Thomson (2011). We, as feminist and critical disability studies scholars, recognize that these fittings and misfittings are dynamic and change, and that policies and practices support certain ways of fitting or misfitting.

The CRPD also recognizes this. Article 1 of the CRPD states: "Persons with disabilities include those who have long-term physical, mental, intellectual or sensory impairments which in interaction with various barriers may hinder their full and effective participation in society on an equal basis with others." It also recognizes that there is considerable diversity among people with disabilities, which shapes the way they experience barriers and discrimination, including for women (Article 6) and children with disabilities (Article 7).

More than a decade ago, I argued (Stienstra 2002) that despite silence on how disability plays a role in international relations and globalization, there was synergy between the two, and the possibility for work that linked them. In recent years, increasing attention has been paid to understanding how disability shapes and is shaped by global development, with a recognition that disability studies itself reflects colonial assumptions, such as the notion of universality, the primacy of Global Northern perspectives and concepts, and the erasure of Indigenous and Global Southern experiences of disabilities, and how it does not pay enough attention to the relationship between colonization and disability (Meekosha 2011; Grech 2011; Connell 2011).

Little of this dynamic discussion around disability and global development has entered into the literature related to Canadian foreign and development policy. Some modest contributions have been made recognizing the bio-medical and rehabilitation focus of much of Canadian foreign and development policies (Stienstra 2003), and examining the neocolonial discourses in Canadian international development NGOs (Wehbi et al. 2009).

USING INTERSECTIONALITY TO FIND DISABILITY AND GENDER

One way of understanding disability in Canadian foreign and development policies is through intersectionality, which suggests that the experiences of women, men, girls, and boys are shaped not only by their identities (or social locations), but also by their interactions with social structures, including sexism, ableism, racism, colonization, and capitalism, among others (Crenshaw 1991; McCall 2005). Intersectionality theory allows us to foreground diversity and difference, and illustrate privilege and oppression in the various ways in which they manifest; highlight the ways that systems and structures create and reinforce inequalities; and explore reflexively our own positions as researchers (Cho et al. 2013).

My understanding of intersectionality has been defined to include Garland-Thomson's (2011) concepts of fitting and misfitting. Fitting is being in sync or in union with the circumstances of one's life, and misfitting refers to disjuncture, inconsistencies, and a jarring relationship with one's environment. Garland-Thomson (2011) argues that "a good enough fit produces material anonymity" (596), and that "the experience of misfitting can produce subjugated knowledges from which an oppositional and politicized identity might arise" (597). She suggests that fitting and misfitting are dynamic processes, constantly in motion within an ever-shifting environment, thus creating and recreating identities.

This argument suggests that disability is not a static lack, or problem for particular bodies, and challenges us to consider how, and in what circumstances, fitting and misfitting affects each of us. Misfitting leads us to recognize that disabilities are part of the human experience rather than exceptional circumstances requiring accommodation. It also suggests that for some women and girls, disability intersects with gender (and global location, Indigenousness and other social locations) to create situations of inequality.

Intersectionality is a tool that has implications for policy and practice (Hankivsky 2012; Hankivsky and Cormier 2011). Specifically, intersectionality examines the implicit assumptions in policies and among policy makers, as well as in policy analysis. Intersectionality-based policy analysis encourages us to leave open the categories of analysis, rather than to assume that one set of power relations, such as gender, is the primary set of inequalities, both present and to be explained. Hankivsky (2014) suggests that an intersectionality-based policy analysis "leaves open, as a matter of investigation, the content and implications of co-constituting relationships between power structures and social locations. Such an analytic method can thus expose less visible or completely overlooked social locations ... and in turn what degrees of privilege or penalty are experienced in relation to existing policies" (260–1).

This intersectional method also moves our analysis beyond the gender–race–class trichotomy, or the tendency to group together identities such as race, religion, class, ability, age, etc., in an unsophisticated or misguided attempt to engage with diversity. This can be thought of as "shallow" or thin intersectionality. Walby et al. (2012) suggest six different ways of addressing inequality in policy. The single approach identifies one primary form of exclusion. The asymmetric approach argues that one inequality is dominant, and although it recognizes others, they are secondary. The parallel forms of inequality approach recognizes that there are multiple forms of inequality but addresses them through separate laws and practices. The additive approach suggests that groups that have multiple disadvantages are doubly or triply disadvantaged, and that disadvantage is cumulative. Walby et al. (2012) argue that there are groups at the intersection of multiple forms of inequality who may be understood as being mutually constituted. Mutual shaping suggests that although separate systems of inequality exist, they affect and shape each other. Providing a rich analysis with complex policy responses requires that we ask what power relations or inequalities are at work, and examine ways in which these diverse relations are mutually constituted or mutually shaped, and their various effects.

Intersectionality-based policy analysis offers a way and some tools to illustrate how disability and gender interact with each other and with other sets of power relations in Canada's foreign and development policies and practices. It also suggests that when we consider gender in Canadian foreign policy, we need to also consider the mutually constituting or shaping relationships that may result from the intersection of disability and other power structures and social locations.

GENDER AND INTERSECTIONALITY IN CANADIAN FOREIGN AND DEVELOPMENT POLICIES

In a 2013 presentation at the University of Ottawa, I argued that Canada's gender equality policies were important but failed to address disability, and as a result, ignored some key situations for women, men, girls, and boys with disabilities in fragile and conflict-affected states (Stienstra 2013). One of the architects of Canada's policy took me aside and gently told me that the gender equality policy did include and address disability, and took intersectionality into account.

Her comments have remained with me, causing some questions and concerns to percolate. In what ways is the policy intentionally and recognizably intersectional? Does it leave open the categories of analysis so as to examine the ways diverse social locations and structures intersect? Is gender predominant in the policy, with disability and other sets of power relations ancillary to gender? Are tools provided to ensure that disability/ability are addressed appropriately in Canadian and global contexts? Were commitments made to disability-specific policy through CIDA and the Department of Foreign Affairs, Trade and Development (DFATD)? What are the implications of the intersectional stance taken (or not) for the inclusion of women and girls with disabilities in Canada's foreign and development policies?

In this chapter, I begin to explore, in a modest way, these questions and possible answers by looking at how CIDA and DFATD's policy on gender addresses disability and if intersectionality plays a role in the policy. I examine CIDA and DFATD's responses to disability, both in policy and in project funding, and ask to what extent they reflect gender equality. This will allow us to consider how the tools of disability rights and intersectionality can be way-finders for Canadian foreign and development policies.

As Tiessen and Baranyi note in the introduction to this book, CIDA has a long history of addressing gender in Canada's development policies, with some effect and leadership. This leadership has been by way of institutional policies and practices, including the gender equality policy adopted in 1999, evaluated in 2008, and renewed with an action plan in 2010. Together with Canada's domestic Gender-Based Analysis Plus (GBA+) framework, we see the outlines of what can be described as a gender-first or asymmetrical intersectional approach in Canadian foreign and development policies.

This approach sets gender equality as the critical framework within which other diversities exist. CIDA's policy on gender equality (CIDA 1999, 2010) includes diversity as one of its principles: "Women and men have different perspectives, needs, interests, roles and resources – and those differences may also be reinforced by class, race, caste, ethnicity or age. Policies, programs and projects must address the differences in experiences and situations between and among women and men" (CIDA 2010, 4). In addition, the policy suggests that using gender analysis throughout the project cycle provides information on "the differences among women and men and the diversity of their circumstances, social relationships and consequent status (e.g. their class, race, caste, ethnicity, age, culture and abilities)" (CIDA 2010, 7). In each of these policies, it is important to note the gender-first or asymmetric construction of the policy. Any other "consequent status" comes after or out of our consideration of gender inequalities.

Canada's GBA+ framework addresses diversity in a slightly different way. It argues that GBA+ "is an analytical tool for examining the potential impacts of policies, programs, and initiatives on diverse groups of women and men, girls and boys, taking into account gender and other identity factors" (Status of Women Canada 2013). In this approach, gender remains a major factor but analysis extends to what they call other intersecting identity factors, such as age, education, language, geography, culture, and income.

This gender-first approach takes its direction from feminist scholars and practitioners who have been arguing for decades about the importance of considering gender in Canadian policies and practices (Sjolander et al. 2003; Dobrowolsky 2009). Yet this acceptance of the importance of gender equality, hard-fought as it was, also brings with it implicit and unexamined assumptions about the predominant place of gender in the context of other sets of power relations.

My purpose in raising these issues is not to undercut the importance of gender equality commitments and analysis, or the huge challenge that those within and outside CIDA (now GAC) have faced and continue to face to have these policies adopted and implemented. Rather, I want to recognize that a gender-first intersectional approach helps us tell a story from particular vantage points – those beginning with the assumption that gender is the most significant factor in understanding inequalities and the best way through which to provide a policy response.

This approach may be less useful for illustrating experiences in which other social locations, including disability, are the dominant factor. A gender-first approach may inadvertently make invisible other power relations at the expense of identifying gender inequalities. A gender-first intersectional approach may not be effective in explaining situations in which other power relations, such as disability, colonialism, or racism, shape the experiences of women, nor in supplying measures to provide redress for these inequalities.

An example from the experiences of girls with disabilities illustrates this point. We know the importance of girls having access to education and that girls in the Global South face many gendered barriers to education. Global initiatives like the United Nations Girls' Education Initiative, Because I Am a Girl, and the Global Partnership for Education have raised the profile of the issue and increased girls' access to education in the Global South. A gender-first approach ensures that we ask why girls are not able to access education, and then develop measures to address this lack of access.

Despite significant global attention and funding in this area, however, girls with disabilities continue to lack access to education at significantly higher rates than girls without disabilities, but comparably low rates to boys with disabilities (Rousso 2003; Nguyen and Mitchell 2014). This lack of access needs to be understood as a result of the mutually shaping relationships of gender and disability, as well as other relations of power, including class and caste. For example, Nguyen and Mitchell (2014, 332) show how in Vietnam, girls and boys with disabilities are excluded from the educational system because of assumptions about disability built into the educational and policy processes, that disability is a medical problem requiring diagnosis, cure, and prevention. Being excluded from education as a result of assumptions about disability shapes the experiences of many girls and boys with disabilities around the world. Trani et al. (2012) argue that although gender is a significant factor in Afghanistan for access to education for children with disabilities, other factors, such as assumptions about the ability of people with disabilities to contribute to society, the age of onset for impairments, and cultural views on war-related impairments versus congenital conditions, are even more significant.

To address disability within an intersectional framework requires paying attention to how disability is constituted within societies, governments, and policies, as well as how it is experienced by girls, boys, men, and women. Canada has been lauded in the international community for its leadership in recognizing disability rights in Canada's Charter of Rights and Freedoms (Stienstra 2016). To what extent do Canadian foreign and development policies and practices reflect a commitment to disability rights and adopt an intersectional approach that addresses both gender and disability?

DISABILITY AND CANADIAN FOREIGN AND DEVELOPMENT POLICIES

For many in the disability community, the so-called golden age of Canada including disability in its foreign and development policies was during the United Nations Decade for Disabled Persons between 1983 and 1992 (Neufeldt and Egers 2003). In particular, Canada showed leadership in shifting the discourse of international norms from a bio-medical model and a charity approach to disability, to one of human rights. This came in part through the presence of leaders in the disability rights movements on Canadian delegations to the United Nations, and Canada's support of the Canadian office of Disabled Peoples' International (DPI). These measures ensured that the Canadian government had advisors from the advocacy movement itself. In 1998, the Canadian government was awarded the Franklin Delano Roosevelt International Disability Award for its international leadership on disability rights.

Following the Decade for Disabled Persons, however, there was a noticeable decline in focus and commitment in Canada's foreign and development policies related to people with disabilities. This was despite the persistent efforts of organizations of disabled people and their families, like the Council of Canadians with Disabilities (CCD) and the Canadian Association for Community Living (CACL). In 1998, CACL argued that the federal government should establish a framework and include disability in its foreign policies. The then Department of Foreign Affairs and International Trade initiated a reference group, with terms of reference, but the group never met (Stienstra 2003).

In 2002, the United Nations began to negotiate a convention on the rights of persons with disabilities. These efforts were successful, and in 2006 the United Nations adopted the CRPD, bringing it into force in 2008.

The Convention opened a new era of human rights for people with disabilities, with organizations for disabled peoples engaged in monitoring and implementing their rights across the globe, including through Disability Rights Promotion International (DRPI). Canada announced its ratification of the CRPD in 2010 at the Vancouver Winter Paralympics.

The Canadian government's approach to disability in global development under the Harper Conservatives between 2006 and 2015 must be understood in the broader context of CIDA and the federal government. In 2006, the Canadian government reframed and cut funding to women's groups within Canada. As Tiessen and Baranyi (in this volume) suggest, the changing approach was also reflected in policy and programming shifts related to gender equality within CIDA. Similar cuts were made to CIDA and development assistance organization funding in 2012. Finally, in 2013, disability organizations received comparable cuts to their operational funding. These cuts to NGOs are part of a larger neoliberal shift that reduced government involvement in some areas, increased corporate involvement, and called for greater competition for public funds.

The effects of these cuts have been significant in each sector. For example, among the disability organizations, the cuts will likely result in the amalgamation or closure of self-representational organizations of people with disabilities, leaving the disability sector primarily led by service or medical organizations, which do not rely on governments for their funding and do not necessarily ensure that their organizations are led by people with disabilities. Similar cuts to service delivery at the provincial and local levels reinforce this "privatization" trend, with increased reliance on family support or charity to deliver disability-related services (Stienstra 2014). These neoliberal shifts are also evident in the overall decline in Canada's official development assistance, and the closure of CIDA and the inclusion of its work in DFATD (now GAC), as well as in the increasing corporate presence and links between corporations and development assistance.

DISABILITY AND DEVELOPMENT ASSISTANCE FUNDING

As a result of its ratification of the CRPD, and according to Article 32, the Canadian government has a responsibility to ensure that its international development programs are inclusive of and accessible to people with disabilities. In its first report on the implementation of the CRPD, the Government of Canada argued:

Canada's development assistance, in conformity with the spirit of the Official Development Assistance Accountability Act, includes programming that promotes human rights and equal opportunities for persons with disabilities by raising awareness of disability issues addressing stigma and discrimination, and reducing barriers to the integration of persons with disabilities into their societies. Between 2001 and 2011, the Government of Canada invested approximately $350 million in international projects for which disability was a principal or significant focus, such as issues associated with landmines, natural disasters, discrimination and poor health and nutrition. (Canadian Heritage 2014, 8)

In its 2011 Federal Disability Report, the government suggests that it spent $66.1 million in 2009–2010 and $76.6 million in 2010–2011 in development assistance spending that included disability as a significant or principal project objective (ESDC 2011, Appendix A). These numbers are illustrative of a broad range of projects and approaches to disability as we discuss below, not all of which are in the same spirit as the understanding of disability found in the CRPD.

To understand how the Canadian government has been addressing disability in practice, we analyzed sixty-nine project profiles that included key words related to disability (disability, disabilities, disabled, and handicap) on the CIDA/DFATD International Project Browser (see table 5.1). For several projects, we examined the project or recipient's website to get further information. The funding was in place between 2001 and 2018 (none of the projects ended before 2006), and included both regular funding and emergency funding for particular crises. We collated each project, noting their title, duration, location, funded organization, and CIDA/DFATD contribution. In addition, we analyzed the project profile, identifying keywords, the targeted sector (e.g. emergency assistance, health, rehabilitation, employment, education, etc.), whether people with disabilities were the central focus of their project or one of multiple populations, the type of recipient organization, whether gender was identified as part of the project, and their approach to disability.

We identified four approaches to disability: (1) prevention/recovery or efforts to prevent, fix, or overcome impairments; (2) inclusion or efforts to include people with disabilities in communities or governments, or to increase accessibility; (3) human rights, which included projects that specifically mentioned the human rights of people with disabilities or people with disabilities claiming their human rights; and (4) capacity building or those projects that aimed to increase the capacity of governments or communities to promote the participation of people with disabilities, or provide specific employment opportunities for people with disabilities.

TABLE 5.1 CIDA/DFATD-funded projects relating to disability

YEAR FUNDING BEGINS	TOTAL PROJECTS (PROJECTS WITH MULTIPLE APPROACHES)	APPROACH (SOME PROJECTS TAKE MULTIPLE APPROACHES)				
		PREVENTION/ RECOVERY	INCLUSION	HUMAN RIGHTS	CAPACITY BUILDING	UNKNOWN
2001	1	0	0	1	0	0
2002	1	0	1	0	0	0
2005	1	1	0	0	0	0
2006	2	0	2	0	0	0
2007	5 (1)	2	2	1	1	0
2008	4 (1)	2	1	1	1	0
2009	8 (2)	5	5	0	0	0
2010	8	3	1	1	2	1
2011	13 (3)	8	2	2	4	0
2012	6 (2)	3	4	1	0	0
2013	13 (1)	11	1	0	2	0
2014	6 (1)	5	1	1	0	0

YEAR FUNDING BEGINS	TOTAL PROJECTS (PROJECTS WITH MULTIPLE APPROACHES)	PROJECT PRIORITIES		GENDER	
		PEOPLE WITH DISABILITIES	MULTIPLE POPULATIONS	YES	NO
2001	1	0	1	0	1
2002	1	0	1	1	0
2005	1	0	1	1	0
2006	2	0	2	1	1
2007	5 (1)	1	4	4	1
2008	4 (1)	1	3	1	3
2009	8 (2)	3	5	4	4
2010	8	0	8	5	3
2011	13(3)	4	9	9	4
2012	6(2)	3	3	4	2
2013	13(1)	4	9	10	3
2014	6(1)	0	6	6	0

These four approaches are directly linked to different understandings of disability, with prevention or recovery seeing disability as within individual bodies and needing to be addressed by medical or rehabilitation expertise, and the other three – inclusion, human rights, and capacity building – recognizing disability as resulting from barriers and discrimination within environments and societies, and thus addressing barriers, building capacity, and implementing rights.

The methods we used do not capture all the disability-related projects funded by CIDA/DFATD during this time period and do not reflect all the development assistance projects undertaken by Canadian organizations related to disability. But this sampling does highlight the projects most clearly associated with disability funded by CIDA/DFATD. This sample gives us a taste of some key themes, priorities, and approaches that the Canadian government supports around disability, and allows us to evaluate how this fits with their commitments under the CRPD. It also enables us to begin evaluating the extent to which CIDA's gender equality policy ensures that disability and gender are addressed.

We identified several key themes in the sample: the majority of projects funded took a prevention or recovery approach to disability; the NGOs that received significant funding had been involved for many years in this area but were not disabled peoples' organizations (DPOs), whereas organizations working primarily on disability issues received very little project funding; most of the projects addressed people with disabilities as part of vulnerable or marginalized populations, having special needs or requiring recovery and reintegration into society; and gender was addressed alongside disability primarily in projects that included disability as one of many priorities.

Prevention or Recovery Focus
Of the project summaries reviewed, almost 58 per cent were focused on prevention or recovery, and roughly 46 per cent were focused on inclusion, human rights or capacity building (see table 5.2). As figure 5.1 illustrates, an increasing proportion of projects are funded that use a prevention/recovery approach. As well, of the total $421,611,513 of funding, roughly 54 per cent was in the area of prevention or recovery, with roughly 50 per cent for projects focused on inclusion, human rights, or capacity building (see table 5.2).

When we analyzed the sector in which the project took place (figure 5.2), we saw a strong emphasis on prevention, rehabilitation, health, and emergency assistance projects, all of which are associated to a significant extent with the perspective that disability is a lack, illness, or condition

TABLE 5.2 Funding by type of project

	FUNDING FOR PREVENTION/ RECOVERY PROJECTS		FUNDING FOR INCLUSION, HUMAN RIGHTS, AND CAPACITY-BUILDING PROJECTS	
YEAR	NUMBER OF PROJECTS	TOTAL AMOUNT ($)	NUMBER OF PROJECTS	TOTAL AMOUNT ($)
2001	0	–	1	4,800,000
2002	0	–	1	14,500,000
2005	1	16,888,643	0	–
2006	0	–	2	19,606,603
2007	2	4,629,182	3	15,000,345
2008	2	62,095,138	2	9,399,922
2009	5	11,506,678	5	5,857,516
2010	3	13,500,000	4	66,499,687
2011	8	32,992,506	6	18,998,303
2012	3	9,743,409	4	11,769,698
2013	11	68,445,000	3	41,175,061
2014	5	9,100,000	1	3,000,000

that needs to be cured, fixed, or prevented. Most projects were involved in more than one sector. Thirteen per cent of the projects had prevention as a sector of activity. In some cases, this was done through preventing disease or distributing vaccines or vitamins, while in others it was through the removal of landmines. Health care initiatives received roughly 25 per cent of the total funding, while rehabilitation initiatives received 20 per cent and emergency assistance roughly 23 per cent. This is in contrast with all of the other sectors, the highest being education (18.8 per cent) and democratic participation (13 per cent). All of the others, including employment, food, sanitation, human rights, and infrastructure, were significantly lower.

Shifting NGO Involvement

Several key NGOs, including Handicap International and Christian Blind Mission, have been active in the disability and global development field for many years and continue to provide leadership in projects in which people with disabilities are the major focus of the project. Handicap

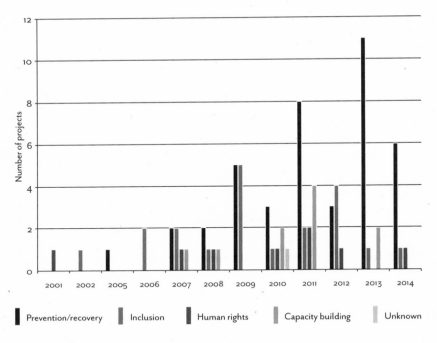

FIGURE 5.1 Approaches to disability in CIDA/DFATD-funded projects

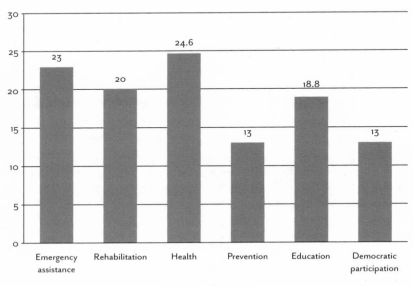

FIGURE 5.2 Funding by sector for prevention/recovery projects, 2005–2014

TABLE 5.3   Handicap International projects funded by CIDA/DFATD

TITLE (LOCATION)	YEAR (DURATION)	AMOUNT ($)	APPROACH
Emergency Rehabilitation Services in Yemen	2014 (9 months)	1,650,000	Prevention/recovery
Typhoon Haiyan in the Philippines – Shelter Assistance	2014 (8 months)	1,650,000	Prevention/recovery
Syria Crisis – Support for Refugees in Jordan and Lebanon	2013 (9 months)	4,000,000	Prevention/recovery
Support for Children with Disabilities in Gaza	2013 (27 months)	945,000	Prevention/recovery
Emergency Interventions for Vulnerable Syrian Refugees (Jordan and Lebanon)	2013 (7 months)	600,000	Prevention/recovery
Assistance to Landmine Survivors (Colombia)	2012 (51 months)	2,296,006	Prevention/recovery
Assistance to Conflict-Affected People in Pakistan	2011 (14 months)	500,000	Prevention/recovery
Haiti Earthquake	2010 (12 months)	500,000	Prevention/recovery
Basic Education of Children with Disabilities in Kenya	2009 (40 months)	378,000	Inclusion

International's work is especially notable, having received approximately $14.5 million from CIDA for ten projects since 2009 (see table 5.3). Their work reflects the shift in philosophy noted by Neufeldt and Egers: "from an expert, curative, institutionalized approach to an increasing emphasis on community-based programming with a greater array of interventions" (2003, 286). Through its experience in emergency response initiatives, Handicap International developed a checklist to assist development agencies with concrete practices that will better ensure the inclusion of people with disabilities in emergency settings. They note that the checklist (Handicap International n.d.) is a much-needed tool for including people with disabilities in emergency assistance projects and reconstruction. It offers concrete suggestions for addressing people's needs with regard to water, education, health, livelihoods, and shelter. Yet the checklist also uses language that continues to portray people with disabilities as vulnerable rather than capable, and identifies women and children with disabilities as being even more vulnerable. This undermines the concrete and practical suggestions around inclusion, and paints people with disabilities primarily as victims rather than agents capable of engaging in political and social life.

The NGO community in Canada, through the Canadian Council for International Cooperation (CCIC) has also begun to recognize that women, men, girls, and boys with disabilities are an important part of global development initiatives, including in crises. For example, in 2010, as part of Canada's response to the earthquake in Haiti, Canadian civil society organizations called on foreign ministers meeting in Montreal to "include persons with disabilities and organizations focused on disability rights in all initiatives and stages of relief, recovery, reconstruction and longer-term development planning" (CCIC 2010). In its own model agreement with CIDA from 2012 to 2016, the CCIC notes the importance of both gender equality and disability inclusion as shared development principles that will guide their cooperative work and strengthen their effectiveness (CCIC 2011).

Despite the shift from a medicalized and individual approach to one guided more by human rights and a socially constructed approach to disability – as well as the leadership taken by some key NGOS – DPOS themselves receive only very modest funding from CIDA in our sampling. This reflects a gap in understanding that disabled people are not just victims, but rather actors. We identified only three projects that came from DPOS, with a total of approximately $5 million in funding (see table 5.4).

These organizations are those in which the direction comes from disabled peoples themselves, and that direction is evident in the prominent place (and usually majority) of people with disabilities on the board of the organization. Two of the organizations – Disabled Peoples' International and the Canadian Centre on Disability Studies – have significant experience in international development work with people with disabilities and are led by people with disabilities. The third group, Parkland Community Living and Supports Society (CLASS), is primarily an organization providing disability service, and arguably not a DPO, although half of its board of directors have direct experience with disabilities. They have long-standing relationships with Indigenous peoples in Canada and Argentina, who provide a foundation for the funded project.

Two universities have also been involved in disability related development projects – Queen's University and York University. Queen's University's long-established international centre on community-based rehabilitation (CBR) received funding for two projects, totaling $6.2 million. The first project addresses barriers to education, health, and vocational services for Bangladeshi children and youth with disabilities, and includes some gender-based training. The second, also in Bangladesh, is focused on providing training for maternal and child health, as well as for disability workers, linking the project to the Canadian

TABLE 5.4 Projects by DPOs funded by CIDA/DFATD

TITLE (LOCATION)	ORGANIZATION	YEAR (DURATION)	AMOUNT ($)	APPROACH
Support to Disabled Aboriginal Children (Mexico)	Parkland CLASS	2012 (37 months)	483,086	Inclusion and human rights
Human Rights Defenders (many Global South countries)	Disabled Peoples' International	2011 (28 months)	312,047	Capacity building and human rights
Inclusive Education for Children with Disabilities (Ukraine)	Canadian Centre on Disability Studies	2008 (58 months)	4,699,922	Inclusion and human rights

government's maternal and child health initiative. Although the field of CBR has shifted considerably from an earlier reliance on a medicalized, individualized approach to disability to one that pays more attention to human rights and addressing poverty (Hartely et al. 2009), CBR continues to be criticized for the lack of participation it affords for disabled people in decision making around their own lives (DPI 2012). Queen's University does not currently have a degree program at any level related to critical disability studies, although in 2013 it initiated a certificate program on international health and disability.

By contrast, the $1.6 million project funded at York University is integrally linked to the university's graduate program in critical disability studies and headed by its founding director, Marcia Rioux, who also co-leads Disability Rights Promotion International. This project is clearly linked to the CRPD and DPOs in the region. Its focus is on enhancing capacity through labour market initiatives. In addition, the project addresses gender directly along with disability.

Portraying People with Disabilities
A third theme illustrates some of the discourse in the data around disability or the portrayal of people with disabilities. Just over three-quarters of the projects included people with disabilities as one of a number of priority populations (figure 5.3). These groups, including people with disabilities, were most often portrayed as vulnerable, marginalized, or disadvantaged, and therefore with special needs or requiring protection, recovery, rehabilitation, and reintegration into society. In several of the projects addressing post-conflict initiatives, a distinction was made between people with disabilities and those with injuries or the war-wounded. This may reflect cultural assumptions about disabilities, as

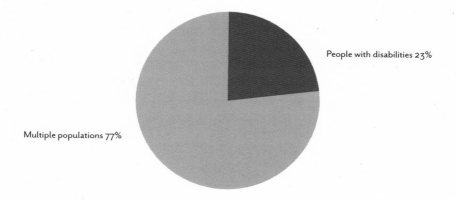

People with disabilities 23%

Multiple populations 77%

FIGURE 5.3 Projects priorities

Trani et al. (2012) illustrate with regard to Afghanistan, where a distinction is made between impairments received in war and those from other
causes, and a different value ascribed to each.

Several project profiles, notably those involved in health-related prevention activities, suggest that their work will reduce "life-long disability."
This understanding renders disability as an illness and something to be
prevented or avoided. The summaries say little about people who live with
these conditions, except to assert that their survival and well-being are at
stake. This again reflects long-standing global approaches to disability,
including one of the World Health Organization's key measurements – the
Disability-Adjusted Life Year (Parks 2014).

The language used in the majority of the project profiles with regard
to people with disabilities reflects the discourse that Wehbi et al. (2009)
found in their analysis of Canadian international NGOs. Although one
of their key findings is the absence of disability in NGO work, we looked
specifically at where disability was present. In this case we found similar
themes around disability. Wehbi et al. argue that when disability is present, ableist language is used. In particular, as we also note, they suggest
that the language used reflects a tragedy discourse of disability – with disability being seen as something to be avoided or pitied because it causes
suffering. Secondly, Wehbi et al. argue the language focuses on vulnerability, which illustrates an individualist approach to disability: "By focusing
the gaze on individuals and their perceived vulnerability, not only do we
locate the problem within the individual, but we also negate any individual and collective resistance efforts" (Wehbi et al. 2009, 416). Finally, they
suggest that the discourse promotes an ideal of normalcy, and promotes

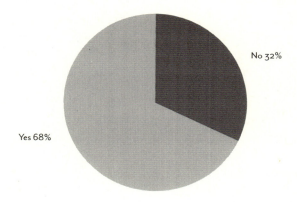

No 32%

Yes 68%

FIGURE 5.4 Is gender included?

work that brings disabled people to normalcy. Again, this is illustrated in the project profiles we identified, with the high proportion of projects focused on prevention, rehabilitation, and health, and few enhancing the capacity of people with disabilities and their representative organizations, or addressing stigma and the exclusion of people with disabilities within their communities and societies.

Gender and Disability
One of the expectations of the gender equality policy is that gender is integrated or mainstreamed in CIDA/DFATD's work. With that in mind, we looked at what proportion of the disability-identified projects funded by CIDA/DFATD also addressed gender. We examined the extent to which the projects' approaches to gender and disability reflected an intersectional approach, and if they did, what type of intersectionality?

More than two-thirds (68 per cent) of the projects we examined addressed gender to some degree in the project profile (see figure 5.4). Almost all of these (88 per cent) were projects that addressed disability as one of a number of vulnerable or marginalized populations. The populations named as vulnerable varied by project, but included women, children, the elderly, and people with disabilities. This suggests the thin version of intersectionality discussed earlier.

Although it is difficult to illustrate this using the project profiles alone, the use of such phrases as "especially for girls and children with disabilities," "the special needs of women, children, people with disabilities, and the elderly" and "disadvantaged groups in the labour market, such as women, youth, and people with disabilities" suggest that although funded organizations recognized the importance of including gender, they had a difficult time linking gender and disability in a substantive way. In many ways, as I have argued elsewhere, disability trumps gender (Stienstra 2015), rendering people with disabilities sexless and genderless.

The projects designed specifically for people with disabilities were divided evenly between those that addressed gender and those that did not. Again we see little understanding of the implications that disability and gender have for people with disabilities. Handicap International's multiple projects for people with disabilities did not generally include a gendered analysis of the project or its outcomes. For example, their project for conflict-affected people in Pakistan, funded in 2011, is directed to "people with long-term physical or intellectual disabilities, people with injuries or chronic diseases, and the elderly" (DFATD 2013a). Their project providing assistance to landmine survivors in Colombia, funded in 2012, targets "children and youth as well as disabled people and persons excluded because of crippling injuries" (DFATD 2013b). Yet we know from the research that the effects of landmines are gendered, with boys most affected by conflict (UNICEF 2013). Parkland's CLASS project for Indigenous peoples in Mexico, funded in 2012, illustrates an appreciation of the intersections of Indigenousness and disability, but not of gender.

One project, from DPI and funded from 2011 to 2013, stands out for its attention to both disability and gender, as well as its inclusion of people with disabilities and their representative organizations as active agents in the project. This project offers a model for a deep intersectional analysis and practice that recognizes how disability and gender mutually shape the experiences of each. Using the CRPD as its basis, the project, called Human Rights Defenders, was initiated to address the awareness, protection, and enforcement of the rights of people with disabilities and to enhance their inclusion and access to services. As part of the project, DPI established two women's global networks for the rights of women with disabilities, particularly young women with disabilities. Despite the exemplary approach taken by DPI in this project, it was funded for a modest ($312,047) albeit wide-ranging project.

CONCLUSIONS: WAY-FINDING, DISABILITY, AND GENDER

Since 2006, the overall direction of Canadian foreign and development policies has changed, though two commitments have remained – Canada's commitment to its gender equality policy and to the implementation of the CRPD. Implementing these requires an intersectional approach that recognizes the mutual shaping of gender and disability-related inequalities. These provide way-finders for Canadian foreign and development policies.

Yet our research found that CIDA/DFATD's approach to disability does not reflect the understandings of disability found in the CRPD. Rather, the Canadian government has invested significant funds in projects focused on a contested area of disability – prevention and recovery. The work promotes the work of medical and rehabilitation "experts" who were consulted on both the problems and the solutions, and who portrayed disabled people as victims, or part of vulnerable populations. This approach is inconsistent with the CRPD and the commitments made by the government in ratifying the CRPD, though it is consistent with the neoliberal approach that we see more generally in cuts to funding for NGOs, changes to the mandate of CIDA, and the involvement of the corporate sector in development assistance. This is one area in which the Canadian government needs to be held accountable to its commitments to the CRPD and the implications of disability rights for its global development work.

In the implementation of the gender equality policy, we see a thin intersectionality at work, although in some projects we find a gender-first or disability-first, or asymmetrical, approach to intersectionality. Very few projects reflect gender and disability as mutually shaping, or as mutually constituting relationships of inequality requiring distinctive policy responses. In order to develop a deeper approach to intersectionality within the gender equality policies at GAC, officials could work to develop tools that reflect these intersections, as well as their implications for development work. As well, the GBA+ framework in Canadian policy and Canada's commitment to the CRPD and other international conventions provides an opportunity to reflect on how to deepen GAC's commitment to intersectionality.

One excellent resource for effectively incorporating disability in policy and program initiatives are DPOs, such as DPI, or university-based projects that are integrally linked to critical disability studies programs. These are at the frontline of work addressing disability rights and have successfully incorporated a deeper understanding of the relationship between disability and gender. These organizations also work to engage disabled people as active agents in constructing and reconstructing inclusive societies. Unfortunately, these organizations have also seen their funding cut and their work marginalized.

The Canadian government has important way-finders at its disposal – including disability rights, DPOs, and intersectionality. The challenge is ensuring that these are used and implemented, especially in these neoliberal times.

REFERENCES

Canadian Council for International Cooperation (CCIC). 2010. "A Canadian Civil Society Statement to the Foreign Ministers Meeting on Haiti." Canadian Council for International Cooperation, 25 January.

– 2011. *CIDA/CCIC Cooperation Agreement*. Canadian Council for International Cooperation, April 25. Accessed 29 October 2014. http://www.ccic.ca/_files/en/media/2011_03_%20CIDA_CCIC_Model_Cooperation_Agreement.pdf.

Canadian Heritage. 2014. *Convention on the Rights of Persons with Disabilities: First Report of Canada*. Canadian Heritage.

Canadian International Development Agency (CIDA). 1999. *CIDA's Policy on Gender Equality*. Canadian International Development Agency.

– 2010. *Gender Equality Policy and Tools: CIDA's Policy on Gender Equality*. Canadian International Development Agency.

Cho, Sumi, Kimberlé Williams Crenshaw, and Leslie McCall. 2013. "Toward a Field of Intersectionality Studies: Theory, Applications, and Praxis." *Signs* 38, no. 4: 785–810.

Connell, Raewyn. 2011. "Southern Bodies and Disability: Re-Thinking Concepts." *Third World Quarterly* 32, no. 8: 1369–81.

Crenshaw, Kimberlé Williams. 1991. "Mapping the Margins: Intersectionality, Identity Politics, and Violence against Women of Color." *Stanford Law Review* 43, no. 6: 1241–99.

Davis, Lennard. 2006. "Constructing Normalcy: The Bell Curve, the Novel and the Invention of the Disabled Body in the Nineteenth Century." In *The Disability Studies Reader*, 2nd ed., edited by Lennard Davis, 3–16. New York: Taylor and Francis.

Department of Foreign Affairs, Trade and Development (DFATD). 2013a. "Project Profile: Assistance to Conflict-Affected People in Pakistan – Handicap International Canada 2011." Department of Foreign Affairs, Trade and Development. Accessed 23 September 2013. http://www.acdi-cida.gc.ca/cidaweb/cpo.nsf/vWebCCEn/C38E3C15C49AAB358525785A00372910.

– 2013b. "Project Profile: Assistance to Landmine Survivors." Department of Foreign Affairs, Trade and Development. Accessed 23 September 2013. http://www.acdi-cida.gc.ca/cidaweb/cpo.nsf/vLUWebProjEn/C57C12706D3B498A85257992003B42A1?openDocument.

– 2013c. *Report to Parliament on the Government of Canada's Official Development Assistance 2012–2013*. Department of Foreign Affairs, Trade and Development.

Disabled Peoples International. 2012. *Position Paper on CBR and WHO's CBR Guidelines 2010*. Disabled Peoples International. Accessed 29 October 2014. http://www.disabledpeoplesinternational.org/documents/DPI%20Position%20Paper%20on%20CBR%20Guidelines%20Final.pdf.

Dobrowolsky, Alexandra, ed. 2009. *Women and Public Policy in Canada: Neoliberalism and After?* Toronto: Oxford University Press.

Employment and Social Development Canada (ESDC). 2011. *2011 Federal Disability Report*. Employment and Social Development Canada. Accessed 29 October 2014. http://www.esdc.gc.ca/eng/disability/arc/federal_report2011/index.shtml.

Garland-Thomson, Rosemarie. 2011. "Misfits: A Feminist Materialist Disability Concept." *Hypatia* 26, no. 3: 591–609.

Grech, Shaun. 2011. "Recolonising Debates or Perpetuated Coloniality? Decentring the Spaces of Disability, Development and Community in the Global South." *International Journal of Inclusive Education* 15, no. 1: 87–100.

Handicap International. N.d. "Disability Checklist for Emergency Response." Handicap International. Accessed 29 October 2014. http://www.handicap-international.de/fileadmin/redaktion/pdf/disability_checklist_booklet_01.pdf.

Hankivsky, Olena, ed. 2012. *An Intersectionality-Based Policy Analysis Framework*. Vancouver: Institute for Intersectionality Research and Policy. Accessed 29 October 2014. http://www.sfu.ca/iirp/documents/IBPA/IBPA_Framework_Complete%20Collection_Hankivsky_2012.pdf.

– 2014. "Rethinking Care Ethics: On the Promise and Potential of an Intersectional Analysis." *American Political Science Review* 108, no. 2: 252–64.

Hankivsky, Olena, and Renee Cormier. 2011. "Intersectionality and Public Policy: Some Lessons from Existing Models." *Political Research Quarterly* 64, no. 1: 217–29.

Hartley, Sally, Harry Finkenflugel, Pim Kuipers, and Maya Thomas. 2009. "Community-Based Rehabilitation: Opportunity and Challenge." *Lancet* 374, no. 9704: 1803–4.

McCall, Leslie. 2005. "The Complexity of Intersectionality." *Signs: Journal of Women in Culture and Society* 30, no. 3: 1771–800.

Meekosha, Helen. 2011. "Decolonising Disability: Thinking and Acting Globally." *Disability & Society* 26, no. 6: 667–82.

Neufeldt, Aldred, and Julie Egers. 2003. "Rise and Ebb of Canada's International Disability Policy and Practice." In *In Pursuit of Equal Participation: Canada and Disability at Home and Abroad*, edited by Henry Enns and Aldred Neufeldt, 196–226. Toronto: Captus Press.

Nguyen, Xuan-Thuy, and Claudia Mitchell. 2014. "Inclusion in Vietnam: An Intersectionality Perspective on Girls with Disabilities and Education." *Childhood* 21, no. 3: 324–38.

Parks, Rachel. 2014. "The Rise, Critique and Persistence of the DALY in Global Health." *Journal of Global Health*: n.p. http://www.ghjournal.org/the-rise-critique-and-persistence-of-the-daly-in-global-health.

Rousso, Harilyn. 2003. *Education for All: A Gender and Disability Perspective.* United Nations Organization for Education, Science and Culture. Accessed 29 October 2014. http://unesdoc.unesco.org/images/0014/001469/146931e.pdf.

Sjolander, Claire, Heather Smith, and Deborah Stienstra, eds. 2003. *Feminist Perspectives on Canadian Foreign Policy.* Toronto: Oxford University Press.

Status of Women Canada. 2013. "What Is GBA+?" Status of Women Canada. Accessed 29 October 2014. http://www.swc-cfc.gc.ca/gba-acs/index-en.html.

Stienstra, Deborah. 2002. "DisAbling Globalisation: Rethinking Global Political Economy with a Disability Lens." *Global Society* 16, no. 2: 109–21.

– 2003. "Less than Equal: Disability and Canadian Foreign Policy." In *In Pursuit of Equal Participation: Canada and Disability at Home and Abroad,* edited by Henry Enns and Aldred Neufeldt, 346–60. Toronto: Captus Press.

– 2013. "Making Disability Visible: Inclusive Reconstruction in Fragile and Conflict-Affected States." *Canadian Centre for International Policy Blog,* 21 May. http://cips.uottawa.ca/making-disability-visible-inclusive-reconstruction-in-fragile-and-conflict-affected-states.

– 2014. "More and Less: DisAbling Women and Girls in 'Austere' Times." Paper presented at the Canadian Political Science Association 2014 meetings, Brock University, 28 May.

– 2015. "Trumping All? Disability and Girlhood." *Girlhood Studies* 8, no. 2: 54–70.

– 2016. "DisAbling Human Rights: Moving from Rights into Access and Inclusion in Daily Life." In *Current Issues and Controversies in Human Rights,* edited by Gordon DiGiacomo, 240–61. Toronto: University of Toronto.

Trani, Jean-Francois, Parul Bakhshi, and Anand Nandipati. 2012. "'Delivering' Education; Maintaining Inequality: The Case of Children with Disabilities in Afghanistan." *Cambridge Journal of Education* 42, no. 3: 345–65.

United Nations Children's Fund (UNICEF). 2013. *Children with Disabilities.* New York: United Nations Children's Fund.

Walby, Sylvia, Jo Armstrong, and Sofia Strid. 2012. "Intersectionality and the Quality of the Gender Equality Architecture." *Social Politics: International Studies in Gender, State & Society* 19, no. 4: 446–81.

Wehbi, Samantha, Lindsay Elin, and Yahya El-Lahib. 2010. "Neo-Colonial Discourse and Disability: The Case of Canadian International Development NGOs." *Community Development Journal* 45, no. 4: 404–22.

World Health Organization and World Bank. 2011. *World Report on Disability.* Geneva: World Health Organization.

PART TWO

Case Studies

Gold 'n' Girls: Why Canada Weds Gender Equality with Mining Capitalism in Burkina Faso

Paula Butler

INTRODUCTION

In Burkina Faso, schoolgirls who become pregnant are likely to drop out of school. This fact was profiled in a Plan International video as an example of problems faced by girls, at the launch of UNICEF's International Day of the Girl Child in 2014.[1] Keeping teenage Burkinabé mothers in school, and educating girls in general, exemplifies the goals of the International Day of the Girl Child, and of Plan International. Few would argue with the value of such goals. In Canada, they are advanced through Plan Canada's Because I am a Girl campaign.[2] With its signature bright pink colour scheme and smiling girls on billboards, and television and internet ads, this campaign has become part of the public landscape. The campaign is enthusiastically supported in many high schools and community service organizations across the country. But there is more to Canada's championing of such girl-child advocacy than meets the eye. The curious echo between "I Am a Girl" and "IAMGOLD," it turns out, is more than serendipitous.

In this chapter, I use Plan Canada's participation in an ongoing (2011–2017) public–private development project in Burkina Faso – a $7.6 million project that involved partnering with the Canadian gold-mining company IAMGOLD in a youth training initiative funded by the Department of Foreign Affairs, Trade and Development (DFATD) – to explore some of the less visible and even troubling aspects of Canada's official championing of the rescue, liberation, and empowerment of girls. I argue that a goal as laudable as supporting the wellbeing of and opportunities for girls in the Global South also functions strategically as an important ideological dimension of Canada's corporate/political agenda to expand a foreign capitalist business and financial presence in the African continent. This is the conclusion I reached from my investigation of the curious connection between gender-sensitized NGO programming with Burkinabé youth and the expanding Canadian mining and investment presence in Burkina Faso. This project reveals the promotion of gender equality as an ostensibly progressive value (equal education for girls) in service of wider private economic objectives.

This is a complex story to unpack because it is lodged in a web of sectors (NGO, government, and corporate), issues (gender equality, education, and mining), and scales (local, national, and international). It is also hard to unpack because – as I would argue – it is not meant to be unpacked. Its unpacking requires a number of analytical tools: a theorization of Canada as a racialized, imperialist settler state; a theorization of gender and neoliberalism; and a theorization of the cultural function of dominant discourses such as philanthropy. In the next section, I present each of these concepts in order to establish a framework for making sense of the Plan Canada–IAMGOLD–DFATD "youth training project" in Burkina Faso. I then provide an overview of Canada's recent aid/investment relations with Burkina Faso in order to set the scene for analyzing the Plan Canada–IAMGOLD project. The remaining sections of the chapter look in detail at what the Burkinabé youth training project has achieved to date.

The program was designed to provide (and advertised as providing) poverty-reducing, employment-focused basic education and vocational training to 10,000 youth, with a strong focus on gender equality. The project was to equip Burkinabé youth to take advantage of jobs that would be generated by the expansion of industrial gold mining. The most recent project report to which I had access, the Semi-Annual Report for Project Year 4 (April to September 2014), indicated that there were a cumulative 2,867 youth in the various training programs, of whom 44 per cent were girls. Of the first class of graduates, twenty-six youth (two girls and twenty-four boys) had been able to find employment (ATIP A0365793_26-000742). One-third of these (eight youth) had employment with wages above the poverty line, which in Burkina Faso is the equivalent of about C$60/month. Notably, local "artisanal" (or small scale) Burkinabé miners displaced for IAMGOLD's Essakane mine reported earning the equivalent of C$60 *per day* prior to the establishment of the Canadian mine (Oved 2014).

THEORIZING CANADIAN INTERNATIONALISM

In line with many scholars (Borrows 2002; Gordon 2010; Heron 2007; Razack 2004; Sherman 2008), I regard Canada as a racialized, capitalist settler-colonizer state. This historical framing positions the era of the Harper government (2006 to 2015) as part of a much longer trajectory. Many of the trends pertaining to foreign aid, trade, and investment that have noticeably intensified since 2006 – principally, support for a private/corporate-sector-led market economy as the primary development and poverty-reduction strategy – were set in motion under previous Liberal and Conservative governments. Moreover, these trends typify a much longer historical alliance between government/monarch and private corporate interests dating back to cooperation between the British Crown and the Hudson's Bay Company in what is now Canada – cooperation that set up the conditions for the gradual displacement, dispossession, and impoverishment of Indigenous peoples. In line with this long-standing logic, the Harper government championed and supported the global expansion of the Canadian private mining sector, especially in South America and Africa, and instigated the negotiation and signing of a record number of Foreign Investment Protection Agreements (FIPAS) with mineral-rich African countries. Later in this chapter I will detail the position of power and influence that Canada occupies in Burkina Faso – a relationship that can credibly be characterized as neo-colonial in nature.

This gives rise to the following question: In the formally post-colonial era, how do neocolonial forms of power come to be accepted and legitimized? Edward Said (1993) and Achille Mbembe (2001) assert that colonial/imperial relations require the production and dissemination of a particular worldview and accompanying discourses – a "central cultural imaginary" – to assuage, justify, and normalize domination. In particular, imperialist states fashion and disseminate representations of themselves as benevolent states; this allows their populations to anaesthetize their objections or any uneasiness ("cognitive dissonance") they may feel by internalizing an identity of themselves as people who do good, not harm. This kind of national cultural imaginary infiltrates routine social life. In Canada today, the discourses and practices of philanthropy, or more specifically "corporatized philanthropy," play a crucial cultural role in normalizing, recasting, and rendering acceptable imperialist relations of domination (see also Kapoor 2013).

CORPORATIZED PHILANTHROPY

"Corporatized philanthropy" is a phenomenon in which the corporate business sector and the charity sector recognize a useful ideological convergence. This convergence centres on a tacit agreement not to offer explanations of poverty, sexism, or social inequality that expose structural/historical causes or call for structural changes that would directly challenge or threaten the status quo. It fosters a Canadian public that wants to help, but does not feel implicated in global inequalities, and it circumscribes the kinds of questions to be asked about poverty and inequality. Responses to social problems are addressed in a manner that keeps intact and reaffirms belief in the free market system, GDP growth as an engine of development, and, implicitly, Western cultural superiority. This generates an appealing but simplistic, and seemingly apolitical, notion of what can be done about poverty and gender inequality.

What makes corporatized philanthropy convincing and thus influential is its capacity to deliver and publicize some positive results "on the ground." For example, as I will indicate later, the Canadian-funded youth training program in Burkina Faso has certainly provided education and training opportunities for youth who would not otherwise have had such access, and a considerable number of these opportunities have gone to girls. One teenage Burkinabé girl was profiled for having defied gender stereotypes by enrolling in a welding program (Oved 2014). Such appealing examples, particularly when widely disseminated in the public domain, serve to significantly shape public awareness and understanding. Public acceptance of and engagement with these simple narratives thus lubricates the expansion of corporate/capitalist power. Disavowing evidence that the West advances its own economic power and privilege at the expense of the populations of impoverished countries, corporate philanthropy as a neoliberal narrative casts Western countries, citizens, NGOs, and corporations as friends, guides, and, at times, rescuers of these very populations.

I call this form of philanthropy "corporatized philanthropy" because it is generated from within a neoliberal corporate ethos. The Harper government and its big business allies came to regard the African continent as an exciting new frontier for profitable foreign private-sector investment. With its economies liberalized and its governance systems at least superficially "democratized," the African continent is now perceived as "open for business." It is logical to anticipate that an intensified Canadian corporate presence in Africa will require enhanced and robust narratives of benevolence. Enter the NGO sector. Although Western NGOs and Christian missions have long been critiqued for their historical roles in providing the soft face of Western imperialism, some also challenged Western power and articulated structural causes of global inequality (Barry-Shaw and Jay 2012). During the era of the Harper Conservatives, such critiques became much harder to sustain. CIDA/DFATD's approach to the NGO sector – an approach characterized by funding uncertainties, delays, cuts, and new procedures and criteria for grant eligibility – arguably "disciplined" the sector. This had the effect of encouraging, if not coercing, many organizations to reframe their public narratives in a manner that cohered with what Brown (2014) has called the "recommercialized" aid agenda. It also favoured the emergence and strengthening of a type of NGO that I call the corporate NGO. A degree of ideological convergence thus appeared among the federal government, large corporations, and such NGOs. One manifestation of this ideological convergence is corporatized philanthropy, one of whose classic tropes is the rescue of the oppressed "Third World" woman and girl (Mohanty 2000). This trope oils the wheels of a Canadian national imaginary in which Canada is presented as a do-good nation – not as a neocolonizer.

GENDER + NEOLIBERALISM = TRANSNATIONAL BUSINESS FEMINISM

When deployed as rhetoric for rescuing girls and women, "gender equality" can be analyzed as a component of the historical legitimization of European/Western colonial domination. The use of sensationalized imagery – such as "forced marriage"[3] or the Harper government's Zero Tolerance for Barbaric Cultural Practices Act – continues a paternalistic/racist traditions in which "othered" women are rescued by Westerners from sati, foot binding, female genital mutilation, militarized rape, the Taliban, and so on, and thus raises the ire of postcolonial/critical race feminists, among others. These critics do not deny the egregious harms done to some women and girls, but rather object to how harms are selectively identified, and used to divide and rule, stereotype "cultural Others," assert a cultural hierarchy, and justify certain kinds of interventions and policy frameworks, while rendering invisible patriarchal and other types of harm perpetrated in and by the West. Simplistic narratives of rescuing girls and women engrain in the Canadian public imaginary a misleading and racially inflected notion of a benevolent, culturally progressive West set in opposition to stereotyped ultra-sexist or simply backward "non-Western" societies. NGOs that bank on the deployment of such narratives play an important cultural role in generating the idea of the noble Canadian, providing Canadians with a comforting, positive understanding of themselves and an image of Canada as a do-good nation in the world (Thobani 2007). This narrative suggests that Canadians, acting in solidarity or as donors, can offer oppressed girls and women opportunities, empowerment, and hope they might not otherwise have.

Secondly, a focus on gender equality also needs to address and problematize the relationship between feminism and neoliberalism. One of the seminal documents of feminist thought, the African-American-women-authored "Combahee River Collective Statement" (1977), characterized the oppression of Black women as the effect of interlocking systems of domination: heteronormative patriarchy, white supremacy, and capitalism. From this perspective, Black women's struggle for gender justice or gender equality (and racial justice) is incompatible with support for capitalism. The Combahee statement powerfully challenged second wave mainstream feminism, which, in the USA and Canada, was dominated by white, middle-class "liberals" with universalist understandings of human rights. Indeed, liberal feminism, ideologically compatible with capitalism, largely informed the approach to gender within official aid agencies and multilateral agencies during the 1980s and 1990s. The OECD (through their Development Assistance Committee) and CIDA both produced gender equality policy guidelines (in 1995 and 1999 respectively) at the same time as both organizations were actively supporting Washington Consensus neoliberal economic policies, whose harmful effects, via structural adjustment policies, on women and children – particularly in African countries – have been thoroughly documented. And yet, the philanthropic narrative of rescuing girls and women renders invisible the way in which it is embedded in the neoliberal ideology and agenda.

Marxist-feminist and feminist international political economy (IPE) scholars have helped make visible the way in which this narrative is embedded in neoliberal ideology by drawing attention to the instrumentalization of "gender equality" in neoliberal capitalism. This trend of instrumentalizing gender equality is captured in the World Bank's use of the slogan "gender equality as smart economics" (World Bank 2006) and the financial sector's enthusiastic embrace of "womenomics" (Elias 2013; Roberts and Soederberg 2012). Peterson and Runyan (2010, 135) note that "it is no accident that gender equality becomes (at least a rhetorical) priority in global governance precisely at the time that neoliberal ideology is globalized." Women are now seen as the "archetypal neoliberal subject" (Roberts and Soederberg 2012); essentialized as "more responsible" (astute financial managers but less risk-taking than men) and more caring, women are regarded as the kinds of subjects required to rescue capitalism from its latest crises (Roberts 2012). Roberts analyzes how the

Canadian securities and risk management firm Ernst and Young began "discovering" and recruiting women as ideal capitalists, and adopting the language of gender equality, and dubs this phenomenon "transnational business feminism." This brand of feminism sees women as able to play important roles in the global market, and sees market-led growth as beneficial for all, including women. By embodying "business feminism," such feminists deny, challenge, and render invisible the contradictions between capitalism and gender equality. The trenchant analysis of the Combahee River Collective is treated as passé.

Transnational business feminism increasingly characterizes the dominant approaches to gender within corporate, governmental, and elite international development circles. Even UN Women has embraced the business woman as a leading development actor, and UN Women Canada has, under the executive leadership of Almas Jiwani, moved ideologically closer to a corporate ethos. Presenting the keynote speech in April 2013 to the Global Connect Women Entrepreneurs Expo and Summit, Jiwani declared:

> Female entrepreneurs are the building blocks for success in any economy as they bring a unique approach to business and have specific skills. Women entrepreneurs have been starting businesses at a higher rate than men and are creating more jobs. They are heavily engaged, motivated and extremely well suited for the emerging workplace. Women entrepreneurs should be celebrated in every society.[4]

If the transnational business feminist is lauded as an outstanding person, women in the Global South are collectively identified as offering a vast untapped ("uncolonized") market for the multinational finance industry (Roberts and Soederberg 2012). Keating et al. (2010, 173) identify microcredit as a key domain for the "macropolitics of dispossession," which entails the subjectification of women as entrepreneurial capitalist subjects, portions of whose microprofits can be appropriated (by the banking industry) while the women are drawn into a neoliberal social order that "renegotiates" the social contract (the commons) in ways that maintain or exacerbate a stratified, depoliticized society. In this manner, "feminist ideas often lend ideological cover to processes of economic restructuring" (Keating et al. 2010, 155).

This rich field of feminist scholarship can be used to analyze the approach to gender equality favoured by the Harper government in concert with wider trends within some domestic and multilateral development agencies and the transnational financial/business sector. Under the Harper government, the shift to a culturally conservative, binary, essentialist, and business-friendly concept of gender supported and encouraged the dissemination of a particular discourse (and related programming) in which the transnational business feminist and the empowered girl function as related subjects who are ideologically in sync with a corporate private sector-led development model.

A final point on gender equality as a concept concerns the distinction between an essentialist "body count" approach – a response to one of feminism's questions, "where are the women?" – and an approach that sees gender as a complex, multiscalar system of power, both material and ideological, tied to the social construction of the gendered body. Although essentialized "body counting" has some value for identifying and attempting to redress some of the effects of patriarchy, this approach is inadequate without an understanding of patriarchy as a system that is ideological, cultural, and material, and that interlocks with transnational capitalism and racism. I will use both "body count" analysis and structural analysis in exploring the effect of Plan Canada's youth training program in Burkina Faso. In order to better set the stage for that analysis, I now present a brief overview of Canada's aid and investment relations with Burkina Faso.

SITUATING THE PLAN–IAMGOLD PROJECT IN CANADA'S RELATIONS WITH BURKINA FASO

The strategic direction of Canada's program in Burkina Faso is to help the country secure a future for children and youth, and stimulate sustainable economic growth. (DFATD 2015a)

This statement from the federal Department of Foreign Affairs, Trade and Development (DFATD) succinctly expresses the twinned strategies (aid and investment) that characterize Canada's policy in many African countries, and that create the ideological framework for the twinning of Plan Canada's project focus on gender equality and youth training/education with IAMGOLD's mining projects. Burkina Faso has been named a "priority country" as part of Canada's Global Markets Action Plan. Although Canada's trade with Burkina Faso has varied considerably, in 2013 it became particularly imbalanced, in Canada's favour: Canada's exports to Burkina Faso were valued at C$51.1 million (mainly in support of mining), while Burkina Faso's exports to Canada were worth a mere C$400,000 (DFATD 2014a). Canada is reported to be the largest source of foreign investment in Burkina Faso since 2008 (DFATD 2014b). To protect Canadian investors (mostly mining companies at present) against political risk, the Canadian government negotiated a FIPA with Burkina Faso, then had its ratification pushed through in 2015 by the unelected interim government that followed former president Blaise Compaoré's forced departure due to mass popular protest.

Gold mining is the leading sector of activity for Canadian interests in Burkina Faso. Following the liberalization of Burkina Faso's mining code in 1993 and 2003 as part of World Bank structural adjustment and heavily indebted poor countries (HIPC) reforms, Canadian mining and exploration firms have been active and successful in the country. Of the country's five currently operating gold mines, three are operated and 90 per cent owned by Canadian companies: IAMGOLD's Essakane mine, SEMAFO's Mana mine, and Endeavour's Youga mine. Two other gold mines, the Taparko-Bouroum mines and the Bissa mine, were explored and brought to the point of production by the Canadian companies High River Gold and Orezone. Another Orezone find, the Kalsaka-Sega mine, was acquired and brought into production by Cluff Gold/Amara Mining.[5] Endeavour expects to bring a second mine, the Houndé mine, into production in the near future with an anticipated 31.4 per cent internal rate of return (Endeavour 2015). The recent opening of an office of the Canadian Institute for Mining, Metallurgy and Petroleum in Ouagadougou is an indication of expectations of long-term Canadian mining presence in the country.

The promotion of foreign-investment-led private mining in African countries has often proved to be the real meaning of the phrase "stimulate sustainable economic growth." For decades under French colonial rule and into the early postcolonial era, cotton production for export drove the country's official economy. In 2009, gold surpassed cotton as Burkina Faso's leading export sector (US Dept. of Commerce 2014, 1), with gold production increasing by 41 per cent between 2010 and 2011 (IMF 2012, 35). The value of gold exports, as reported by the Government of Burkina Faso, was US$377 million in 2009 and US$936 million in 2010, and the value of government income from gold mining was US$32 million in 2009 and US$98 million in 2010 (approximately 10 per cent of the export value) (ATIP A0033574_2-00055). The benefits to some Canadians of gold extraction in Burkina Faso are considerable. Using the posted cash cost per ounce and production volumes in 2013 when the average gold price was US$1,250/ounce, I calculate approximate net revenues in 2013 for the three Canadian mines in current operation in Burkina Faso as US$277.3 million – in one year alone.[6]

Canadian business with Burkina Faso is not limited to mining. For example, in 2014, Windiga Energy won a $50 million contract to build a solar energy plant in Burkina Faso (DFATD 2014b). Significantly, the president and CEO of Windiga Energy is Benoît La Salle, who was chair of the board of directors of Plan Canada (2007 to 2009) when the first Memorandum of Understanding was signed with IAMGOLD. During his tenure as Plan Canada chair, La Salle was CEO of the second-largest gold mining company operating in Burkina Faso, SEMAFO. He also served as the chair of the Canadian Council on Africa, an agency set up to encourage and support commercial and business relations between Canada and African countries.

By comparison with these business interests, Canada's aid program (including humanitarian assistance) in Burkina Faso for 2012–2013 was valued at $40.76 million.[7] This sets Burkina Faso among Canada's top ten aid recipients in Africa. Since 2000, this aid has been significantly focused on two sectors: private sector development (averaging approximately 40 per cent) and basic education (approximately 60 per cent).[8] Currently, the largest private sector development project, valued at C$10 million for the period 2009 to 2015, is support for a national microfinance strategy, and C$5 million went to a Financial Centre for Entrepreneurs/Agricultural Financial Centre during 2008 to 2015. DFATD's Canadian nongovernmental partners implementing microfinance work include the Quebec-based bank Développement international Desjardins and Groupe-conseil Interalia SENC, a firm that offers technical services in project management, business, and human resources. One of DFATD's 2013–2018 regional aid projects for West Africa (based in Ouagadougou) is a C$2 million project to set up a training institute in applied solar technology. The executing agency for this training project is Polytechnique Montréal.[9] Here we see the interesting interconnections among the private sector (the construction contract won by Windiga for the solar energy plant), official aid, and Canadian colleges and NGOs, including La Salle's connections to both Windiga and Plan Canada.

The solar technology training project points to education as the other major sector for Canadian aid in Burkina Faso. Over the period 2001–2016, three large Canadian aid disbursements totalling C$94.4 million were made to basic education, and Canada has indicated its intention to contribute to this sector up to 2020. In fact, Canada has taken a leading role, coordinating a pooled donor fund to finance the national budget of the Ministry of Basic Education and Literacy (French acronym, MENA), particularly in school construction, the supply of teaching resources, and the "modernized" management of a national school system. Plan

International is one of the leading foreign NGOs working in the education sector in Burkina Faso (Maclure et al. 2007, 13). Touorouzou (2006)
acknowledges the strong interest in and support for the country's education sector and for gender equality in education on the part of foreign
donor countries and multilateral agencies, but charges that the sector is
too controlled by foreign agencies. Maclure et al. (2007, ii) concur: "the
degree to which policy-oriented educational decision-making is a democratic process (or even one that is nationally led as opposed to donor-led)
is far from evident."

In recent years, only a small part of CIDA/DFATD funding has been
specifically earmarked for gender equality programming in Burkina
Faso: grants totalled just under C$400,000 for consultations on "gender
and development" during the 2006 to 2012 period. Notably, a new private sector project will invest C$6 million over five years (2014–2019) in
women-run businesses producing parboiled rice – a project that exemplifies the Harper government's enthusiasm for "business feminism," as
discussed earlier. When not specifically targeting women, most CIDA/
DFATD aid programs in Burkina Faso claim to ensure the inclusion of
women and report sex-disaggregated results; some incorporate gender sensitivity training.[10] The prospectus for DFATD's West Africa solar
energy training project states that 20 per cent of those trained, as techni-
cians and engineers, are to be women (DFATD 2015a).

We can now situate the DFATD-funded Plan–IAMGOLD project within
this overview of Canadian investment and aid portfolios in Burkina Faso.
In bridging the private/for-profit and the private/not-for-profit sectors,
the Plan–IAMGOLD project expresses an underlying coherence in policy objectives. The five-year project, titled "Capacity building of youth
to grow the economy – private-public partnership for corporate social
responsibility in Burkina Faso," was funded as follows: IAMGOLD, C$1
million; Plan Canada, C$0.9 million; and DFATD, C$5.7 million.

What can we understand from this sketch of Canadian investment and
aid priorities in Burkina Faso? There is a pairing of strategic interventions
in both the economic (mining, solar power) and cultural (education, gender equality, corporate social responsibility [CSR]) realms, with the two
working in sync. We can also observe extensive economic benefits for
Canadian mining and exploration firms, mining services and equipment
exporters, other businesses, consultants, financial institutions, NGOs, and
colleges – benefits that may even exceed the benefit of Canadian aid to
Burkinabé citizens. This clearly validates Brown's (2014) assessment of
renewed motives, under the Harper Conservatives, of commercial and

financial national self-interest in Canada's aid and trade programming in low income countries. What is also apparent is the high degree of Canadian influence in at least two major sectors of Burkinabé society: mining and education – strategic economic and cultural realms.

PLAN CANADA: CORPORATIZED PHILANTHROPY AND THE EMPOWERMENT OF GIRLS

Although child sponsorship has been and remains a mainstay of Plan Canada's programming, by the 1990s Plan Canada began expanding and adapting its programming to changing global circumstances. Articulating its raison d'être as reducing child poverty and advancing the rights of children, Plan Canada launched the Because I Am a Girl campaign in 2009, in conjunction with follow-up to the Beijing Platform of Action on the girl child. In 2011, Plan Canada played a lead role in persuading the UN to establish the International Day of the Girl Child, and the G8 to adopt the Muskoka Initiative on Maternal, Newborn and Child Health. The Muskoka Initiative was often touted by the Harper government as a flagship of its foreign aid program.

During the period 2005 to 2013, while many Canadian NGOs suffered cuts in government grants, funding uncertainty, and overall budgetary reductions, Plan Canada saw dramatic growth in its revenues. Plan Canada was historically an organization with minimal government funding, being primarily dependent, rather, on an individual donor base, but this began to change. During 2006 to 2011, an average of 10 per cent of funding came from government grants, jumping to 19.4 per cent in 2012, and 25.7 per cent and 27.3 per cent in 2013 and 2014, respectively (Plan International Canada, Annual Review and Financials 2007 to 2014). The organization's overall annual revenues grew from $58.1 million in 2005 to $166.4 million in 2013 – almost tripling in only eight years. The largest overall budgetary increase occurred between 2010 ($115.4 million) and 2011 ($141.2 million), coinciding with the first year (2011) of the CIDA-funded Plan–IAMGOLD project. In addition to securing much larger government grants, Plan Canada received donations from a number of large and medium-size corporations and businesses. Over the past five years, these have included IAMGOLD, Ernst and Young, Danier, Birks, Olsen Europe, Groupe Marcelle, Sears Canada, Dubai Cares (of the United Arab Emirates), ING Direct, Stikeman Elliott LLP, MasterCard Foundation, Cassels Brock and Blackwell LLP, Sun Life Financial, Ardene, Jean Machine, and CanEducate (a charity formed by employees of Barrick

Gold), among others (Plan International Canada, Annual Review and Financials 2008 to 2013).

Since 2006, Plan Canada has consistently allocated about 14 per cent of its total annual budget for fundraising. Between 2009 and 2013, the annual fundraising budget increased from just under $13 million to over $23 million (Plan International Canada, Financial Reports 2009 to 2013). Such amounts have made possible a widely visible marketing campaign, with Plan Canada and Because I Am a Girl running ads on prime time Canadian television, on Google bars and other social media sites, in magazines, on billboards on heavily populated streets such as Toronto's Yonge Street, and, periodically, in Toronto's subway cars.

Plan Canada's annual reports from 2006 to 2013 reveal a surprisingly weighted representation on the board of directors of persons with expertise in the fields of corporate law, securities, financial services, and banking. Board members did not appear to possess expertise or credentials in the fields of human rights, gender, or development. Only one board member was known for extensive experience in the not-for-profit international development sector.[11] I noted earlier that the chair of the board of directors from 2007 to 2009 was the president of the mining company SEMAFO, which owns the second-largest gold mine in Burkina Faso (the Mana mine), and that it was during his tenure as board chair that Plan Canada signed its first Memorandum of Understanding with IAMGOLD. Another long-term board member from 2007 to 2013 was a partner at the law firm Stikeman Elliott LLP, whose specializations include corporate mining law, international investment law, and risk management for the mining sector. The ideological leanings of such a board seem apparent. Without access to the minutes of Plan Canada board of directors meetings, which would offer more detailed insights into the decision-making processes of this board, I can only examine the board composition to conclude that it would tend to consider development from a private sector, big business perspective, and about CSR from a mining company perspective; it would, one can reasonably conclude, be open to and even enthusiastic about partnering Plan Canada with such companies. In the context of the Devonshire Initiative, which was set up in 2009 to respond to widespread public criticisms of the mining sector's human rights and environmental violations and failure to generate socio-economic benefits for populations in "host countries," such partnering is exactly what happened. CIDA/DFATD championed this project principally as a means of giving concrete expression to the government's new CSR policy, "Building the Canadian Advantage."

THE PLAN–IAMGOLD PROJECT: ASSESSING GENDER EQUALITY AND OPPORTUNITIES FOR GIRLS

I turn, finally, to a closer examination of the youth training project. Although the project has diverse objectives – and was pitched in different ways to different audiences – my discussion here is limited to one aspect: Plan Canada's effort to make gender equality a key component. As the project has not yet reached its completion point – 31 March 2017 – my observations are based on project reports to date (specifically, the reports from years one to three, and the semi-annual report on year four, up to 30 September 2014).

As indicated in the DFATD project browser profile, the training of youth aged thirteen to eighteen was to be linked to "labour market needs in the mining sector and its sub-sectors." The primary expected result was: "Youth (50% girls) of the project zones participate in improved pre-vocational and vocational training in line with market needs to increase their employability." Training consisted of two types: access to "basic education" (literacy, numeracy, and trades) at the Centres d'éducation de base non formelle (CEBNF), and professional vocational training at the Centres de formation professionnelle (CFP). (Later, training was added at the Rural Promotion Centres.) Two areas of Burkina Faso were identified for the project – Centre Nord and Sud-Ouest; neither was in the immediate vicinity of IAMGOLD's Essakane mine. A labour market study commissioned by the project and conducted in May 2012 identified a market demand for almost 32,000 jobs in these two regions up to 2020, of which some 29,000 were in agriculture and food processing, almost 3,000 in skills such as masonry, plumbing, two-wheel mechanics, and steel construction, and 300 in mining-related jobs. These market study findings line up only weakly with the stated objectives and claims of the project, to equip youth for employment to be generated by the expanding mining industry. Indeed, the labour market survey – conducted only in year two of the project – noted that none of the existing training centres offered programs in food processing, mining-related employment, or other emerging fields such as information technology or cellphone repair. Rather, youth continued to be trained in traditional skills such as carpentry, mechanics, and tailoring, all relatively poorly paid work. A major challenge identified by the labour market survey was thus to improve the content and quality of vocational training. Its findings led to the introduction of short courses in animal husbandry and other food and agriculture-related vocations. Students were also trained in entrepreneurship for self-employment.

From the outset, this project demonstrated a strong commitment to maximizing female youth participation in the training opportunities, working toward male–female parity, and shifting attitudes and beliefs about gender roles and competencies. Burkina Faso's adoption of a national gender policy offered validation of the gender equality agenda. The all-stakeholder workshop held in Ouagadougou in September 2011 to discuss, refine, and launch the project included content on gender equality indicators for results-based project evaluation. All training components, for instance of instructors and "training of trainers" sessions (conducted by educators from the British Columbia-based College of the Rockies), incorporated "gender sensitive" approaches and taught gender equality ("l'égalité des sexes") as a topic. The mining company IAMGOLD was expected to send female mine personnel with technical expertise to visit the training centres as role models; IAMGOLD was also expected to make internships available to female youth.

During project year three, a comprehensive "gender audit" was conducted (February to September 2013). It exposed and confirmed many of the anticipated barriers and problems related to equal participation of girls in the training programs. These included a lack of female instructors, a lack of separate toilets at some training centres, instances of sexual violence and harassment from male instructors and students at the training centres (which were often located far from students' homes), pregnancy, early marriage, domestic chores and responsibilities expected of girls that interfered with the time required to attend the education centres, and unwillingness of parents or spouses to pay training costs. These problems were often referred to as "barrières socio-culturelles," or being socio-cultural in nature. Also noted was the "voluntary" segregation of girls into training for traditionally female occupations – such as dressmaking and hairdressing – all of which had typically low rates of remuneration and were not deemed to be pathways out of poverty. Further, although participation of female youth approached 50 per cent in the basic education centres (CEBNF), this dropped off considerably (34 per cent) in the higher-skill vocational centres (CFP). All these circumstances militated against female youth being able to benefit equally to male youth in training opportunities, employment, and higher incomes and improved livelihoods.

Project organizers took many steps to address these issues. In year four, a gender code of conduct was developed to be adhered to at all training centres, with a view to ensuring the safety and rights of female students, along with measures to deal with violations. Public outreach and communication campaigns were conducted in the communities where students were being recruited in order to shift attitudes among parents and community leaders regarding female youth participation and the types of skills they could learn. Gender sensitization was also extended to potential employers. Steps were taken to set up child-care facilities in conjunction with the centres to enable young mothers to attend training. Teaching manuals were revised to avoid gender stereotypes. As a result of all these initiatives, there were higher levels of female enrolment, and a trickle of female students opted for nontraditional fields of study, such as welding and two-wheel mechanics. (Significantly, no male students opted for the traditionally "female" trades.) However, considerable male–female disparity remained. Of the fifty-three youth who qualified for scholarships, only fifteen were girls. Of the 171 youth who passed graduation tests offered at the centres, only thirty-three were girls (ATIP A0365793_24-00740). Inadequate recruitment of female trainers persisted. Indeed, the gender audit noted that: "to address gender inequality in the centres implies addressing the full range of social and cultural challenges and factors, notably poverty, unequal access to resources between men and women, gender-based violence (such as rape, assault, unplanned pregnancy, and early marriage), domestic roles of girls and women, and inequality in decision-making" (my translation) (ATIP A0365788_5-000598).

CLOSING THOUGHTS: HOW GOLD *COULD* EMPOWER GIRLS... AND BURKINABÉ PEOPLE

Acknowledging that an extraordinary amount of work has gone into this project to date (and I have touched on only one aspect), I end this chapter with several critical reflections that open up alternative ways of thinking about Canada's involvement in the lives of Burkinabé youth, girls in particular.

The first point concerns the project's approach to alleviating youth unemployment and poverty, and the myths surrounding mining as an employment-generating sector. Western-owned industrial mining in African countries more often exacerbates unemployment, as tens and even hundreds of thousands of local artisanal miners are fenced out of metal-rich concessions, or as peasants lose access to grazing or agricultural land and lose livelihoods (Butler 2015, 212–15; Luning 2008). At IAMGOLD's Essakane gold mine in Burkina Faso, 16,000 people were displaced and "relocated" to make room for the mine. An international NGO that conducted extensive field-based research (using qualitative and quantitative methods) among female members of the displaced population identified a host of negative impacts from the displacement.

These included decreased agricultural and livestock-rearing activity, reduced quality and quantity of food, increased hunger that particularly affected the health of children and pregnant women, lack of work, and out-migration (or abandonment) of male family members (FIAN International). Open pit industrial gold mining is not a labour intensive industry – a widely known fact – something that was confirmed by the project's own labour market survey. Although the country's population in 2010 was sixteen million, only 4,000 people were employed in the industrial mining industry (ATIP A0033574_2-00055). This figure increased to between 6,000 and 8,000 by 2014 (US Dept. of Commerce 2014) but is still relatively minimal. By comparison, a 2006 IMF study estimated that 200,000 Burkinabé artisanal miners worked at more than 200 "non-industrial" mine sites (Werthmann 2009, 18). During 1986 to 1997, 47 per cent of all gold production was carried out by artisanal miners (Gueye 2002). Also, unlike male-dominated industrial mining, women are actively involved in many aspects of artisanal mining. Gueye (2002) estimated that 45 per cent of the people working at artisanal mine sites in Burkina Faso were female. Werthmann (2009) cites economic opportunity as the main draw for Burkinabé girls and women into artisanal mining; she found that girls who were employed pounding ore could earn the equivalent of C$135 to $210 a month (far above the poverty line at C$60 a month) and met a female pit owner who claimed to have earned the equivalent of C$300,000 from one artisanal mine. The owner used the funds to "acquire three plots of land in her home town on which she constructed houses that she rents out" (Werthmann 2009, 19). These accounts reveal a clear competition for resource-based wealth between Burkinabé citizens and foreign investors, and replace the notion that Burkinabé women need rescuing and assistance from Western actors with the notion that they might benefit more from an absence or withdrawal of foreign mining presence.

Although there are a host of technical, social, and environmental problems associated with artisanal mining – problems that are chronically cited by Western industrial miners – such problems have viable solutions. Western mining companies generally do not want African countries to prioritize artisanal mining because it may mean losing access to lucrative resources. Given that, in the context of this project, DFATD, Plan Canada, and IAMGOLD claim to increase opportunities for employment and reduce poverty for male and female Burkinabé youth, why has no consideration been given to opportunities in artisanal mining? None of the jobs for which the project is training Burkinabé youth is likely to generate monthly incomes comparable to what can be obtained from small-scale mining. (As noted in the introduction, by September 2014 – midway through year four of a five-and-a-half-year project – only eight graduates of the centres were employed with wages above the poverty line.) Furthermore, one of the strategies repeatedly identified by those interested in how mining can bring developmental benefits to African countries is "beneficiation," or in-country processing of metals and minerals (see publications from the United Nations' Africa Mining Vision). Such value-added industries – gold jewellery-making, for instance – are both greater sources of employment and add more to the country's GDP. Currently, most of Burkina Faso's gold is exported unprocessed. Such options and possibilities appear to be outside the conceptual framework and partisan motives of this project.

Secondly, a few comments on the gender equality agenda of this project are warranted. As indicated in the quotation above from the project's gender audit, movement toward gender equality is a complex, long-term process (Kloosterman et al. 2012). The project reports' repetition of the term "socio-cultural barriers" to explain gender inequalities can be read as a pejorative depiction of Burkinabé culture as being inherently too traditional or too sexist. It is illuminating to compare the gender equality record of the Canadian mining industry. As a sector, Canadian mining has above-average wages and salaries. However, women represent only 16 per cent of its workforce and are still most commonly found in the lowest-paid (usually clerical) positions (Mining Association of Canada 2013, 44). A sample taken in September 2011 of thirty Canadian companies with operations in African countries showed that among 340 company directors and senior executives, only 8 per cent of these positions were held by women (Butler 2015, 169). These discrepancies persist despite Canadian women having had, in a formal sense, equal access to university education for training as mining engineers, geologists, and other related professional fields for decades. Such facts recast patriarchal social relations as relevant to both Burkina Faso and Canada, and underscore the peculiarity of gender equality champions DFATD and Plan Canada partnering with the mining sector.

Patriarchal power also intersects with racialized colonial/imperial structures of domination that affect contemporary relations between Burkina Faso and Canada. Reconceptualizing gender beyond a binary "body count" paradigm, and rather as a structural relation of power tied to notions of femininity and masculinity, allows us to understand how racialized patriarchy shapes inter-state relations, especially between enriched and impoverished nations (Peterson and Runyan 2010, 76–85). Recalling the history of inter-state relations becomes important. For instance, Thomas Sankara, president of Burkina Faso from 1983 to 1987, is regarded by many as one of the continent's outstanding leaders. Among many achievements, his efforts to promote gender equality, as part of a socialist–nationalist development vision, were significant (Touorouzou 2006, 7). Sankara was one of the first African leaders to champion women's rights; he appointed women to cabinet positions, introduced changes in family law to outlaw polygamy and to give women property ownership and inheritance rights, and publicly advocated for dignity and respect for women (Harsch 2013, 366–7). He prioritized literacy, education, primary health care, peasant-based agriculture, the eradication of corruption, and national economic self-reliance. His integrity, youth, and championing of African/Burkinabé creativity and energy remain inspirational to many people, including young African women.[12] However, his political vision, which resisted foreign economic domination and championed Burkinabé economic self-reliance – including national management of the mining sector in the interests of collective benefits (Luning 2008, 389–90) – alienated major Western nations. Sankara was assassinated and replaced by his colleague Blaise Compaoré, who assumed the presidency and remained in power for twenty-seven years. During his tenure, Compaoré oversaw a restructuring of the nation's economy in line with the neoliberal prescriptions of the World Bank and Western donors. We cannot know how differently the country might have fared under a longer Sankara leadership. What we do know is that Canadian private mining interests flourished in a Compaoré-led Burkina Faso. If Canada claims to champion gender equality and improved lives for girls and women, as it purported to do under the Harper Conservatives, then does it also support leaders like Sankara with comprehensive visions and policies that address gender equality as part of a wider set of nationalist and African-centric equity and development objectives? Or would such visions be "feminized" and ridiculed as unrealistic?

I want to conclude by suggesting that those Canadians who participate enthusiastically and good-heartedly in Plan Canada and Because I Am a Girl fund-raising activities have little understanding of the wider picture I have mapped out in this chapter; it could be argued, in fact, that those involved in the neoliberal power structure do not want individual participants to know, and largely prevent them from knowing. The knowledge of these individuals is shaped in a particular direction: it is important that they know of certain subjects – the girls who need rescuing (or in this case, vocational training), and the business feminist-cum-philanthropist – but they must not know about the gold and its terms of extraction, nor about the many other Canadian organizations benefitting handsomely from aid contracts in Burkina Faso. Such an observation perhaps holds true on the other side of the story as well – in which youth in Burkina Faso from impoverished families embrace training opportunities without being aware of the larger picture. Neoliberal power – primarily accountable to private actors rather than to the public – requires such systems of secrecy and subterfuge. Nevertheless, the story leaks out. The story that emerges from this limited study of the DFATD-funded Plan–IAMGOLD collaboration in Burkina Faso is troubling: Canadian actors collaborate to polish Canada's international reputation as a nation that cares about girls and gender equality, even while Canadian private for-profit and not-for-profit organizations benefit from Burkina Faso's resource wealth. From this wealth, Burkinabé girls, like Burkinabé people more generally, remain largely excluded.

NOTES

1 The event, entitled Empowering Adolescent Girls: Ending the Cycle of Violence, occurred on 10 October 2014. It featured a keynote speech by Nigel Chapman, CEO of Plan International. See https://vimeo.com/122000600.

2 Plan International Canada is the legal name of the organization; I refer to it throughout the paper as Plan Canada. Because I Am a Girl is a program of Plan Canada.

3 "Child, early and forced marriage" is a theme that the Canadian government, through DFATD, has recently profiled, as has Plan Canada. See http://www.international.gc.ca/rights-droits/childmarriage-mariageenfants/index.aspx?lang=eng and http://plancanada.ca/media-backgrounder-child-early-and-forced-marriage (accessed 26 February 2014).

4 UN Women National Committee Canada. "Almas Jiwani to Deliver Keynote Speech at the Global Connect Women Entrepreneurs Expo & Summit 2013." Marketwired, 2 April 2013. Accessed 25 November 2014. http://www.marketwired.com/press-release/almas-jiwani-deliver-keynote-speech-global-connect-women-entrepreneurs-expo-summit-2013-1780984.htm.

5 This mine was closed in 2014 due to lower than expected ore grades and lower returns.

6 If one subtracts the 10 per cent interest of the Government of Burkina Faso, this still leaves the Canadian shareholders with approximately US$250 million for the year.

7 As reported by DFATD, "Where We Work: Burkina Faso," updated 18 February 2015. See http://www.international.gc.ca/development-developpement/countries-pays/burkina-faso.aspx?lang=eng. Accessed 26 February 2015.

8 These are my estimates based on a review of CIDA- and DFATD-funded projects in Burkina Faso listed on DFATD's projects browser.

9 In addition to being infamous for the mass murder of female engineering
   students in 1989, Polytechnique Montréal is one of the host institutions for
   the federal government's $25 million Canadian International Institute for
   Extractive Industries and Development project.

10 For all the projects mentioned in this paragraph, see DFATD project browser:
   http://www.acdi-cida.gc.ca/cidaweb/cpo.nsf/fWebCSAZEn?ReadForm&idx
   =00&CC=BF. Accessed 26 February 2015.

11 Ian Smillie, who headed CUSO in the 1980s and later played a leading role in
   the development of the Kimberly Process to control trade in illicit "conflict
   diamonds." .

12 See, for instance, this "praise video" to Thomas Sankara by the Nigerian
   journalist Adeola Fayehun: https://www.youtube.com/watch?v=0c-wLOipffY.
   Accessed 1 January 2015.

REFERENCES

Barry-Shaw, Nikolas, and Dru Oja Jay. 2012. *Paved with Good Intentions: Canada's Development NGOs from Idealism to Imperialism.* Halifax: Fernwood Publishing.

Borrows, John. 2002. *Recovering Canada: The Resurgence of Indigenous Law.* Toronto: University of Toronto Press.

Brown, Stephen. 2014. "Undermining Foreign Aid: The Extractive Sector and the Recommercialization of Canadian Development Assistance." In *Rethinking Canadian Aid*, edited by Stephen Brown, Molly den Heyer, and David R. Black, 277–95. Ottawa: University of Ottawa Press.

Butler, Paula. 2015. *Colonial Extractions: Race and Canadian Mining in Contemporary Africa.* Toronto: University of Toronto Press.

Chant, Sylvia, and Caroline Sweetman. 2012. "Fixing Women or Fixing the World? 'Smart Economics,' Efficiency Approaches, and Gender Equality in Development." *Gender and Development* 20, no. 3: 517–29.

Combahee River Collective. 1977. "The Combahee River Collective Statement." Combahee River Collective. Accessed 11 November 2016. http://circuitous. org/scraps/combahee.html.

Department of Commerce (US). 2014. *Doing Business in Burkina Faso: 2014 Country Commercial Guide for U.S. Businesses.* Washington, DC: United States Department of Commerce. Accessed 26 February 2015. http://photos.state. gov/libraries/burkinafaso/1135087/cissemx_001/2014%20Country%20 Commercial%20Guide%20FINAL.pdf.

Department of Foreign Affairs, Trade and Development (DFATD). 2014a. "Fact Sheet: Burkina Faso; Canada's Priority Market." Department of Foreign Affairs, Trade and Development, 18 June. Accessed 26 February 2015. http:// international.gc.ca/global-markets-marches-mondiaux/markets-marches/ burkina.aspx?lang=eng.

– 2014b. "Minister Fast Congratulates Windiga on $50 Million Contract Win in Burkina Faso." Department of Foreign Affairs, Trade and Development, 19 June. Accessed 26 February 2015. http://news.gc.ca/web/article-en.do?nid=859359.

– 2014c. "Canada–Burkina Faso Relations." Updated 27 November. Accessed 26 February 2015. http://www.canadainternational.gc.ca/burkinafaso/bilateral_relations_bilaterales/Canada-Burkina_Faso.aspx?lang=eng.

– 2015a. "Burkina Faso: International Development Projects." Department of Foreign Affairs, Trade and Development. International Development Project Browser. Updated 1 January. Accessed 26 February 2015. http://www.acdi-cida.gc.ca/cidaweb/cpo.nsf/fWebCSAZEn?ReadForm&idx=00&CC=BF.

– 2015b. "Project Profile: Capacity-Building of Youth to Grow the Economy: A Public-Private Partnership." Department of Foreign Affairs, Trade and Development. International Development Project Browser. Updated 1 January. Accessed 26 February 2015. http://www.acdi-cida.gc.ca/cidaweb/cpo.nsf/vWebCSAZEn/20C477E0EDCA3CE6852579450037F6DF.

Development Assistance Committee. 1999. DAC Guidelines for Gender Equality and Women's Empowerment in Development Cooperation. Paris: Organisation for Economic Co-operation and Development. Accessed 1 January 2015. http://www.oecd.org/dac/gender-development/28313843.pdf.

Elias, Juanita. 2013. "Davos Woman to the Rescue of Global Capitalism: Postfeminist Politics and Competitiveness Promotion at the World Economic Forum." International Political Sociology 7, no. 2: 152–69.

Endeavour Mining. 2015. "Endeavour Mining Updates Houndé Project Economics Following Increase in Mineral Reserves to 2.1 Moz." Endeavour Mining, 19 February.

FIAN International and FIAN Burkina Faso. 2015. "Women's Perspectives on the Impact of Mining on the Right to Food: The Human Right to Adequate Food and Nutrition of Women and Children of Communities Affected by Mining and Displacement in Essakane, Burkina Faso." Heidelberg, Germany: FIAN International.

Gordon, Todd. 2010. Imperialist Canada. Winnipeg: Arbeiter Ring.

Gueye, Djibril. 2002. "Small-Scale Mining in Burkina Faso." London: International Institute for Environment and Development, and World Business Council for Sustainable Development.

Harsch, Ernest. 2013. "The Legacies of Thomas Sankara: A Revolutionary Experience in Retrospect." Review of African Political Economy 40, no. 137: 358–74.

Heron, Barbara. 2007. Desire for Development: Whiteness, Gender and the Helping Imperative. Waterloo: Wilfrid Laurier University Press.

International Monetary Fund (IMF). 2012. Burkina Faso: Fourth Review under the Three-Year Arrangement under the Extended Credit Facility and Request *for Modification of Performance Criteria and Augmentation of Access – Staff Report; Debt Sustainability Analysis; Press Release on the Executive Board Discussion; and Statement by the Executive Director for Burkina Faso.* IMF Country Report No. 12/159, International Monetary Fund, June. Accessed 26 February 2015. https://www.imf.org/external/pubs/ft/scr/2012/cr12159.pdf.

Kapoor, Ilan. 2013. *Celebrity Humanitarianism: The Ideology of Global Charity.* New York: Routledge.

Keating, Christine, Claire Rasmussen, and Pooja Rishi. 2010. "The Rationality of Empowerment: Microcredit, Accumulation by Dispossession and the Gendered Economy." *Signs* 36, no. 1: 163–76.

Kloosterman, Jeanette, Esther Benning, and Rex Fyles. 2012. "'Measuring the Unmeasurable': Gender Mainstreaming and Culture Change." *Gender and Development* 20, no. 3: 531–45.

Luning, Sabine. 2008. "Liberalisation of the Gold Mining Sector in Burkina Faso." *Review of African Political Economy* 35, no. 117: 387–401.

Maclure, Richard, Benoit Kabore, Colette Meyong, Daniel Lavan, and Karen Mundy. 2007. *Civil Society and the Governance of Basic Education: Partnership or Cooptation? Burkina Faso Country Field Study.* Ottawa: Comparative and International Development Centre, and OISE/UT, 31 July. Accessed 1 January 2015. http://www.oise.utoronto.ca/cidec/UserFiles/File/Research/Civil%20 Society/BurkinaFasoCS_BasicEdGovnce.pdf.

Mbembe, Achille. 2001. *On the Postcolony.* Berkeley: University of California Press.

Mining Association of Canada. *Facts and Figures of the Canadian Mining Industry 2013.* Ottawa: Mining Association of Canada.

Mohanty, Chandra Talpade. 2000. "Under Western Eyes: Feminist Scholarship and Colonial Discourses." In *Theories of Race and Racism: A Reader*, edited by Les Back and John Solomos, 302–23. London and New York: Routledge.

Oved, Marco Chown. 2014. "After the Gold Rush." *Toronto Star*, 1 December.

Peterson, V. Spike, and Anne Sisson Runyan. 2010. *Global Gender Issues in the New Millennium.* 3rd ed. Boulder, CO: Westview Press.

Plan International. 2014. *The State of the World's Girls 2014.* Surrey, UK: Plan International. Accessed 1 January 2015. http://plan-international.org/girls/ reports-and-publications/the-state-of-the-worlds-girls-2014.php?lang=en.

Plan International Canada. 2006a. "Creating Leaders, Creating Change." Annual report. Plan International Canada. Accessed 1 January 2015. http://plancanada. ca/downloads/2006-Annual-english.pdf.

– 2006b. Financial statements, 30 June.

– 2007a. Financial statements, 30 June.

– 2007b. "You + Plan: A Brighter Future for Impoverished Children Worldwide." Annual review and financials.

– 2008a. Annual review and financials.

– 2008b. Financial statements.

– 2009. "Delivering Sustainable Results through Responsible Spending." Annual review and financials.

– 2010. "A Plan to Improve the Lives of Children." Annual review and financials.

– 2011. "A Plan to Improve the Lives of Children." Annual review and financials.

– 2012. "A Plan to Improve the Lives of Children." Annual review and financials.

– 2013. "Making a Difference." Annual review and financials.

– 2014. "Changing the World for the Better." Annual review and financials.

Razack, Sherene. 2004. *Dark Threats and White Knights: The Somalia Affair, Peacekeeping, and the New Imperialism*. Toronto: University of Toronto Press.

Roberts, Adrienne. 2012. "Financial Crisis, Financial Firms ... and Financial Feminism? The Rise of 'Transnational Business Feminism' and the Necessity of Marxist-Feminist IPE." *Socialist Studies* 8, no. 2: 85–106.

Roberts, Adrienne, and Susanne Soederberg. 2012. "Gender Equality as *Smart Economics*? A Critique of the 2012 *World Development Report*." *Third World Quarterly* 3, no. 5: 949–68.

Said, Edward. 1993. *Culture and Imperialism*. New York: First Vintage Books.

Sherman, Paula. 2008. *Dishonour of the Crown: The Ontario Resource Regime in the Valley of the Kiji Sibi*. Winnipeg: Arbeiter Ring.

Thobani, Sunera. 2007. *Exalted Subjects: Studies in the Making of Race and Nation*. Toronto: University of Toronto Press.

Touorouzou, Some. 2006. "Gender Bias in Education in Burkina Faso: Who Pays the Piper? Who Calls the Tune? A Case for Homegrown Policies." *Journal of Contemporary Issues in Education* 1, no. 1: 3–19.

Werthmann, Katja. 2009. "Working in a Boom-Town: Female Perspectives on Gold-Mining in Burkina Faso." *Resources Policy* 34, no. 1–2: 18–23.

World Bank. 2006. *Gender Equality as Smart Economics: A World Bank Group Gender Action Plan (Fiscal Years 2007–2010)*. Washington: World Bank Group. Accessed 15 November 2014. http://siteresources.worldbank.org/INTGENDER/Resources/GAPNov2.pdf.

Chapter 7

Canada, Women, and Artisanal Mining in the Democratic Republic of the Congo

Julia Hartviksen and Rebecca Tiessen

INTRODUCTION

In this chapter, we interrogate Canada's commitment to addressing gender inequality in the Democratic Republic of the Congo (DRC). The central argument guiding our analysis in this chapter is the failure on the part of the Government of Canada (GoC) under the Harper Conservatives (2006 to 2015) to sustain a gender equality (GE) approach in development programming in the DRC, specifically in artisanal small-scale mining (ASM). ASM is the source of employment for nearly one in five people in the DRC and represents a major source of income for the country. Mining-related activities involve men and women; therefore, development programs associated with ASM must provide opportunities for promoting gender equality. Our research, however, points to minimal efforts to address gender inequality in ASM among Canadian-funded initiatives in the DRC; a highly paternalistic and superficial approach to gender issues, such as the near-exclusive focus on sexual and gender-based violence (SGBV); and a missed opportunity to extend the focus on ASM to include women's economic opportunities and gender equality in this sector, including a failure to focus on the complexity of women's economic participation and the tensions surrounding the related consequences to this failure.

The DRC has experienced years of conflict, violence, and humanitarian emergencies. High rates of SGBV have resulted from this protracted crisis, and SGBV remains an important area of focus for a country that continues to struggle to build peace, promote economic growth, and ensure political stability. SGBV continues to be a serious issue in the DRC, and consequently women's "victimhood" has dominated much of the focus among donor commitments to the DRC. This has eclipsed the complexity of gender relations in the DRC and the diverse needs and opportunities for women and men. For example, women play an important role in the economic sector, and empowering women with economic opportunities is an important focus for development efforts. We contend that women's participation in productive labour cannot, on its own, eliminate the range of gender inequalities faced by women; particularly if it is promoted through the lens of what Paula Butler (in this collection) refers to as corporatized philanthropy. However, attention to women's roles in – and gendered barriers to – economic activities is a specific area of focus for this particular analysis of ASM in the DRC, given its absence in the literature.

Examples of women's contributions to the economic sector can be found in ASM in mining communities and as crossborder traders, among other economic activities. Although the GoC has demonstrated an interest in ASM-related activities in the DRC, the Harper Conservatives did little, if anything, to understand the range of actors involved in – and effected by – the mining sector in the country. In this chapter, we argue that the GoC's near-exclusive focus on SGBV in its projects relating to gender in the DRC reinforces gender essentialism and overshadows the complexity of gender issues and gender inequality, specifically within the context of ASM. The Canadian government has been weak in terms of articulating a clear policy around gender, particularly in relation to women and the complex and diverse roles they assume in the mining sector in the DRC; this has shaped the projects on the ground, which serve as a reflection of GoC policy. Further, under Harper, Canada remained out of touch with ongoing efforts towards regulation and certification of conflict minerals in the DRC, which increasingly aim to recognize women as key players in ASM. This lack of clear policy and directed projects geared towards addressing women in the mining sector in the DRC reaffirms the simplistic perceptions of inequality and gender relations in recent Canadian development programming on a broader scale.

We begin the chapter by providing a brief introduction to the DRC, followed by a discussion of the focus on SGBV by the Department of Foreign Affairs, Trade and Development (DFATD)[1] in its gender-focused projects. We then turn to ASM and Canada's commitments to ASM in the country, followed by contextual information on women's role in the mining sector, drawing on a growing body of literature documenting women's (limited and contentious) economic contributions to this sector of the economy. Little has been written to date on the role of women in ASM. We advance this knowledge by drawing on some key reports and documents that shed light on women's participation in the mining sector more broadly and on ASM more specifically. We also document the important literature on SGBV in the DRC, finding that it is significant and highly linked to mining-related activities. Subsequently, we analyze Canada's efforts to address gender and/or women's issues in the DRC, with a particular lens to determine the extent to which these efforts have been directed at women's contributions to the ASM sector. We conclude with some final reflections on the lost opportunities to date and the potential for new and gender-sensitive programming through DFATD's toolkit for Promoting Gender Equality in the Extractive Sector, as well as some reflections on potential policy directions for Canada's contributions to gender equality in the ASM sector in the DRC.

In 2014, the DRC was added to Canada's list of "countries of focus," joining twenty-four other countries for which Canada has made a priority. The GoC, and DFATD in particular, has invested in development programs in the DRC for many years and continues to play a significant role, operating numerous development projects in the DRC. The thematic focus for Canada in the DRC is based on five pillars: "Promoting good governance and consolidating peace through institutional capacity-building; consolidating macroeconomic stability and growth; improving access to social services and reducing vulnerability; combatting HIV/AIDS; and supporting dynamism at the community level" (DFATD 2014a). Furthermore, at the time this chapter was written, the official GoC website pertaining to the DRC defined Canada's goal in the DRC as: "to help establish a more democratic, prosperous, and equitable state – one that will be able to reduce poverty sustainably and secure the future of its children and youth. Canada also provides humanitarian assistance to communities in the DRC affected by conflict" (DFATD 2014a). Between 2012 and 2013, Canada contributed $51.31 million in development assistance in the DRC (DFATD 2014b). Among the many projects that DFATD supports in the DRC, support to the African Minerals Development Centre is one of the more important ventures, with a contribution of $15 million. The goals of this project include a sustainable mining sector (DFATD 2014c). Of particular relevance is a reflection on Canada's "modest but growing trade relationship with the DRC ... and Canadian investments in the DRC, notably in the mining sector" (DFATD 2014b).

Several other projects and the funding allocated for each project in the DRC are available on the GoC website. Support to victims of sexual violence in the DRC is highlighted as one of Canada's flagship programs in the DRC. No dollar figures, however, are mentioned in relation to this specific program, unlike the funding allocations clearly available for other projects, such as peacekeeping efforts ($300 million) (DFATD 2014b). The focus on victims of sexual violence includes supporting and providing capacity for the health care system to improve primary health care "for those most vulnerable: women and children" (DFATD 2014b). Consequently, the projects that address women's concerns, we argue, also perpetuate the tropes that frame women as victims and view them through narratives of feminine vulnerability in the DRC; this ignores women's involvement in ASM and simplifies complex gender relations surrounding mineral development in the DRC, which has earned the unenviable title of the "rape capital of the world" (BBC News 2010; Palermo and Peterman 2011).

CASE STUDY CONTEXT: DEMOCRATIC REPUBLIC OF THE CONGO

The DRC's colonial and postcolonial history is characterized by conflict and civil war, which has, in turn, fed into foreign representations of the country as "fragile," particularly in the context of international aid. In the 2013 special issue of the *Review of African Political Economy*, the contributors to this special issue challenged the representations of the DRC as a failed state, as well as the "chaos" often associated with such illustrations (Larmer et al. 2013, 5). These representations and their consequences are also highly gendered – a key argument guiding this analysis that we will turn to later in this chapter.

Taking these problems of representation into account, it is nonetheless important to note that the complex history of conflict in the DRC has factored into the exacerbation of the precarity of life in the region. The roots of the ongoing insecurity and violence are linked to Belgian colonialism, which forged a relationship predicated on violence and reinforced an oppressive state and submissive population (Larmer et al. 2013, 2). Shifts towards privatization in the post-independence state under President Mobutu Sese Seko contributed to a landscape in which informal economies sprouted up, which in turn provoked conflict over land and access to resources, and led to forced displacements, as well a broader context of increased, post-independence violence (Larmer et al. 2013, 3). Although the DRC is no longer experiencing a formal conflict, it retains "an image as a country in a state of quasi-anarchy and chaos" (Kabamba 2010, 271). The DRC is also presented as a fragile state characterized by high rates of poverty, ongoing political instability, and violence. Between 2002 and

2010, the DRC was ranked among the top three "most fragile states" in the world (Carment et al. 2013, 136). Ongoing challenges for the DRC include its inability to control rebel group activities and the provision of basic security to the citizens of the country (Carment et al. 2013, 136). Contributing to this construction of the DRC as an othered, dangerous place, is the characterization – and arguably the caricaturizaton – of the country's high rates of SGBV.

Certainly, SGBV has played an important – and devastating – role in shaping the DRC's recent history. Men and women – civilians and combatants alike – have suffered greatly as a result of the conflict in the DRC by virtue of a number of related challenges, including internal displacement, institutional breakdown, the erosion of family support structures, the decline in agricultural productivity, and, often related to many of these challenges, high rates of rape and sexual violence. Inadequate institutional support at the state level has meant that many of those who are responsible for SGBV have gone unpunished. The estimates for the number of rapes in the DRC since 1996 are staggering, with 35,000 reported rapes, though many other cases and forms of SGBV go unreported (IRIN 2006; Schroeder 2005). The effects of these high rates of SGBV have been long-term and wide-reaching, resulting in physical and psychological injuries, including high rates of HIV/AIDS infections, early and unwanted pregnancies, and disruptions to quality of life, including opportunities for women and men to become married and/or active members of society. Women who have been rejected by their communities due to stigma associated with sexual violence often find themselves in precarious economic situations and resorting to "survival prostitution," whereby women and girls provide sexual favours in exchange for food and/or shelter, or other material goods (Bosmans 2007; Schroeder 2005).

As more information about the extent of SGBV and its implications becomes available, we can better assess the long-term implications for women and girls, and for gender equality in the country. In response to this growing awareness of SGBV in conflict, the United Nations has introduced several reports and resolutions. Among these international commitments are the 2003 United Nations High Commissioner for Refugees (UNHCR) Guidelines for Prevention and Response: Sexual and Gender-Based Violence Against Refugees, Returnees and Internally Displaced Persons; Resolution 1325, accepted in 2000; Security Council Resolution (SCR) 1820 on sexual violence in armed conflict, adopted in 2008; SCR 1888, which created the Special Representative of the Secretary-General on Sexual Violence in Conflict, adopted in 2009; and SCR 1889 which provided a mandate for monitoring and evaluating initiatives for women, peace, and security, adopted in 2009 (see UNHCR 2011 for a more complete list and explanation of the different UN commitments to date). Canada signed on to these commitments and continues to work on these commitments through National Action Plans on Women, Peace and Security at the national level, and ongoing reporting on the achievements to date. In 2014, Canada reaffirmed its commitment to addressing SGBV at the Global Summit to End Sexual Violence in Conflict, held in London, UK, underscoring the necessity of translating policies into practice. These important initiatives are useful starting points for addressing one key issue in the DRC and elsewhere. However, the characterization of the DRC as being fragile and unstable, and having high rates of SGBV, does not give a full picture of the diverse risks for men and women in the DRC and the ways in which communities – particularly of women – navigate and negotiate within economic and productive activities in such conditions.

These problematic caricatures of the DRC are countered by the reality on the ground and the ways in which communities and individuals work towards building alternative livelihoods and forms of social organization, despite persisting levels of insecurity. The complex array and production of social relations as they play out on the ground challenges the ways in which Western aid and Western representations isolate the DRC as a place of violent anarchy (Côté 2014). The social relations that emerge through ASM represent both a challenge to these representations, in that they are illustrative of economic potential, livelihood sustenance, and relations of exploitation and, at times, of violence. As such, aid projects aiming to address this sector must consider the complex characteristics of these activities in developing a greater, more nuanced approach.

Artisanal Mining in the DRC

ASM has come to play a significant role in the economic sector of the DRC, particularly since the 1990s and 2000s, replacing traditional agricultural practices as a central economic activity for those living in rural poverty, and as a means towards economic stability (Larmer et al. 2013, 5). Recent estimates suggest that 18 per cent of the DRC's population is economically sustained through ASM activities (Perks 2011, 178). It is estimated that two million people participate in ASM as miners in the DRC, with many more working in service activities related to mining in ASM communities (Perks 2011, 181). Key minerals that are sourced from the DRC and enter global commodity chains include artisanally mined gold, diamonds, tantalum, tin, and tungsten (the 3Ts) (Côté 2014). Further, 90 per cent of minerals coming out of the DRC originate from ASM activities, while globally only 15 per cent of minerals are mined in ASM sites (Perks 2011, 181; Hayes 2008).

ASM is often associated with violence and conflict, linked to Africa's so-called "resource curse," which is said to perpetuate conflict in the region (Bush 2008, 362). Globally, clashes between large-scale mining operations and artisanal miners have also been said to contribute to conflict, violence, and insecurity; as large-scale mining companies increasingly gain a foothold in the DRC, conflict around mining operations will likely continue. The poor working conditions, health hazards, and environmental effects of the largely unregulated mining activities contribute to these associations (Perks 2011, 177–8).

However, as Larmer et al. (2013) reiterates, current research suggests that minerals and mineral extraction are not the main cause of violence in the DRC, and also that they represent the means to an alternative source of livelihood and economic well-being. Following Butler's analysis (in this collection), that capitalism's (and more specifically neoliberalism's) relationship to gender must be problematized, we also recognize that ASM can create spaces for alternative livelihoods and productive labour outside of the mainstream economic order. ASM is also increasingly regulated through legal shifts occurring on the ground in the DRC: for instance, ASM in the DRC is regulated by the 2002 Mining Code, which stipulates that only Congolese citizens (men and women), certain companies involved in the ASM sector, and certain foreign nationals with appropriate permissions can mine in this subsector in the DRC (Côté 2014, 9). ASM is arguably a source of great economic potential for communities involved in the activity (Perks 2011, 178). Nonetheless, there are important risks and adverse effects related to participation in the ASM sector; it is therefore critical for policymakers to engage with the complexity of social relations around ASM to understand these diverse issues and the related gendered effects.

The OECD highlights some of the diverse risks in the supply chain of mineral extraction from conflict-affected and high-risk areas for diverse actors. Mineral producers risk being implicated in forced labour practices, including child labour, extortion or illegal taxes from miners, torture and degrading treatment, sexual violence, and other serious violations of international humanitarian law (OECD 2013, 35). Various people and communities may be drawn to ASM, and the effects of these activities on social life is varied. On the one hand, the promise of economic benefits attract labourers – yet on the other, the highly migratory nature of the work; the use of drugs, prostitution and alcohol in ASM communities; and the debt and poverty that labourers can incur as a result can also lead to more precarious situations (Perks 2011, 181). In some cases, local governing officials and miners may engage in complex relations of bribery, and may threaten or clash with traditional governance structures, contributing to "generalised social insecurity" in these communities (Perks 2011, 182). Simultaneously, ASM sites themselves sometimes rely on exploitative relationships between those who own/profit from the mine, and miners and community members (BSR 2010, 1). As well, writes Perks, "The multi-ethnic composition of most ASM communities further complicates approaches to gender issues, as tribal values and practices vary significantly, and occur within the void of an overarching traditional governance structure" (2011, 183). A report on violence against women in the DRC highlights some of the specific issues women in ASM may face pertaining to SGBV, including the presence of a large group of young men employed in the mining sector who are far from home and who engage in high rates of alcohol and drug consumption, which the authors of the report argue creates "a combination that diminishes moral responsibility and increases violent tendencies" (ITUC 2011, 21). Perpetration of sexual violence extends also to state and nonstate security workers who work around the mines. These two constituencies are identified as contributing to the demand for sex-trade. Women employed in the ASM sector may need to supplement their incomes with money earned through sex-trade (ITUC 2011). We return to some of the gender-specific risks and realities in the section below.

Although ASM is seen as a vector for community organization and productive labour *outside* formal political and economic structures, it is important to note that everyone involved in the mining industry in the DRC can face health and safety challenges. ASM practices involve several risks, especially given the generally low level of technical mechanization and regulation, and the physical dangers involved. In some areas, particularly in the eastern part of the country, more than half of ASM operations are controlled by armed groups (BSR 2010, 1). Further, as we discuss later in this chapter, ASM's effects are gendered and affect women in particular ways.

The DRC, as part of the Great Lakes region, has been moving towards the regulation of conflict minerals in the region. In particular, the International Conference of the Great Lakes Region (ICGLR) Regional Certification Mechanism creates a framework for certification, database records, formalization, revenue transparency, harmonization of laws, and whistleblowing, all of which can create a safer environment for ASM, and help ensure that workers can maintain livelihoods and employment activities. While it remains important to emphasize that the ICGLR Regional

Certification Mechanism places considerable emphasis on the links between mining activities, conflict, occupational hazards, and insecurity, the mechanism is nonetheless representative of a shift towards mediation of the risks and illegal activities around ASM.

The Role of Women in Artisanal Mining in the DRC

In the section above we document some of the risks of ASM-related activities for women, including SGBV and prostitution. Understanding these gendered risks is an important dimension of understanding the broader challenges surrounding the ASM sector; however, these risks are only one aspect of community participation in ASM. It thus remains important to contextualize the challenges faced by women (and opportunities for women) participating in mining activities. ASM should not be represented as solely a violent space for women, particularly because ASM activities provide women with alternative forms of labour beyond the domestic sphere. Nonetheless, mining itself is often a highly masculinized activity (Lahiri-Dutt 2011, 2), and gender-related issues other than violence remain central to a deeper analysis.

An important starting point is the sheer number of women involved in ASM work. Women comprise as much as 50 per cent of the labour force in ASM in Africa more broadly (Perks 2011, 178; Hayes and Perks 2012, 529), and one study has noted that in some contexts, approximately 30 per cent of women also perform the same tasks as men in mining-related activities, including digging, processing, and providing transport services. The tasks that are generally assigned to women in ASM work include sorting minerals, particularly diamonds, from gravel (Gagnon 2009, 1–2) and other tasks. A 2014 Partnership Africa Canada (PAC) study on the gendered dimensions of ASM in the DRC provides cutting-edge information about the diverse roles and tasks ascribed to women in artisanal gold mines, including such roles as "transporteuses," who carry sand and stone from the extraction site to the crushers; "hydrauliques," who carry water for the purpose of cooling the crushers; "songeuses," who prepare the ground-up sand to be washed by wetting it with water to make mud; and "laveuses," who then wash the sand. The task of "bizalu" requires women to recoup the discarded sand that is then rewashed by the "twangaises" so that the gold that is extracted can be sold. A final category of work accorded to women in ASM are the "souteneuses," who provide support during the difficult phase of digging the gold pit (Côté 2014, 16). The research conducted by staff at PAC offers important insights into the nature of the work performed by women, as well as the titles of jobs that have been defined and adopted in the ASM communities in the DRC. Women, therefore, provide essential services in mining communities directly within mining operations. Women also play a key role in the cross-border trading of minerals. In the province of South Kivu, for example, 70 per cent of traders are women (Tegera and Johnson 2007). Mining communities also serve as unique spaces in which micro-enterprises thrive, enterprises that are likewise often established and run by women (Perks 2011, 179). These examples highlight the diverse and significant ways that women contribute to the ASM-based economy in the DRC.

Women typically are paid lower wages than their male counterparts for their roles in the mining process (Gagnon 2009, 2), and women's work is systematically undervalued in relation to the same work performed by men (Côté 2014, 17). Furthermore, the few women who own gold pits are represented by a man who serves as the manager of the pit (Côté 2014, 16). In addition, women do not always have access to – or control over – their incomes generated from mining-related activities (Côté 2014, 17). These challenges pose important socio-economic risks for women and reinforce gender-based inequality in ASM communities – challenges that are reinforced through legal issues women also face. For example, the 2002 Mining Code provides no specific stipulations to address the economic and social inequalities that persist within ASM activities (Côté 2014, 10). Examples of discrimination faced by women in ASM provide important evidence of the broader challenges women face in this sector (BSR 2010). Several other challenges are important to highlight, as they provide opportunity for a deeper analysis of the issues noted above – including discrimination in hiring and compensation arrangements in ASM work, as well as discrimination arising from lack of access to education and credit. Women may also face loss of livelihoods in cases where land has been appropriated for ASM. Women are forced to adapt to new economic realities when their means of generating income (such as from farming) are obliterated. Women also play multiple roles within the gendered division of labour, including productive (generally paid labour), reproductive (unpaid work in support of family and household needs that facilitates productive labour, in addition to child-bearing and child-rearing), and community roles (support and unpaid work provided outside the household), and may therefore find themselves bearing the burden of significant reproductive responsibilities, including time spent collecting water or firewood, preparing food, and caring for members of the family (DFATD 2014d; Moser 1989; PAC 2014). Upon completing a day's work in and around mining sites, women also engage in other productive and reproductive activities after the workday is over, adding to the burdens of labour they endure (Côté 2014, 16) as part of their socially constructed and assigned gender roles.

The risks of SGBV associated with ASM are particularly acute for women, particularly in "remote areas where mines are still controlled by military forces" (Mallo 2012, 4721; BSR 2010, 1). SGBV can be exacerbated by high rates of alcohol and drug consumption, as well as lack of protection against domestic violence, and can contribute to high rates of sexually transmitted infections (STIs). These SGBV-related risks pose additional health issues, particularly maternal health issues that can be caused by untreated STIs, as well as lack of sanitation and malnutrition. As this section has demonstrated, the range of risks and challenges women face in the mining sector is significant, and illustrates that the risks women face are not limited to SGBV. Clearly, addressing SGBV remains a priority for future ASM projects. However, the near-exclusive attention paid to SGBV by the Harper government overshadowed the diverse contributions of women to ASM and the related issues and challenges they face. The complexity of women's involvement in the ASM sector is thus erased by narratives emphasizing feminine vulnerability that are increasingly perpetuated by foreign donors, including Canada, and NGOs. Ignoring the complexity of the gendered dimensions of mining, we argue, diminishes international efforts to address community-based ASM risks and reproduces ill-advised programs based on narratives of women's vulnerability and victimhood.

CANADA'S COMMITMENTS TO GENDER, SECURITY, AND THE MINING SECTOR IN THE DRC

Canada has supported the efforts of the international community in raising awareness of – and acting on – inequality and SGBV in conflict and postconflict communities. Canada's National Action Plan for the implementation of UN Security Council Resolutions on Women, Peace, and Security (DFATD 2010), for example, consists of major commitments, including supporting the active and meaningful participation of women in peace operations and peace processes as well as decision making and management of conflicts; increasing the effectiveness of peace operations, including the protection and promotion of the rights and safety of women and girls; improving the capacity of Canadian staff to help prevent violence and to protect the human rights of women and girls in peace operations, fragile states, and conflict-affected communities; promoting and supporting relief and recovery efforts in fragile states and conflict-affected countries while simultaneously taking into account the differential experiences of women, men, boys, and girls; and increasing the account-ability of leadership in peace operations.

At the time of announcing Canada's commitment to the National Action Plan on Women, Peace, and Security, the Harper government, through CIDA, pledged increased support (80 per cent of bilateral assis-tance) to a list of twenty "countries of focus," seven of which are located in Africa but did not, at that time, include the DRC (DFATD 2012). Crit-ics argued that the Harper Conservatives had "turned their backs on Africa" and had a declining interest in Africa overall (Akuffo 2012; Black 2012; MacDonald and Ruckert 2013). It is worth noting, however, that under the Harper Conservatives, overall foreign aid to the DRC had steadily and marginally increased between 2006 and 2014 (NSI 2012). Canada provided official development assistance (ODA) to the DRC in the amount of US$70 million in 2006, US$40 million in 2008, US$70 mil-lion in 2010, and US$62 million in 2012 (NSI 2012). In 2014, the year that the DRC joined Canada's list of countries of focus, the amount allocated in foreign aid spending amounted to US$74 million, making the DRC the eighth highest recipient of funds allocated for developing countries (NSI 2012; OECD 2014). Prior to the Conservative party taking power in 2006, Canada had maintained a steady commitment to the DRC, with funds ranging from US$14 million in 2001 to nearly US$50 million in 2005, and a particularly high amount in 2003, with Canada's donor support to the DRC totalling US$125 million (NSI 2012). Thus, the general trend of incre-mental growth in ODA support to the DRC continued through the period of Harper Conservative leadership; however, the 2014 commitment of US$74 million is only slightly larger than during the years prior to the DRC becoming a "country of focus."

When the list of countries of focus was updated in 2014, two coun-tries were removed (Pakistan and Bolivia), and the list featured a growing interest in mining opportunities in Africa in general, and in the DRC in particular (Abadie 2011). This renewed commitment to an African country, along with a growing interest in mining-related investments, raises import-ant questions about the GoC's commitment to gender equality in mining communities. In order to evaluate Canada's investments in the DRC, par-ticularly in terms of Canada's efforts to address gender equality in mining communities, we consulted grey material (documents and policy briefs) available online, in addition to submitting an Access to Information and Privacy (ATIP) request to DFATD. Key words used in our ATIP request were "programs" and "policies" relating to "gender, women, small-scale mining, large-scale mining, sexual- and gender-based violence, and the DRC."[2] The time frame used for analyzing these documents was 2006 to 2014.[3]

The list of projects generated was extensive, consisting of sixty-six ongoing and terminated projects, each spanning several months or years, and in partnership with other humanitarian or aid organizations and institutions, including the Red Cross, UNICEF, UNHCR, and the World Food Programme. Much of the more detailed information and project records were held by aid partners on the ground, making the acquisition of certain documents costly and time consuming.[4]

Interestingly, the majority of projects on the list we received have already been terminated, making the acquisition of additional information on these projects more difficult. A significant number of terminated projects that turned up in our search addressed issues around food aid, nutrition, health, security, water, and sanitation. Current projects continue to emphasize food aid, nutrition, and health, and there is an increasing emphasis on providing assistance to victims of sexual violence, particularly women and girls. These projects are among the longest running projects in our list, from 2013 ongoing until 2018.

The language used to describe the projects, including the projects dealing with violence against women and girls, tended to emphasize vulnerability, humanitarian emergency, conflict, and violence, as well as a generalized severe lack of basic services. Broadly speaking, this operates to portray the DRC through a Western lens that characterizes and frames the DRC as ungoverned, chaotic, and lacking in the most basic conditions for survival (Larmer et al. 2013; Kabamba 2010, 271). These discourses matter; the reproduction of these tropes occurs on a material level, through the types of projects that are implemented as a result. Indeed, although the issues addressed by the projects, both ongoing and terminated, reflect important areas, the danger in approaching the situation from this perspective is that it will result in the continuation of short-term, band-aid fixes that fail to address the complexities and nuances of social relations.

A number of gaps persist in addressing issues, especially in relation to the ASM sector as it pertains to gender. In particular, our ATIP request failed to generate information on any projects that addressed both gender issues and ASM. Further, although no mining-related projects were presented in our ATIP request, one project dealing with mining in the region was identified through a general search of the DFATD project database.

Despite a broad lack of engagement with mining projects by DFATD in the DRC, the treatment of gender in the region illustrates a compartmentalization, rather than integration or mainstreaming, of gender in all projects. This highlights the ways in which the Harper government in particular viewed gender as a separate issue, rather than an important axis of difference that permeates social relations and is an integral component to development in all contexts. This reproduces an essentialized understanding of how gender operates. As we have highlighted, the complexity of gender relations in the ASM sector calls for a more integrated and nuanced approach to policy, rather than merely ticking a box.

As such, not only do projects tend to cast women as victims of conflict rather than as active participants in social relations, they also tend to perpetuate the homogenized understandings of the DRC as conflict ridden, chaotic, and violent. This approach erases the dimensions of organization and social engagement in the region; this is particularly problematic given the significance of artisanally mined minerals in global commodity chains. Further, there remains a key gap in terms of women's productive work, given that only one terminated project that focused specifically on women was found through our search, dealing with microcredit programs for women[5] in the region. As such, the complexity of the tensions and contradictions surrounding women's productive labour is erased by the gender essentialist narrative underpinning Canadian development efforts in the DRC. An ongoing project geared towards community economic stability was also found, and emphasized the role of women in communities. Broadly speaking, the lack of women-focused economic empowerment projects, and economic projects more widely, points to the erasure of women as agents of social relations and economic livelihoods, and their presentation as, solely, victims. While sexual violence is a key issue in the DRC, it does not occur in isolation from other social relations and productive activities. Similar issues surrounding a general silence on gender discourse can be found in the case of Haiti, as shown by Stephen Baranyi and Shantelle Binette (in this collection), who note the absence of references to "gender equality" in any official statements or press releases concerning Haiti since 2010, and the near-exclusive emphasis on women's vulnerability and victimhood as it pertains specifically to violence. However, unlike the research conducted by Baranyi and Binette, our analysis did not include field-based research and interviews with those responsible for implementing programs and projects. The limitations identified here thus speak to an overall failure of national-level commitments by the Harper Conservatives to mainstreaming gender in ASM programs in the DRC.

As noted above, women play a key economic role in the activities of ASM communities; and yet this is met by a lack of projects committed to engaging with women's economic participation and inclusion as key players in social relations in the DRC. Projects instead reinforce the conceptualization of women as victims of conflict, rather than incorporating a nuanced understanding of the complexity of gender and social relations in this context. The gendered relations around social reproduction in ASM communities – relations that are rooted in traditional, heteronormative understandings of labour – are reflected in the kinds of projects DFATD has supported; this perpetuates victimhood narratives rooted in problematic gendered assumptions in aid policy.

SOME POSITIVE SIGNS AHEAD

Advocates and researchers promoting an improved understanding of women's roles in ASM in the DRC and elsewhere, as well as the gender-related effects of mining in development, have made some inroads as of 2014. One initiative resulting from this work is a research projected supported by the International Development Research Centre (IDRC) that aims to fill the knowledge gap pertaining to women's economic contribution to ASM. The findings from this research will likely be a key resource in understanding the ways in which women engage in and are influenced by ASM activities in the Great Lakes region. While governments may be looking for ways to understand and integrate ASM into formal economic structures in developing aid policy, this research promises to highlight the gendered aspects of ASM in the region, which continues to be unaddressed by government policies (Côté 2014).

A significant advancement on the part of the GoC is the introduction and adoption of Canada's 2014 toolkit for Promoting Gender Equality in the Extractive Sector. Drawing on the Sustainable Economic Growth Strategy introduced by CIDA, DFATD recognized that "women play a central role as income earners in lifting themselves, their families, and their communities out of poverty. Yet they face significant hurdles to full and effective participation in economies." (DFATD 2014d, 2). The toolkit provides a broad and comprehensive discussion of the nature and effect of women's participation in the extractive sector, beginning with a reaffirmation of many of the issues highlighted earlier in this paper in terms of discrimination, sexual violence, inequality of opportunity, increasing reproductive workloads, etc. The introduction to the toolkit goes even further to situate these issues in the context of the manner in which they disrupt gender equality dynamics within communities engaged in extractive industries. Several tip sheets accompany this DFATD toolkit; these are indispensable in terms of improving our understanding of the effects on women and why gender equality matters in the area of extractive industries, but also in terms of highlighting the roles of – and opportunities for – different actors in building economic foundations, improving resource governance capacity, and supporting local economic development. The tips sheets and the introductory material provided in the toolkit are therefore important advances in terms of the GoC's commitments to addressing gender equality in the extractive industry and in ASM in particular. However, these tips sheets and toolkit are limited by the general nature in which the findings are presented, and the effects on women are generalized by region. For example, the toolkit makes note of the large number of men and women whose livelihoods depend on ASM, with estimates of "100 million men and women around the world" (DFATD 2014d, 5). Women's participation, however, ranges across regions, with an overall estimation of 30 per cent participation as ASM miners globally and highly varying rates of participation within regions, such as: "10–50 percent of miners in some Asian countries, 10–30 percent in Latin America, and 40–100 percent in Africa" (DFATD 2014d, 4; World Bank 2012). The data used for this summary is attributed to the 2012 World Bank toolkit, reinforcing the need for up-to-date and country-specific information. Additional research is therefore of utmost importance to an improved investment in policies and programs supporting gender equality in the DRC. Researchers must also, however, involve communities in their research, to "reflect on the initiatives that have been undertaken in different contexts by different actors, and ask whether the ideas developed in one corporate, political or cultural context can or should be applied to others" (Lahiri-Dutt 2011, 2).

CONCLUSIONS

The findings from our analysis of Canadian commitments to gender equality in ASM in the DRC under the Harper Conservatives point to several key weaknesses in incorporating a gender lens in development programming. Attention to gender and women's issues, when they are addressed at all, has been limited to SGBV, and therefore is not a demonstration of effective gender mainstreaming practice. Advancements in 2014 towards the development of a DFATD training guide (see DFATD 2014d) for improving gender programming in ASM display a potential for a future of gender mainstreaming. Yet ongoing effort is needed to ensure that women are not essentialized (see introduction, this volume) or framed as mere victims of development processes. Furthermore, women are frequently instrumentalized in conflict settings for the purpose of attracting aid (Carpenter 2013, 3); in doing so, Western countries like

Canada perpetuate victimhood narratives rooted in an Orientalism that erase the complexity of women's productive labour on the ground.

Canada's approach to development programming in the DRC between 2006 and 2014 largely entrenches gender essentialism by contributing to the erasure of the dynamism of women's roles in the region, particularly with regard to the ASM sector. The silence on gender equality in Canada's policies and commitments surrounding ASM in the DRC highlights the failure of the GoC to engage with women's diverse participation in and the social relations surrounding ASM activities. Simplified and highly generalized representations of women as exclusively victims and vulnerable to SGBV in the DRC limits our understanding of the roles and contributions of women within ASM communities in the DRC. In so doing, the GoC has not answered the question, "where are the women" (Enloe 2000), and ignores women's and men's diverse roles, responsibilities, identities, and contributions to ASM.

The emphasis on insecurity and violence, rather than on the diversity and complexity of economic activities within the ASM sector and the social relations they espouse, perpetuates a form of Othering[6] through the aid that is provided. This form of Othering frames the issues in the DRC as existing within a binary of security/insecurity, and ignores the ebbs and flows of conflict, violence, and inequality that are the context necessary for understanding the complexity of social relations. In her critique of the male/female or masculine/feminine binary, Mary Schippers (2007) suggests that gender roles operate in complex, interlocking ways. ASM activities present a challenge to the binaries that are otherwise reinforced through aid policy. Aid policy that reinforces the traditional division of labour also perpetuates hegemonic masculinities that cast women as victims and men as victimizers; as we have attempted to show, productive and social relations in the DRC differ from this caricature in complex and nuanced ways. This harkens back to Eriksson Baaz and Maria Stern's challenge of the "fearless fighters and submissive wives" binary in the DRC in the context of female soldiers (Baaz and Stern 2012, 711); likewise, women involved in mining continue to challenge the active–passive dichotomy with regard to masculinity and femininity in the diverse and shifting roles they take on in ASM. It is important to keep in mind that mining is a highly masculinized field; yet within ASM, women and men are actively involved in diverse ways (Lahiri-Dutt 2011, 2). The complex relations around ASM activities, including women's participation and vulnerability in these settings, challenge hegemonic forms of masculinity and femininity, and should also serve as further areas for research toward developing a more nuanced approach to policy, one that focuses on the everyday aspects of social relations in conflict settings in order to better understand the dynamics of masculinity and femininity in these contexts (Parahsar 2014).

As the findings presented in this chapter suggest, there is a great need for careful and context-specific research that can inform both policy and practice. The gaps in the GoC's draft toolkit for promoting gender equality in the extractive industry make the case for more information on local community experiences. Mining companies have also jumped on the bandwagon, providing important summaries of why gender matters in resource extraction activities. Rio Tinto, for example, has developed such a guide, and although not specific to ASM, it points out that some companies have developed a greater benchmark for addressing gender in the minerals sector. While this may be an interesting development in the corporate sector, we also concede that simply inserting women or gender into corporate social responsibility guidelines does not trouble the ways in which corporate, neoliberal agendas may simply instrumentalize women as ideal neoliberal subjects, and does not challenge existing inequities (see Roberts and Soederberg 2012; Butler, this collection).

In this chapter, we have highlighted the significance of gender inequality in the extractive sector. The findings pertaining to Canada's efforts to understand gender equality in the mining sector are highly generalized and require detailed research and analysis that can guide specific programs. We have drawn several practical recommendations from our findings, including:

- The GoC, under Liberal party leadership as of November 2015, could take a leadership role in the promotion of community-driven development opportunities – and community-based (rather than Canadian-derived) benefits – in ASM communities. An improved understanding of the community-based opportunities and benefits must start with understanding the nature and extent of women's participation in the ASM sector in country-specific studies, as well as community-specific analyses, given that conditions and experiences can differ greatly from one community to the next. Drawing on the expertise of researchers working in development NGOs and research groups such as PAC, and the wealth of information acquired by staff working on the Great Lakes region in Africa will shed additional light on the experiences of women and the nature of gender inequality surrounding ASM in the DRC.
- Policy makers must ensure that research translates into better visibility of the role of women, women's issues, and gender inequality in

the extractive sector, particularly in ASM. This can translate into the allocation of funding to standardize gender mainstreaming in Canadian-funded mining initiatives, as well as funding for existing research and advocacy groups internationally and locally within the DRC who are best placed to inform program planners.

- Ongoing collaboration with gender experts in local community contexts and more broadly within the DRC allows for additional opportunities to mitigate some of the negative effects of mining investments, and potentially opportunities for alternative resource development strategies.

- These guidelines require the support of many actors, not the least of which are local, regional, and national governments. Gender sensitization and awareness raising is therefore crucial for in-country decision makers who are responsible for promoting community-based economic opportunities as part of a broader strategy to promote women's empowerment and gender equality.

- Shining a spotlight on SGBV remains important and should not be eliminated from the GoC's commitments to the DRC or elsewhere. However, more effort is needed to ensure that gender is mainstreamed into development programming and ASM projects. In doing so, the GoC must begin with an understanding of the masculinities that perpetuate inequality and disadvantage for certain groups and privilege for others. Investing in gender equality requires creating opportunities for empowerment and building on improved knowledge of the diverse and key contributions of all groups, including women as active agents in ASM – in sex-trade work, but also in the diverse productive roles involved in ASM. Improved knowledge of women's roles and contributions will lend additional support to advances in gender-sensitive programming and legal reform.

- Training and sensitization in gender mainstreaming and gender analysis must extend to mining companies operating within the DRC, in an effort to promote gender equality and improved mining standards. Mechanisms to ensure gender is mainstreamed can include monitoring and evaluation practices, consider the gendered implications of mining activities, and recognize the complexity and gendered dimensions of productive roles in the ASM sector. The use of gender equality and women's economic empowerment as key indicators of program success could serve as a starting point for mining companies' commitment to improving the contentious standards of the industry.

- A comprehensive approach to a gender-sensitive lens on ASM must also focus on legal reform and protection for those who face forced relocation or other legal matters stemming from ASM initiatives. Promoting gender equality in legal reform could address some of the gender-based inequalities arising from ASM projects and could ensure adequate compensation for those who may lose land to mining initiatives.

NOTES

1 With the change of government in 2015, the Liberals changed the title of DFATD to Global Affairs Canada (GAC). We refer to the DFATD, as it was the institutional title at the time of collecting data for this chapter.
2 We also consulted the DFATD project database, which turned up similar information to our ATIP request.
3 We chose this time frame particularly because it encompasses the Conservative Party of Canada's mandate at the time of writing this chapter, and also to limit the breadth of our request.
4 Nonetheless, we acknowledge and are grateful for the hard work of DFATD professionals processing our request, given the complexity and diffuse spread of information available.
5 Microcredit programs have remained a contested form of development, often creating shortsighted solutions to larger problems of economic inequality. Although part of the mainstream development agenda, these programs have been critiqued for lack of long-term viability and for imposing debt, among other issues.
6 See: Edward Said, *Orientalism* (London: Penguin Books, 2003).

REFERENCES

Abadie, Delphine. 2011. "Canada and the Geopolitics of Mining Interests: A Case Study of the Democratic Republic of Congo." *Review of African Political Economy* 38, no. 128: 289–302.
Akuffo, Edward. 2012. "A New Love for Africa." *OpenCanada*, 15 October. Accessed 28 December 2014. https://www.opencanada.org/features/a-new-love-for-africa.
BBC News. 2010. "UN Officials Call DR Congo 'Rape Capital of the World.'" 28 April. Accessed 14 November 2014. http://news.bbc.co.uk/2/hi/africa/8650112.stm.
Black, David. 2012. "Between Indifference and Idiosyncrasy: The Conservatives and Canadian Aid to Africa." In *Struggling for Effectiveness: CIDA and Canadian Foreign Aid*, edited by Stephen Brown, 246–68. Montreal and Kingston: McGill-Queen's University Press.

Bosmans, Marleen. 2007. "Challenges in Aid to Rape Victims: The Case of the Democratic Republic of the Congo." *Essex Human Rights Review* 4, no. 1: 1–12.

Bush, Ray. 2008. "Scrambling to the Bottom: Mining, Resources and Underdevelopment." *Review of African Political Economy* 35, no. 117: 361–6.

Business for Social Responsibility (BSR). 2010. *Conflict Minerals and the Democratic Republic of Congo: Responsible Actions in Government Engagement, Supply Chains and Capacity Building.* Business for Social Responsibility, May. Accessed 9 November 2014. http://www.bsr.org/reports/BSR_Conflict_Minerals_and_the_DRC.pdf.

Carment, David, Yiagadeesen Samy, and Joe Landry. 2013. "Transitioning Fragile States: A Sequencing Approach." *Fletcher Forum of World Affairs* 37, no. 2: 125–51.

Carpenter, Charli. 2013. *"Innocent Women and Children": Gender, Norms and the Protection of Civilians.* Aldershot, UK: Ashgate.

Department of Foreign Affairs, Trade and Development (DFATD). 2012. "CIDA's Aid Effectiveness Agenda." Department of Foreign Affairs, Trade and Development. Accessed 4 November 2014. http://www.acdi-cida.gc.ca/acdi-cida/ACDI-CIDA.nsf/eng/CAR-31183317-VMC.

– 2014a. "Where We Work: Democratic Republic of the Congo." Department of Foreign Affairs, Trade and Development. Accessed 22 December 2014. http://www.international.gc.ca/development-developpement/countries-pays/drc-rdc.aspx?lang=eng.

– 2014b. "Canada–Democratic Republic of Congo Relations." Fact sheet. Department of Foreign Affairs, Trade and Development. Accessed 22 December 2014. http://www.canadainternational.gc.ca/congo/bilateral_relations_bilaterales/canada_drc-rdc.aspx?menu_id=7&lang=eng.

– 2014c. "Project Profile: Support to the African Mineral Development Centre." Department of Foreign Affairs, Trade and Development. Accessed 22 December 2014. http://www.acdi-cida.gc.ca/cidaweb/cpo.nsf/projen/A033536001.

– 2014d. "Promoting Gender Equality in the Extractive Sector: A Tool Kit." Draft document. Department of Foreign Affairs, Trade and Development.

Côté, Gisèle Eva. 2014. *Women in the Artisinal Gold Mining Sector in the Democratic Republic of Congo.* Ottawa: Partnership Africa Canada. http://cirdi.ca/wp-content/uploads/2014/01/Women-in-the-Artisanal-Gold-Sector-in-DRC.pdf.

Eftimie, Adriana, Katherine Heller, John Strongman, Jennifer Hinton, Kuntala Lahiri-Dutt, and Nellie Mutemeri. 2012. *Gender Dimensions of Artisanal and Small-Scale Mining: A Rapid Assessment Toolkit.* World Bank. Accessed 14 November 2014. http://siteresources.worldbank.org/INTEXTINDWOM/Resources/Gender_and_ASM_Toolkit.pdf.

Enloe, Cynthia. 2000. *Bananas, Beaches and Bases: Making Feminist Sense of International Politics.* Berkeley and Los Angeles: University of California Press.

Erikkson Baaz, Maria, and Maria Stern. 2012. "Fearless Fighters and Submissive Wives: Negotiating Identity among Women Soldiers in the Congo (DRC)." *Armed Forces and Society* 39, no. 4: 711–39.

Gagnon, Monia. 2009. "Artisanal Diamond Mining and Gender: An Overview." Diamond Development Initiative. Accessed 9 November 2014. http://www. ddiglobal.org/login/resources/ddi-gender-backgrounder-may-2009-en.pdf.

Hayes, Karen. 2008. "Artisanal and Small-Scale Mining and Livelihoods in Africa." Amsterdam: Common Fund for Commodities.

Hayes, Karen, and Rachel Perks. 2012. "Women in the Artisanal and Small-Scale Mining Sector of the Democratic Republic of the Congo." In *High-Value Natural Resources and Peacebuilding*, edited by Päivi Lujala and Siri Aas Rustad. New York: Earthscan.

International Trade Union Confederation (ITUC). 2011. *Violence against Women in Eastern Democratic Republic of Congo: Whose Responsibility? Whose Complicity?* Brussels: International Trade Union Confederation. Accessed 22 December 2014. http://www.ituc-csi.org/IMG/pdf/ituc_violence_rdc_eng_lr.pdf.pdf.

IRIN. 2006. "Rape on the Rise in North Kivu, as Fighting Displaces 70,000." Kinshasa: IRIN, 10 February. http://www.irinnews.org/printreport. aspx?reportid=58097.

Kabamba, Patience. 2010. "Heart of Darkness: Current Images of the DRC and Their Theoretical Underpinning." *Anthropological Theory* 10, no. 3: 265–301.

Lahiri-Dutt, Kuntala, ed. 2011. *Gendering the Field: Towards Sustainable Livelihoods for Mining Communities*. Canberra: ANU E Press. Accessed 7 November 2014. http://www.oapen.org/download?type=document&docid=459251.

Larmer, Miles, Ann Laudati, and John F. Clark. 2013. "Neither War nor Peace in the Democratic Republic of Congo (DRC): Profiting and Coping amid Violence and Disorder." *Review of African Political Economy* 40, no. 135: 1–12.

MacDonald, Laura, and Arne Ruckert. 2013. "Continental Shift? Rethinking Canadian Aid to the Americas." *OpenCanada*, 16 September. Accessed 28 December 2014. http://opencanada.org/features/ continental-shift-rethinking-canadian-aid-to-the-americas.

Mallo, Stephen. 2012. "Mitigating the Activities of Artisanal and Small-Scale Miners in Africa: Challenges for Engineering and Technological Institutions." *International Journal of Modern Engineering Research* 2, no. 6: 4714–25.

Moser, Caroline. 1989. "Gender Planning in the Third World: Meeting Practical and Strategic Needs." *World Development* 17, no. 11: 1799–825.

North-South Institute (NSI). 2012. "Canadian Foreign Aid 2012." Canadian International Development Platform. Accessed 28 December 2014. http://cidpnsi. ca/blog/portfolio/canadas-foreign-aid.

Organization for Economic Cooperation and Development (OECD). 2013. *OECD Due Diligence Guidance for Responsible Supply Chains of Minerals for Conflict-Affected and High-Risk Areas.* 2nd ed. OECD Publishing. Accessed 22 December 2014. http://www.oecd.org/corporate/mne/GuidanceEdition2.pdf.

– 2014. "Aid at a Glance Charts." Organization for Economic Cooperation and Development, 16 December. Accessed 28 December 2014. https://public.tableausoftware.com/views/AidAtAGlance/ DACmembers?:embed=y&:display_count=no?&:showVizHome=no#1.

Palermo, Tia, and Amber Peterman. 2011. "Undercounting, Overcounting and the Longevity of Flawed Estimates: Statistics on Sexual Violence in Conflict." *Bulletin of the World Health Organization*, December. Accessed 14 November 2014. http://www.scielosp.org/scielo. php?pid=S0042-96862011001200017&script=sci_arttext&tlng=es.

Parashar, Swati. 2014. "(En)Gendered Terror: Feminist Approaches to Political Violence." In *The SAGE Handbook of Feminist Theory*, edited by Mary Evans, Clare Hemmings, Marsha Henry, Hazel Johnstone, Sumi Madhok, Ania Plomien, and Sadie Wearing. London: SAGE Publishing.

Perks, Rachel. 2011. "Towards a Post-Conflict Transition: Women and Artisanal Mining in the Democratic Republic of Congo." In *Gendering the Field: Towards Sustainable Livelihoods for Mining in Mining Communities*, edited by Kuntala Lahiri-Dutt. Canberra: Australian National University Press.

Roberts, Adrienne, and Susanne Soederberg. 2012. "Gender Equality as *Smart Economics*? A critique of the 2012 *World Development Report.*" *Third World Quarterly* 3, no. 5: 949–68.

Schippers, Mimi. 2007. "Recovering the Feminine Other: Masculinity, Femininity and Gender Hegemony." *Theory and Society* 36: 85–102.

Schroeder, Emily. 2005. *A Window of Opportunity in the Democratic Republic of the Congo: Incorporating a Gender Perspective in the Disarmament, Demobilization and Reintegration Process.* New York: PeaceWomen. http://www. peacewomen.org/node/89910.

Tegera, Aloys, and Dominic Johnson. 2007. *Rules for Sale: Formal and Informal Cross-Border Trade in Eastern DRC.* Goma: Pole Institute. http://www.pole-institute.org/sites/default/files/regard19_anglais.pdf.

United Nations High Commissioner for Refugees (UNHCR). 2011. *Action Against Sexual and Gender-Based Violence: An Updated Strategy.* UNHCR, Division of International Protection, June. Accessed 4 November 2014. http://www.unhcr. org/4e1d5aba9.pdf.

Chapter 8

Discourse and Whole-of-Government: The Instrumentalization of Gender in the Kandahar Provincial Reconstruction Team

Sarah Tuckey

INTRODUCTION

Speaking about the next phase of official development assistance in Afghanistan in 2010, then minister of international cooperation Bev Oda devoted a substantial portion of her speech to development for women and girls in the country. The speech was largely dedicated to Canada's role in bringing change to Afghanistan, a country known for being embroiled in more than thirty years of bitter conflict and being on the receiving end of near-constant international intervention. Minister Oda highlighted Canada's particular contributions in health care, education, and humanitarian assistance, but the real successes that she showcased were in the substantial increase in girls attending school, women receiving access to microfinance and other loans, and women becoming a part of the political process. In particular, Oda cited Canada's influential role as being behind these successes; indeed, Canada's "continued commitment to advancing the cause of women and girls in Afghanistan would be crucial to ensuring a brighter future for all Afghans."

Similarly, in 2012, foreign affairs minister John Baird and Rona Ambrose, minister for public works and government services and minister for the status of women, issued a statement on the status of women's rights in Afghanistan, noting that "the protection and advancement of women's rights has been, and continues to be, a key pillar of Canada's foreign policy. This is especially true in Afghanistan, where promoting and protecting human rights, including women's rights, is a central theme of Canada's post-2011 engagement" (DFAIT 2012).

This is not the first instance of high-ranking Canadian ministers highlighting the importance of rescuing Afghanistan's women and girls. Research by Claire Turenne-Sjolander and colleagues (see Smith and Turenne-Sjolander 2013, and Turenne-Sjolander and Trevenen 2011) has identified previous occasions where women and girls have figured prominently in public rhetoric surrounding Canadian foreign commitments overseas. Indeed, Oda, Baird, Ambrose, minister for international cooperation Julian Fantino, and Prime Minister Stephen Harper, to name a few, have on numerous occasions made direct reference in speeches to the plight of Afghan women and children in relation to Canadian military, diplomatic, and development intervention. On 13 March 2006, when discussing the humanitarian effort displayed by the Canadian Armed Forces in the country, Harper remarked in an address that "already a great deal has been accomplished. Reconstruction is reducing poverty; millions of people are now able to vote; women are enjoying greater rights and economic opportunities than could have been imagined under the Taliban regime; and of Afghan children who are now in school studying the same things Canadian kids are learning back home."

On 23 May 2007, while speaking to Canadian troops during an official visit to Kandahar Province, Harper presented the positive connection between the plight of Afghan women and children and Canada's involvement much more plainly: "This progress hasn't all been achieved by men and women in uniform. But none of it could have been achieved unless you had put yourselves on the line. Because of you, the people of Afghanistan have seen the institution of democratic elections, the stirring of human rights and freedoms for women, the construction of schools, healthcare facilities and the basic infrastructure of a functional economy." In 2012, during a speech to the Economic Club of Canada, Minister Fantino highlighted a personal, paternal connection to Canada's intervention in Afghanistan: "On a trip to Afghanistan as Associate Minister of Defence, I saw young Afghan girls heading to school, wearing their backpacks. And it reminded me of my own grandchildren. I was impressed then, and I remain so, knowing that these girls were going to school because of the assistance Canada provided."

Successes in Afghanistan for women and children are almost always directly tied to Canada's (deeply paternalistic) involvement. For the Harper Conservatives and their contemporaries, this discursive use of the plight of Afghan women and girls is deliberate and politically charged (Enloe 1990, 2000; Ferguson 2005). As noted by Turenne-Sjolander and

Trevenen (2011, 102–3), Afghan women and children figure prominently within a narrative of Canada as a "good international citizen" and a "protector of the weak," akin to the model of a "stern but righteous father who must protect his family." Mazurana et al. (2005, 21–2) argue that this narrative is not just a common trend, it is also ironic, and dangerous within the post-9/11 context. Through such narratives, "those who have been campaigning for the protection and promotion of women's and girls' human rights and for increased gender awareness in international relations and intervention are now seeing these same agendas manipulated to validate military invasion and occupation" (Mazurana et al. 2005, 21–2). As highlighted by Smith and Turenne-Sjolander (2013), and as demonstrated in the quotes above, many of "the speeches of Stephen Harper are value-laden and replete with constructions of Canada informed by assumptions that are gendered, racialized, and colonial" (xxv). In the context of Canada's intervention in Afghanistan, the narrative of passive women and children in need of assertive, paternalistic protection appears in support of the Canadian whole-of-government (WOG) approach in Kandahar, which aims to first securitize, then democratize and provide development for develop the people of this heavily war-torn, fragile region.

In this chapter, I use a critical feminist theoretical approach, which provides space for analysis via collaborative public management theory to conduct a discourse analysis on the publicly accessible policy documents of the Kandahar Provincial Reconstruction Team (K-PRT). This analysis reveals that the Canadian government has instrumentalized gender equality for military intervention purposes in its WOG approach. This is significant, given that the K-PRT was meant to represent Canada's best example of the WOG approach – an example of joined-up government, under the umbrella of collaborative public management – in its international relations abroad. The *Independent Panel on Canada's Future Role in Afghanistan* (the "Manley Report") (2008) and the fifteen Afghanistan Quarterly Reports to Parliament, released by the Canadian government as the official reports on the successes and failures of the WOG approach in Kandahar, represent the rhetorical presentation of the K-PRT to the Canadian public and the world. A discourse analysis of these documents reveals that Canada's government continues to support rather than transform the current hegemonic,[1] patriarchal, masculine worldview.

This support for the status quo is all the more troubling given the collaborative context within which Canada intervened in Kandahar from 2005 to 2011. The WOG approach called for Canada's development commitments to be accompanied by diplomatic and defence initiatives, as all three branches of governance were considered equally important in the pursuit of Canada's goals in the country. With Canada's development commitments directly tied to diplomacy and defence issues, the government pledged that Canada's work in Afghanistan would be more efficient, and its goals of achieving long-term peace and stability in the region would be reached. Like the merging of the Department of Foreign Affairs and International Trade (DFAIT) the Canadian International Development Agency (CIDA) in 2013, the proposed equal collaboration of many government departments on one large project promised greater efficiency and quicker results (Brown 2015). In theory, the governmental resources for Canada's commitments to gender equality in Afghanistan grew considerably larger.

However, what the Manley Report and the Quarterly Reports reveal in their language is a continued marginalization of gender equality efforts in favour of using women and children to justify increased militarization and securitization of the K-PRT. This argument has been made by other critical feminist scholars in other areas of Canadian foreign policy, such as the Muskoka Initiative on Maternal, Newborn and Child Health put forward by the Harper Conservatives and in Canadian official development assistance (ODA) (Carrier and Tiessen 2013; Swiss 2012). Despite the larger collaborative platform through which transformative gender equality policy and programming could be integrated, in the K-PRT, gender equality remains a political issue of "saving the women and children," and is found only when it supports increased securitization of the Kandahar region.

THE KANDAHAR PROVINCIAL RECONSTRUCTION TEAM: THE MYTH OF WHOLE-OF-GOVERNMENT AND GENDER EQUALITY

In 2005, Canada's development, diplomatic, and defence institutions joined together within the model of a Provincial Reconstruction Team (PRT) in one of the most dangerous regions of Afghanistan. At the time, the K-PRT was one of twenty-five PRTs spread across the different regions and provinces of Afghanistan. PRTs began as a concept devised in late 2001 by the United States to facilitate civil–military cooperation. They were designed to consist of "soldiers, diplomats, and civilian subject-matter experts, working together to extend the authority of the Afghan government by supporting reconstruction efforts" (Holland 2009, 9–10; 2010, 278). A PRT is a unique collaborative entity, as it is commanded by a military officer, usually a lieutenant colonel, and is similarly structured to a military base (Manley et al. 2008, 23; Holland 2010, 278). Despite its military-heavy structure, the K-PRT was intended to be Canada's best test of the WOG approach, and for the Canadian government, when it came to addressing the challenging nature of resolving conflict while simultaneously conducting development work in Afghanistan, the K-PRT presented a welcome opportunity.

With the Canadian Forces (CF) scheduled to rotate out of the military leadership position of the International Security Assistance Force (ISAF) in the summer of 2004, the Liberal government explored a new project for the Canadian military, and "welcomed the idea of NATO expanding the ISAF presence gradually to cover all of Afghanistan, relieving US forces by taking over the PRTs that the United States had established throughout the country" (Marten 2010, 217; Stein and Lang 2007, 132). The operation of a PRT provided Canada with a reason to remain in Afghanistan at a diminished capacity, while continuing to give the CF a large role overall. When Canada elected to take over the K-PRT in 2005, General Rick Hillier, then commander of the CF, commended the Canadian WOG concept, as his vision of the future role of Canada in Afghanistan was "based on the 'three-block war' model developed by US Marine Commandant Gen. Charles Krulak: that peace operations, humanitarian assistance, and combat would from now on be comingled missions existing side by side, block to urban block, in the new threat environment of failed states" (Marten 2010, 218). Thus, spanning a six-year period from 2005 to 2011, Canada's physical location in Afghanistan became centred in the province of Kandahar, at Camp Nathan Smith in Kandahar City, and took a WOG approach within the K-PRT (Holland 2009, 10; Kowaluk and Staples 2009; Stein and Lang 2007).

The unique opportunity of the K-PRT is its potential for increased collaboration among the major Canadian government departments engaged in the theatre of Afghanistan. Theory on collaborative public management approaches suggests that higher levels of cooperation among members increases general public goods and improves the welfare and well-being of large communities (Vigoda and Gilboa 2002, 101). Thus, collaboration such as what is seen in the structure of the K-PRT is "frequently referred to as another mechanism for conflict management" (Vigoda and Gilboa 2002, 101). However, research has shown that with collaboration, "many public managers are both unitary leaders of unitary organizations *and* work with other organizations and with the public through networks. As such, public managers must work with both autonomy and interdependence, and they must be both authoritative and participative" (O'Leary et al. 2009, 12; emphasis in original). Thus, collaborative public management approaches such as the model of the K-PRT may in fact bring about conflict, particularly within highly formal and dependent networks of public managers, as their focus is often spread across a wider array of issues (O'Leary et al. 2009, 12). Theory suggests that this conflict is not inevitable, but it is predictable if it is not properly managed (O'Leary et al. 2009, 12). Collaborative processes such as the WOG approach, therefore, are often prone to conflict due to their more complicated structure.

Yet with this potential for increased collaboration, including heightened communication, greater allocation of resources, and increased variety of personnel on the ground, there is also the potential for a mainstreamed discussion of gender issues across the Department of National Defence (DND), the former DFAIT, the former CIDA, the RCMP, and other major departments working within the K-PRT. As elaborated by Salahub (2006, 2), "Canada's current whole-of-government approach toward fragile states provides a unique opportunity to ensure policy coherence across departments and to continue to demonstrate Canada's leadership on gender equality and women's rights throughout all international policy sectors." Indeed, it has been well documented that a gender-sensitive approach leads to better development, higher security of the population, and stronger diplomatic ventures to ensure a stable democratic government and economy (Mazurana et al. 2005; Paducel and Salahub 2011; Salahub 2006). It is therefore highly logical that the collaborative WOG approach could be coupled with a gender-sensitive approach to continue to improve the Kandahar region. However, others at the now-defunct North-South Institute "demonstrated that these emerging policy frameworks contain few considerations of the gender dimensions of state fragility, or the constraints/opportunities for promoting gender equality in different states of fragility" (Baranyi and Powell 2005a, 3).

Thus, the K-PRT may in fact face conflict due to its very structure, leading to a difficulty in properly accommodating an important gender equality focus, thereby being less efficient and productive on gender issues than promised by both theory and the Canadian government. Indeed, a superficial understanding of gender equality can be seen in the language of the Manley Report and Quarterly Reports. In the section that follows, I conduct a discourse analysis of the above-mentioned documents, using a critical feminist theoretical framework. This discourse analysis reveals that on the surface there is concern for Afghan women and girls, and that overall, the Canadian government makes it clear that gendered issues are funded and that information on such endeavours are made available to the public (see also Swiss and Barry this volume). However, the presentation of gender equality as a benefit of the Canadian WOG approach, in which gender is often only equated with women, is found only when women and children are discussed as passive victims, and only in conjunction with efforts to securitize and militarize Canada's WOG efforts in Kandahar.

DISCOURSE ANALYSIS AND THE WHOLE-OF-GOVERNMENT POLICY DOCUMENTS

Using a discourse analysis informed by critical feminist theory will bring information to light that cannot be gleaned directly from the language in each of these reports. This form of discourse analysis follows from feminist post-structural and postmodern theory, which have "contributed the view that language and discourse are powerful in shaping reality and defining political interests" (McKeen 2001, 38; see also Ferguson 2005, 13). Furthermore, feminist theory identifies that political discourses are borne by institutions of hegemonic masculinity, in which male bodies have historically and continually dominated and in which a particular form of masculinity has become the norm, and thus that any analysis should be conducted "through the deconstruction of the texts and discourses emerging from these institutions, sometimes 'reading' what is not written, or what is 'between the lines,' or what is expressed as symbols and in procedures" (Kronsell 2006, 108–9). Finally, critical feminist theory values the good that can be achieved from collaboration, thus providing an avenue through which to critique the theoretical appeal of the WOG approach. By taking a critical feminist lens as the basis for a discourse analysis of the reports, this chapter provides further insight into what the Canadian government is saying about gender equality when it discusses women and men in the WOG approach in Kandahar.

The Manley Report and the Afghanistan Quarterly Reports to Parliament present a unique pool of written public resources for a critical discourse analysis of the K-PRT. The Manley Report, commissioned by the Conservative Canadian government in the fall of 2007, marked a turning point in Canada's WOG approach in Afghanistan. As accounted by Baranyi and Paducel (2012, 112):

> In 2007–08 the war continued to escalate, placing the government
> of Canada's policies under increased public scrutiny. Prime Minister
> Stephen Harper responded by convening an independent panel,
> led by John Manley, a prominent Liberal politician. In early 2008
> Harper instructed officials to implement the Manley Report's central
> recommendation: that Canada should more closely integrate its
> WOG resources in Afghanistan, particularly by redirecting at least 50

per cent of Canada's development assistance to Kandahar to support the almost 3,000 Canadian military personnel there.

Thus, in the pivotal year 2007, roughly halfway through Canada's WOG commitment in Kandahar, funds earmarked for development became redefined as security funds. Indeed, data collected by Baranyi and Paducel (2012, 112–13) "suggests that Canada spent about $9 billion in Afghanistan from 2005 to 2010, of which about $7.8 billion (87 per cent) went to military operations via the Department of National Defence (DND) and only $1.23 billion (13 per cent) to humanitarian and development via CIDA and OGDs [other government departments]." As well, the projects that this money supported bypassed many Afghan state institutions in an attempt to put a Canadian stamp on development in Kandahar and "win the hearts and minds" of local Afghans, resulting in an undermining of the legitimacy of the Afghan state and its ability to deliver core public services to its population (Banerjee 2009, 2010, 2011, 2012; Baranyi and Paducel 2012, 114). For a process that is theoretically considered to be horizontally balanced and holistically inclusive, these highly skewed numbers present a far less balanced picture of Canada's WOG approach.

Analyzing the text of the Manley Report itself, there is an imbalance regarding the limited space the document gives to a discussion of gender equality. Moreover, where that discussion is found, it is connected solely with Afghan women, and with the need to increase military spending and presence in order to protect them. Indeed, the report highlights a speech made by Harper in 2007, in which he states plainly that "there can be no progress in Afghanistan without security – the security provided by the sacrifice and determination of our men and women in uniform ... Without security, development workers cannot provide reconstruction or humanitarian assistance; police and corrections officers cannot ensure justice and peace; diplomats cannot help build democracy and enhance human rights" (Harper 2007, cited in Manley et al. 2008, 53). The collaborative aspect of the Canadian WOG approach in the K-PRT is clearly intended to favour military intervention first and foremost. In the section entitled "Security," the report highlights the deplorable treatment of Afghan women by the Taliban, connecting the emphasized importance of security with the need to address women's issues in the country (Manley et al. 2008, 12).

After the Manley Report, the Quarterly Reports were the Canadian government's opportunity to present to parliament, and the Canadian public at large, their perspective on the objectives and projects of the K-PRT, including the three signature projects and the six priorities for

Afghanistan. Like the Manley Report, in the Quarterly Reports the Canadian government made it clear that any WOG collaboration in Afghanistan required securing the area first and foremost. Indeed, the February 2007 report highlighted that "the challenges in Afghanistan are complex and diverse. The security situation will continue to be challenging. Political, social and economic development will be difficult until there is more stability and security" (Government of Canada 2007, 5). The report further highlights that "Canada's objectives – like those of the Afghan government and our international partners – are focused firmly on the longer term and the future. We believe in the Afghan people and in their desire to have a country where security, development and good governance replace the chaos, violence and destitution of the past" (Government of Canada 2007, 5). This dedication to the Afghan people, however, is underscored by the security threat Afghanistan poses to Canada and its allies, and how this threat effects and is received by Canada itself. Securing and developing Afghanistan is not simply an altruistic "humane internationalist" mission by Canada, but an assurance that inhabitants of Afghanistan will not return to countries in the West with acts of terrorism (Black 2014). The report stresses its obligation in this regard: "we have a responsibility to inform Canadians – those who serve on the front lines in Afghanistan, who establish the security and provide aid and development assistance, and the Canadian public at large – of the results of our military, diplomatic, development and reconstruction efforts. Canadians want to know whether there is progress being made and how we measure that progress. They have a right to know" (Government of Canada 2007, 5–6).

This positionality is interesting, as it is understood from previous critical feminist research on this topic that Canada has placed itself in a paternalistic, patriarchal relationship with Afghanistan (Turenne-Sjolander 2013; Turenne-Sjolander and Trevenen 2011). Beyond Canada's commitments to the K-PRT and the people of Afghanistan, is Canada's promise to its Western allies that it would do its part to protect the world from these barbaric "others" who dwell in this conflict-ridden part of the world (Turenne-Sjolander 2013). Turenne-Sjolander (2013, 249) has identified this Othering of the Afghan people in many of Harper's speeches, noting that "through these portrayals, Afghan women and children have no agency; they are constructed as backward and subjugated, in need of rescue from Canadian (Western) men." This conceptualization, first identified by Chandra Mohanty in 1984, also brings to light the Western world's patronizing view of the "Third World" as a place of ignorant, poor, uneducated, tradition-bound, domestic, family-oriented, victimized women, who are seen in opposition to the educated, independent, and empowered Western woman (Turenne-Sjolander 2013, 249). This understanding naturally requires that men in the Third World, and in Afghanistan, be "consistently painted as devoid of humanity and, as a result, as somehow subhuman, or even non-human. They stand as the antithesis of progress and development (at least, as these are defined in Canada and the West)" (Turenne-Sjolander 2013, 250). Throughout the reports, this is where Canada makes the connection to gender, or more specifically to the victimhood of Afghan women and children, regarding its WOG role in Kandahar.

Liam Swiss (2012, 135) argues that there has been a "securitization" of Canadian aid, and that "it has been conducted at the expense of other development objectives in Canada's aid program, including its nearly thirty-five-year focus on women's rights and gender equality." In discussing the work of Canada's WOG approach as seen in the K-PRT, the 2007 report makes clear the necessity of the large amount of military troops stationed in Kandahar to protect the program:

> The environment in which our troops and personnel are working is extremely difficult and dangerous. The insurgents, with their methods of violence and terror, are present throughout the area. They seek ruthlessly and relentlessly to disrupt all efforts toward achieving normalcy and progress. They do this through violence and intimidation, including by attacking Afghan government officials, labourers, teachers, women and children. (Government of Canada 2007, 8)

Furthermore, subsequent reports highlight an ever-expanding presence of foreign troops in the region (Government of Canada 2009b). Discussion of gender is relegated to the victimized bodies of Afghanistan's women and children. Moreover, the mention of government officials, labourers, and teachers alongside this distinction suggests that Afghan women cannot be expected to hold any of these positions. From this reading, it is apparent that Canada's WOG approach in Kandahar was to rescue and protect what it considered to be the vulnerable and helpless female and youth demographics. In the September 2008 report, the Canadian government stated this explicitly as part of its list of priorities and benchmarks through to 2011 and the end of Canada's command of the K-PRT. Under the priority in which Canada pledges to "provide humanitarian assistance for extremely vulnerable people, including refugees, returnees and internally displaced persons," Afghan women are singled out as among those with the most chronic disadvantages (Government of Canada 2008b, 6).

Yet in both the Manley Report and the Quarterly Reports, Canada commends itself for helping to increase the roles that women and girls play in Afghan society (Manley et al. 2008, 25; Government of Canada 2007, 14). For example, mention is made of Canada's support of the National Solidarity Program (NSP), which was developed by the Afghan government to promote rural development and improved governance in the difficult to control southern provinces, where Kandahar is located (Government of Canada 2007, 13). The discourse surrounding this program is vague at best, but the report does make mention of women as community leaders within the NSP. They are mentioned as sitting on community development councils throughout the country, yet despite testimony in the March 2011 report that women and men have been found to be on equal footing through the NSP (Government of Canada 2011a, 11), there is no clear indication if any Afghan women have had or continue to have central roles in the province of Kandahar, or if their roles held or hold any significant power within such community councils. A 2010 report mentions a record number of women candidates – 69 – being voted into the Afghan parliament – however, despite mentioning that over 400 women competed for such seats, no conclusive numbers of successful candidates representing Kandahar have been publicly released by the Conservative government (Government of Canada 2010c, 2010d).

The reports also make reference to Canada's efforts to ensure that women are enrolled as voters for Afghanistan's democratic elections process – another aspect of Canada's priority to ensure an improvement in governance and democratic institutions in the nation. The December 2008 report stated that Canada's quarterly result on this priority saw that "over 3.2 million eligible voters had been registered under phases I–III (October–December), approximately 40% of whom were women," with the 2011 targets being a 70 per cent voter turnout for men and a 40 per cent voter turnout for women (Government of Canada 2008c, 25–6). The March 2009 report, however, dropped the percentage of women voters to 38 per cent (Government of Canada 2009a, 10). Concerns were raised in later Quarterly Reports regarding the apparent regression of certain Afghan laws repealing the internationally recognized human rights of women, and greater attention was paid to the rule of law in order to guarantee women's participation in democratic governance (Government of Canada 2009a, 2009d, 2010a). Indeed, Canada made renewed financial commitments to strengthen Afghanistan's rule of law, including improving the prisons in Kandahar.

An increase in spending on military and security measures accompanied these commitments, highlighting how this aspect of the WOG approach was prioritized in the province. The March 2009 report explicitly stated that "improving the rule of law means improving police and prisons. More than that, it means improving Afghanistan's justice system with more capable judges and lawyers. It means suppressing corruption. And it means enabling the greater exercise of human rights – including the rights of women and girls" (Government of Canada 2009a, 2). As was demonstrated by Swiss (2012) regarding gender equality in Afghanistan and by Carrier and Tiessen (2013) regarding the Conservative harnessing of the Muskoka Initiative, this statement in the report underscores the use of gender equality, specifically the rights of women and girls, as a policy instrument to justify the increase in spending on military and security measures in Kandahar. From a critical feminist perspective, this sort of reasoning displayed by the Conservative government to the Canadian public is meant to create a direct and positive connection between militarization and securitization and the human rights of Afghan women and girls.

Much is praised in the reports surrounding Canada's WOG work on illiteracy in the Kandahar region, particularly among women and children. The June 2008 report highlights that school enrolment for children in Afghanistan overall has increased from fewer than one million pupils to almost six million, with a third of those pupils being girls (Government of Canada 2008a, 5). The report claims that "the reintroduction of girls into the formal school system will help break the cycle of illiteracy among Afghan women, resulting in numerous positive effects in all facets of life in Afghanistan for generations to come" (Government of Canada 2008a, 5–6). In Kandahar specifically, the report highlights that scarcely 5 per cent of women in the region can read, in comparison to 26 per cent for Kandahari men (Government of Canada 2008a, 11). As part of the second signature project, in which Canada pledged to build and repair fifty schools in the Kandahar region, significant plans are highlighted to increase women's literacy rates and conduct teacher training for women (Government of Canada 2008c, 7; 2009a, 7–8). During the last quarter of 2008, the Canadian government highlighted an increase in intensive vocational and literacy training in the region, with "some 10,949 adults, including 8,984 women, preparing to complete a 10-month literacy course in January 2009" (Government of Canada 2008c, 7). Yet despite the positive gains for young women and girls in Afghanistan, some reservation and skepticism regarding Canada's motives for reporting these improvements remains.

This skepticism is given merit when the types of literacy programs Canada has elected to support are considered from a critical feminist and collaborative theory position. For example, in the June 2009 report, the Canadian government highlights that progress was made in "literacy training for Afghan National Police; vocational training; and approval of a \$1.5-million skills-for-employment project at the Kandahar Technical School, an initiative to develop market-relevant skills among young men and women" (Government of Canada 2009b, 6). As part of the signature projects, most of Canada's money continued to go to building and repairing the pledged fifty schools, but a good portion of the allocated funds also went to the Afghan National Police, a security-based and military-trained Afghan institution. Any additional funds for women were mentioned as an addition, although they were present nonetheless. Later in 2009, the Canadian government reported increased funding for the creation and training of a new group of women officers to guard female inmates at Kandahar City's Sarpoza prison (Government of Canada 2009c, 7). As noted by Swiss (2012) and identified in the priorities examined above, the transition towards increased military-related spending can be seen in the expanding efforts to uphold the rule of law in places one would least expect it to be funded – in literacy programs and in programs for improving the livelihoods of women.

The reports also make reference to the strides Canada has taken to ensure child and maternal health rates improve in the country. Carrier and Tiessen (2013, 186) discuss the importance that the Harper government has placed on this in the Muskoka Initiative, noting that it "focused primarily on women in their role of mothers and on the necessity of 'saving' them." Evidence of this same treatment of women is seen in the Quarterly Reports. For example, in the September 2008 report, focus is paid to preparing for a severe winter and anticipated floods in the southern region of Afghanistan in 2008 and 2009. As part of this preparation, the report highlights that "approximately 3,800 families are targeted in Kandahar, along with 9,000 children under the age of five and 4,500 pregnant and lactating women" (Government of Canada 2008b, 20). Moreover, within Canada's humanitarian assistance goals, measles and tetanus vaccinations for Kandahari women and children are emphasized (Government of Canada 2008a, 12). From a critical feminist perspective, research shows that this essentialized view of women as "pregnant and lactating" is not surprising. Indeed, as Carrier and Tiessen (2013, 184) note, "Canadian internationalism under the Harper government is predicated on a view of women as mothers and caregivers in need of rescuing, as opposed to individuals with agency who are defined by much more than their reproductive capacity." Throughout the many Quarterly Reports available to the public, this perspective on women as "pregnant and lactating" or "giving birth" is demonstrated numerous times.

For example, in the December 2008 report, the Canadian government again highlights the victimized and essentialized nature of Afghan women and girls, and Canada's role in protecting their bodies from harm, stating:

> Women and girls comprise the largest category of vulnerable people in Afghanistan, facing barriers to education, health care and other necessary services. In Kandahar City, Canadian funded construction of an obstetrical unit at Mirwais Hospital was completed in the quarter. The first facility of its kind in all of Afghanistan, this project is part of an Afghan government initiative to increase the numbers of women giving birth with the aid of trained birth attendants. This facility is expected to receive 1,000 patients every year. Canada is also supporting renovation of the hospital's female surgical wing and operating theatre. (Government of Canada 2008c, 9)

This statement makes it clear that the government's proclaimed dedication of resources to Afghan women and girls in Kandahar remains primarily focused on them as mothers and caregivers, and as vessels of reproductive capability. This trend continues into 2010, with the mid-year report highlighting a health program funded by Canada entitled the Emergency Micronutrient Initiative, which aimed "to reduce nutritional deficiencies and health complications among pregnant women and children under the age of five: 140,000 children received packets of multiple micronutrient powders, while 78,000 pregnant or lactating women received iron and folic acid supplements" (Government of Canada 2010b, 1). There is no clear indication in any of the reports if there are any dedicated health programs for women beyond those solely for reproductive health.

CONCLUSION

In 2009, in a speech given on a panel regarding the future of Afghanistan at the Munich Security Conference, minister of national defence Peter MacKay had this to say about Canada's WOG approach in Afghanistan:

> Canada has been on the leading edge of putting into practise what NATO has come to call the "Comprehensive Approach." This is something I've been engaged on since I was Foreign Minister and, now, as Defence Minister. I strongly support the "comprehensive approach." But I'd like to suggest that this is really nothing more than what I would call a "Common Sense Approach." If we have learned nothing else from conflicts around the world – whether

Afghanistan, the Middle East, Africa – we must have learned that security is the necessary precursor for sustainable development; democratic governance and prosperity. But military and civilian efforts must be integrated. There is no military solution to the insurgency in Afghanistan – any more than there is elsewhere.

Military engagement is simply not sufficient in and of itself. Long term security cannot exist in the absence of justice and prosperity. And this isn't sophisticated strategic doctrine. It is common political and human sense that tells us that people in war torn, fragile, disintegrating or disintegrated societies want stability; want good governance from their leadership; want their dignity; and, frankly, want hope.

What's my take-away from this experience? If we don't go comprehensive – with an integrated civ/mil, multi-national, and multi-organizational approach, and all that means in terms of building, rebuilding and restoring governance, prosperity and hope – we put our mission fundamentally at risk and we should seriously consider whether we go at all. (Wells 2009)

For the Canadian government, intervention in Afghanistan cannot happen without military involvement, and yet at the same time, Canada cannot expect improvement without civilian integration in the form of diplomatic and development assistance. Yet this chapter has demonstrated that MacKay and his contemporaries often fail to mention the critical role a gender equality approach can play when presented with the opportunity to apply it across such a "comprehensive" foreign policy playing field. If gender is mentioned at all, it is relegated to issues facing "women" or "women and children" only. What is more, it is clear that in such contexts, women and children have been instrumentalized to condone the emphasis on security and military intervention within the collaborative intentions of the K-PRT.

What the language and recommendations of the Manley Report and the Quarterly Reports demonstrate to the Canadian public is that the Canadian government continues to regard Afghan women and girls as passive victims of circumstance, and considers the collaborative benefits of a mainstreamed gender equality discussion of little importance. The victimized women come to represent hope within a war-ravaged nation, and women who must be protected and saved at all costs, if not for their own well-being than for their reproductive potential. By looking at public government documents through a discourse analysis informed by critical feminist theory, it is clear that gender was instrumentalized for the purpose of maintaining a heightened military presence and focus within the K-PRT, and that gender equality was not encouraged intrinsically, but used rather to present Canada as the patriarchal saviour of Afghanistan's vulnerable women and youth. The language of these documents reveals the Canadian government's continued support of the instrumentalization of gender, despite the potential within the collaborative aims of the WOG approach for increased prioritization of gender equality.

There are opportunities to shift this kind of thinking, and present some long-term policy recommendations to Canada's future governments regarding the commitment to gender equality in WOG intervention. As was noted at the outset of this chapter, an increase in capacity, resources, and communication through a WOG approach allows for an increased ability to mainstream a gender equality perspective. Theoretically, opportunities exist for greater communication and collaboration across departments on critical social issues, such as gender equality and the issue of entrenched and hegemonic patriarchal norms. Approaching gender equality policies in joined-up government efforts requires an expert leadership with an invested interest in achieving real gendered change, using the experiences and reports generated from other successful examples of gender equality work in WOG approaches, such as in Haiti (Baranyi and Paducel 2012; see also Baranyi and Binette, this volume). Previous research by Baranyi (2011), as highlighted in Baranyi and Paducel (2012, 118), indicates that Canada, through the former CIDA, has nurtured societal democratic growth through modest support to women's organizations and civil society organizations.

However, transformational change cannot come through a quick fix, and can only be achieved via concerted educational efforts and long-term governmental commitments. The concepts of patriarchy and hegemonic masculinity are profoundly anchored in processes of socialization, therefore the response to these antiquated ideas must be equally thorough. Ultimately, policy must commit to creating new ways of socialization, and this is no easy task. Within the right context, using collaborative networks of experts, such as academics, NGOs, civil society organizations, and grassroots women's organizations, as in the case of Haiti, can bring about a greater understanding of the causes of gender inequality, and may increase awareness and support for programs that promote more transformative approaches to gender equality. Moreover, using groups with different perspectives allows for an intersectional analysis; as noted by Stienstra (in this volume), "intersectionality-based policy analysis encourages us to leave open the categories of analysis, rather than to assume that one set of power relations, such as gender, is the primary set of inequalities, both present and to be explained." If Canada were to invest resources into supporting such collaborative intersectional connections, a mainstreaming of transformational gender equality perspectives into policy could be possible.

Concrete policy recommendations for Canada's WOG approach and the integration of gender equality must therefore start with an idea that is neither new nor innovative, but that often gets lost: the push for mandatory gender experts at every policy table and every program meeting. Moreover, equal collaboration among the various government departments should be considered compulsory. For true collaboration to take place, this must be enforced at the highest levels of government, namely the ministerial level, as well as politically emphasized at the prime ministerial level. For gender equality issues to take centre stage within the Canadian WOG approach, gender experts must be present at all times, and must not be marginal to the conversation. In this way, a true and genuine understanding of what gender means can be mainstreamed throughout the vested government departments. Gender equality concepts, terms, and mainstreaming approaches must be taught and enforced, from the ministerial level down, in order to reach a common understanding across the collaborative organizations. To this end, the expertise of gender-focused NGOs, civil society organizations, and academics can be harnessed to foster a deeper understanding of the connection between effective collaboration and gender equality in Canadian foreign policy endeavours.

Government commitment to revitalizing and supporting gender equality networks within Canadian civil society is an essential part of that strategy (such as the North-South Institute, or the Women, Peace and Security Network – Canada). It is equally important for the Canadian government to support the placement of gender experts in all areas and at all levels of the WOG approach. Ultimately, policy that harnesses the education and advocacy of actors invested in the Canadian WOG approach, and introduces a fundamental shift in the behaviour of the Canadian government towards gender equality, will tip the scales in favour of governance that values a transformational understanding of gender as being more than about women and girls alone.

NOTES

1 Hegemonic masculinity refers to the powerful role that certain forms of masculinity wield in a gender-hierarchical society. Masculinity theory, as informed by critical feminist perspectives, understands masculinity and femininity as separate from the corporeal bodies they are assumed to be naturally

attached to (Parpart and Zalewski 2008, 11). R.W. Connell (1987; 1995; 2005) argues that although there can be multiple forms of masculinity and femininity underlying the concept of gender and the struggle for power that one singular form of these has over all others, there can be no corresponding form of hegemonic femininity: all forms of femininity are in some ways subordinate (Whitworth 2004; Parpart and Zalewski 2008, 11).

REFERENCES

Banerjee, Nipa. 2009. "Afghanistan: No Security, No Governance." *Policy Options*, November.
– 2010. "Aid Development for a Secure Afghanistan." *Policy Options*, November.
– 2011. "Letter from Kabul." *Policy Options*, April.
– 2012. "Aid and Keeping Hope Alive in Afghanistan." *Policy Options*, April.
Baranyi, Stephen. 2011. "Canada and the Travail of Partnership in Haiti." In *Fixing Haiti: MINUSTAH and Beyond*, edited by Andrew Thompson and Jorge Heine, 205–28. Tokyo and New York: United Nations University Press.
Baranyi, Stephen, and Anca Paducel. 2012. "Whither Development in Canada's Approach toward Fragile States?" In *Struggling for Effectiveness: CIDA and Canadian Foreign Aid*, edited by Stephen Brown, 108–34. Montreal and Kingston: McGill-Queen's University Press.
Baranyi, Stephen, and Kristiana Powell. 2005a. *Bringing Gender Back into Canada's Engagement in Fragile States: Options for CIDA in a Whole-of-Government Approach*. Ottawa: North-South Institute.
– 2005b. *Fragile States, Gender Equality and Aid Effectiveness: A Review of Donor Perspectives*. Ottawa: North-South Institute.
Black, David. 2014. "Humane Internationalism and the Malaise of Canadian Aid Policy." In *Rethinking Canadian Aid*, edited by Stephen Brown, Molly den Heyer, and David Black, 17–33. Ottawa: University of Ottawa Press.
Brown, Stephen. 2015. "15 Proposals for Canadian Foreign Aid." *CIPS Blog*, Ottawa: Centre for International Policy Studies, 11 January. http://cips. uottawa.ca/15-proposals-for-canadian-foreign-aid.
Carrier, Krystel, and Rebecca Tiessen. 2013. "Women and Children First: Maternal Health and the Silencing of Gender in Canadian Foreign Policy." In *Canada in the World: Internationalism in Canadian Foreign Policy*, edited by Heather Smith and Claire Turenne-Sjolander, 183–200. Don Mills, ON: Oxford University Press.
Connell, R.W. 1987. *Gender and Power: Society, the Person, and Sexual Politics*. Stanford: Stanford University Press.
– 1995. *Masculinities*. Berkeley: University of California Press.
– 2005. *Masculinities*. 2nd ed. Berkeley: University of California Press.

Department of Foreign Affairs, Trade and Development (DFATD). 2014. "History of Canada's Engagement in Afghanistan 2001–2014." Department of Foreign Affairs, Trade and Development. http://www.international.gc.ca/afghanistan/history-histoire.aspx?lang=eng.

Enloe, Cynthia. 1990. *Bananas, Beaches and Bases: Making Feminist Sense of International Politics*. Berkeley: University of California Press.

– 2000. *Maneuvers: The International Politics of Militarizing Women's Lives*. Berkeley: University of California Press.

Ferguson, Michaele. 2005. "'W' Stands for Women: Feminism and Security Rhetoric in the Post-9/11 Bush Administration." *Politics and Gender* 1, no. 1: 9–38.

Government of Canada. 2007. *Canada's Mission in Afghanistan: Measuring Progress*. Report to Parliament, February. http://epe.lac-bac.gc.ca/100/205/301/afghanistan/www.afghanistan.gc.ca/canada-afghanistan/assets/pdfs/260207_report_e.pdf.

– 2008a. *Canada's Engagement in Afghanistan: Setting a Course to 2011; Report to Parliament, June 2008*. Ottawa: Library and Archives Canada Cataloguing in Publication. http://epe.lac-bac.gc.ca/100/205/301/afghanistan/www.afghanistan.gc.ca/canada-afghanistan/documents/q108/index.aspx.htm.

– 2008b. *Canada's Engagement in Afghanistan, Report to Parliament, September 2008*. Ottawa: Library and Archives Canada Cataloguing in Publication. http://epe.lac-bac.gc.ca/100/205/301/afghanistan/www.afghanistan.gc.ca/canada-afghanistan/documents/r11_08/index.aspx.htm.

– 2008c. *Canada's Engagement in Afghanistan, Report to Parliament, December 2008*. Ottawa: Library and Archives Canada Cataloguing in Publication. http://epe.lac-bac.gc.ca/100/205/301/afghanistan/www.afghanistan.gc.ca/canada-afghanistan/documents/r02_09/index.aspx.htm.

– 2009a. *Canada's Engagement in Afghanistan: Report to Parliament, March 2009*. Ottawa: Library and Archives Canada Cataloguing in Publication. http://epe.lac-bac.gc.ca/100/205/301/afghanistan/www.afghanistan.gc.ca/canada-afghanistan/documents/r03_09/index.aspx.htm.

– 2009b. *Canada's Engagement in Afghanistan: Report to Parliament, June 2009*. Ottawa: Library and Archives Canada Cataloguing in Publication. http://epe.lac-bac.gc.ca/100/205/301/afghanistan/www.afghanistan.gc.ca/canada-afghanistan/documents/r06_09/index.aspx.htm.

– 2009c. *Canada's Engagement in Afghanistan: Quarterly Report to Parliament for the Period of July 1 to September 30, 2009*. Ottawa: Library and Archives Canada Cataloguing in Publication. http://epe.lac-bac.gc.ca/100/205/301/afghanistan/www.afghanistan.gc.ca/canada-afghanistan/documents/r09_09/index.aspx.htm.

– 2009d. *Canada's Engagement in Afghanistan: Quarterly Report to Parliament for the Period of October 1 to December 31, 2009*. Ottawa: Library and Archives

Canada Cataloguing in Publication. http://epe.lac-bac.gc.ca/100/205/301/afghanistan/www.afghanistan.gc.ca/canada-afghanistan/documents/r12_09/index.aspx.htm.

– 2010a. *Canada's Engagement in Afghanistan: Quarterly Report to Parliament for the Period of January 1 to March 31, 2010*. Ottawa: Library and Archives Canada Cataloguing in Publication. http://epe.lac-bac.gc.ca/100/205/301/afghanistan/www.afghanistan.gc.ca/canada-afghanistan/documents/r01_10/index.aspx.htm.

– 2010b. *Canada's Engagement in Afghanistan: Quarterly Report to Parliament for the Period of April 1 to June 30, 2010*. Ottawa: Library and Archives Canada Cataloguing in Publication. http://epe.lac-bac.gc.ca/100/205/301/afghanistan/www.afghanistan.gc.ca/canada-afghanistan/documents/r06_10/index.aspx.htm.

– 2010c. *Canada's Engagement in Afghanistan: Quarterly Report to Parliament for the Period of July 1 to September 30, 2010*. Ottawa: Library and Archives Canada Cataloguing in Publication. http://epe.lac-bac.gc.ca/100/205/301/afghanistan/www.afghanistan.gc.ca/canada-afghanistan/documents/r09_10/index.aspx.htm.

– 2010d. *Canada's Engagement in Afghanistan: Quarterly Report to Parliament for the Period of October 1 to December 31, 2010*. Ottawa: Library and Archives Canada Cataloguing in Publication. http://epe.lac-bac.gc.ca/100/205/301/afghanistan/www.afghanistan.gc.ca/canada-afghanistan/documents/r12_10/index.aspxlangeng.htm.

– 2011a. *Canada's Engagement in Afghanistan: Quarterly Report to Parliament for the Period of January 1 to March 31, 2011*. Ottawa: Library and Archives Canada Cataloguing in Publication. http://epe.lac-bac.gc.ca/100/205/301/afghanistan/www.afghanistan.gc.ca/canada-afghanistan/documents/r03_11/index.aspxlangeng.htm.

– 2011b. *Canada's Engagement in Afghanistan: Quarterly Report to Parliament for the Period of April 1 to June 30, 2011*. Ottawa: Library and Archives Canada Cataloguing in Publication. http://epe.lac-bac.gc.ca/100/205/301/afghanistan/www.afghanistan.gc.ca/canada-afghanistan/documents/r06_11/index.aspxlangeng.htm.

– 2011c. *Canada's Engagement in Afghanistan: Fourteenth and Final Report to Parliament*. Ottawa: Library and Archives Canada Cataloguing in Publication. http://epe.lac-bac.gc.ca/100/205/301/afghanistan/www.afghanistan.gc.ca/canada-afghanistan/documents/r06_12/index.aspxlangeng.htm.

Holland, Kenneth. 2009. *Canadian–United States Engagement in Afghanistan: An Analysis of the "Whole of Government" Approach*. Ottawa: Pearson Peacekeeping Centre.

– 2010. "The Canadian Provincial Reconstruction Team: The Arm of Development in Kandahar Province." *American Review of Canadian Studies* 40, no. 2: 276–91.

Kowaluk, Lucia, and Steven Staples, eds. 2009. *Afghanistan and Canada: Is There an Alternative to War?* Montreal: Black Rose Books.

Kronsell, Annica. 2006. "Methods for Studying Silences: Gender Analysis in Institutions of Hegemonic Masculinity." In *Feminist Methodologies for International Relations*, edited by Brooke Ackerly, Maria Stern, and Jacqui True. Cambridge: Cambridge University Press.

Mamuji, Aaida. 2012. "Canadian Military Involvement in Humanitarian Assistance: Progress and Prudence in Natural Disaster Response." *Canadian Foreign Policy Journal* 18, no. 2: 208–24.

Manley, John, Derek Burney, Jake Epp, Paul Tellier, and Pamela Wallin. 2008. *Independent Panel on Canada's Future Role in Afghanistan.* Ottawa: Government of Canada.

Marten, Kimberly. 2010. "From Kabul to Kandahar: The Canadian Forces and Change." *American Review of Canadian Studies* 40, no. 2: 214–36.

Mazurana, Dyan, Angela Raven-Roberts, Jane Parpart, and Sue Lautze. 2005. "Introduction: Gender, Conflict, and Peacekeeping." In *Gender, Conflict, and Peacekeeping*, edited by Dyan Mazurana, Angela Raven-Roberts, and Jane Parpart, 1–26. Oxford: Rowman and Littlefield.

McKeen, Wendy. 2001. "The Shaping of Political Agency: Feminism and the National Social Policy Debate, the 1970s and Early 1980s." *Studies in Political Economy* 66: 37–58.

O'Leary, Rosemary, Beth Gazley, Michael McGuire, and Lisa Blomgren Bingham. 2009. "Public Managers in Collaboration." In *The Collaborative Public Manager: New Ideas for the Twenty-First Century*, edited by O'Leary, Rosemary, and Lisa Blomgren Bingham. Washington, DC: Georgetown University Press.

Paducel, Anca, and Jennifer Salahub. 2011. *Gender Equality and Fragile States Policies and Programming: A Comparative Study of the OECD/DAC and Six OECD Donors.* Ottawa: North-South Institute.

Parpart, Jane, and Marysia Zalewski. 2008. *Rethinking the Man Question: Sex, Gender and Violence in International Relations.* London and New York: Zed Books.

Patrick, Stewart, and Kaysie Brown. 2007. *Greater than the Sum of Its Parts? Assessing "Whole of Government" Approaches to Fragile States.* New York: International Peace Academy.

Peterson, Spike, and Anne Sisson Runyan. 2010. *Global Gender Issues in the New Millennium.* 3rd ed. Boulder, CO: Westview Press.

Salahub, Jennifer. 2006. *Canada's Whole-of-Government Approach to Fragile States: The Challenge of Gender Equality.* Ottawa: North-South Institute.

Smith, Heather, and Claire Turenne-Sjolander. 2013. "Introduction: Conversations without Consensus: Internationalism under the Harper Government." In *Canada in the World: Internationalism in Canadian Foreign Policy*, edited by

Heather Smith and Claire Turenne-Sjolander, i–xxvii. Don Mills, ON: Oxford University Press.

Stein, Janice Gross, and Eugene Lang. 2007. *The Unexpected War: Canada in Kandahar*. Toronto: Penguin Group.

Swiss, Liam. 2012. "Gender, Security, and Instrumentalism: Canada's Foreign Aid in Support of National Interest?" In *Struggling for Effectiveness: CIDA and Canadian Foreign Aid*, edited by Stephen Brown, 135–58. Montreal and Kingston: McGill-Queen's University Press.

Travers, Patrick, and Taylor Owen. 2008. "Between Metaphor and Strategy: Canada's Integrated Approach to Peacebuilding in Afghanistan." *International Journal* 63, no. 3: 685–702.

Turenne-Sjolander, Claire. 2013. "Canada and the Afghan 'Other': Identity, Difference, and Foreign Policy." In *Canada in the World: Internationalism in Canadian Foreign Policy*, edited by Heather Smith and Claire Turenne-Sjolander, 238–54. Don Mills, ON: Oxford University Press.

Turenne-Sjolander, Claire, and Kathryn Trevenen. 2011. "Constructing Canadian Foreign Policy: Myths of Good International Citizens, Protectors, and the War in Afghanistan." In *Readings in Canadian Foreign Policy: Classic Debates and New Ideas*, edited by Duane Bratt and Christopher Kukucha. 2nd ed. Toronto: Oxford University Press.

Vigoda, Eran, and Etai Gilboa. 2002. "The Quest for Collaboration: Toward a Comprehensive Strategy for Public Administration." In *Public Administration: An Interdisciplinary Critical Analysis*, edited by Eran Vigoda, 99–117. New York: Marcel Dekker.

Wells, Paul. 2009. "Verbatim: Peter McKay on the Future of Afghanistan." *Maclean's*, February 9.

Whitworth, Sandra. 2004. *Men, Militarism and UN Peacekeeping: A Gendered Analysis*. Boulder, CO, and London: Lynne Rienner.

Chapter 9

The Gendered Politics of Deceit in Egypt: The Instrumentalization of Women's Rights for an International Geostrategic Agenda

Nadia Abu-Zahra, Ruby Dagher, Nicole Brandt, and Khalid Suliman

INTRODUCTION

While John Baird, Canada's minister of foreign affairs in 2014, prepared for the Global Summit to End Sexual Violence in Conflict (organised by the British government), fifty-four women were raped in detention by policemen in Egypt for protesting against the 2013 military coup that ousted Egypt's first freely elected president (Middle East Monitor 2014). Among the incidents documented: two of the women became pregnant; two were raped more than fourteen times in a single day (within the camp of the Central Security, or the riot police); one was suspended naked in her cell; some were forced to watch pornographic films; others were forced to wipe the prison floors with their naked bodies; and one was raped daily for a complete week in one of the police stations (Middle East Monitor 2014). Canada's silence on the systematic rape of Egyptian women amid a conference combating sexual violence against women speaks volumes about Canada's approach to Egyptian trade, aid, and diplomatic relations, and the implications of this approach for gender equality in Egypt.

This chapter tells the short story of Canada's policy and relations with Egypt from 2001 to 2015, with a brief sojourn into the prior twenty years to understand Egypt's economic shifts and their gendered effects. The first part of the chapter, sections 2 to 4, focuses on the years 2001 to 2011. In this part, we describe Canada's and Egypt's commitments to gender equality, the use of state feminism in Egypt to subdue criticism, and how women's rights, while substantially advanced through Canada–Egypt cooperation, were nevertheless instrumentalized to deflect attention from deeper structural issues in both Egypt and Canada.

The second part of the chapter, sections 5 through 7, highlights some of the losses felt in the years 2007 to 2015, particularly the latter few years. In this part of the chapter, we graph the drop in aid, explain the changes within Canada's aid architecture, and take a hard look at the consequences for women and girls, and for feminist activists (women and men), who played so important a role in the 2011 revolution and post-election period. The years 2013 to 2015, as indicated in the beginning of this chapter, will forever signify a violent turn against women in Egypt.

The final, and most damning, part of the chapter is a brief history of the way that international intervention has collaborated with the Egyptian military to emasculate the Egyptian labour force and bring the labour movement – led in no small part by Egyptian women – to its knees. This part of the chapter presents the devastation wrought by decades of international economic dependence, and a searingly unaccountable military regime propped up by foreign money and weapons. Egyptian women and men have never before had such defined and constrictive gendered roles, complete with symbolisms of superiority and inferiority in the extreme. The all-powerful father figure rules over the feminized masses, for the greater good of the mother country – *umm al-dunya*, Egypt as mother of the world. And in the midst of this extreme representation of gender – likened in *Forbes* to that of the Pharaohs – Canada has weapons to barter and petrochemicals to pull. The scramble to privatize Egypt's last remaining sectors – energy, water, and transport – has begun.

Through a detailed analysis of Egyptian and Canadian media reports, government documents, and promotional material (e.g. ministerial websites), this chapter explores the implications of the Canadian policy shift from gender equality to a charity approach toward women and girls, set within a much larger reliance on and ideological belief in the market. Can Canada's economic interests align with the needs and wishes of Egyptians? Can advancing these economic interests serve also to promote gender equality? To best understand the gendered human costs of a Canadian foreign affairs and aid policy that strengthens and upholds the Egyptian military's hold over Egypt's government and economy, this chapter takes a long look at Canada–Egypt relations in the early years of the millennium.

A PERSONAL, TRANSNATIONAL COMMITMENT TO GENDER EQUALITY, 2001–2011

The Government of Canada's website describes the relationship between Canada and Egypt as a "mutually beneficial partnership, founded on a common interest in peace, stability and security in the Middle East" (Government of Canada 2012). Interestingly, that partnership is felt at the individual level, fostered by civil servants in both Canada and Egypt who maintain a commitment to ongoing positive relations and gender equality.

Despite criticism of Canada's gender-based aid on a structural level (Tiessen 2014; Carrier and Tiessen 2012; Baranyi and Powell 2005), gender was often an important focus of Canada's aid to Egypt, due to the "long-standing commitment to the promotion of gender equality" by many Canadian International Development Agency (CIDA) staff members (Tiessen 2014, 205). This ongoing commitment of CIDA staff members represents gender-based aid that is not always structural, but personal.

This is particularly relevant to Canada–Egypt relations, given that aid and foreign policy toward Egypt has the potential to be influenced by the individual civil servants who implement and/or define it. For example, Canada and Egypt exchange diplomats-in-training, a tradition for a decade and a half, in recognition of citizen-level ties through immigration and business relationships (Bell et al. 2009). The commitments of individuals to a strong Canada–Egypt bilateral relationship have a history of shaping Canadian public policy, including gender policy, in positive ways for both Canada and Egypt.

Canada has been providing development assistance to Egypt since 1976, with a gendered focus as far back as 1993 (CIDA 2001). Women and girls have comprised the overwhelming majority of the beneficiaries of Canada's indicative $150 to $200 million budget over ten years (CIDA 2001, 14).[1] This indicative budget was to be spent on *(a)* improving the economic conditions of women by supporting the development of small and medium enterprises (SMES), *(b)* supporting and improving basic education and human resource development for women and girls, and *(c)* funding projects that helped build synergy between *(a)* and *(b)* (CIDA 2001).

These were considered key areas of intervention for "reducing *gender* inequalities in access to and control over the resources and benefits of development, and advancing women's equal participation with men as decision-makers in shaping the sustainable development of their societies" (CIDA 2001, 21, emphasis added). In essence, Canada had committed to help provide a much-needed holistic approach to gender equality as part of bilateral Canada–Egypt relations.

STATE FEMINISM IN EGYPT, 2001–2011

Despite the best of intentions, however, efforts toward gender equality came to be dominated from the mid-1950s onward by undemocratic state institutions in Egypt. State-driven efforts to bring women into the workforce (rather than recognize their unpaid labour) overshadowed and ignored repressive gendered laws (Azzam 2013). The term "state feminism" was coined to capture some of the scepticism surrounding policies perceived as superficial and two-faced (Saleh 2012).

When repressive gendered laws were eventually changed, the changes were so top down that they were nicknamed after then president Anwar Sadat's wife: "Jihan's laws" (Azzam 2013). The limited feminisms allowed under state feminism were trumpeted as controversial (Abu-Zeid 1999, 31) because they advocated a removal of religion from politics (Karam 1998; Wassef and Guenana 1999; Ahmed 1992), in a context in which, until the present, the majority of the multifaith population saw purpose in maintaining ties between religion and politics (Gallup 2011). In reality, however, such feminisms – often, although not always, championed as they were by Egypt's wealthy political elites – were well aligned with state feminism, and were useful in maintaining an international image of liberalism amid severe socio-political repression.

Under President Hosni Mubarak, for example, the military officer who ruled Egypt for an unbroken thirty-year period, female activists were obliged to register and operate under the control of the Ministry of Social Affairs (which would retain the power to dissolve any organization) and the Ministry of the Interior, the approval of which was required for public meetings, rallies, and protest marches (*Law on Civil Association and Institutions*, Law No. 32 of 1964 and Law No. 153 of 1999, cited in Al-Ali 2000).

By the end of Mubarak's rule, Egypt ranked 125th out of 134 countries assessed in the Global Gender Gap Report (WEF 2010). Violence against women was prominent, particularly sexual harassment (Hassan et al. 2008). Egypt continues to suffer high female illiteracy (58 per cent), as well as significant gaps between female and male literacy, labour force participation, and political participation (ratios of 0.77, 0.30, and 0.02, respectively) (WEF 2010).

In part to mask the most egregious of these figures – the 0.02 male–female ratio of political participation – Mubarak created 64 women-only positions (i.e. no male candidates) in 2009 in a newly expanded 518-member parliament for the 2010 elections (Ramadan 2012). Of all the actions toward gender equality in Egypt from the 1950s to the present, this was perhaps most emblematic of the policy of state feminism at the cost of social justice.

Canada's greatest contributions to gender equality in Egypt – powerful changes in the legal system – were therefore nevertheless hampered by the harnesses of state feminism. Laws that Canada sees itself as instrumental in supporting (CIDA 2005) were nicknamed "Suzanne's laws," again, after the president's wife (Saleh 2012).

These laws represented big strides in the feminist movement in Egypt: a 2005 child custody law that was more gender-equal, prison sentences for men who failed to pay alimony, a law reversing the requirement for a woman to have her husband's permission in order to travel, and an amended pension law "to allow men to receive the pension of their deceased wives" (Dawoud 2012). Yet they were spearheaded by Suzanne Mubarak's National Council for Women, which she led from 2000 until 2012 (Abdel Rahim and Fracolli 2016). As such, they further entrenched the belief among Egyptians that state feminism was the only feminism the state would tolerate.

THE INSTRUMENTALIZATION OF WOMEN'S RIGHTS, 2001–2011

Competing feminisms co-existed despite repression, and were part of a wider social justice movement (Eft 2011; Karam 1998) that flew in the face of state feminism, pointing out how women's rights were instrumentalized to present a façade of human rights in the midst of heavy state control and some of the worst conditions for women in the world.

Canada – either intentionally or unintentionally – quietly sidestepped the minefield of gender equality in the political sphere, and instead honed in on the economy and workforce participation. Even this, however, was a notable position to take, in a context where up to 60 per cent of the economy is dominated by the patriarchal structure of the military (Abul-Magd 2011; Eltahawy 2014; Hauslohner 2014).

Canadian aid helped enable a more gender-sensitive environment for SME development (Bytown Consulting and C.A.C International 2008), and enhance educational access and completion rates for women (CIDA 2005), and aimed to reduce poverty, especially among "women and children/youth" (CIDA 2001, vi).

Lastly, Canada was able to take strides in spheres of mutual agreement, such as extreme and culturally specific (to the Nubian minority in Egypt) practices like female circumcision. In 2007, Canada was one of eight international partners credited with helping Egypt bring in a prohibition on female genital mutilation – a campaign that was as personal as it was political in its involvement of ordinary citizens from both Canada and Egypt (Bytown Consulting and C.A.C. International 2008, 17). Although such advances were indicative of positive change, they were nevertheless safely within the realm of state feminism, and a comfortable distance from any kind of political change.

The key problem with such an instrumentalization of women's rights by consecutive undemocratic, military rulers of Egypt is that the state feminism these rulers allowed was always at the expense of true political change toward gender equality in all spheres. State feminism does not address the multiplicity of oppressions that Egyptian women face. It is politically opportunistic in its portrayal of Egypt as pro-women (Azzam 2013), "using women to hide the real authoritarian face of the system" (Ramadan 2012). It is a monopolization of legitimacy and funding (Gray 2012) that, despite its positive results (Azzam 2013), conceals a stifling of discourse and an enforced lack of diverse voices.

Canada's own instrumentalization of women's rights is covered elsewhere in this volume (Stienstra, this volume), and Canada, too, benefits from including gender in aid, diverting attention from Canada's ranking in the Global Gender Gap Report (behind some other countries with a far lower per capita income, such as the Philippines and Nicaragua) (WEF 2014), and a higher percentage of poverty among single mothers and Indigenous people (Canadian Encyclopedia 2014). As much as Canada gains in its international reputation from promoting gender equality, these gains are nevertheless outshone by the business gains of certain kinds of aid and foreign policy strategies.

CANADIAN AND EGYPTIAN BUSINESS INTERESTS, 2007–2015

After the Conservatives were elected to federal government in January 2006, Prime Minister Stephen Harper first chose Josée Verner (2006 to 2007) and then Bev Oda (2007 to 2012) as minister for international cooperation responsible for CIDA. While no major changes for Egypt were implemented under Verner's leadership, the arrival of Minister Oda led to a sustained re-evaluation of CIDA's programs. She commissioned a series of "business case studies" detailing each receiving country's developmental needs and, more importantly, Canada's economic and political interests related to its involvement and support.

Although this link between development and Canadian business interests was not new, the Harper era ushered in a more sustained and effective politicization of several key programs. This had immediate consequences on the personal connections that had inspired gender equality projects for the previous decade. Since the arrival of the Conservatives, the number of project officers working on the Egypt Country Program decreased drastically: by 2011, the program had dwindled from three project officers and a program manager in 2007 to one project officer and a program manager whose file was not solely dedicated to Egypt. The change was also felt in the field office and resulted in the loss of key personnel, including the gender advisor in early 2012.

This loss of personnel, combined with the budget re-evaluations (subsequent to the business case studies), jeopardized gender equality projects and efforts. Examples of projects that were initiated in 2001 but dropped in 2011 include:

- over $27.5 million to strengthen the livelihoods, economic opportunities, and income levels of women through support to SMEs (the majority of which are led by women);
- over $12.5 million for civil society groups and government institutions to help improve the legal, policy, and societal norms related to gender; and
- over $50 million related to the education of children and youth, with a significant emphasis on women and girls. (OECD 2014; IDRC 2014a; DFATD 2014a)

These and other projects were dropped from receiving full support – up to $20 million per annum for ten years – to nearly no support, with a paltry $1 million for all aid to Egypt per annum from 2011 onward, as shown in figure 9.1.

Furthermore, the graph also demonstrates a decrease in disbursements, especially dramatic in 2009 (after the budget re-evaluations of 2007/2008), falling short of Canadian commitments made from 2001 to 2011. Despite this drop in disbursements, certain ongoing programs (lingering from the 2001 commitments) achieved impressive results, which went unreported or underreported in public government communications; Canada's Gender Equality Development Facility, for example, supported 1,689 staff (1,067 female, 622 male) from 26 Egyptian civil society organizations that promote gender equality, and particularly civil and economic empowerment (DFATD 2014c). The lack of public emphasis on gains in gender equality contrasts starkly with the heavy public emphasis on achievements in economic growth and women's gains in the market (accessing jobs, developing SMEs, accessing economic growth tools, etc.).

This heavy emphasis on the market rather than gender equality marks a trend from 2008 onward. The few projects approved by CIDA since

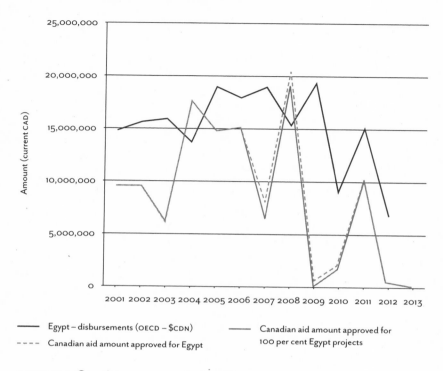

FIGURE 9.1 Canadian government's aid to Egypt, 2001–2013

2008 (the year the business case studies were completed) have been overwhelmingly related to trade, youth unemployment, and SMEs, with women cursorily added as one of the multiple beneficiaries. In addition to Egypt-specific funding, a 2011–2015 $11 million assistance package for the Middle East and North Africa region has followed similar priorities: youth unemployment and capacity building for Egyptian journalists (Government of Canada 2011). The economic objectives of the program are "to create employment through market reforms, stimulating invest-ment and promoting private sector participation" (DFATD 2014b). As for women, the program anticipates reducing female unemployment by 10 per cent by 2015 through their inclusion in the list of project beneficiaries.

The Canadian Government's own website highlights the precarious conditions that women face in Egypt:

[W]omen face substantial social – and often legal – restrictions on their activities, leading to low female participation in the economy and in social and political institutions. According to the World

Economic Forum Global Gender Gap Report 2012, Egypt ranks 126 out of 135 countries in equality between women and men. (DFATD 2014b)

Unfortunately, the change or realignment of Canada's aid focus has both affected the gender-specific emphasis on women when dealing with SMES, and ignored much of the analysis regarding the conditions and needs of women. Gender equality has ceased being a primary emphasis for Canada's Egypt program, and has instead been replaced by a more politicized assistance program catering to elite business interests (Dagher 2014). Before going into more detail on the connections between aid, trade, and the business elite, however, the following section explores the consequences of these policy shifts.

THE GENDERED CONSEQUENCES OF DROPPING GENDER AMID AN ARRESTED REVOLUTION, 2011–2015

The revolution that overthrew Mubarak in 2011 at last broke the muzzles on feminist activism, which for so long had struggled to move beyond state feminism (Ramadan 2012, 34–6). A powerful voice of feminism emerged "to create a novel approach to social justice for women, one created by us and for us" (Farouq 2014). The instrumentalization of women's rights to deflect domestic and international criticism could no longer continue after the fall of Mubarak, and state feminism could not longer serve as an effective "tool to depict the president as the defender of women and liberalism" (Ramadan 2012, 34).

Despite repression, feminists had long been part of the wider workers and peasant struggles ongoing in Egypt, particularly from 2004 to 2011. Over 100 collective actions per year took place in the early 2000s, growing to over 200 per year in the years 2004 to 2006 (Chalcraft 2011, 51). When global investment patterns forced up food and energy prices in 2007 and halved the economy in late 2008 (Hanieh 2009, 77–8), the number of protests rose dramatically to over 600 per year – the most important of which was led by 3,000 women (Alexander 2009). This four-day strike and occupation of a textile factory – the largest textile company in Africa and the Middle East, with textiles being the second-largest industry in Egypt (Hanieh 2013, 57) – catalyzed even more strikes in subsequent years (Chalcraft 2011, 51).

Between 2011 and 2013, an eight-person committee joined together to pen a vision for a gender equality built on existing international models, while taking "the opportunity to critique these existing concepts and paradigms, to examine these frameworks and come up with ideas of our own" (Farouq 2014):

> [We tried] to integrate non-tangible aspects of contribution into our development model. One of these non-tangible aspects was the concept of serenity. The concept of enabling a sense of serenity within every woman was novel. If we could achieve this, then this would contribute to her empowerment.
>
> We saw that this form of justice really exists in providing Egyptian women with integrated resources: health, education, media, self-actualization, infrastructure are all needed to help women achieve serenity. (Farouq 2014)

These feminists faced strong and ongoing opposition to their attempts to integrate social justice into their discourse, as state feminism had functioned for so long and so effectively as to remove wider social justice issues from the ascribed "women's" (not gender) agenda. The minister of defence wasted no time in cracking down through gender-based violence: General Abdel Fattah el-Sisi (Minister from 2012 to 2014) proudly explained in an international public statement that "virginity tests" carried out on beaten, detained women were to "protect" them "from rape" (BBC 2014; Amnesty 2012).

Few to no journalists covered the quiet story of an intersectional feminist movement (intersectional for tackling the multifaceted forms of oppression facing Egyptian women and girls, including class, race, gender, and age) rising to supplant the former suppressive state feminism of unelected Egyptian military rulers. And in very little time, it was violently crushed. In less than three years, a military coup quashed efforts to launch a mass movement for social justice and gender equality. On 14 August 2013, security forces killed at least 1,000 civilians in Rab'a al-Adawiya Square in Cairo, many of whom were women. The executive director of Human Rights Watch called it "one of the world's largest killings of demonstrators in a single day in recent history":

> This wasn't merely a case of excessive force or poor training. It was a violent crackdown planned at the highest levels of the Egyptian government. Many of the same officials are still in power in Egypt, and have a lot to answer for. (Human Rights Watch 2014)

Indeed, the very same official who instituted the "virginity tests" installed himself as ruler, and Canada quickly – although not immediately, thanks to the shrewd intervention of gender-aware civil servants – recognized him as Egypt's legitimate leader.

Following the 2013 coup, women and girls from across Egypt have been kidnapped, imprisoned, tortured, and killed (Osman 2011). Dress restrictions have been reinstated, university students have been forbidden from political activity, stop-and-search procedures have been instituted, and sexual harassment rates have risen sharply (AED 2014). Indeed, sexual harassment, discriminatory laws, and a surge in violence and trafficking since the coup have made Egypt the worst country in the Arab world to be a woman (Thomson Reuters Foundation 2013). The gendered consequences of dropping gender and human rights from a Canadian foreign affairs and development agenda in Egypt have been staggering. Canada's silence amid mass violations and overt gender-based violence has sent a strong, implicit message of support to Egypt's patriarchal military.

GENDER-BASED VIOLENCE AND STATE FEMINISM, 2013–2015

Meanwhile, the symbol of state justice, the Egyptian judiciary, has suppressed rather than upheld women's rights (Annis 2014). In November 2013, when Egyptians marched to commemorate the International Day for the Elimination of Violence against Women, fourteen women between the ages of seventeen and twenty were condemned to prison for eleven years (Carlstrom 2013). A girl of eleven years of age was sentenced to ten years' imprisonment for carrying a yellow balloon emblazoned with the symbol of freedom: four outstretched fingers, signifying the square where protests were held and the site of a massacre by the Egyptian military (Abdul Rahman 2013). Given that the institutions meant to protect and uphold women's rights – the judiciary, state ministries, the police, and the army – are instead attacking them, women see such protests for democracy as essential to attaining their rights (Glacier 2013).

Yet women involved in protests have not been the only ones to suffer gender-based violence. In January 2014, a nineteen-year-old "was arrested while heavily pregnant ... during the first day of voting on Egypt's new constitution" (Berger 2014).

[M]ass arrests took place in Cairo and other major cities throughout the country. Hamdy said she was detained as she walked past a police station on her way to a doctor's appointment. Despite her repeated claims that she had not taken part in any protests, she was imprisoned at a police station and charged with violating the draconian protest law imposed in November.

...

Hamdy said a police officer told her following her arrest: "You will give birth in prison, just so you know." ... She was moved from her police cell to hospital ... [and] after the delivery, Hamdy was once more restrained in her hospital bed. (Berger 2014)

Notwithstanding Canada's relative silence, international condemnation has poured in (Carter Center 2014). The response from Egypt to this criticism has been to adhere to its longstanding tradition of state feminism. On 10 December 2014, Egypt's pyramids and Sphinx were lit in orange as part of a campaign by UN Women to end gender-based violence. UN Women executive director Phumzile Mlambo-Ngcuka said in a statement, "We need this eye-catching colour everywhere so that the message is loud and clear: we all need to work together to stop violence against women and girls right now" (Egyptian Streets 2014).

As eye-catching as it may have been, spotlighting the pyramids did little to serve the women kept captive in Egypt's prisons, the struggle for gender equality amid legal and political discrimination, and the perpetuation of gender-based violence by the judiciary, police, and army. Rather, it was an act powerfully reminiscent of the tools used to subdue feminist activism in Egypt, through state feminism and the instrumentalization of women's rights by both domestic and international actors profiting from stark inequality.

COMMERCIAL INTERESTS AND PATRIARCHY, 1981–2015

The dividing line in Egypt is often mistakenly portrayed as being between political Islam on the one hand, and secularism and Christianity, allied with the international community, on the other hand. This division serves to uphold rather than challenge gender inequality, and conveniently conceals a far more tangible and longstanding divide (Chalcraft 2007, 2012a, 2012b, 2014; Mitchell 1999) between Egypt's military and economic elite, allied with international exploitative industries, and Egypt's eighty-two million population, a quarter of whom live under the poverty line (World Bank 2015) and who – with the exception of the years 2011 to 2013 – have never had a government elected in free and fair elections.

Understanding the class divide in Egypt is critical to understanding the obstacles to gender equality. Strikes were closely tied to gender equality issues, after decades of rulers emasculating the domestic economy for the profit of political and military elites. One of the key actors in enforcing patriarchy and gender inequality has, surprisingly, been the international institution charged with promoting human development: the World Bank. Emboldened by over three decades of structural adjustment programs that broke the back of the Egyptian labour movement – lengthening the working week and dropping pensions, family allowances, annual leave, wages (from 60 per cent of per capita GNP in 1984 to 13 per cent in 2007), severance pay, and, most importantly, regulations over hiring and firing – the World Bank has since argued against maternity leave on the grounds that it causes female unemployment and informalization (Hanieh 2013, 52–3; Hanieh 2011b, 13).

Women have been the principal losers in the liberalization of the Egyptian economy from the 1980s to the present. Following Mubarak's opening of the economy (1981 to 1991), which caused rural poverty to double and urban poverty to increase more than 150 per cent, a 1992 law allowed for the eviction of hundreds of thousands of agricultural workers (Hanieh 2011b, 12–13). This continues to affect women in particular; in 2003 women constituted over half the agricultural labour force (World Bank 2003, 199–200). As "literally just a handful of families" profit immensely (Hanieh 2011a), nearly 70 per cent of the Egyptian population survives on food rations, and another 19 per cent have nothing to eat at all (UN News Centre 2013).

An historic dependence on US food aid dates back to the early 1960s, and by the late 1970s, Egypt was taking in about a fifth of all US food aid globally, not least because the guarantee of cheap food helped ruling regimes retain legitimacy, and the US could offload its agricultural surpluses (Hanieh 2013, 30). Yet the reliance on food aid has artificially propped up an unsustainable inequality, and the profit of the rich has come at a high cost: as of 2013, 31 per cent of Egyptian children under the age of five were stunted for lack of food (UN News Centre 2013). As speculative developers double the size of Cairo (Mitchell 1999), its squatter communities of six million people are left to starve (Hanieh 2011b, 12–13).

The war of commercial interests against labour rights and gender equality intensified in the years 2000 to 2015. Import tariffs in this period were halved, the market was flooded (dropping domestically produced sales by half in the textile sector from 2000 to 2004), and support was cut to Egyptian firms (Hanieh 2013, 57–8). Once again, these measures have disproportionately and negatively affected women. Handicapping the domestic industry led to increased pressure to squeeze the labour force – which in textiles was mostly women – in order to "attract investment." Worse measures followed: corporate profits were allowed to leave Egypt with zero tax, while subsidized inputs, including land, flowed to wealthy corporations (Hanieh 2013, 57). In 2005, corporate tax was cut from

40 per cent to 20 per cent, and the highest personal income tax bracket was cut from 32 per cent to 20 per cent; meanwhile, the poor were slapped with a sales tax in 1991 and subsidy cuts (Hanieh 2011b, 14).

Recognizing the deep socio-economic inequality in Egypt helps to situate feminist movements. The popular feminist movement had none of the funding and endowed legitimacy that was enjoyed by state feminism (Ramadan 2012, 35), but it did find a home among wider social justice struggles in Egypt. A clear look at privatization – which has eaten up $15.7 billion of public assets, often at below-market value prices – from 1998 to 2008 reveals that the worst affected are university educated women, who in 2006 comprised nearly a quarter of all female unemployment (Hanieh 2013, 72). Nearly half of all girls and women aged fifteen to twenty-four are unemployed – double the rate of men (DFATD 2014b) – yet the recommendations of the World Bank have been to use women's vulnerability to bring down costs: given the gendered wage gap, argued the World Bank, more women could be employed in textiles to lower expenditures, as exemplified by the *maquiladoras* in Mexico (World Bank 2003, 64).

Egyptian women are blind neither to the effects of privatization, nor the consequences for their lives of World Bank recommendations. Such a strong connection between a movement toward gender equality and macroeconomic fluctuations is not unique to Egypt. This makes the continued Canadian policy to rely on market forces to support gender equality in Egypt even more worrisome. In the years 2011 to 2015, Canadian aid to Egypt concentrated on youth employment and economic opportunities (IDRC 2014b, 2014c), with the goal, as mentioned above, "to create employment through market reforms, stimulating investment and promoting private sector participation" (DFATD 2014b). The public sector once accounted for 59 per cent of employment in Egypt, but "promotion of private sector participation" led to half of this labour force losing their livelihoods from 1994 to 2001 (Hanieh 2011b, 12–13). In textiles, where women predominate, privatization in the years 2000 to 2008 meant nearly a third (100,000) of workers lost their jobs, with the remainder receiving wage cuts (Hanieh 2013, 60). Women in Egypt, as has happened elsewhere in the world, were hardest hit by privatization and market reforms, and were fully cognizant of the connections between these measures – promoted by countries like Canada – and gender inequality.

CANADA–EGYPT MILITARY TIES AND INEQUALITY, 2013–2015

Beyond aiding and abetting the widening of the gap between the rich and poor, men and women, in Egypt, the international community partnered with the key patriarchal institute responsible for gross inequality in Egypt: the military. It received $1.3 billion a year in military aid from 1987 onward, and engaged – together with international firms and Gulf-based conglomerates – in the privatization of real estate, tourism, telecommunications, banks, food, and steel (Hanieh 2013, 32–3, 50–2).

> [T]he largest single builder of Cairo's new neighborhoods, far larger than the builders of Dreamland [advertised as "the world's first electronic city"], is the Egyptian army. Military contractors are throwing up thousands of acres of apartments on the city's eastern perimeter to create new suburban enclaves for the officer elite. (Mitchell 1999)

The military "pays no taxes, employs conscripted labor, buys public land on favorable terms and discloses nothing to Parliament or the public" (Kirkpatrick 2011). Despite owning up to 60 per cent of the Egyptian economy (as mentioned above), the military keeps its budget secret, and its industries "unaudited and untaxed" (Hauslohner 2014).

Since the 2013 coup, Canada has been a chief beneficiary of this extensive military control of the Egyptian economy. Military exports from Canada to Egypt jumped 182,873 per cent after the coup, from less than $4,000 to over $7.2 million (DFATD 2014d). This at a time when global Canadian arms exports slid by $320 million (Ling 2015). With Egypt buying Canadian arms while the rest of the world reduces their purchases, it is small wonder that Canada's Foreign Affairs Minister in 2014 saw Egypt as "tremendously important" (Adam 2014) and congratulated a military general who garnered a vote in 2014 of 96.9 per cent (even the dictator Mubarak dared not inflate his own false claims beyond 88 per cent or 94 per cent). Critics interpreted Canada's fawning as the result of successful marketing by Egypt's military at best (Saunders 2015) or commercial interest at worst (Mackrael 2015).

The latest commercial venture to be promoted by Egypt's military is the privatization of energy, transport, and water (including wastewater) – the only remaining sectors awaiting privatization (as of 2015). Canada took an interest. According to a DFATD internal document, "investment mostly in the petro-chemical sector … [constituting] increasing commercial interests" warrants warm relations with Egypt (CIDA 2013, 37). Privatization of wastewater has begun (although not by Canada), through public–private partnerships (Hanieh 2013, 55).

Petroleum, petrochemicals, and mining are extractive industries that could either serve public sector development and social improvement for Egypt's eighty-two million populace, or serve private interests in Egypt and Canada. Egypt's leaders (and Canada's) appear to have chosen the latter. In Cairo, power shortages are rampant, water shortages seriously affect public health, and issues with basic infrastructure disrupt the daily lives of Egyptians (Farid 2016; Aswat Masriya 2015; Hussein 2014). Rather than use local resources to alleviate shortages, however, the Egyptian military looks to Canada for an arrangement to privately share the profits.

Canada is ready to step in, and Canadian oil and gas companies have increased their activities in Egypt (Halais 2015).

> Canada and Egypt's Ministry of Petroleum and Mining are agreeing to cooperate in Egypt's oil and gas and mining sectors to help address energy needs, strengthen Egypt's regulatory system and create jobs for Egyptians. Canada's history demonstrates that the extractives sector can help build a country and contribute to its prosperity. (DFATD 2015)

Nor will Canada be the only country to do so: Egypt plans to increase its exports in extractive industries, and an Egyptian Economic Development Conference in 2015 promoted precisely these types of exports (Middle East Magazine 2014).

A "STRONG MAN" FOR EGYPT, 2013–2015

The untold story in Canada–Egypt business relations is the toll this will take on gender equality, in very real and material terms. Negative gendered stereotypes now permeate the Egyptian public discourse over governance: since the coup, General (now President) el-Sisi has masculinized political power while feminizing subjection and citizenship. He has promoted himself internationally as a champion for women, while women supporters have written to local newspapers to declare their allegiance. One female journalist encapsulated the trend with this statement:

> As long as el-Sisi has called us to go out to support him, we have to reply. Frankly, he does not need to call or give an order, he needs only wink with his eye, and all of us will respond to the call. The

man is beloved by the Egyptians, and if he wants to marry three women in addition to his own wife, we are under his command, and if he wants us to be odalisques, we will not hesitate to lay down our lives for him. (Sharif 2013)

General el-Sisi actively engages with such statements, and responds in kind. Speaking to an audience of women at a conference, he beamed:

You have raised my spirits so so much. Now I realize how brave Egyptian women are. I don't say compliments, I pray to God to deserve all of this love. I am in dire need to talk to you, since I know that my words will reach all people by talking to you. You write a new history for Egypt, to confirm your ability to achieve the impossible. I feel about you, as I feel about poor citizens. (Rabie 2014)

In the eyes of many Egyptians – females and males – el-Sisi is a symbol of manhood and masculinity. For them, he is the strong man, the *zakar* – a term for virility, power, and prowess. Shaaban Abdel-Rahim, a popular Egyptian singer "of the people" (*sha'bi*), launched a song entitled "el-Sisi rajil zakar," or "el-Sisi Is a *Real* Man" (*Al-Masry Al-Youm* 2013).

That only a "real" man can lead Egypt – or anything, for that matter – is a vast step backward for the Egyptian and international feminist movement. The discourse of the strong man and the prostrating women has removed all trace of gender equality from power and governance. The good woman, in this discourse, is one who loves her leader devoutly, "responds to his wink," and is "under his command." The good woman does not protest. She does not call for democracy. And she does not, under any circumstances, call for gender equality.

That Canada has blithely followed and actively supported this path for Egypt is a death knell to feminist activists. When General el-Sisi as minister of defence defended his "virginity tests" on women in 2011, Canada initially called out the Egyptian president. However, now that el-Sisi is president, fifty-four women can be raped under his watch and Canada keeps its silence. Such selective silences, including condemning violence against Christians while staying silent on violence against Muslims – in the thousands – prompted award-winning Canadian journalist Haroon Siddiqui (2013) to nickname Canadian elected representatives "Harper and his Christian crusaders." In repeating el-Sisi's self-promotion as bringing "order and democracy" to Egypt, Canada is furthering a dangerous agenda that contradicts gender equality under the guise of defending women.

CONCLUSION

The story of Canada's policy and relations with Egypt from 2001 to 2015 does not have a happy ending. State feminism in the years 2001 to 2011, and revived with a vengeance in 2013 to 2015, has displaced broad-based feminist movements and their counterparts in the struggle for labour rights – labour rights being a particular aspect that cannot be divorced from gender equality. Canada's early efforts to promote gender equality were based on sound theory and practice – such as funding legal reform and education, and focusing on gender equality in resource access, control, and decision making – but were nevertheless instrumentalized to serve state interests. For the key funding recipients – dominated by relations of the successive military leaders of Egypt – the appearance of gender equality has always taken priority over the actualization of gender equality. A true social movement of men, women, girls, and boys should not require ministerial approval or be subject to ministerial veto for every move and every action of every component organization and individual.

Then, starting in 2007, the sound gender equality theory and practice was dropped from Canada's aid policy to Egypt, and "business case studies" provided rationales for cutting funding to the former mainstays of legal reform, education, and the promotion of gender equality in resource access, control, and decision making. Aid shrank to 5 per cent of its former levels, gender equality was dropped as a program priority, and women and girls became a cursory add-on to market-based programs. Instead of understanding the drastic effect that privatization had on labour rights and gender equality, Canada advocated for more of the same, with terrible consequences (DFATD 2014b). Following a decade of privatization of more than $15.7 billion of public assets, and a severe constriction of domestic industry, women's employment – which had primarily been in these sectors – plummeted. Women's rights as workers disintegrated: maternity and parental leave, gendered wage equality, regulations over hiring and firing, consumer subsidies, the working week, pensions, family allowances, annual leave, and severance pay were all squeezed for the sake of "competition."

Meanwhile, with Canada egging them on, exploitative industries are becoming even cozier with Egypt's military elite. Canada, we are told, needs good relations with these military elites because of our "investment mostly in the petro-chemical sector ... [constituting] increasing commercial interests" (CIDA 2013, 37). At least we are upfront about it (except that it took a Freedom of Information request to obtain the document containing that statement). The fact that this is the same military that raped fifty-four women seems peripheral, at least at a world conference on sexual abuse. And so it continues: Egypt's military dominates the economy, claiming free labour (prisoners), subsidized land and resources, and luxurious tax cuts. Egypt's president stands as the symbol of manhood, while women labour on in textile factories, beaten into submission by policies promoted not only by private profiteers but also the World Bank – and pro-privatisation Canada.

So how to end on a note of hope, if not happiness? The movement in Egypt toward gender equality has not been extinguished. Nor has the – not unsubstantial – movement toward gender equality within the current Canadian civil service. If those with the know-how and understanding of intersectional inequalities – gender, class, race, faith, ability, age, and others – have the opportunity to build a collective movement together, much can change for the better. We have argued in this chapter that gender inequality in Egypt, and Canada's role in diminishing or exacerbating it, can only be understood in the context of the deep class divide that shears Egypt's eighty-two million people from a small, resource-controlling elite. Conversely, however, once that context is understood, and once Canada – as a member of the international community – ceases to support the elite at the expense of the majority, the majority will have far greater power to advocate for gender equality and social justice.

To return, then, to the questions posed at the beginning of this chapter: Can Canada's economic interests align with the needs and wishes of Egypt's population? Can advancing these economic interests also serve to promote gender equality? Indeed they can, though certainly not if Canada continues to envision our economic interests in terms of benefitting a few wealthy corporations (and individuals). We have much to benefit, and Egypt has much to benefit, if we commence (or return to) seeing people as more than just production machines, and the earth's contents and water as more than just profits to be exploited. Consider the long-term losses of keeping women and men at near-starvation levels, with nearly 70 per cent of Egyptians on food rations, 19 per cent with not even that, and a third of children stunted (UN News Centre 2013). Or the losses of female unemployment rates double those of men, together with gendered wage gaps? The gains of these people, the gains of anyone in Egypt, Canada, or elsewhere, are the gains of all.

However, telling that to the politicians making the policy (or overruling them through democracy), the military dominating the Egyptian economy, and the companies who extract the wealth at the cost of the (recently) disenfranchised, will perhaps be the greatest task ahead. Doubtless, within the wider movements in Egypt and Canada, among

workers and civil servants, those who believe in true gender equality will
be forging the way.

NOTES

1 CIDA established an indicative budget of between $15 and $20 million (for
its entire Official Development Aid portfolio, not just the gender equality
component). However, there was no official Treasury Board approval to
ensure an approved commitment.

REFERENCES

Abdel Rahim, Sara, and Erin Fracolli. 2016. "Egypt's National Council for
Women: A Substitute for Civil Society?" Tahrir Institute for Middle East Policy. Accessed 7 December 2016. https://timep.org/commentary/egypts
-national-council-for-women-a-substitute-for-civil-society.
Abdul Rahman, Ahmad. 2013. "Egypt Claims the Release of the Girls Accused
of Carrying Balloons with the Rabiaa Slogan." *Egypt Today*. http://www.
egypttoday.co.uk/also-in-the-news/20131027/159959.html.
Abul-Magd, Zeinab. 2011. "The Army and the Economy in Egypt." *Jadaliyya*.
Accessed 14 January 2015. http://www.jadaliyya.com/pages/index/3732/
the-army-and-the-economy-in-egypt.
Abu-Zeid, Nasr Hamid. 1999. "The Woman Affair between the Hammer of
Modernity and the Anvil of Tradition." Translated by Khalid Suliman. *Journal
of Comparative Poetics* 19: 29–65.
Adam, Mohammed. 2014. "Don't Legitimize Egypt's Regime." *Ottawa Citizen*, 7
May. http://ottawacitizen.com/news/world/dont-legitimize-egypts-regime.
Ahmed, Laila. 1992. *Women and Gender and Islam*. New Haven: Yale University
Press.
Al-Ali, Nadje. 2000. *Secularism, Gender and the State in the Middle East: The
Egyptian Women's Movement*. Cambridge: University of Cambridge Press.
Alexander, Anne. 2009. *Egypt's Strike Wave: Lessons in Leadership*. Economic and
Social Research Council, Non-Governmental Public Action Programme.
Al-Masry Al-Youm. 2013. "With Video, Shaaban Abdel Rahim in a New Song:
El-Sisi Is a Masculine Man, and His Thought Is Creative." *Al-Masry Al-Youm*,
31 October. http://www.almasryalyoum.com/news/details/334308.
Amnesty International. 2012. *Egypt: A Year after 'Virginity Tests,' Women Vic-
tims of Army Violence Still Seek Justice*. Amnesty International. http://www.
amnesty.org/en/news/egypt-year-after-virginity-tests-women-victims-army-
violence-still-seek-justice-2012-03-09.

Annis, Roger. 2014. "Mass Protests Grow as Military Drags Egypt Back to Dictatorship." *Bullet*, no. 928. http://www.socialistproject.ca/bullet/928. php#continue.

Aswat Masriya. 2015. "Egypt: Dollar Crisis and Fuel Shortages Biggest Obstacles Facing Industrial Sector in 2016." allAfrica. Accessed 26 November 2016. http://allafrica.com/stories/201512310737.html.

Azzam, Lubna. 2014. "State Feminism and Women's Legal Rights in Egypt." *Diplomacy and Foreign Affairs*, 8 February. http://diplomacyandforeignaffairs.com/state-feminism-and-womens-legal-rights-the-role-of-national-council-for-women-in-todays-egypt.

Baranyi, Stephen, and Kristiana Powell. 2005. *Fragile States, Gender Equality and Aid Effectiveness: A Review of Donor Perspectives.* Ottawa: North-South Institute and CIDA.

BBC News. 2014. *Egypt: Abdul Fattah Al-Sisi Profile.* BBC News, 16 May. http://www.bbc.com/news/world-middle-east-19256730.

Bell, Michael, Michael Molloy, David Sultan, and Sallama Shaker. 2009. "Practitioners' Perspectives on Canada–Middle East Relations." In *Canada and the Middle East: In Theory and Practice*, edited by Paul Heinbecker and Bessma Momani, 20–3. Waterloo: Wilfrid Laurier University Press.

Berger, Carol. 2014. "Egyptian Detainee Handcuffed to Bed after Having Baby Is Released." *Guardian*, 20 February.

Bytown Consulting and CAC International. 2008. *Evaluation of CIDA's Implementation of Its Policy on Gender Equality.* Gatineau, QC: Canadian International Development Agency. http://www.oecd.org/derec/canada/42174775.pdf.

Canadian Encyclopedia. 2014. "Poverty." *Canadian Encyclopedia.* http://www.thecanadianencyclopedia.ca/en/article/poverty.

Canadian International Development Agency (CIDA). 2005. *Canadian International Development Agency Departmental Performance Report 2005.* Gatineau, QC: Canadian International Development Agency. http://publications.gc.ca/collections/collection_2012/sct-tbs/BT31-4-27-2005-eng.pdf.

– 2011. *Egypt Country Development Programming Framework 2001–2011.* Gatineau, QC: Canadian International Development Agency. http://lnweb90.worldbank.org/Caw/CAWDoclib.nsf/0/DC190DE8F21698F085256CD200698093/$file/Egypt.pdf.

– 2013. *Reviewing CIDA's Bilateral Engagement: Countries of Focus and Modest Presence Partners: Qualitative Assessment.* Ottawa: Canadian International Development Agency.

Carlstrom, Gregg. 2013. "Egyptian Women Get Jail Terms over Protests." Al-Jazeera, 28 November.

Carrier, Krystel and Rebecca Tiessen. 2012. "Women and Children First: Maternal Health and the Silence of Gender in Canadian Foreign Policy." In *Canada in* the World: Perspectives on Canadian Foreign Policy, edited by Heather Smith and Claire Turenne-Sjolander, 183–200. Don Mills, ON: Oxford University Press.

Carter Center. 2014. "Carter Center Closes Egypt Office; Calls for Stronger Protections for Democratic Rights and Freedoms." Carter Center, 15 October. http://www.cartercenter.org/news/pr/egypt-101514.html.

Chalcraft, John. 2007. "Popular Protest, the Market and the State in Nineteenth and Early Twentieth Century Egypt." In Subalterns and Social Protest: History from Below in the Middle East and North Africa, edited by Stephanie Cronin, 69–90. London: Routledge.

– 2011. "Labour Protest and Hegemony in Egypt and the Arabian Peninsula." In Social Movements in the Global South: Dispossession, Development and Resistance, edited by Sara Motta and Alf Gunvald Nilsen, 35–58. London: Palgrave Macmillan.

– 2012a. "Egypt's Uprising, Mohammed Bouazizi, and the Failure of Neoliberalism." Maghreb Review 37, nos. 3–4: 195–214.

– 2012b. "Horizontalism in the Egyptian Revolutionary Process." Middle East Report 262: 6–11.

– 2014. "Egypt's 25 January Uprising, Hegemonic Contestation, and the Explosion of the Poor." In The New Middle East: Protest and Revolution in the Arab World Gerges, edited by Fawaz A. Gerges, 155–79. Cambridge: Cambridge University Press.

Crina Boros, Crina. 2013. "POLL – Egypt Is Worst Arab State for Women, Comoros Best." Thomson Reuters Foundation, 12 November. http://www.trust.org/item/20131108170910-qacvu/?source=spotlight-writaw

Dagher, Ruby. 2014. "CIDA, the Mining Sector, and the Orthodoxy of Economic Conservatism in Harper Decision Making." In How Ottawa Spends 2014–2015: The Harper Government – Good to Go?, edited by G. Bruce Doern and Christopher Stoney, 192–204. Montreal and Kingston: McGill-Queen's University Press.

Dawoud, Aliaa. 2012. "Why Women Are Losing Rights in Post-Revolutionary Egypt." Journal of International Women's Studies 13, no. 14: 159–69.

Department of Foreign Affairs and International Trade (DFAIT). 2011. "Canada Announces $11-Million Assistance Package for Egypt and Middle East-North Africa Region." Department of Foreign Affairs, Trade and Development.

– 2012. "Canada-Egypt Relations." Department of Foreign Affairs and International Trade. http://www.canadainternational.gc.ca/egypt-egypte/bilateral_relations_bilaterales/index.aspx?lang=eng.

Department of Foreign Affairs, Trade and Development (DFATD). 2014a. http://www.international.gc.ca/international/index.aspx?lang=eng.

– 2014b. "Canada's Development Assistance in Egypt." Department of Foreign Affairs, Trade and Development. http://www.international.gc.ca/development-developpement/countries-pays/egypt-egypte.aspx?lang=eng.

– 2014c. "Project Profile: Gender Equality Development Facility." Department of Foreign Affairs, Trade and Development. http://www.acdi-cida.gc.ca/cidaweb/cpo.nsf/vWebCSAZEn/63EA29CFE92B2BB085256FCF0036F7C6.

– 2014d. *Report on Exports of Military Goods from Canada.* Department of Foreign Affairs, Trade and Development. http://www.international.gc.ca/controls-controles/report-rapports/mil-2012-2013.aspx?lang=eng.

– 2015. "Baird Promotes Democracy, Security and Prosperity in Egypt." Department of Foreign Affairs, Trade and Development, 9 February.

Donnelly, Jack. 2000. *Realism and International Relations.* Cambridge: Cambridge University Press.

Drolet, Julie. 2010. "Feminist Perspectives in Development: Implications for Women and Microcredit." *Journal of Women and Social Work* 25, no. 3: 212–23.

Eft, Natalie Darlene. 2011. "Advocating for Greater Political Participation: Feminisms in Egypt and the Muslim Brotherhood" PhD diss., Georgetown University, ProQuest Dissertations Publishing.

Egyptian Streets. 2014. "Egypt's Pyramids Turn Orange to End Violence against Women." *Egyptian Streets.* http://egyptianstreets.com/2014/12/11/egypts-pyramids-turn-orange-to-end-violence-against-women.

Eltahawy, Mona. 2014. "Women of the Arab Spring: 'We now need a sexual revolution, not just a political one.'" *Telegraph,* 17 June.

European Alliance for Democracy and Human Rights (AED). 2014. *Save Cleopatra: Report on Women's Rights Violation in Egypt till June 2014.* European Coalition for Democracy and Human Rights. Accessed 26 November 2016. http://elmarsad.org/ar/wp-content/uploads/2014/06/TheWomenBooklet.pdf.

Farid, Doaa. 2016. "70 Million Reliant on Food Subsidies in Peril amid Government Austerity and Mismanagement." *Daily News Egypt,* 2 March. http://www.dailynewsegypt.com/2016/03/02/70-million-reliant-on-food-subsidies-in-peril-amid-government-austerity-and-mismanagement.

Farouq, Marwa. 2014. *Social Justice for Women in Egypt.* Unpublished manuscript.

Gallup. 2011. "Egypt from Tahrir to Transition." Gallup World. http://www.gallup.com/poll/157046/egypt-tahrir-transition.aspx.

Garikipati, Supriya. 2013. "Microcredit and Women's Empowerment: Have We Been Looking at the Wrong Indicators?" *Oxford Development Studies* 41 (sup1): S53–S75.

Glacier, Osire. "Women in the Egyptian Revolution." 2013. Tolerance Canada. Accessed 30 January 2013. http://www.tolerance.ca/Article.aspx?ID=157663&L=en.

Gray, Jessica. 2012. "Egypt's Feminist Union Undergoing Reincarnation." *United Press International*, 30 January.

Halais, Flavie. 2015. "Arms, Oil and Market-Based Development: DFATD's New Strategy in Egypt." *Devex*, 2 February. Accessed 4 February 2015. https://www.devex.com/news/arms-oil-and-market-based-development-dfatd-s-new-strategy-in-egypt-85409.

Hanieh, Adam. 2009. "Hierarchies of a Global Market: The South and the Economic Crisis." *Studies in Political Economy* 83: 61–84.

– 2011a. "Egypt's Uprising: Not Just a Question of Transition." *Monthly Review*, 14 February.

– 2011b. "Beyond Mubarak: Reframing the 'Politics' and 'Economics' of Egypt's Uprising." *Studies in Political Economy* 87: 7–27.

– 2013. *Lineages of Revolt: Issues of Contemporary Capitalism in the Middle East.* Chicago: Haymarket Books.

Hassan, Rasha, Komsan Nehad, and Aliyaa Shoukry. 2008. *"Clouds in Egypt's Sky": Sexual Harassment from Verbal Harassment to Rape.* Cairo: Egyptian Centre for Women's Rights (ECWR).

Hauslohner, Abigail. 2014. "Egypt's Military Expands Its Control of the Country's Economy." *Washington Post*, 16 March.

Human Rights Watch, 2014. *All According to Plan: The Rab'a Massacre and Mass Killings of Protesters in Egypt.* Human Rights Watch. https://www.hrw.org/report/2014/08/12/all-according-plan/raba-massacre-and-mass-killings-protesters-egypt.

Hussein, Walaa. 2014. "Egypt Faces Power Cuts, Potential Drought." *AlMonitor*. Accessed 26 November 2016. http://www.al-monitor.com/pulse/en/originals/2014/09/egypt-water-nile-shortage-power-cuts.html.

International Development Research Centre (IDRC). 2014a. http://idris.idrc.ca/app/Search.

– 2014b. *Exploring the Differential Impact of Two Modalities of Microfinance on Vulnerable Segments of Society in Egypt.* International Development Research Centre. http://idris.idrc.ca/app/Search?request=directAccess&projectNumber=107746&language=en.

– 2014c. "HarassMap: Using Crowdsourced Data in the Social Sciences." International Development Research Centre. http://www.idrc.ca/EN/Misc/Pages/ProjectDetails.aspx?ProjectNumber=106623.

Karam, Azz. 1998. *Women, Islamism, and the State: Contemporary Feminisms in Egypt.* London: Macmillan.

Kirkpatrick, David. 2011. "Egyptians Say Military Discourages an Open Economy." *New York Times*, 17 February.

– 2014. "International Observers Find Egypt's Presidential Election Fell Short of Standards." *New York Times*, 29 May.

LahaOnline. 2004. "Egyptian Women Reject Western Concepts for Liberation."
LahaOnline, 4 June. Translated by Khalid Suliman. http://www.lahaonline.
com/articles/view/4331.htm.

Ling, Justin. 2015. "Data Shows Canada Upping Arms Sales to Human Rights
Abusers." *Vice*, 6 January. http://www.vice.com/en_ca/read/data-shows
-canada-upping-arms-sales-to-human-rights-abusers-786.

Mackrael, Kim. 2014. "Commercial Motives Driving Canada's Foreign Aid, Documents Reveal." *Globe and Mail*, 8 January.

McDonald, Laura. 2008. "Islamic Feminism." *Feminist Theory* 9, no. 3: 347–54.

Middle East Magazine. 2014. "Current Affairs: Egypt Economic Development
Conference." *Middle East Magazine*, November. Accessed 26 November 2016.
http://www.themiddleeastmagazine.com/wp-mideastmag-live/2014/11/
current-affairs-egypt-economic-development-conference.

Middle East Monitor. 2014. "54 Documented Cases of Women Being Raped
While Detained in Egypt." *Middle East Monitor*, 4 July. https://www.middle
eastmonitor.com/news/africa/12544-54-documented-cases-of-women
-being-raped-while-detained-in-egypt.

Mitchell, Timothy. 1999. "Dreamland: The Neoliberalism of Your Desires." *Middle
East Report* 210 (spring): 28–32.

Osman, Tarek. 2011. *Egypt on the Brink: From the Rise of Nasser to the Fall of
Mubarak*. New Haven: Yale University Press.

Rabie, Dalia. 2014. "Sisi and His Women." *Mada Masr*, 25 May.

Ramadan, Nada. 2012. "Envisioning and Defining a New Egypt: Women and
Gender in the January 25th Uprising and Transitional Process." Master's thesis,
Georgetown University, Washington, DC.

Saleh, Heba. 2012. "Egyptian Women Fear Regression on Rights." *Financial Times*,
1 October.

Saunders, Doug. 2015. "Canada Sells 'Rule of Law' to Countries Like Egypt. But
Whose Rule? What Law?" *Globe and Mail*, 21 March.

Sharif, Ghada. 2013. "El-Sisi, You Need Only Wink with Your Eye." *Al-Masry
Al-Youm*, 25 July. Translated by Khalid Suliman. http://www.almasryalyoum.
com/news/details/198680.

Siddiqui, Haroon. 2013. "Canada Should Campaign for Democracy in Egypt."
Toronto Star, 18 August.

Swain, Ranjula Bali. 2012. *The Microfinance Impact*. New York: Routledge.

Tiessen, Rebecca. 2014. "Gender Equality and the 'Two CIDAS': Successes and Setbacks between 1976 and 2013." In *Rethinking Canadian Aid*, edited by Stephen
Brown, Molly den Heyer and David Black, 195–209. University of Ottawa Press.

UN News Centre. 2013. "Hunger, Poverty Rates in Egypt Up Sharply over Past
Three Years – UN Report." UN News Centre. Accessed 9 February 2015. http://
www.un.org/apps/news/story.asp?NewsID=44961#.VNlEoMYntl8.

Wassef, Nadia, and Nemat Guenena. 1999. *Unfulfilled Promises: Women's Rights in Egypt*. West Asia and North Africa Region: Population Council.

World Bank. 2003. *Trade, Investment, and Development in the Middle East and North Africa: Engaging with the World*. Washington, DC: World Bank.

– 2015. *Egypt, Arab Republic of – Country Partnership Framework for the Period FY2015-19*. World Bank. Accessed February 9 2015. http://documents. worldbank.org/curated/en/773051468197407822/Egypt-Arab-Republic-of-Country-partnership-framework-for-the-period-FY2015-19.

World Economic Forum (WEF). 2010. The World Economic Forum. Global Gender Gap Report 2010. Retrieved online 1 February 2015 from http://www. weforum.org/reports/global-gender-gap-report-2010.

– 2014. *Global Gender Gap Report 2014*. World Economic Forum. Accessed 26 November 2016. http://www3.weforum.org/docs/GGGR14/GGGR_Complete Report_2014.pdf.

Chapter 10

The Erasure of Gender in
Canada–Haiti Cooperation?

Stephen Baranyi and Shantelle Binette[1]

The fate of gender in Canada's international policies is generating lively debate among activists, parliamentarians, officials, and scholars. Some lament what they see as the marginalization or distortion of gender in Canada's international engagement, particularly under the Conservative governments, which governed from 2006 to 2015. In his original work on this issue, Liam Swiss (2012) argued that there was an inverse correlation between Ottawa's increased funding for conflict and security assistance, notably via the Stabilization and Reconstruction Task Force (START) and its Global Peace and Security Fund (GPSF), and its decreasing support for women's rights and gender equality (GE) abroad. Where support for GE has survived, it has done so in an instrumentalized and securitized form, because it advances other Western priorities such as security in Afghanistan. Even there, the ideal of GE was downgraded to "equality between men and women," under former minister of international cooperation Bev Oda.

Rebecca Tiessen (2014a) reinforced that analysis by suggesting that despite the Maternal, Newborn and Child Health Initiative and a high-profile stand against early and forced marriage, successive Harper governments indeed instrumentalized women and girls to promote other Canadian foreign policy goals. In so doing, they engineered a major shift from an agency-based, intersectional and therefore potentially transformative approach to gender, to an essentialist framing of women and girls as victims requiring our protection or charity. Those discursive changes are analyzed more extensively from a critical feminist perspective in an article on the "erasure of gender" (Tiessen and Carrier 2015). In it, the authors added nuances on how some "insider-activist" officials resisted changes pushed by the Harper government. Despite such resistance, they concluded that discursive changes had negative effects on cooperation, such as through the non-renewal of GE funds in several country programs, and through increased funding for less-controversial activities like women's participation in elections and girls' access to education – the results of which could be easily measured and reported to parliament. Tiessen also explored negotiations between insider activists and their political masters in "Gender Equality and the 'Two CIDAs'" (2014b), calling for new research on the results of such negotiations, given the creation of the Department of Foreign Affairs, Trade and Development (DFATD).

Those analyses offer important insights into the changing articulation of gender and other agendas in Ottawa. Swiss framed all conflict and security assistance as securitization and as a loss for GE, but that assumption tended to downplay substantive differences between distinct forms of assistance to promote security in different fragile states. For example, it did not help distinguish between aid used to win hearts and minds in the context of a counter-insurgency campaign in Afghanistan, versus aid used to support the training of women police officers in the context of more legitimate security sector reform in Haiti (Baranyi and Paducel 2012). It ignored the possibility that assistance coded as "peace, conflict, and security" could actually promote GE. Swiss also downplayed the possibility that agency by activists inside and outside the Canadian state enabled GE programming to survive despite official directives. However, in their chapter in this volume, Swiss and Barry (chapter 1) confirm the effect of pro-GE agency, at least for macro-level spending patterns. Our paper builds on Swiss and Barry's new data and responds to Tiessen's invitation for further research by looking more carefully at the case of Haiti – a case that does not fit the binary trade-off between security and gender evoked by some critics.

Salahub's study of gender in Canada–Haiti cooperation (2008) already documented the existence of strong women-focused programming by the Canadian International Development Agency (CIDA) during the post-9/11 era. Through its Kore Fanm Fund, CIDA supported Fanm Yo La's promotion of women's participation in the 2005/2006 elections in Haiti – as voters and as candidates. After the elections, the Kore Fanm Fund as well as Rights and Democracy supported activists who successfully pushed for legislative changes such as the criminalization of rape. CIDA also supported projects to strengthen the capacities of the Ministry

for the Condition of Women and Women's Rights (MCFDF). Yet Salahub noted that only 52 per cent of CIDA's projects in Haiti mentioned
women or gender in their reports on results (Salahub 2008, 58). Meanwhile, the Department of Foreign Affairs and International Trade (DFAIT)
championed the inclusion of GE in the resolutions mandating the UN Stabilization Mission in Haiti (MINUSTAH). The Royal Canadian Mounted
Police (RCMP) was trying to increase the 15 per cent share of women
police deployed to Haiti via the Canadian Police Arrangement (Salahub
2008, 63), and Correctional Services of Canada (CSC) was planning to
rehabilitate or build prison facilities for women. Salahub cautioned that
it was hard to ascertain the strength of GE in the activities of other government departments, given that it had not been rigorously assessed. She
ascribed Canada's mixed record of uneven buy-in to senior levels of government, as well as to weak commitments by government leaders in Haiti
– reminding us that gendered politics should be studied on both sides of
the development cooperation coin.

This paper picks up the Canada–Haiti story in 2007, when Salahub
ended her research. We have focused on Haiti for several reasons. First,
Canada's cooperation with Haiti has been one of its largest programs
since 2004, displacing Afghanistan in the top spot after the 2010 earthquake before settling into the third spot behind Mali and Tanzania, but
still ahead of Afghanistan in current plans (DFATD 2013a). Second, Canadian institutions have a long association with the women's movement in
Haiti. Canada educated many of the exiled women who became leaders
in the democratic movement during the 1980s. CIDA supported the institutionalization of the women's movement and the creation of the MCFDF
in the 1990s.[2] Third, unlike Afghanistan, Haiti has not recently been at
war. It has been plagued by protracted governance crises, violence, and
natural disasters. Those conditions and the mix of international actors
cooperating under the UN umbrella have enabled the construction of a
security-development nexus that differs from the militarized line-up in
Afghanistan (Baranyi 2011b) – opening up distinct spaces for the promotion of GE in that context. Fourth, with the exception of Salahub's
pivotal piece, the modest amount of literature on Canada–Haiti cooperation does not delve into the gender dimensions of that relationship.[3]
Given our contacts and experience, we are well-positioned to access
gender-disaggregated data on Canadian cooperation in that fragile and
conflict-affected state, building on the official evaluation of CIDA's programming there (DFATD 2015a).[4] Haiti is therefore a relevant place for us
to look at how GE has evolved, in Canada's international cooperation.

Responding to the critiques raised by Swiss and Tiessen, we explore the following issues: How has gender been framed discursively and put into practice in Canada's cooperation with Haiti, particularly since 2007? To what extent has gender been instrumentalized, securitized, or erased by post-9/11 priorities in practice? Why or why has it not been instrumentalized, securitized, or erased – in terms of the interplay between Canadian, Haitian, and global agency, norms, institutions, and power relations?

The last question evokes the theoretical framework through which we approach our subject. Our starting point is similar to Tiessen's critical, intersectional feminist approach. We are interested in the gender dimensions of international cooperation at the level of discourse and practice. We seek to comprehend the gendered construction of cooperation by officials in Canadian state agencies and by other Canadians such as feminist activists, as well as by their Haitian interlocutors. We also strive to understand how those social forces are embedded in wider normative frames, power relations (where class, race, gender, and age intersect in complex ways, as explained by Stienstra in chapter 5 of this volume), and evolving world orders. As noted elsewhere (Baranyi and Paducel 2012; Baranyi 2014), we share concerns highlighted by postcolonial feminist and other critics of the security–development nexus (Duffield 2001; Varynen 2010), yet our approach is rooted in Coxian critical theory (Cox 1987) and is therefore more sensitive to the diversity of arrangements that are socially constructed in different historical contexts.

In the next section, we analyze the gender dimensions of Canada–Haiti cooperation in three parts. First, we provide an overview of GE in Canada–Haiti cooperation, mainly at the discursive level. Second, we undertake a quantitative and qualitative examination of the gender dimensions across the portfolio formerly managed by CIDA – covering humanitarian assistance, and economic and social development, as well as some governance projects. Third, we focus on the domain of security and justice, managed mostly by DFAIT/DFATD. At all levels, we look at overall GE spending trends in the portfolio, at women-focused projects and at the record of gender mainstreaming in other projects. We also begin using critical security and development theory to explore how gender is manifested and why it has been socially constructed as such in that particular time and place. The chapter ends with our thoughts on the implications of this case for wider debates on the gendered character of international cooperation in fragile states.

Beyond the literature reviewed above, this chapter is based on open source research, as well as internal documents obtained from DFATD and other official agencies. It is also informed by confidential conversations and email exchanges with over forty Canadian and Haitian government, civil society, and UN informants, mainly in Ottawa and Port-au-Prince, in 2014 and 2015.[5]

GENDER DIMENSIONS OF CANADA–HAITI COOPERATION

The Big Picture, 2007–2015

Canada has a long history of engagement with Haiti, with cooperation dating back generations. After participating in the US-led military intervention in 2004, Canada began using a whole-of-government (WOG) approach to manage its scaled-up engagement in Haiti (Baranyi 2011a). That approach was buttressed by the creation of DFAIT's START in 2005. Indeed, Haiti has been one of the top Canadian official development assistance (ODA) partners since 2004, with cumulative aid disbursements amounting to over C$1 billion from 2006–2013 (DFATD 2015a, viii). CIDA's annual ODA disbursements to Haiti averaged C$100 million from 2006–2009, reached over C$245 million per year from 2009–2011, and decreased to less than C$83 million in 2012–2013 (see table 10.1). START committed more than C$80 million from the GPSF during the 2006–2013 period, yet CIDA's portfolio accounted for the majority of Canada's disbursements in Haiti. Even if we add all the assistance through the Canadian Police Arrangement to START/GPSF's side of the ledger, CIDA's Haiti portfolio dwarfed DFAIT expenditures by a factor of approximately eight to one over the 2004–2014 decade (Baranyi 2014).

The gender dimensions of Canadian discourse vis-à-vis Haiti have followed trends in Canada's broader international policies, as identified by Tiessen (2014a). Between 2010 and 2014 there was little mention of the term "gender equality" in official statements or press releases concerning Haiti, consistent with the shift in terminology from "gender equality" to "equality between women and men" under Minister Oda. When women were mentioned, they were portrayed as either vulnerable victims of violence requiring Canada's intervention, or recipients of services provided by generous Canadian citizens. Minister Julian Fantino's January 2013 address exemplified that view. In his words: "Due to the generosity of Canadian taxpayers ... more than three million Haitian women, newborns and children have access to free health services in 63 health institutions nationwide through Canada's assistance" (DFATD 2013b).

There is also no indication of GE being a priority in Canada–Haiti cooperation, or any evidence of transformative GE results in any public

TABLE 10.1 Gender equality focus of CIDA's aid program in Haiti, 2006–2013 (CAD)

	2006–07	2007–08	2008–09	2009–10
0	57,465,719.7	69,064,380	88,691,778	144,724,927
1	23,461,504.8	7,527,831	17,015,954	62,442,065
2	23,461,504.8	21,766,396	27,628,610	38,521,591
3	5,337,900.0	5,208,765	1,307,756	1,140,887
T	109,726,629.3	103,567,372	134,644,098	246,829,470

	2010–11	2011–12	2012–13
0	132,558,932	44,781,936	18,338,755
1	68,372,485	40,229,875	19,646,921
2	46,006,106	65,364,437	44,708,502
3	250,918	249,990	50,000
T	247,188,441	150,626,238	82,744,178

Methodological notes for figure 10.1 and table 10.1: Data downloaded from DFATD's Open Data Historical Project Dataset (DFATD 2014e). We sorted by project browser country ID (column AQ), cut out all but "HT," sorted by country/region name (column AS), cut out all but "Haiti," sorted by gender equality (marker), and summed the totals in column "Amount Spent" (AX) for each marker.

statements by ministers after 2009. Indeed, when the word "women" was mentioned, it was typically preceded by a number indicating the amount of women who were recipients of Canadian assistance. The complete absence of GE at the level of public discourse and its translation into an essentialist view of women is problematic, and seems to confirm the hypothesis of the erasure of gender in Canada's programming in Haiti.

Nonetheless, Swiss and Barry's observation (this volume) of disconnections between ministerial discourses and GE spending suggests that we should look more carefully at Canada's actual practices in Haiti. This chapter carefully reviews evidence suggesting that despite clear shifts at the level of official pronouncements, the promotion of GE endured in Canada's actual cooperation with Haiti.[6] Moreover, it documents what could be the start of a shift back to a more transformative conception of GE, through the visible statements by Canada's ambassador to Haiti, Paula Caldwell, at the presentation of Haiti's Policy for Gender Equality and Action Plan for Gender Equality in 2015.

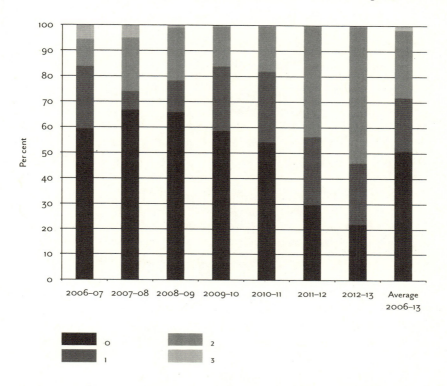

FIGURE 10.1   Gender equality focus of CIDA's aid program in Haiti, 2006–2013

Gender in the (Ex-)CIDA Portfolio

CIDA's priorities in Haiti have varied during this period, reflecting changing Canadian thematic emphases as well as evolving Haitian development
plans. Though the packaging has changed, four priorities have remained
constant since 2007: humanitarian assistance; children and youth (including maternal, newborn, and child health, as well as education); economic
growth, with an emphasis on food security since 2009; and governance
(DFATD 2014a; Baranyi 2014).

DFATD's Historical Project Data Set (HPDS) details the expenditures
of CIDA (which merged into DFATD in 2013) in Haiti, coding all disbursements to indicate the extent to which GE goals and results were
registered.[7] The HPDS data suggest that almost half of CIDA's programming in Haiti made GE a priority. As illustrated in figure 10.1 and detailed
in table 10.1, 49 per cent of programming since 2006 had GE either as a
principal (coded as 3), intermediate (coded as 2), or immediate (coded
as 1) priority. There was also a notable increase in the percentage with

positive GE results at the intermediate and immediate outcome levels, from 35 per cent in 2006–2007 to 78 per cent in 2012–2013.

Yet figure 10.1 and table 10.1 indicate a significant drop between 2008 and 2013 of programming coded as having GE as a principal objective and outcome. That decline coincides with the 2008 decision by Minister Oda to reject her officials' proposal to scale up programming to promote GE systematically in Haiti. Such an integrated program would have included a renewal of the Kore Fanm Fund; an expansion of support to the MCFDF to strengthen its country-wide presence and policy role within government; and stronger gender mainstreaming in the rest of the portfolio. Minister Oda supported only the last element, while giving a green light to more women- and girl-focused projects in areas like health and education.[8]

The increase in activities with GE as an intermediate and immediate outcome, illustrated in figure 10.1, may reflect the results of CIDA's attempt to mainstream GE as a cross-cutting theme. Indeed, an official evaluation of Haiti–Canada cooperation (DFATD 2015a) suggests that CIDA's cooperation has led to positive gender outcomes in some sectors, despite GE not always being integrated or systematically monitored across the portfolio. To understand the extent to which GE was prioritized or compromised by such decisions, we need to look at the qualitative dimensions of funding in different sectors and projects.

According to the official evaluation (DFATD 2015a, 16), CIDA's programming in Haiti's health sector since 2010 has shown mixed GE results. Priorities have been shaped by needs identified by the Interim Reconstruction Commission and the Ministry of Public Health (DFATD 2015a, 11), and align well with Canada's broader priorities, notably the country's commitment to the 2010 Muskoka Initiative. Accordingly, investments have concentrated on providing maternal and child health care (C$33 million), improving management of the national health system (C$30 million), reconstructing the hospital in Gonaïves (C$29.25 million), fighting HIV/AIDS (C$20 million), and vaccination (C$15 million) (DFATD 2015a, 11). Though Canada's engagement contributed to substantial progress in reducing maternal mortality, the majority of CIDA's programming in this sector neglected to prioritize gender beyond the participation of female beneficiaries.

CIDA's programming in the education sector has prioritized improving student access, retention, and graduation, while reducing the gaps in these areas between girls and boys, as well as improving pedagogical and management practices (DFATD 2015a, 12). Consequently, the Credit for School Fees program was developed to offer school fee loans to parents and improve quality of classroom instruction. Since 2008, it has enabled 9,944 children to attend school, 57.6 per cent of whom were girls. That achievement is substantial, though just as in the health sector, the program was limited to simply increasing the number of female beneficiaries instead of addressing the deeper roots of inequality that perpetuate disparities in student performance. Still, other programming included training for teachers on the integration of GE in their pedagogy, and supporting the development of GE-focused human resources practices in community-based institutions like parent committees (CCHC 2015, 29).

Projects in economic development and food security have also had mixed results, landing somewhere on the spectrum of having significant, lasting gender results and none at all. For example, the credit component of the Agriculture Finance and Insurance System in Haiti project permitted approximately 25,000 women to increase their productive capacity and generate revenue, with positive effects on the quality of life of children and families (DFATD 2015a, 13). A number of projects led by Canadian organizations in this sector worked in partnership with women's groups to prioritize the strategic needs of women, and provided large-scale training and awareness campaigns (DFATD 2015a, 16). Yet while the Cayes-Jérémie road project (C$75 million from 2008 to 2014) included a quota of 30 per cent women's participation in the project, there is little publicly available evidence[9] of that quota being filled, or any publicly available documentation of women obtaining work after their training (DFATD 2015a, 16).

Nonetheless, CIDA's programming in the governance sector has had notably positive GE results, with some projects taking a transformational approach by empowering women to be agents of change, not simply regarding them as bodies to fill quotas or privileged recipients of services. For example, the Support for the Rights of Children and Youth and the Participation of Vulnerable Populations program managed by Rights and Democracy in 2010–2012 educated 2,224 adults and 4,035 students on gender-based violence; provided legal support for fifteen minors and twenty-two girls who were victims of sexual assault; published five reports on the living conditions of prison inmates; and financed a fund that supported original studies on migration, incarceration, and domestic violence against women (DFATD 2014b; 2015a, 16). The program included training that empowered women to become leaders in community decision making and supported NGOs that were instrumental in passing the constitutional amendment requiring a 30 per cent quota for women in state activities (DFATD 2014a). Canada's governance programming also contributed to equipping women who were active in Haiti's political parties with the technical knowledge and protection required to participate in the 2015 elections as candidates, trainers, or campaign managers (CCHC 2015, 30).

CIDA's governance programming also included support to professionalize the Haitian National Police (PNH). Within that framework, the C$16.5 million project for Initial Training and Professional Development for the Haitian National Police's Managerial Staff (FIPCA-PNH), executed by Quebec-based institutions in partnership with the National Police Academy (ANP), also has a significant gender component (DFATD 2014d). Based on agreements with CIDA, FIPCA and the ANP took meaningful steps to accommodate the health, security, and privacy needs of women students and staff onsite. In 2012, the first cohort of forty-one student cadres included five women officers (12 per cent of that cohort). In 2013, the second cohort of thirty-seven student cadres included only two women (5 per cent).[10] At FIPCA's insistence and after being reminded by Haitian President Michel Martelly that this was inconsistent with the new national quota of 30 per cent female representation in the public service, the ANP launched a special recruitment process for women. Although that effort only generated one female officer out of thirty-four cadres (2.5 per cent) in 2014, it generated six women officers out of thirty-nine cadres (15 per cent) in the fourth cohort, admitted in 2015.[11]

With Canadian technical assistance, the ANP also worked to mainstream gender across its curriculum. It effectively eliminated gender-biased language and integrated gender sensitivity in all teaching modules – for example on ethics, personal security, human resource management, community policing, equipment, and weapons management (ANP 2013; Ménard 2013). However, in-class observation and conversations with Canadian and Haitian staff, as well as with a range of student cadres in June to July 2014, suggest that gender sensitivity is still practiced unevenly by instructors and by student cadres. It also suggests that the PNH high command has only begun to internalize the principles of GE. As one senior Haitian government official put it: "As long as the chiefs don't change, norms will not be applied."[12]

Canadian partners are aware of those institutional challenges. As one report noted:

> The fifth year of the FIPCA-PNH project constitutes the last opportunity to consolidate gains in equality between men and women inside the ANP and in the management practices of PNH graduates. This year offers a unique time frame to permit cadres, managers and personnel of the ANP, supported by Canadian partners, to complete planned activities, refine what has been built, evaluate results, draw

"lessons learned" and appropriate themselves of associated adminis-
trative and pedagogical responsibilities. (Ménard 2014, 13, translated
by the authors)

Given the ambitions of this pioneering effort and its enduring challenges,
it will be important to assess its gendered results at the end of the project
in 2016.

In sum, despite its almost complete erasure from ministerial discourse, GE remained an important dimension of CIDA's engagement on
the ground in Haiti, from 2007 to 2014. Although funding for programming with GE as a principal goal declined after 2006, programming that
included GE results at the level of intermediate and immediate outcomes
more than doubled. That included a critical mass of women and girl-cen-
tred projects in sectors such as health, education, economic development,
and governance. Some of those projects were framed in traditional terms,
but others were at least implicitly about empowering women (and sometimes men) to challenge patriarchy, impunity, and privilege. This calls into
question broad claims about the instrumentalization or erasure of gender
in Canada's programs. Still, we should recall that Conservative decision
makers blocked a proposal that would have scaled up Canada's GE programming in Haiti. As a result, Canada and Haiti lost the Kore Fanm
Fund, with negative consequences. A key Haitian official identified that
sudden halt in funding as a major setback for the MCFDF, as no other
donor filled the gap left by CIDA's withdrawal.

Yet CIDA officials adapted by finding other venues through which to
support the MCFDF. Through the Strengthening of Public Management
Project (PARGEP), the governments of Canada and Quebec supported
the participatory elaboration of the Haitian Policy for Equality between
Women and Men, unveiled in March 2015 (ENAP 2015). Through the
Technical Support in Haiti (PATH) project, CIDA backed the elaboration
of the National Action Plan for Equality between Women and Men, presented in May 2015 (CIDA 2015). Ambassador Caldwell was present at
both events, pointedly underscoring Canada's longstanding and ongoing
support for governmental initiatives that "will inevitably lead to durable
progress and structural changes for all of society" (authors' translation
from le Nouvelliste 2015, 10). As such, Canada quietly but steadily supported the crafting of the strategic documents enshrining the Haitian
state's commitments to a transformative approach to gender mainstreaming in all areas of public policy over the coming decades.[13]

The continuation of GE programming despite changing priorities at
the upper echelons of political power suggests that GE activists within

the state bureaucracy, buttressed by international norms and the creative agency by partners in countries like Haiti, can redirect some attempts to shift priorities. However, discursive shifts and the loss of the Kore Fanm Fund remind us that insider activists cannot resist all political pressures. Clearly, programming practices reflect a complex negotiation of agendas between bureaucrats and their masters, at both ends of cooperation relationships – as suggested by Tiessen, Swiss, and Barry (this volume).

Gender in the START/GPSF Portfolio

Internal DFATD documents support Salahub's suggestion (2008) that, notwithstanding Canada's championing of a gender-sensitive mandate for MINUSTAH, the gender dimension of the department's material cooperation with Haiti was not particularly stellar. As shown in table 10.2, just under half of its Haiti projects took women stakeholders' views into account at the design stage, and less than a third resulted in the protection of women or their access to significant project benefits. The otherwise rigorous summative evaluation of START's Haiti portfolio was almost gender-blind (DFAIT 2009; Baranyi 2011a). As a result, the evaluation shed no light on whether major projects like strengthening the Office of the Inspectorate General reinforced that unit's capacity to discipline police officers who violated the rights of female colleagues or clients.

Some officials were aware of that blind spot. They worked hard to promote gender sensitivity and a broader emphasis on the "software" side of security and justice programming. As a result, the multi-annual strategy formulated after the earthquake included a significant gender dimension (MAÉCI 2010). Its contextual analysis highlighted the vulnerability of women and children in post-earthquake internally displaced person (IDP) camps as a significant security issue. It mentioned the vulnerability of those groups and of disabled persons in disputes over land, property, and inheritance rights. It also noted problems associated with the lack of separate detention facilities for women and minors in many prisons. The document did not systematically analyze the gender dimensions of wider rule-of-law issues such as impunity for violence against women (beyond the camps for IDPs) or what Haitian women's organizations were already doing to support victims and/or to advocate institutional reforms, yet its second cross-cutting objective was to:

> reinforce local capacities to counter threats to the security and physical integrity of women and children, notably in camps for displaced persons, in communities and in detention centres. That includes training and sensitizing police and correctional officers services in

TABLE 10.2 Gender dimensions of START/GPSF projects in Haiti, 2006–2013

TIME FRAME AND SAMPLE SIZE	WOMEN PARTICIPATED IN PROJECT DESIGN	ADDRESSED VIOLENCE AGAINST WOMEN	GAVE WOMEN ACCESS TO RESOURCES	AVERAGES
2006–9 (8 PROJECTS)	4 (50%)	3 (38%)	1 (13%)	2.66 (33%)
2010–13 (13 PROJECTS)	5 (38%)	3 (23%)	5 (38%)	4.33 (33%)
TOTALS (21 PROJECTS)	9 (43%)	6 (29%)	6 (29%)	7 (33%)

Sources: DFATD 2014f, 2014g, and 2014h. Though this data is only indicative, the sample includes 21 of the 43 projects supported by START/GPSF in Haiti from 2006 to 2013.

the needs of children and women, establishing specialized units in this area, as well as rehabilitating or constructing prison infrastructures to allow the separate detention of women and minors. (MAÉCI 2010, 12, translated by the authors)

Informed by that outlook,[14] START/GPSF approved several projects with significant gender elements. The most visible was perhaps the Frontline Justice project, managed by Lawyers Without Borders Canada (ASFC). With C$2.5 million funding from DFAIT, ASFC collaborated with the Port-au-Prince Bar Association and the Movement of Haitian Women for Education and Development (MOUFHED) in 2011 to 2013, to provide legal assistance to women and other vulnerable persons displaced by the earthquake, mostly in the capital area. Women accounted for 65 per cent of the 1,900 persons who received legal assistance. In some cases, that led to significant justice outcomes, such as for the 300 persons who received official birth or death certificates enabling them to claim social benefits. ASFC notes that over seventy Haitian legal personnel also received professional training (ASFC 2013, 2014). START/GPSF was unable to renew funding beyond 2013, yet ASFC obtained other Canadian funds to support Haitian team members' efforts to continue offering legal services to women and other "oppressed" Haitians.[15] Though women and other "victims" of displacement were prominent in the conception of this project, the partnership has since taken a potentially more transformative direction.

START also made a modest C$1 million contribution, through UN Women, to strengthen services for victims of gender-based violence, particularly in IDP camps in the capital and in Léogâne. This involved providing gender training for PNH officers deployed in the camps, as well as strengthening their capacity to work collaboratively with statutory and civil society institutions offering medical or legal assistance to victims. The final UN Women (2013) report suggests that the project significantly enhanced the capacities of PNH and other officials to assist victims of gender-based violence, in conjunction with other agencies. However, some officials doubt those claims and suggest that there may have been duplication of training programs coordinated by the PNH and by NGOs like ASFC in some communities.[16]

Since 2007, START has provided about C$10 million of phased funding to support the deployment of CSC officers to Haiti. That began with the deployment of a small contingent of senior officers posted to MINUSTAH to provide policy and planning mentoring to their Haitian counterparts in the Directorate of Penitentiary Administration (DAP). It grew into the deployment of twenty-five Canadian officers during the period following the earthquake – to help the DAP manage the prison crisis, as well as to support the construction and effective administration of a new model prison at Croix-des-Bouquets.

Although there is no publically available data on the proportion of female CSC officers who were deployed through that channel, the report on the last deployment notes that six of the eighteen officers deployed (33 per cent) were women (CSC 2013). Similarly, while START's data (DFATD 2014g) suggests that the CSC deployments were not particularly gender-sensitive, project reports tell a more nuanced story. For example, one report notes that women and juvenile detainees were released from Les Cayes prison "through the advocacy and mentoring efforts by CSC/MINUSTAH" (CSC 2012, 2). Furthermore:

> CSC/MINUSTAH advocated for more recreation time at both the women's facility in Pétionville and the young offender facility in Delmas 33. At Pétionville, CSC ... was instrumental in advocating for repairs ... in perimeter infrastructure to help ... augment hygiene conditions, as well as securing a supply of sanitary pads and mentoring officials on the need and manner to ration them. (CSC 2012, 7)

With regard to infrastructure, most of the detention facilities built with GPSF funding, such as the Croix-des-Bouquets prison, were intended for men – which seems appropriate given that men comprise the lion's share of detainees in Haiti. Yet some facilities were constructed specifically for women: for example, the rehabilitation of the Cap-Haïtien prison included the construction of three cells for women and minors, enabling their separate incarceration from adult men (PADF 2010). Those interventions did not transform gender relations in Haiti's prisons, yet they modestly enhanced the conditions for some women within those confines.

Though only partly funded through START/GPSF, the deployment of Canadian police personnel to MINUSTAH via the Canadian Police Arrangement has been another mechanism for Canadian engagement in Haiti's security reforms. As such, Canada deployed approximately eighty-five Canadian police officers per year via MINUSTAH from 2006 onward, making it the largest Canadian police deployment in the world. Yet officials had great difficulty increasing the share of women officers deployed from the level noted by Salahub for 2006. Of the eighty-one police officers deployed in early 2014, ten (12 per cent) were women (UNSG 2014, 22). That share increased in 2015, when thirteen of the fifty-seven Canadian UN Police (23 per cent) deployed via the Canadian Police Arrangement were women (UNSG 2015, 19). In part, that reflects the difficulty of finding female Canadian police officers who are able to deploy to Haiti for postings of six months or more. It also reflects Ottawa's decision to prioritize Canadian strengths like community policing in its police deployments – unlike the Norwegians, for example, who prioritized gender-based violence in their police cooperation. Despite this, Canadian police women occupied key positions in the program, including as the francophone interface between Norwegian trainers and PNH personnel in 2014.[17]

In sum, our data suggest that despite its inauspicious beginnings in Haiti from a GE angle, START/GPSF gradually developed a more gender-sensitive programming framework and several women-focused projects; it also integrated gender transversally in some of its larger security-sector projects. After the earthquake, START moved beyond an urgent-action, victim-centred approach by investing in the hardware and software of Haitian institutions and by strengthening their capacities to effect some gender-sensitive changes. Despite such adaptation, only about 33 per cent of the START/GPSF portfolio was gender sensitive. This nuanced picture does not fit the neat security–GE trade-offs observed by Swiss and Tiessen in other contexts. Nor does it fit neatly with the tendency for gender to become instrumentalized by foreign humanitarian actors, as observed by Côté (2014) after the earthquake.

CONCLUSIONS

In line with the patterns observed by Tiessen and others, there is no doubt that ministerial views and discourses on Haiti shifted remarkably after 2007 and that this had negative effects on Canada's GE programming in Haiti. Minister Oda rejected her officials' proposal to scale up GE programming in Haiti, greatly restricting Canada's ability to support the MCFDF and civil society institutions genuinely promoting GE. Minister Fantino further shifted toward an essentialist, victim-based discourse on Haitian women, which affected CIDA programming after the earthquake. Those political shifts go some way to explaining why the proportion of GE-focused Canadian aid to Haiti decreased after 2007.

What is more surprising is that gender remained an important dimension of CIDA–Haiti cooperation – in quantitative and qualitative terms. The proportion of CIDA aid with GE as an intermediate and immediate outcome actually increased after 2007. It remained significant in traditional areas like maternal and child health, as well as in education, but also in the areas of economic growth and governance. Much of that involved conventional support for maternal and child health, and education, or for women's participation in elections as voters. But it also involved supporting advocacy – by a lucid Haitian women's movement – for legislative and practical changes to transform relations between men and women, from the household to the workplace and indeed to the sphere of state power. So while it is accurate to say that CIDA's GE programming in Haiti has been weakened in recent years, it is important to recognize the extent of creative adaptation rather than assuming that GE disappeared from the scene.

Perhaps the most interesting finding is that the GE dimensions of security and justice-sector programming, managed mostly by DFAIT/START, also evolved during this period. From its modest beginnings in the first generation of START programming in Haiti, security and justice assistance was adapted through a gender-inclusive strategy – through projects focused on women's rights as well as the mainstreaming of gender in larger projects like prison reform and training for mid-level and senior police officers, including a small number of women police cadres.

Those patterns support our initial skepticism about a clear trade-off between security assistance and GE programming, and about the erasure of gender from Canadian cooperation practices. The situation in Haiti, one of Canada's largest country programs since 2004, is much more complex. GE was marginalized discursively in Canada–Haiti cooperation, but in practice it was adapted rather than being erased or instrumentalized to serve other policy goals.

More research is certainly required to understand these complex trends. There is a particular need to assess the gendered results of security and justice programming, since neither the FIPCA project nor the START/GPSF portfolio were adequately covered by the evaluation of CIDA programming from 2006 to 2013.[18] Yet the question requiring the most research and analysis is the question of why these uneven advances have materialized. So far, our explanation for the uneven advances of Canada's gender programming in Haiti is the agency of CIDA, DFAIT, and other Government of Canada officials who pushed for innovations in spite of the views of their superiors. That certainly fits the suggestion mooted by Tiessen of negotiations between "insider activists" and Conservative decision makers. Yet we still know little about how the agency of Haitian officials and activists, international GE norms, and gendered relations of power influenced negotiations among Canadian and Haitian actors at the project, program, or strategic levels.

In order to understand these dynamics, it would be useful to trace the micro-level processes through which a sample of strategies and projects were socially constructed in Ottawa, Port-au-Prince, and elsewhere. In terms of CIDA, these processes could include the bureaucratic formulation and political rejection of the GE program in 2008, and the adaptation of projects that carried some of its goals forward. They could also include the social construction (and non-approval) of START/GPSF's 2010–2014 Haiti strategy – of GE-sensitive GPSF-funded initiatives like the deployment of Canadian corrections and police. The gendered construction and results of the FIPCA project deserve particular attention in this context. Further analysis could also include the careful study of how gender was integrated into the Canada–Haiti cooperation strategy announced in June 2015 (CIDA 2015), building on the evaluation report released that year (DFATD 2015a).

Such research may also enable us to make full use of a critical, intersectional theoretical framework to analyze the social construction of gender in Canada–Haiti cooperation. That could provide a stronger basis on which to move beyond the binary of security versus gender, while contributing to more nuanced generalizations about the gender dimensions of the security–development nexus in Canada's engagement in different fragile and conflict-affected states.

In the meantime, this case study suggests that despite the creative preservation of GE in Canada–Haiti cooperation, there is considerable scope for renewal over the coming years. At the declaratory and policy levels, high-level officials (on both sides of the bilateral relationship) could more consistently emphasize the importance of GE in their cooperation, as Canadian diplomats have started doing again in Port-au-Prince.

When the Canadian government eventually shares more information on the Canada–Haiti country strategy announced in June 2015, it could ensure that gender analysis and GE promotion are more prominent than they were in the first announcement. Ottawa could also explicitly link its new cooperation strategy to the GE action plan adopted by the Haitian government (with Canadian support) in the same year.

New projects and broader practices that could flow from such an approach include:

- Institutional support to the MCFDF, to strengthen its links to the countrywide governmental GE network and its partnerships with local women's (and men's) organizations, as well as its ability to collaborate with other ministries to mainstream gender in all public policies, from gender-sensitive budgeting to gender-sensitive results-based management across all portfolios (as per the action plan).
- Renewed support to the dynamic but under-resourced Haitian women's movement, by re-establishing a mechanism like the Kore Fanm Fund or by providing budget support to the MCFDF to enable it to take on that responsibility (as suggested in the action plan).
- Strengthening the gender dimension of results-based programming in Canada's cooperation across the priority sectors of economic growth, democratic governance, rule of law, and security, as well as health and education. That should include working with Haitian partners to increase the number of female beneficiaries, as well as supporting the agency of women and men working to transform attitudes, laws, and practices.

Joint monitoring and evaluation of gendered results across the Canada–Haiti cooperation portfolio could be another strategic domain of collaboration, particularly as gendered monitoring and evaluation is flagged as a priority in the action plan. The Mutual Accountability Framework being negotiated by the two governments offers another opportunity to codify joint commitments in this regard. Finally, Canadian and Haitian decision makers could do much more to support policy research in this area, through the establishment of a GE observatory or by supporting networks of Haitian (and Canadian) researchers already active in this domain. As noted in the action plan, evidence-based research can inform social input into relevant public practices. Having invested heavily in developing that action plan, Canada now has the strategic opportunity to support its implementation in the near future.

NOTES

1 A draft of this paper was presented at the Canadian Association for the Study of International Development (CASID) annual conference at Brock University in St Catharines on 29 May 2014.

2 This summarizes the story as told to one of the authors by a lifelong Canadian educator and supporter of the Haitian women's movement.

3 For reviews of that case-specific literature, see Baranyi 2011a and 2014, as well as Baranyi and Paducel 2012.

4 In 2013 to 2014, Baranyi was the external expert for the official evaluation of ex-CIDA programming in Haiti.

5 Our primary research was carried out in Port-au-Prince and in Ottawa, mainly from April to June 2014, and February to June 2015.

6 There is some validity to governmental reports on the implementation of gender-sensitive principles in programming in Haiti (DFATD 2014c, 2014h). Yet independent analysts are correct in noting that those reports do not provide enough data to systematically assess Canada's gendered engagement in Haiti or elsewhere (Woroniuk and Minnings 2014).

7 The data set only includes funding disbursed by CIDA. Funding disbursed by DFAIT/START and other Canadian departments is not available in the HPDS, and those agencies do not share GE-coded data with the public. For the base data and additional explanations of how we used it, see the Annex. Those trends are consistent with earlier observations based on other measurement scales. A background document for the CIDA-commissioned review of its GE policy (Bytown 2007) suggested that from 1998 to 2006, the GE-focused content of its programming in Haiti averaged only 2.8 per cent – and varied from a high of 6.8 per cent in 2001 to 2002 to a low of 1.6 per cent in 2004 to 2005 (180). This corresponds roughly to trends for GE as a principal objective and results, noted in figure 1, for 2006 to 2013. Similarly, Salahub's figure of 52 per cent is only slightly higher than the total proportion of the country program that took women or GE into account during the 2006 to 2013 period. However, we cannot conclude that there was a decrease of GE programming in Haiti after 2006 because these data are not strictly comparable. See Swiss and Barry (this volume) for a broader explanation of the HPDS, its coding procedures, and their limits.

8 From background conversations with CIDA officials in Port-au-Prince on 8 June 2009, as well as in Ottawa on 21 November 2009 and 16 September 2011; and a conversation with a key Haitian government official on 10 June 2014.

9 An internal document (CCHC 2015, 27) suggests that the majority of beneficiaries of the Cayes-Jérémie road project who received training in heavy machine

operation and road maintenance were female. It also indicates that small businesses were developed from the project, but does not specify whether they are owned by women. Because this document has not been made public, we stand by the results of the public synthesis report of the evaluation (DFATD 2015a).

10 This reflects the current proportion of women at middle (5 per cent) and senior (3 per cent) levels of the Haitian National Police. Yet it is far below the target of 30 per cent set by the 2013 constitutional amendment. See Ménard 2013: Tableau 1.

11 This analysis of FIPCA's GE plans and results is based on a reading of internal documentation, background conversations with four Canadian and four Haitian officials or project personnel, and participant observation at the ANP, mostly in Port-au-Prince on 3, 6, 9, 11, and 13 June 2014. It is also informed by one author's correspondence with ANP officials on 4 September 2014, as well as by conversations with Haitian and Canadian officials at the ANP on 6 February 2015.

12 From a background conversation with a senior Haitian government official, Port-au-Prince, 10 June 2014.

13 See Gouvernement d'Haiti 2015a and Gouvernement d'Haiti 2015b for references to those strategic documents (and to Canadian support for their production).

14 Although the draft strategy was not officially adopted, DFATD officials claim that it informed their programming efforts. Our project-level research supports that claim.

15 From background conversations with two Canadian officials, a Canadian NGO worker, and three Haitian NGO staff, in Port-au-Prince, 2, 6, and 9 June 2014. The word "oppressed" comes from the name of the NGO that emerged from the partnership with ASFC, namely Défense des opprimées/opprimés. See http://www.frontlinedefenders.org/fr/node/23601, accessed on 3 November 2014.

16 From background conversations with a Canadian official and a Haitian official, Port-au-Prince, 6 and 9 June 2014.

17 From background conversations with three Canadian police officers assigned to MINUSTAH/UN Police, as well as a senior Haitian government official, Port-au-Prince, 4 and 9 June 2014.

18 An evaluation of START's global program was conducted in mid-2014, in a matter of weeks. Though we have not been able to obtain a copy of the evaluation, conversations with START officials suggest that it does not offer a deep assessment of Haiti programming or of its gender dimensions because of its global scope and its short execution time frame. A more rigorous evaluation of START programming was apparently underway in 2016.

REFERENCES

Académie nationale de police (ANP). 2013. "Programme de formation continue des commissaires. Code:220. Le programme." Port-au-Prince: Académie nationale de police.

Avocats sans frontières Canada (ASFC). 2013. "Rapport final: Projet Justice de première ligne en Haiti." FPSM 09-156. Avocats sans frontières Canada.

– 2014. "Haiti: Front Line Justice." Avocats sans frontières Canada. Accessed 20 May 2014. http://www.asfcanada.ca/en/lwbc-in-action/lwbc-programmes/18/haiti-program.

Baranyi, Stephen. 2011. "Canada and the Travail of Partnership in Haiti." In *Fixing Haiti. MINUSTAH and Beyond*, edited by Andrew Thompson and Jorge Heine, 205–28. Tokyo: United Nations University Press.

– 2011b. "Special Issue: Cooperation for Reconstruction, Peace and Transformation in Haiti." *Journal of Peacebuilding and Development* 6, no. 3.

– 2014. "Canada and the Security-Development Nexus in Haiti: The 'Dark Side' or Changing Shades of Grey?" *Canadian Foreign Policy Journal* 20, no. 2: 163–75.

Baranyi, Stephen, and Anca Paducel. 2012. "Whither Development in Canada's Engagement in Fragile States?" In *Struggling for Effectiveness: CIDA and Canadian Foreign Aid*, edited by Stephen Brown, 108–34. Montreal and Kingston: McGill-Queen's University Press.

Bytown Consulting. 2007. "Profile of CIDA Investments. Evaluation of CIDA Gender Equality Programming." Ottawa: Bytown Consulting.

Canadian International Development Agency (CIDA). 2015. "Project Profile: Technical Support in Haiti." Canadian International Development Agency. Accessed 28 July 2015. http://www.acdi-cida.gc.ca/cidaweb/cpo.nsf/projen/A033889001.

Centre de coopération Haiti-Canada (CCHC). 2015. "État des lieux EFH : Version finale Mai 2015." Centre de coopération Haiti-Canada.

Côté, Denyse. 2014. "Anpil fanm tonbe, n'ap kontinye vanse: luttes féministes en Haiti." *Revue possibles* 38, no. 1: 209–23.

Correctional Services Canada (CSC). 2012. "Deployment of CSC Officers to MINUSTAH. Final Project Report to GPSF." Correctional Services Canada.

– 2013. "Deployment of CSC Officers to MINUSTAH. 2012–2013 Final Report to GPSF." Correctional Services Canada.

Cox, Robert. 1987. *Production, Power and World Order: Social Forces in the Making of History.* New York: Columbia University Press.

Department of Foreign Affairs and International Trade (DFAIT). 2009. "Summative Evaluation of START's Global Peace and Security Fund: Haiti. Final Report." Ottawa: Department of Foreign Affairs and International Trade.

– 2010. "Building Peace and Security for All: Canada's Action Plan for the Implementation of United Nations Security Council Resolutions on Women, Peace
and Security." Department of Foreign Affairs and International Trade.

Department of Foreign Affairs, Trade and Development (DFATD). 2013a. "Report
on Plans and Priorities 2014–15." Ottawa: Department of Foreign Affairs, Trade
and Development.

– 2013b. "Development in Haiti." Department of Foreign Affairs, Trade and
Development. Accessed 4 August 2014. http://www.acdi-cida.gc.ca/acdi-cida/
acdi-cida.nsf/eng/NAT-18123021-NJJ.

– 2014a. "Haiti." Department of Foreign Affairs, Trade and Development.
Accessed 9 May 2014. http://www.acdi-cida.gc.ca/acdi-cida/acdi-cida.nsf/En/
JUD-12912349-NLX#a2.

– 2014b. "Project Profile: Support for the Rights of Children and Youth and the
Participation of Vulnerable Populations." Department of Foreign Affairs,
Trade and Development. Accessed 9 May 2014. http://www.acdi-cida.gc.ca/
cidaweb/cpo.nsf/vLUWebProjEn/36B5B9417087ECA1852574C2003719D9.

– 2014c. "2012–2013 Progress Report: Canada's Action Plan for the Implementation of United Nations Security Council Resolutions on Women, Peace and
Security." Department of Foreign Affairs, Trade and Development. Accessed
4 August 2014. http://www.international.gc.ca/START-GTSR/women_
report_2012-2013_rapport_femmes.aspx.

– 2014d. "Project Profile: Initial Training and Professional Development for the
Haitian National Police's Managerial Staff." Department of Foreign Affairs,
Trade and Development. Accessed 9 May 2014. http://www.acdi-cida.gc.ca/
cidaweb/cpo.nsf/projen/A032561001.

– 2014e. "Open Data Historical Project Dataset." Department of Foreign Affairs,
Trade and Development. Accessed 26 July 2014. http://www.international.
gc.ca/department-ministere/open_data-donnees_ouvertes/dev/historical_
project-historiques_projets.aspx?lang=eng.

– 2014f. Email to the authors about START's Haiti projects, 22 May.

– 2014g. Email to the authors about START's Haiti projects, 26 May.

– 2014h. Email to the authors about START's Haiti projects, 2 June.

– 2015a. *Evaluation of Canada-Haiti Cooperation 2006–2013: Synthesis Report*.
Department of Foreign Affairs, Trade and Development. Accessed 28 July
2015. http://www.international.gc.ca/department-ministere/evaluation/2015/
dev-eval-canada-haiti01.aspx?lang=eng.

– 2015b. "Document d'information. Engagement renouvelé du Canada en
Haïti (2015–2020)." Department of Foreign Affairs, Trade and Development. Accessed 20 June 2015. http://www.international.gc.ca/media/dev/
news-communiques/2015/06/12b_bg.aspx?lang=fra.

Duffield, Mark. 2001. *Global Governance and the New Wars: The Merging of Development and Security*. London and New York: Zed Books.

École nationale d'administration publique (ENAP). 2015. "PARGEP: Projet d'appui au renforcement de la gestion publique en Haïti." École nationale d'administration publique. Accessed 28 July 2015. http://international.enap.ca/6473/Description-sommaire.enap.

Gouvernment d'Haïti. 2015a. Ministère à la Condition féminine et aux Droits des femmes (MCFDF). "Politique d'égalité femmes-hommes 2014–2034." Ministère à la Condition féminine et aux Droits des femmes.

– 2015b. "Plan d'action national d'égalité femmes-hommes 2014–2020." Ministère à la Condition féminine et aux Droits des femmes.

Ménard, Suzanne. 2013. "Projet FIPCA-PNH. Volet: Égalité entre les femmes et les hommes. Avril 2012–mars 2013." Unpublished report.

– 2014. "Projet FIPCA-PNH. Plan de travail, Égalité entre les femmes et les hommes. Mars 2014–mars 2015." Unpublished report.

Ministère des affaires étrangères, commerce et développement (MAÉCD). 2014. "Évaluation de la coopération en Haiti, 2006–2013: Rapport synthèse." Ministère des affaires étrangères, commerce et développement.

Ministère des affaires étrangères et du commerce international/Fonds pour la paix et la sécurité mondiales (MAÉCI/FPSM). 2010. "Stratégie pluriannuelle pour Haïti, 2010–2014." Ottawa: Ministère des affaires étrangères et du commerce international.

Nouvelliste. 2015. "Vers la matérialisation de l'égalité de genre." *Nouvelliste*, 29 May.

O'Connell, Helen, and Wendy Harcourt. 2011. *Conflict-Affected and Fragile States: Opportunities to Promote Gender Equality and Equity?* London: UK Department for International Development.

Paducel, Anca, and Jennifer Salahub. 2011. *Gender Equality and Fragile States Policies and Programming: A Comparative Study of the OECD/DAC and Six OECD Donors*. Ottawa: North-South Institute.

Pan-American Development Foundation (PADF). 2010. "Réhabilitation de la prison civile du Cap Haitien: Rapport intérimaire au FPSM." Pan-American Development Foundation.

Salahub, Jennifer E. 2008. "Canada, Haiti, and Gender Equality in a 'Fragile State.'" In *Fragile States or Failing Development? Canadian Development Report 2008*, edited by Stephen Baranyi and Roy Culpepper, 49–68. Ottawa: North-South Institute.

Swiss, Liam. 2012. "Gender, Security, and Instrumentalism: Canada's Foreign Aid in Support of National Interest?" In *Struggling for Effectiveness: CIDA and Canadian Aid Policy*, edited by Stephen Brown, 135–58. Montreal and Kingston: McGill-Queen's University Press.

Tiessen, Rebecca. 2014a. "Canada's Changing Priorities (2006–2014) and What They Mean for the Promotion of Gender Equality in Development." *Undercurrent Journal* 10, no. 2: 54–8.

– 2014b. "Gender Equality and the 'Two CIDAs': Successes and Setbacks between 1976 and 2013." In *Rethinking Canadian Aid*, edited by Stephen Brown, Molly den Heyer, and David Black, 195–210. Ottawa: University of Ottawa Press.

Tiessen, Rebecca, and Krystel Carrier. 2015. "The Erasure of 'Gender' in Canadian Foreign Policy under the Harper Conservatives: The Significance of the Discursive Shift from 'Gender Equality' to 'Equality between Women and Men.'" *Canadian Foreign Policy Journal* 21, no. 2: 95–111.

United Nations Secretary-General (UNSG). 2014. *Report of the Secretary-General of the United Nations Stabilization Mission in Haiti.* S/2014/162. United Nations Secretary-General.

– 2015. *Report of the Secretary-General of the United Nations Stabilization Mission in Haiti.* S/2015/157. United Nations Secretary-General.

UN Women. 2013. *Promoting Security and Outreach Services in Order to Resolve the Issue of Gender-Related Violence in Temporary Shelters in Haiti: Final Report to the Government of Canada.* UN Women.

Varynen, Tania. 2010. "Gender and Peacebuilding." In *Palgrave Advances in Peacebuilding. Critical Developments and Approaches*, edited by Oliver Richmond, 137–53. Houndsmill, UK: Palgrave Macmillan.

Walby, Kevin, and Jeffrey Monaghan. 2010. "'Haitian Paradox' or Dark Side of the Security-Development Nexus? Canada's Role in the Securitization of Haiti, 2004–2009." *Alternatives: Global, Local, Political* 36, no. 4: 273–87.

Woroniuk, Beth, and Amber Minnings. 2014. "Worth the Wait? Reflections on Canada's National Action Plan & Reports on Women, Peace & Security." Ottawa: Women, Peace and Security Network-Canada.

Chapter 11

Not High on Our Radar? The Harper Government and Missing and Murdered Aboriginal Women in Canada

Heather Smith

The scale and severity of violence faced by Indigenous women and girls in Canada – First Nations, Inuit and Métis – constitutes a national human rights crisis.

– Amnesty International (2014, 2)

It isn't really high on our radar, to be honest.
  – Prime Minister Stephen Harper, when asked about the possibility of a national inquiry into missing and murdered women in Canada (CBC News, 2014b)

We condemn it. Even though some might prefer that we kept quiet. The discomfort of the audience is of small concern, particularly in the context of a crime that calls to heaven for justice. If this body does not act to protect young girls, who will?
    – Former minister of foreign affairs John Baird on enforced marriage,
30 September 2013

Minister of foreign affairs John Baird gives voice to a kind of "swaggering white knight to the rescue" discourse that seemed to pervade the (now former) Conservative federal government's statements about gender and race-based violence outside Canadian borders. Yet at home, the 1,200 Aboriginal[1] girls and women who have been murdered or gone missing do not merit the same rhetorical place in government discourse. Surely, as Warren Kinsella (2014) has argued, missing and murdered Aboriginal women "deserve more than a shrug." Kinsella (2014) writes: "If it had been a bunch of white girls who had been killed or disappeared, there would be no collective societal shrug taking place. Holy God Almighty, there'd be a hue and a cry like none this nation had ever seen. You'd have mild-mannered suburbanites storming Parliament Hill with pitchforks and torches if we were talking about 20 Midget 'A' teams, or the entire population of Tilt Cove, Newfoundland, or Greenwood, B.C. But it's aboriginal women. And so nobody's enraged and nobody's storming Parliament Hill."

The contrast between the relative silence and apparent dismissiveness of the Conservative federal government toward missing and murdered Aboriginal women and a clear posturing of the "outraged protector of the most vulnerable abroad," as expressed by Baird's bullhorn diplomacy, is as striking as it is disheartening.

This chapter takes this rhetorical gap as its starting point. After setting the parameters for the chapter, I will turn my attention to unpacking components of the foreign policy discourse articulated by Minister Baird, labelled by the Department of Foreign Affairs, Trade and Development (DFATD) as "the freedom, security and dignity agenda." As will be seen, both the framing of Canada and the rhetorical turns of phrase that shape the discourse around child, early, and forced marriage provide us with the means to compare the discourse or lack thereof relating to missing and murdered Aboriginal women in Canada.

Turning to the crisis of missing and murdered Aboriginal women, I will begin with an overview of the case of missing and murdered Aboriginal women, and will show that there is no comparable set of ministerial or prime pinisterial statements. Given the overwhelming silence in official press statements and speeches, I turn to media statements as a means by which to highlight the various ways in which the Conservative federal government demonstrated an apparent apathy. I then explain the gap by arguing that in order to see the missing and murdered Aboriginal women in Canada as a crisis, the Conservative government would have needed to see colonialism in ways that were not celebratory. The gap is explained, as well, by a long-standing narrative of Canada as a good international citizen, which I believe the Conservatives saw no electoral value in disrupting. The chapter concludes with two recommendations. First, I recommend that everyone gets engaged and educates themselves. Second, highlighting the arguments of Aboriginal leaders, families, and NGOs, there is clear evidence to support the need for a culturally appropriate national inquiry. These recommendations stand even with the election of a new Liberal majority federal government.

SETTING THE PARAMETERS

Before I turn to my analysis, I present three significant qualifiers that set the parameters for this chapter. First, I am not an Indigenous woman. I make my home in Prince George, British Columbia, and I am a visitor to the Lheidli T'enneh (Lheidli T'enneh 2014) traditional territory. I am not seeking to represent the views of Indigenous peoples, but rather, and consistent with the position taken by Franke Wilmer (2009, 188), "what follows is my understanding of Indigenous perspectives rather than a representation of those perspectives."

Second, while my work may be viewed as adopting a postcolonial approach, the use of the term "postcolonial" is entirely inappropriate when discussing the experience of Aboriginal peoples in Canada. Indigenous scholars Marie Battiste (2000) and Linda Tuhiwai Smith (1999) have both argued that the use of "post" implies that colonialism is in the past. According to Battiste (2000, xix), "post-colonial societies do not exist." The invocation of the postcolonial is actually seen as part of a colonial project.

Postcolonial theory does provide nuanced framework for analyzing the cultural legacy of colonialism and for a reinvigorated critique of an imagined postcolonial world. Critical insights from Said (1978) and Spivak (1998), among others, have fostered new debates and discussions of the nature of an ongoing form of colonialism and the oppression of the subaltern (Spivak 1998; Gramsci 2006). Thus, although the term postcolonial makes little sense in the day-to-day realities of many subaltern groups, the employment of postcolonial theory facilitates a comprehensive analysis of the continued violence against the subaltern (Spivak 1998) and ongoing acts of colonialism that marginalize specific groups. This said, I do not describe the work here as postcolonial.

Third, and finally, I would like to address one possible justification for the inclusion of this chapter in the broader volume. The inclusion of a chapter on the lives and deaths of Canada's Aboriginal women serves to demonstrate the validity of the term "Global South," as defined in the introduction to this volume. The focus is instead on disrupting the homogenizing implications of simplified state-based analyses, and understanding of the inequalities that exist within states. However, in my research to date, I have been unable to find language invoking the Global South in narratives and documents related to Aboriginal peoples in Canada. There are, however, a variety of examples in the press of political elites and Aboriginal leaders invoking the concepts of the "Third World" or the "developing world" when referring to Canada's First Peoples or when inferring conditions often associated with developing states

(Anderson 2009; Mackay and Niigaanwewidam 2011; Angus 2011; United Nations Special Rapporteur 2013).

The term "Fourth World" has also been widely used by critical scholars and Indigenous community leaders to highlight the nature of inequality and failures to address social injustices faced by Aboriginal communities in Canada. Grace Ouellette (2002) underscores how feminist analyses of Indigenous women's oppression have not been adequate in depicting the nature and extent of inequality and injustice faced by such a highly marginalized group of peoples. Another important Canadian contributor to understanding the "Fourth World" in the Canadian context is George Manuel (1974), who in his book *The Fourth World* argues for a radically different perspective on international politics, based on shared experiences of colonialism, limited rights, oppression, and injustice. The Fourth World is an extension of "Third World" conditions of poverty and "underdevelopment" to include those who are politically and economically disadvantaged in systems of extreme inequality combined with substantial discrimination.

However, the framing of the living conditions of Aboriginal peoples as "Third World" or "Fourth World" is problematic. I do not dispute the massive inequality faced by Canada's Aboriginal peoples. I am concerned about the politics of naming. Although it is difficult to ascribe meaning or intent to all the various speakers cited above, I suspect that the use of the term "Third World" is often meant to draw attention to the disparities and to shame Canada and Canadians into action. The concept, then, has instrumental value (see introduction, this volume). However, it is also a concept with a contested history and complicated lineage. Although it may be seen as being informed by anti-colonialism, invoking images of liberation from hegemonic powers, it also has Eurocentric origins and has informed a discourse of modernization that held up the so-called First World as the model (Dirlik 2004, 133–4). I am concerned that the assumptions of the discourse of modernization deny the agency of Aboriginal peoples, obfuscate the richness of their cultures, and silence their ways of knowing. All of this to say that although the terms "Third World" or "Fourth World" have been used by the media, by Canadian political elites, and by Aboriginal leaders, they are not terms I will adopt here. Nonetheless, the definitions of these terms hold key notions that continue to define the lives of highly marginalized groups such as Indigenous peoples, particularly the high rates of inequality, poverty, and discrimination.

A FREEDOM, DIGNITY, AND SECURITY AGENDA?

In September 2013, DFATD announced that a set of Canadian federal ministers were in New York City to promote a "freedom, dignity and security agenda." This agenda focused on the championing of a broad range of human rights. As expressed by Minister Baird at the United Nations General Assembly in September 2013: "whether the issue is religious freedom, sexual freedom, political freedom or any other freedom, some people ask: What business is it of ours? What interest do we have in events outside our borders? Our business is a shared humanity. Our interest is the dignity of humankind."

The emphasis on human dignity and human rights did not actually begin with those set of ministerial statements in 2013. Rather, the emphasis on human dignity and human rights can be found in speeches and statements by Baird from early in his tenure as minister of foreign affairs. At the United Nations General Assembly in September 2011, Baird set the tone for his approach to Canadian foreign policy and identified themes that would become central to his articulation of the Canada he sought to present. The emphasis on human dignity and human rights seemed to reach its peak in 2013. A few statements in 2014 invoked dignity, but the rhetorical fervor of earlier speeches was absent.

In spite of the apparent shift in discourse, the government's promotion of this agenda can nonetheless provide a basis for our analysis. This discourse includes elements that are consistent with the vision of Canada articulated by Prime Minister Stephen Harper, and thus speaks to a coordinated effort to frame Canadian efforts abroad. As well, as noted above, the discourse included a focus on child, early, and forced marriage.

The speeches by the then minister of foreign affairs were rife with images of Canada – a Canada that both Baird and Harper sought to articulate to the world, and indeed to Canadians. When we examine Baird's speeches since 2011, there are several themes related to Canada and the world that merit our attention.

First, consistent with statements by Prime Minister Harper, Baird repeatedly noted that Canada had a principled foreign policy and that such an approach was a "Canadian tradition" – a tradition marked by "standing for what is principled and just, regardless of whether it is popular, or convenient, or expedient," a tradition based on Canadian values. The same notion was expressed in the 2013 Speech from the Throne (Government of Canada 2013): "Canada stands for what is right and good in the world. This is the true character of Canadians – honourable in our dealings, faithful to our commitments, loyal to our friends. Confident partners, courageous warriors and compassionate neighbours ... Canada seeks a world where freedom – including freedom of religion, the rule of law, democracy and human dignity are respected." Moreover, according to the government discourse, Canada's principled foreign policy is based on the strength of those values, and a willingness to stand up for those values and not to compromise those values. In the words of Baird (in a September 2012 address to the Montreal Council on Foreign Relations), in reference to child, early, and forced marriage: "Our government is standing up for these girls, even when it's not always expedient to do so. We don't shy away from such tough conversations." As Adam Chapnick has observed, this Canadian "diplomatic personality" is marked by "an aggressive assertion of Canadian strength," which "emphasize[s] Canada's distinctiveness" (Chapnick 2012, 153). Baird became fairly well known for his bullhorn diplomacy, particularly around child, early, and forced marriage – a distinct approach from his quiet diplomacy on other matters, as Epprecht and Brown (this volume) elaborate.

In this bullhorn diplomacy, not only does the discourse frame Canada as principled and assertive, it is infused with assumptions of moral authority. Just as Prime Minister Harper's discourse related to Afghanistan constructed a virtuous and righteous Canada, the discourse articulated by Baird is rife with assumptions of a "virtuous and moral" Canada (Turenne-Sjolander 2013, 242). For example, in his September 2012 address to the Montreal Council on Foreign Relations, Baird stated: "in this storm of change, Canada stands as a beacon of light, built around our fundamental values of freedom, democracy, human rights and the rule of law. We have a clear vision of what it takes to build the conditions in which people live with the dignity others crave." Canada has a clear vision. Canada will stand up for the oppressed and marginalized where other states will not. In the words of Baird: "I am not going to stay quiet on an issue that is morally wrong and deserved to be condemned."

A moral and moralizing Canada is not new. Not only have previous governments been accused of moralizing, but the sense of superiority that infused such statements has been critiqued widely (See Turenne-Sjolander 2013; Stairs 2003; Nossal 2000). For the purposes here, what is particularly significant is that, in contrast to Baird and Harper's moralizing, the rights and privileges that are assumed to be inherently Canadian were not universally applied abroad, and in fact are inconsistent with Canada's actions abroad – as well as at home. After delineating a set of "Canadian values" in a 2014 speech at Fourth Annual John Diefenbaker Defender of Human Rights and Freedom Awards Ceremony, Baird laments that, "unfortunately, while these values are universal in application, they are not universally applied. Many people around the world continue to struggle and face oppression in pursuing their beliefs." Baird implies that all Canadians enjoy the rights and freedoms that are promoted abroad, that Canada is the beacon, and the model that others should adopt.

Not only does the discourse on dignity rhetorically draw boundaries between Canada and other countries, it constructs "others" who are not only "not quite as virtuous or possessing of the same moral superiority" (Turenne-Sjolander 2013, 242), and also constructs vulnerable others in need of Canada's support. Baird repeatedly claimed, as he did in his September 2012 address, that "as citizens of a global community, we have a solemn duty to defend the vulnerable, to give voice to the voiceless, to challenge the aggressor, and to promote and protect human rights and human dignity, at home and abroad." Again consistent with the discourse related to women in Afghanistan (Turenne-Sjolander 2013; Bell 2010; Tuckey, this volume, chapter 8), there are claims to giving voice to the voiceless. Those whom Canada is saving are cast as lacking a voice (and thus agency), but Canada will speak for them. Moreover, according to Baird, it is our "duty" and our "obligation" to give voice to the voiceless. It is in this construction of duty and obligation that we can identify as the present-day invocation of the "white man's burden" to protect and speak for the subaltern woman. As Colleen Bell notes: "the so-called burden on the shoulders of the white man was to enlighten and morally improve subject populations" (Bell 2010, 65). In the current context, "the acclaimed moral character of the West's burden today is derived not merely from an imperative to 'improve' the conditions of Southern populations, but derives from Western values themselves, which are taken to offer the requisite capabilities to achieve success" (Bell 2010, 65–6). To claim to give voice to the voiceless is to deny those in a geographical space abroad their own voice and to claim the right to speak for them. It is statement rife with imperial and colonial assumptions that have long had a presence in Canadian foreign policy.

Finally, we turn to the particular framing of gender-based (and race-based) violence that is expressed in speeches by Baird. Baird regularly expressed outrage at the treatment of girls and women abroad. In September 2012 at the United Nations, he raised the issue of forced marriage, calling it "barbaric" (a widely employed term by the Harper Conservatives) and stating, "wherever they occur, assaults on human dignity are unacceptable." In Baird's speeches about women subjected to early and forced marriage, he would often evoke a particular image as though to humanize such women. One example is the story of Habiba, whose "journey from girlhood to womanhood is too fast and too brutal. No girl deserves to have her childhood robbed from her." Baird drew on a moral imperative to give voice to the voiceless, or to speak *for* the subaltern (Spivak 1998).

Baird's evocation of a moral imperative is embedded in a highly essentializing discourse around helpless victims and vulnerable bodies (Tiessen 2015; Baranyi and Tiessen, this volume) that Canada must protect. The performativity of a foreign policy moral imperative is best captured in a statement made by Baird in 2013 at the United Nations General Assembly: "As I close, I cannot help but reflect on three young girls, and my heart breaks for them: The child bride: 'It was the day I left school.' The girl who was a victim of rape and sexual violence. The refugee: 'I want to go home.' We are not here to achieve results for governments or political leaders. We are here to protect and defend these three girls and seven billion other members of the human family."

Our hearts, Baird tells us, should break for the girls subjected to gender- and raced-base violence abroad. But should our hearts not also break for the Aboriginal girls and women found beaten and near death beside muddy rivers, lost on northern Canadian highways, and taken from the downtown eastside of Vancouver?

#MMIW: MISSING AND MURDERED INDIGENOUS WOMEN

#MMIW is a hashtag for missing and murdered Indigenous women. If you use this hashtag to search Twitter, you will find daily reminders of the work undertaken by Aboriginal leaders, social justice activists, women's rights activists, and everyday people to bring attention to the tragedy of missing and murdered Indigenous women in Canada. The numerous tweets using this hashtag seek to draw our attention to the decades old issue of missing and murdered Indigenous women in Canada.

The Native Women's Association of Canada (NWAC) database documents a trail of loss and death back to the 1960s, and of the 582 cases included in their 2010 report, 55 per cent had taken place in the 2000s (NWAC 2010, 20; see also Human Rights Watch 2013). A recent report by the Royal Canadian Mounted Police (RCMP), titled *Missing and Murdered Aboriginal Women: A National Operational Overview*, puts the number of missing and murdered Aboriginal women between 1980 and 2012 at 1,181 (RCMP 2014, 3).

Report after report reminds us that Aboriginal woman in Canada are overrepresented as victims of violent crime. As noted in the 2013 Human Rights Watch report, which focused on issues of policing and the Highway of Tears, "Indigenous women and girls are far more likely than other Canadian women and girls to experience violence and to die as a result ... [B]etween 1997 and 2000, the rate of homicide overall for

Aboriginal women was 5.4 per 100,000, compared to 0.8 per 100,000 for non-Aboriginal women – almost seven times higher" (Human Rights Watch 2013, 25). Evidence from NWAC shows that most of the women were young, often mothers; that the majority went missing in Western provinces; and that the majority went missing from urban areas: "Taking a broad look at the different locations where women and girls have disappeared, it was found that over 70% of women and girls went missing from an urban area, 22% were last seen in a rural area and 7% disappeared from a reserve" (NWAC 2010, 27; see also RCMP 2014, 9). NWAC research further shows that "Aboriginal women and girls are as likely to be killed by an acquaintance or stranger as they are by an intimate partner" (NWAC 2010, ii). The 2014 RCMP report suggests that Aboriginal women "were less often killed by a current or former spouse (29% compared to 41%)" (RCMP 2014, 13), and "were most often murdered by an acquaintance (30% compared to 19%)" (RCMP 2014, 12). It is important to note that "the acquaintance category can be broken down further to include close friends, neighbours, authority figures, business relationships, criminal relationships and casual acquaintances (i.e. a person known to the victim that does not fit in the other acquaintance categories)" (RCMP 2014, 12).

The root causes of this epidemic have been widely discussed. In 2004, Amnesty International produced *Canada: Stolen Sisters*. This study focused on a set of factors that "too long neglected, have contributed to a heightened – and unacceptable – risk of violence against Indigenous women in Canadian cities" (Amnesty 2004, 2).

> The social and economic marginalisation of Indigenous women, along with a history of government policies that have torn apart Indigenous families and communities, have pushed a disproportionate number of Indigenous women into dangerous situations that include extreme poverty, homelessness and prostitution.
>
> Despite assurances to the contrary, police in Canada have often failed to provide Indigenous women with an adequate standard of protection.
>
> The resulting vulnerability of Indigenous women has been exploited by Indigenous and non-Indigenous men to carry out acts of extreme brutality against them.
>
> These acts of violence may be motivated by racism, or may be carried out in the expectation that societal indifference to the welfare and safety of Indigenous women will allow the perpetrators to escape justice. (Amnesty 2004, 2)

In a 2014 report, the Canadian House of Commons Special Committee on Violence Against Indigenous Women (Government of Canada 2014b, 4) included "domestic violence, human trafficking, substance abuse, prostitution, poverty, limited access to health and social services, racism and the after-effects of the residential school system" as root causes. Neither the Special Committee report nor the RCMP report include reference to colonialism as a root cause, though the NWAC study addresses colonialism in its 2010 report:

> The experiences of violence and victimization of Aboriginal women do not occur in a vacuum. Violence is perpetuated through apathy and indifference towards Aboriginal women, and stems from the ongoing impacts of colonialism in Canada. While this process is rooted in history, the impacts of colonization continue to affect Aboriginal peoples, and perhaps more profoundly Aboriginal women, today. (NWAC 2010, 7; see also United Nations Special Rapporteur 2013; Inter-American Commission 2014, 123)

One thousand two hundred missing and murdered Aboriginal women in Canada is a crisis, and it is a crisis that has been acknowledged by Aboriginal leaders, families who have lost a loved one, survivors, the United Nations, and the Inter-American Commission on Human Rights, among others. The Conservative federal government, however, did not frame it as a crises in any of their reports. Conservative cabinet ministers neither regarded it as a crisis nor were outraged in a similar manner to Baird's outrage regarding the violence faced by girls and women abroad. In over 120 speeches and news statements released in 2014 to 2015, and throughout the website for the former minister of Aboriginal affairs and northern development Bernard Valcourt, there is only one reference to missing and murdered Aboriginal women. In a 12 May 2014, statement designed to essentially dismiss the report of the Special UN Rapporteur, Minister Valcourt claimed that "ending violence against women and girls, including violence against Aboriginal women and girls, is a priority for the federal government. Through Economic Action Plan 2014, the Government of Canada committed to investing an additional $25 million over five years to reduce violence against Aboriginal women and girls, putting money into concrete resources." A search of ministerial speeches on the Status of Women Canada website reveals a similar, unfortunate pattern. In over forty speeches delivered in 2013 to 2014 by either former ministers Rona Ambrose or Kellie Leitch, there are only two instances in which the word Aboriginal is used. One is a reference to Aboriginal youth (SWC 2013b) and the other is a reference to taking action to protect Canada's most vulnerable, including Aboriginal women, from human trafficking (SWC 2013a). There is also a news release dedicated to the promotion of the federal government's Action Plan (Government of Canada 2014a) that includes claims of Canadian leadership in standing up for "victims of crime" (SWC 2014), and statements such as the one made by Valcourt that "ending violence against women and girls ... is a priority for the Government of Canada."

And although there is no "official" discourse comparable to the lamentations of Baird for the practices of child, early, and forced marriage abroad, there is a media discourse. Statements to the media by Prime Minister Harper and Minister Valcourt, however, did little to undo the sense that the federal government was not making the issue of missing and murdered Aboriginal women in Canada a priority. Take for example the comment from Prime Minister Harper, noted above, that a national inquiry "isn't really high on our radar." Harper claimed that an inquiry would be expensive and that there were already plenty of studies done, and now was the time for action (CBC News 2014b). The responses to Prime Minister Harper's comments were swift and damning. Tanya Kappo (2014) of the Sturgeon Lake Cree Nation said that the statement by Prime Minister Harper, and one by Minister Valcourt that same week, "confirmed their feelings of indifference, disregard and utter lack of respect for indigenous people." Grand Chief Stewart Phillip of the Union of British Columbia Indian Chiefs (2014) stated, "these recent condescending, disgusting and racist comments greatly underscores the dire need for a national inquiry ... Prime Minister, the inquiry is very high on our radar."

Minister Valcourt also spoke to the media in December 2014, as mentioned above, and in his statement he claimed that there was a lack of respect for Aboriginal women and girls on reserve and claimed an inquiry was not needed because "if we're honest here, it's apparent what part of the problem is" (Kennedy 2014). In an interview that used incredibly problematic terms like "the ultimate solution," Valcourt reinforced the message from Prime Minister Harper that an inquiry was not needed, and he "argued that the issue of violence against indigenous women is 'too important' to use an inquiry as an 'excuse' for not taking action." The minister also referred to the brutal beating of the Aboriginal teenager Rinelle Harper as "a situation" (Kennedy 2014).

Response to Valcourt's statements was swift. He was accused of victim blaming, and the Nuu-chah-nulth Tribal Council (2014) demanded an "immediate public apology and retraction of these insensitive, disrespectful, prejudiced, and absolutely unacceptable comments." Their open letter also stated:

> The hypocrisy of the Minister's superior attitude about the "Canadian" way of doing things is even more astounding. The social issues faced by First Nations communities today are internationally recognized as the direct result of an aggressive and systematic colonial campaign of oppression, cultural assimilation, physical and emotional abuse, and economic deprivation perpetrated on our people by the Government of Canada over hundreds of years. (Nuu-chah-nulth Tribal Council 2014)

Betty Ann Lavallee, national chief of the Congress of Aboriginal Peoples, highlighted that the majority of the missing and murdered Aboriginal women went missing in urban centres, and also demanded an apology from the minister. She wrote:

> To deny the reality of their lives and deaths is to dishonour the memory of these women and girls. The minister owes an apology to their families. To put all the blame on Aboriginal men on reserve is dishonest. The minister owes an apology to them as well. To mislead the public about this national tragedy in a manner that perpetuates colonialism is a disservice to every Canadian. The minister owes an apology to us all. (Lavallee 2014)

After the tragic death of a young Aboriginal woman named Tina Fontaine in August 2014, Prime Minister Harper was asked about a national inquiry. He said there would be no inquiry and went on say, "It's very clear that there has been very fulsome study of this particular ... of these particular things. They're not all one phenomenon ... We should not view this as a sociological phenomenon. We should view it as crime" (CBC News 2014a). He further claimed that the RCMP report showed that these cases got solved and so we should leave it in their hands.

With these statements, Prime Minister Harper compartmentalized the missing and murdered Aboriginal women from broader society and isolated their lives and the context in which they lived. His statement reveals a disregard for the missing and murdered Aboriginal women of Canada, and in his dismissal of "sociology" he also dismisses the broad social, political, historical, and economic context in which we all live and which is the source of deeper systemic problems. His words deny the systematic discrimination identified by human rights groups and Aboriginal women's advocates (Human Rights Watch 2013, NWAC 2010; Inter-American Commission 2014). In a stinging editorial in the *Globe and Mail*, Rashmee Singh (2014) explained how this framing of the issue as being a criminal matter and not sociological accomplished four things:

> First, the claim obscures the effects of colonialism in rendering Aboriginal women far more vulnerable than other Canadian women to violence. Second, it individualizes accountability for the problem. Third, it prevents a consideration of any response beyond criminal justice intervention. Finally, it completely sidesteps any discussion of proactive responses that can be put in place to address the conditions that render Aboriginal women so vulnerable to violence. (Singh 2014)

Harper's referral to the police as the solution to these individualized criminal problems indicated a clear insensitivity to the fear and distrust at the heart of the relationship between many police forces – the RCMP in particular – and aboriginal peoples (see Human Rights Watch 2013, 34).

Statements to the media by Prime Minister Harper and Minister Valcourt show us that silences about colonialism in formal government reports are reinforced by constructions of missing and murdered Aboriginal women in Canada as criminal cases rather than a sad reflection on our society and history. There is an historical and sociological amnesia. Calls for an inquiry are minimized, depoliticized, and cast as somehow seeking to delay action, even when these calls come from girls who have survived brutal beatings and from families who have suffered the loss of their loved ones. Canadians are told there have been plenty of studies, and while indeed there have been plenty of studies, the ones that officials like Harper are referring to have been produced by the same organizations – such as the RCMP – that are also the source of many complaints regarding their handling of the cases of missing and murderered Aboriginal women. The inquiry is cast as an unnecessary cost, and that somehow we already know the answers. Baird's heart breaks for girls abroad who have been raped, while Valcourt calls the beating of Rinelle Harper a "situation." Baird says Canada will stand up for human dignity and human rights, but clearly only for those who live abroad. Why is there such a gap? Why is there such denial? When will the Canadian government listen to the voices of the voiceless in Canada?

There is a longstanding narrative that Canada is not a colonial country. Prime Minister Harper expressed this idea at the 2009 meeting of the

G20, where he stated in a press conference that "Canada has no history of colonialism" (Wherry 2009). In other speeches and statements, the prime minister celebrates colonialism. While in London in 2006, addressing the Canada-UK Chamber of Commerce, Prime Minister Harper discussed Canada's colonial past, stating: "Now I know it's unfashionable to refer to colonialism in anything other than negative terms. And certainly, no part of the world is unscarred by the excesses of empires. But in the Canadian context, the actions of the British Empire were largely benign and occasionally brilliant." When minister of citizenship, immigration and multiculturalism Jason Kenney spoke to the Empire Club of Canada in Toronto on 29 April 2012, he, too, celebrated the legacy of the British empire.

Not only have Prime Minister Harper and Minister Kenney celebrated Canada's colonial past, other government pronouncements and speeches seem to strike Aboriginal peoples from Canada's history. Take for example the founding of Canada in the 2013 Speech from the Throne, where it was stated:

[W]e draw inspiration from our founders, leaders of courage and audacity. Nearly 150 years ago, they looked beyond narrow self-interest. They faced down incredible challenges – geographic, military, and economic. They were undaunted. They dared to seize the moment that history offered. Pioneers, then few in number, reached across a vast continent. They forged an independent country where none would have otherwise existed. (Government of Canada 2013)

Assembly of First Nations National Chief Shawn Atleo was quick to respond that "Canada was not empty," and that "[i]t was not, as they say terra nullius, the doctrine of discovery that says there was no one here … The Indigenous nations pre-existed the establishment of Canada" (APTN 2013). The current government does not see Canada's history as one that includes Aboriginal peoples. It is a government that does not include colonialism as a source of ongoing structural violence against Aboriginal girls and women. Without that ability to see the past and the present in terms consistent with the experiences of Aboriginal peoples, the Harper government would never have seen 1,200 missing and murdered Aboriginal women as a crisis.

It is true that on 11 June 2008, Prime Minister Harper stood up in the House of Commons and stated: "The treatment of children in Indian Residential Schools is a sad chapter in our history," noting that the assimilationist policies of the day were motivated by a desire "to kill the Indian in the child." However, given the politics of apology, whether or not the apology was meaningful is up for debate, as is to whom it was meaningful. Henderson and Wakeham (2009) acknowledge that the apology was important for residential school survivors, but they also note that colonialism is never referred to in the speech, and that "the absence of the word 'colonialism' from the prime minister's apology enables a strategic isolation and containment of residential schools as a discrete historical problem of educational malpractice rather than one devastating prong of an overarching and multifaceted system of colonial oppression that persists in the present" (2). In effect, residential schools are removed from the broader colonial framework in which it was embedded – just like missing and murdered Aboriginal women.

Another interpretation of the apology by Willow Anderson (2012) is that Canada's identity in terms of its relationship with Indigenous peoples is contested. She also discusses how the way in which the apology is written distances the current government from past practices, minimizes blame, and uses language that "distances the government from words that have a connotation of greater violence and deliberateness (colonialism, racism) and projects a faceless and ethereal villain" (Anderson 2012, 578). She also analyzed the comments of those responding to the apology: most felt that the apology was appropriate, some felt it was too late or not strong enough, and some opposed the apology altogether. The tensions Anderson reveals relate directly to the second explanation for the rhetorical gap.

Second, and most unfortunately, Canadian governments and some Canadians have a long history of being unwilling to see the contradictions between how Canada presents itself to the world and who Canada and Canadians actually are, or at least to acknowledge the realties of some Canadians. Baird's statements abroad and the kind of Canada that he seeks to construct – principled, righteous, virtuous, moral, a protector – is an image of Canada as a good international citizen. The treatment of Aboriginal peoples has long been the Achilles heel of Canadian human rights promotion (Lackenbauer and Cooper 2007), and Baird's posturing is consistent with patterns of behaviour of previous governments (Stairs 2003; Nossal 2000). Baird promoted the cultural ideals that underpin and support a particular image of Canada – a Canada to which Canadians may aspire but also a Canada that obfuscates and denies domestic realities.

I would argue that the "real" Canada is obscured by rhetoric and bullhorn diplomacy, and does not sell well either abroad or at home. The construction of the apology, noted above, is a prime example of selling Canada's past in a way that allows Canadians to distance themselves from their past, to make it not about them. It in effect places an historical time stamp on colonial behaviour, allowing Canadians to see themselves as the virtuous, moral people that Baird sought to portray. But what if the Conservative federal government were to have acknowledged that the tragedy of missing and murdered Indigenous women was a crisis? What are the political implications of this acknowledgement, and how are decisions about making such an acknowledgement couched in such primary objectives as winning elections and appealing to a conservative constituency (Nossal 2013)? Even though a recent Angus Reid (2014) poll indicated wide support for a national inquiry, and the same poll identified missing and murdered Aboriginal women as the number one issue facing Aboriginal peoples, the Conservative government failed to make an inquiry a priority, even with Baird's notice of resignation in February 2015.

RECOMMENDATIONS AND REFLECTIONS

Although I cannot and do not speak for Aboriginal peoples, as a concerned Canadian citizen and ally, I offer two key recommendations. My first recommendation is for increased public engagement. I had little faith in the Conservative government to take the issue of missing and murdered Aboriginal women seriously. However, the public became engaged through the electoral process and has now elected a Liberal majority government. This is a vital and necessary step, because Prime Minister Justin Trudeau has made a commitment to create a national inquiry. Nonetheless, the public must stay engaged with this issue and must engage others in our communities. Canadians who invest in improved awareness and education can counter the challenges of Canada's historical amnesia; by joining with community activists on this issue, there is great potential for changing the status quo. The Aboriginal women and men of my community who have shared their experiences with me, who have acted as cultural liaisons, and who have acknowledged me as an ally have had a profound effect on my life, and what they have taught me is too expansive to share here. I do believe that together we can challenge the indifference that characterized the Conservative approach and at least partially disrupt the colonial mentality that is embedded in our culture.

A second recommendation is to demonstrate to Canadians and all communities the clear and pressing need to treat missing and murdered Aboriginal women as a priority. As such, a national inquiry offers a first level of commitment to prioritizing this matter. Although Prime Minister Trudeau has committed to a national inquiry, any inquiry must be culturally appropriate, and the process must be guided by the insights of Aboriginal leaders, thus avoiding some of the procedural issues that plagued British Columbia's Missing Women's Commission (NWAC 2012) and the work of the House of Commons Special Committee on Violence Against Indigenous Women (NWAC 2015). Even if the actions identified by the inquiry mimic those suggested by Aboriginal activists and human rights activists, the process itself needs to be part of a larger national healing process, and could function as a way to educate Canadians. Rinelle Harper, a sixteen-year-old Aboriginal girl left for dead beside a Manitoba river, has called for a national inquiry, and says she is calling for one because "there are far too many women who lost their lives who cannot do the same" (Current 2015). An inquiry, in some small way, could recognize the lives lived and lives lost. For Rinelle, Tina, Tamara, Betty, Ramona, Roxanne, and thousands of Aboriginal girls and women – we need an inquiry. We must protect human rights and human dignity abroad as well as at home.

NOTES

1 In this chapter I often use the words Aboriginal and Indigenous interchangeably, and I will use the words in the way they are used in the particular documents or sources I am citing. One will find that different actors use different terms. However, in the Canadian government context, Aboriginal is the umbrella term often used to refer to First Nations, Inuit, and Métis. See AANDC 2014.

REFERENCES

Aboriginal Affairs and Northern Development Canada (AANDC). 2014. "Aboriginal Peoples and Communities." Aboriginal Affairs and Northern Development Canada. Accessed 25 January 2014. http://www.aadnc-aandc.gc.ca/eng/110010 0013785/1304467449155.

Amnesty International. 2004. *Stolen Sisters: A Human Rights Response to Discrimination and Violence against Indigenous Women in Canada*. Amnesty International. http://www.amnesty.ca/sites/default/files/amr200032004 enstolensisters.pdf.

– 2014. *Violence against Indigenous Women and Girls in Canada: A Summary of Amnesty International's Concerns and Call to Action*. Amnesty International, 7 February. http://www.amnesty.ca/get-involved/lead-in-your-community/violence-against-indigenous-women-and-girls-in-canada-a-summary.

Anderson, Mallory. 2009. "Former FSIN Chief Contests for AFN National Chief." *Sage* 13, no. 10.

Anderson, Willow J. 2012. "Indian in the Drum House: A Critical Discourse Analysis of an Apology for Canada's Residential Schools and the Public's Response." *International Communication Gazette* 74, no. 6: 571–85.

Angus, Charlie. 2011. "Attawapiskat's Impact: Canada's Katrina Moment." *Huffington Post*, 2 December . http://www.huffingtonpost.ca/charlie-angus/attawapiskat-reserve_b_1126595.html.

Angus Reid. 2014. "Three-Quarters of Canadians Back Inquiry on Murdered or Missing Aboriginal Women." Angus Reid, 23 October. http://angusreid.org/three-quarters-of-canadians-back-inquiry-on-murdered-and-missing-aboriginal-women.

APTN. 2013. "In Throne Speech Response Atleo Says Canada 'Was Not an Empty Land.'" APTN, 16 October. http://aptn.ca/news/2013/10/16/in-throne-speech-response-atleo-says-canada-was-not-an-empty-land.

Battiste, Marie. 2000. "Introduction: Unfolding the Lessons of Colonization." In *Reclaiming Indigenous Voice and Vision*, edited by Marie Battiste, xvi–xxx. Vancouver: UBC Press.

Bell, Colleen. 2010. "Fighting the War and Winning the Peace: Three Critiques of War in Afghanistan." In *Canadian Foreign Policy in Critical Perspective*, edited by J. Marshall Beier and Lana Wylie, 58–71. Toronto: Oxford.

CBC News. 2014a. "Harper Rebuffs Renewed Calls for Murdered, Missing Women Inquiry." CBC, 22 August.

– 2014b. "Full Text of Peter Mansbridge's Interview with Stephen Harper." CBC, 17 December. http://www.cbc.ca/news/politics/full-text-of-peter-mansbridge-s-interview-with-stephen-harper-1.2876934.

Chapnick, Adam. 2012. "A Diplomatic Counter-Revolution: Conservative Foreign Policy, 2006–11." *International Journal* 67, no. 1: 137–54.

Current. 2015. "Rinelle Harper Speaks Up for Missing and Murdered Indigenous Women." CBC Radio, 28 January. http://www.cbc.ca/thecurrent/episode/2015/01/28/rinelle-harper-speaks-up-national-inquiry.

Department of Foreign Affairs, Trade and Development (DFATD). 2013a. "Canada Promotes Freedom, Dignity and Security Agenda at United Nations." Department of Foreign Affairs, Trade and Development, 23 September. http://www.international.gc.ca/media/aff/news-communiques/2013/09/23a.aspx?lang=eng.

Dirlik, Arif. 2004. "Spectres of the Third World: Global Modernity and the End of the Three Worlds." *Third World Quarterly* 25, no. 7: 131–48.

Gilmore, Scott. 2015. "Canada's Race Problem? It's Even Worse than America's." *Maclean's*, 22 January.

Government of Canada. 2013. "Seizing Canada's Moment: Prosperity and Opportunity in an Uncertain World." Speech from the Throne. 16 October. http://news.gc.ca/web/article-en.do?nid=781019.

– 2014a. *Action Plan to Address Family Violence and Violent Crimes against Aboriginal Women and Girls.* Government of Canada. http://www.swc-cfc.gc.ca/violence/efforts/action-eng.pdf.

– 2014b. House of Commons Special Committee on Violence Against Indigenous Women. *Invisible Women: A Call to Action; A Report on Missing and Murdered Indigenous Women in Canada.* http://www.parl.gc.ca/HousePublications/Publication.aspx?DocId=6469851&Language=E&Mode=1&Parl=41&Ses=2.

Gramsci, Antonio. 2006. "History of the Subaltern Classes." In *Cultural Themes: Ideological Material,* edited by Meenakshi Durham and Douglas Kellner. Oxford: Blackwell Publishing.

Henderson, Jennifer, and Pauline Wakeham. 2009. "Colonial Reckoning, National Reconciliation? Aboriginal Peoples and the Culture of Redress in Canada." *English Studies in Canada* 35, no. 1: 1–26.

Human Rights Watch. 2013. *Those Who Take Us Away: Abusive Policing and Failures in Protection of Indigenous Women and Girls in Northern British Columbia, Canada.* Human Rights Watch. http://www.hrw.org/sites/default/files/reports/canada0213webwcover_0.pdf.

Inter-American Commission on Human Rights. 2014. *Missing and Murdered Indigenous Women in British Columbia, Canada.* Inter-American Commission on Human Rights. http://www.oas.org/en/iachr/reports/pdfs/Indigenous-Women-BC-Canada-en.pdf.

Kappo, Tanya. 2014. "Stephen Harper's Comments on Missing, Murdered Aboriginal Women Show 'Lack of Respect.'" CBC News, 19 December.

Kennedy, Jason. 2014. "Valcourt Urges First Nations, Provinces to Take Action on Murdered Aboriginal Women." *Ottawa Citizen,* 12 December.

Kinsella, Warren. 2014. "Missing, Murdered Aboriginal Woman Deserve More Than a Shrug." *Toronto Sun,* 2 September.

Lackenbauer, Whitney, and Andrew Cooper. 2007. "The Achilles Heel of Canadian International Citizenship: Indigenous Diplomacies and State Responses." *Canadian Foreign Policy* 13, no. 3: 99–119.

Lavallee, Betty Ann. 2014. "Betty Ann Lavallee: Valcourt's Approach to Missing Aboriginal Women is Dishonourable." *Ottawa Citizen,* 19 December.

Lheidli T'enneh. 2014. "Welcome." Lheidli T'enneh. Accessed 16 March 2014. http://www.lheidli.ca.

Mackay, James, and Niigaanwiwedam James Sinclair. 2011. "Canada's First Nations: A Scandal Where the Victims Are Blamed." *Guardian,* 11 December.

Manual, George. 1974. *The Fourth World: An Indian Reality.* Toronto: Collier-Macmillan Canada.

Native Women's Association of Canada. 2010. "What Their Stories Tell Us: Research Findings from the Sisters in Spirit Initiative." Native Women's Association of Canada. http://www.nwac.ca/sites/default/files/imce/2010_NWAC_SIS_Report_EN.pdf.

– 2012. "Inter-American Commission on Human Rights Holds Hearing on Disappearances and Murders of Aboriginal Women and Girls in British Columbia." Native Women's Association of Canada, 27 March. http://wacns.ca/pipermail/wac-ns-sc_wacns.ca/attachments/20120327/9a513d75/attachment-0002.pdf.

– 2015. "More than Invisible, Invisible to Real Action: NWAC's Response to the Special Committee on Violence Against Indigenous Women (SCVAIW)." 4 February. https://nwac.ca/2014/03/nwacs-official-response-to-the-special-committee-on-violence-against-indigenous-women.

Nossal, Kim Richard. 2000. "Missing Diplomacy and the 'Cult of Initiative' in Canadian Foreign Policy." In *Worthwhile Initiatives? Canadian Mission-Oriented Diplomacy*, edited by Andrew Cooper and Geoffrey Hayes, 1–12. Toronto: Irwin Publishing.

– 2013. "The Liberal Past in the Conservative Present: Internationalism in the Harper Era." In *Canada in the World: Internationalism in Canadian Foreign Policy*, edited by Heather Smith and Claire Turenne-Sjolander, 21–35. Don Mills, ON: Oxford University Press.

Nuu-chah-nulth Tribal Council. 2014. "Open Letter in Response to Minister Valcourt's Recent Statements on Missing and Murdered Indigenous Women." CTV News, 22 December. http://london.ctvnews.ca/open-letter-in-response-to-minister-valcourt-s-recent-statements-on-missing-and-murdered-indigenous-women-1.2158676.

Ouellette, Grace. 2002. *The Fourth World: An Indigenous Perspective on Feminism and Aboriginal Women's Activism*. Halifax: Fernwood Publishing.

Royal Canadian Mounted Police (RCMP). 2014. *Missing and Murdered Aboriginal Women: A National Operational Overview*. Royal Canadian Mounted Police. http://www.rcmp-grc.gc.ca/pubs/mmaw-faapd-eng.htm.

Said, Edward. 1978. *Orientalism*. New York: Random House.

Singh, Rashmee. 2014. "Stephen Harper Is Wrong: Crime and Sociology Are the Same Thing." *Globe and Mail*, 4 September.

Smith, Linda Tuhiwai. 1999. *Decolonizing Methodologies: Research and Indigenous Peoples*. London: Zed Books.

Spivak, Gayatri Chakravorty. 1998. "Can the Subaltern Speak?" In *Marxism and the Interpretation of Culture*, edited by Cary Nelson and Lawrence Grossberg, 271–313. Urbana and Chicago: University of Illinois Press.

Stairs, Denis. 2003. "Myth, Morals and Reality in Canadian Foreign Policy." *International Journal* 58, no. 2: 239–56.

Status of Women Canada. 2013a. "Speaking Notes for The Honourable Rona Ambrose, P.C., M.P. Minister of Public Works and Government Services and Minister for Status of Women on the occasion of an announcement of funding to PACT-Ottawa." Status of Women Canada, 24 June. http://www.swc-cfc.gc.ca/med/spe-dis/2013/0624-eng.html.

– 2013b. "Speaking Notes for the Honourable Dr. K. Kellie Leitch, P.C., O.Ont., M.P. Minister of Labour and Minister of Status of Women on the occasion of an announcement of Government of Canada funding to the Students Commission of Canada." Status of Women Canada, 12 September. http://www.swc-cfc.gc.ca/med/spe-dis/2013/0912-eng.html.

– 2014. "Government of Canada Releases Action Plan to Address Family Violence and Violent Crimes against Aboriginal Women and Girls." Status of Women Canada, 15 September. http://www.swc-cfc.gc.ca/med/news-nouvelles/2014/0915-eng.html.

Tiessen, Rebecca. 2015. "Gender Essentialism in Canadian Foreign Aid Commitments to Women, Peace and Security." *International Journal* 70, no. 1: 84–100.

Turenne-Sjolander, Claire. 2013. "Canada and the Afghan 'Other': Identity, Difference, and Foreign Policy." In *Canada in the World: Internationalism in Canadian Foreign Policy*, edited by Heather Smith and Claire Turenne-Sjolander, 238–54. Don Mills, ON: Oxford University Press.

Union of British Columbia Indian Chiefs. 2014. "UBCIC Repudiates Harper Government's View and Supports National Inquiry into Missing and Murdered Indigenous Women." Union of British Columbia Indian Chiefs, 19 December. http://www.ubcic.bc.ca/News_Releases/UBCICNews12191401.html#axzz3QeGORLcA.

United Nations Special Rapporteur on the Rights of Indigenous Peoples. 2013. "Statement upon Conclusion of the Visit to Canada." 15 October. http://unsr.jamesanaya.org/statements/statement-upon-conclusion-of-the-visit-to-canada.

Wherry, Aaron. 2009. "What Was He Talking about When He Talked about Colonialism?" *Maclean's*, 1 October.

Wilmer, Franke. 2009. "Where You Stand Depends on Where You Sit: Beginning at Indigenous-Settler Reconciliation Dialogue." In *Indigenous Diplomacies*, edited by J. Marshall Beier, 187–206. New York: Palgrave Macmillan.

Looking Back and Moving Forward

Stephen Baranyi and Rebecca Tiessen

This book was inspired by many intellectual and practical experiences, yet the catalyst for its emergence occurred at a conference of the Canadian Association for the Study of International Development (CASID) in May 2014. On one panel, several contributors to this volume presented draft papers and received encouraging feedback from participants. At another session on gender and development, Jane Parpart cited her earlier assessment of gender mainstreaming (GM) in the field, renewing the case for using critical analysis to inform the search for change:

> [W]hile some argue for scaling down GM's more transformative goals ... critical development scholarship ... suggests a different approach. These scholars urge mainstream development institutions to move beyond WID [women in development] in order to understand the more fluid, complex nature of gendered practices. They emphasise the critical role of societal forces in both opposition to and support for gender equality, both within mainstream development organisations and broader society. They highlight the need for more research into and publicity about the impact of gendered hierarchies and gendered structural inequality on people around the world. This ambitious agenda will require innovative leadership, openness to a changing world and the ability to learn from others. It will also require practical short-term strategies along with more protracted, subtle efforts towards gender transformation. While

daunting, these approaches do hold out the possibility for creating a
fairer, more equitable gendered world. (Parpart 2014, 392–3)

In this chapter, we take up Parpart's challenge of harnessing critical
scholarship to "understand the more fluid, complex nature of gendered
practices" (2014, 392–3) in Canada's current relations with the world. Then
we look forward at how practice and scholarship could inform each other in
the next phase of efforts to renew "gender+" mainstreaming, notably under
the federal government that emerged from the elections in October 2015.

INCONSISTENCY, INSTRUMENTALIZATION, PATERNALISM, AND ESSENTIALISM

Most chapters in this volume grapple with the difficulty of making sense
of Canada's position on gender equality due to apparent inconsistencies
under successive Harper governments – between discourse, policy, and
programming; across different countries; and over time. On the surface,
the Conservatives' attention to women and girls (notably their commitments to maternal health and ending child, early, and forced marriage)
suggests continuity and even innovation with regard to Canada's international commitments. However, the policy commitments and programs
that emerged from these issue-based foci have not always had gender
equality as a core goal or outcome. Under the Harper Conservatives,
Canadian commitments have often contradicted broader goals of gender
equality and broader human rights.

Guided by different strands of critical or postcolonial theory, the
chapters in this book carefully document such inconsistencies and contradictions. Keast (chapter 2) juxtaposes the Conservatives' high-profile
yet paternalistic framing of maternal, newborn, and child health (MNCH)
with their unwillingness to address gendered power relations in broader
strategies to promote public health. Smith (chapter 11) demonstrates how
the Canadian state continues to present itself as a progressive force in the
world, notably as a leading force in the struggle against early and forced
childhood marriage, while almost ignoring violence against women in
Aboriginal communities in Canada. Epprecht and Brown (chapter 3) contrast minister of foreign affairs John Baird's loud, "homonationalist," and
instrumental defence of lesbian, gay, bisexual, transgender, and intersex
(lgbti) persons' rights with Canada's promotion of economic or security
interests that actually undermine those constituencies' human rights.

The case studies also document inconsistencies at the country level.
Nadia Abu-Zahra and her co-authors (chapter 9) show how Canada's

position in Egypt shifted from supporting official, market-oriented gender mainstreaming for over a decade, to acquiescing to the military coup in 2013 and supporting a regime that brutally supressed the rights of women and other citizens who promoted their gender, labour, and other rights within an Islamic framework. Though less jarring, the study of Canada–Haiti relations by Stephen Baranyi and Shantelle Binette (chapter 10) also documents inconsistencies between the erasure of gender in official Canadian pronouncements, enduring gender-sensitive programming on the ground, and the loss of the Women's Rights Fund, Rights and Democracy, and other instruments that were crucial for promoting gender equality and broader change in Haiti.

Sarah Tuckey's chapter (chapter 8) revisits the Afghanistan case to highlight the instrumentalization of women and girls for military rationales. Others critical feminists analyzed Ottawa's paternalistic discourse of "protecting the weak" and "giving voice to the voiceless" like "vulnerable women and girls" in the post-9/11 era (Turenne-Sjolander and Trevenen 2010, 102–3). Tuckey updates that analysis by looking at the gender dimensions of whole-of-government engagement in Kandahar, as they are reflected in the Harper government's reports to parliament. She extends her postcolonial analysis to expose the Canadian government's framing of Afghan men as barbaric "others."

Kate Grantham (chapter 4) examines the use of essentialist language to suggest that sex trade workers are "in need of saving" – in Canada and around the world. As explained by Epprecht and Brown, such essentialist statements stem from the conservative ideologies that inspire the Conservatives' support base; not surprisingly, we find plenty of evidence to show that they have influenced Canadian public policy at home and abroad. Paula Butler (chapter 6) explores how Plan International's Because I Am a Girl campaign instrumentalizes girls to legitimize other activities, namely to sanction Canada's mining investments in Burkina Faso. In their chapter on Canada–Congo relations, Julia Hartviksen and Rebecca Tiessen (chapter 7) document how essentialist tropes include framing women in mining communities exclusively as victims of sexual violence, failing to take into account their diverse roles as miners and as agents in communities surrounding mining sites. They also show how such failures represent missed opportunities for a more comprehensive assessment of community-based needs, as well as for the promotion of broader human rights on the basis of such comprehensive assessments.

CONTINUITIES, COUNTERPOINTS, AND COMPLEXITY

Several authors in this volume add layers of complexity to this narrative of inconsistencies, instrumentalization, and essentialism. Some chapters show how certain problematic trends predate the election of the Conservatives in 2006. For example, the chapter on Egypt shows how under the Liberals, there was also a tendency to operationalize gender as WID, namely as the promotion of women's access to the fruits of capitalist development. In Afghanistan, as noted by Tuckey, it is the Liberals who initiated Canada's multi-dimensional engagement in 2001; they were also the first Canadian government to use women's rights to justify what the Conservatives eventually called the whole-of-government approach. The strategic point to retain, here, is that the challenges facing a more transformative approach to gender run deeper than the convictions of a particular party; as such, a strategy to renew a gender+ approach must go beyond calling for a new approach by the Liberal government.

Several chapters also document how the Conservatives did not entirely erase gender-sensitive programming in practice, despite their obvious discursive shifts. In their careful analysis of Canadian International Development Agency (CIDA) spending patterns, Liam Swiss and Jessica Barry (chapter 1) show that overall spending on gender decreased slightly after 2006 – and that this cannot be ascribed entirely to changed coding practices. In their case study, Baranyi and Binette demonstrate how at some levels, Canada's spending on gender increased in Haiti, one of Canada's largest development partners. They document innovative attempts to promote gender equality in sectors like public security, democratic governance, and access to justice. Yet they also show how the Conservatives' decision to eliminate programs like those of Rights and Democracy undermined some of their innovations.

Deborah Stienstra's chapter (chapter 5) challenges us to rethink our categories of analysis in this domain. In her discussion of how Canada's policies on gender and disabilities evolved in tandem, she shows how different policy networks promoted "gender first" and "disability first" approaches instead of promoting a truly intersectional approach. One consequence is that disabled persons' organizations and women's organizations who adopted more transformative approaches in their work were unable to make common cause when faced with funding cutbacks under the Conservatives. On that basis, Stienstra calls on practitioners and scholars to move beyond their essentialist biases (gender- or disability-first) and embrace the possibility of a truly intersectional approach to analysis and action.

One of the novel contributions of this volume is the range of explanations offered for the complex patterns of change and continuity in Canadian policies and practices on gender. Swiss and Barry suggest that sustained spending on gender, despite rhetorical shifts under the Conservatives, may be due to pushback from activist officials, buoyed by the OECD Development Assistance Committee's (DAC) and other international norms that Canada had already accepted. Baranyi and Binette document similar dynamics in the Haitian case, adding that Haitian feminists collaborated with Canadian counterparts to save solid gender programming, despite the Conservatives' inclinations. Several thematic chapters document similar trans-institutional and transnational dynamics, yet Epprecht and Brown add new elements in documenting how norm entrepreneurship by ministers like Baird, and the Conservatives' electorally based need to show a more compassionate face, converged with the opportunism of officials to drive the emergence of Conservative positions on lgbti rights or early and forced marriage. Finally, the chapters on mining as well as the case studies on Afghanistan and Egypt remind us that Canada's economic and geopolitical interests also shape the distinctive framing and use of gender in different instances.

Taken together, these chapters offer a fascinating composite explanation of why there has been continuity and change, innovation and loss under Conservative governments since 2006. Indeed, they highlight the complex interplay of several factors:

- Agency and networks of influence: the agency of certain politicians and their relations with particular electoral constituencies; the activism of gender champions within the government bureaucracy; and the agency of feminist or other civil society organizations outside the state – in Canada as well as in partner countries like Haiti or Egypt.
- Norms: changing and enduring domestic attitudes towards gender, charity, protection, etc.; evolving international norms such as OECD DAC guidelines for gender mainstreaming in international development, UN Security Council Resolution 1325, etc.
- Structures: transnational economic, political, and military relations of power that underpin colonial, paternalistic, homophobic, Islamophobic, etc., discourses and practices.

Informed by postcolonial or other critical theories, several authors also remind us how such structures tend to be unstable, leaving openings for creative agency and practical change.

POST-2015 OPTIONS: POLICY AND PRACTICE

Initial signals from the Liberal government elected in October 2015 are encouraging in this regard. The deliberate appointment of women as half of the new Cabinet; the visible inclusion of ministers from other historically marginalized constituencies such as Indigenous peoples, ethnic minorities, and persons with disabilities; and the justification of those decisions "because it's 2015" all point to a possible Canadian realignment with international norms in this and other areas of public policy. The challenge, of course, will be to follow through on those promising signals by renewing gender-based policy and practice from the macro to the micro levels. Most chapters in this volume offer pointed recommendations that the new Canadian government, Parliament, Canadian civil society organizations and their partners in the world could follow to translate the new symbolism into fundamentally different outcomes.

At the policy level, several authors urge the new federal government to unambiguously recommit to gender – rather than adopting a traditional WID approach. That would include reaffirming the relevance of the Gender-Based Analysis Plus (GBA+) framework across all international portfolios, including diplomacy, trade, development, and security. In this regard, it is quite encouraging to note that the mandate letter for the minister of status of women explicitly instructed her to "Work with the Privy Council Office to ensure that a gender-based analysis is applied to proposals before they arrive to Cabinet for decision-making" (Trudeau 2015a, 2).

A recommitment to gender mainstreaming should also include reinvesting in capacity, at Global Affairs Canada (GAC) and in other governmental departments, to ensure the consistent application of a transformative, intersectional approach to gender in thematic and country strategies, in partnerships and projects, as well as in the monitoring and evaluation of those initiatives. Supporting insider activists, instead of pushing them to the margins, could be a crucial part of bringing gender equality and its implementation back to the top of the agenda in Ottawa. Reviving the gender network inside GAC, offering GBA+ training to more officials, and using expert groups more creatively, as well as consistently funding such initiatives, would go some way to using existing "way-finders," as suggested by Stienstra.

Some chapters offer detailed recommendations for how gender mainstreaming could be revitalized in partner countries. For example, the chapter on Haiti shows how a clear commitment to a gender and development (GAD) approach and renewed support to Haiti's Ministry for the Condition of Women and Women's Rights would signal Canada's re-engagement on gender. Targeted funding for women's organizations and other social movements pushing for more inclusive development could enable them to redouble their advocacy to close key law-practice gaps, for example on the implementation of the 30 per cent quota for women in the public service. Canada could enhance training for police, and judicial and health sector personnel responsible for implementing programs against sexual and gender-based violence (SGBV). Ottawa could invest more in women's contributions to food security, rural development, and sustainable mining. It could embrace joint evaluation, by Canadian and Southern partners, of the gendered results of aid, trade, and investment in key partner countries like Haiti. Ensuring that the Mutual Accountability Framework under discussion connects with the Haitian Action Plan for Equality between Women and Men (developed with Canadian support) would be useful in this regard.

Left alone, governments are unlikely to implement such changes across the board. This volume's analyses of the multiple forces and factors underpinning current policies suggest that the re-engagement of parliamentarians and civil society networks is essential to fuel policy and programmatic change. Advocacy groups in Canada have been promoting the need for increased investment in women's groups at home and abroad. More inclusive approaches would enable civil society organizations to support "subaltern voices" in their attempts to influence policy and practice, on the ground and in the North. As noted in several chapters, recognizing the special knowledge of activists (women, labour, disabled persons, lgbti, etc.) and bringing them back into policy and programming could be an important step towards more inclusive results.

These examples remind us that it is not enough to critique existing Canadian practices and call for "rethinking." As suggested in this book, successive Conservative governments returned to a traditional WID approach because of its appeal to key constituencies. Electing a government with a different vision and social base is a necessary but not a sufficient part of a strategy to renew policy and practice in this domain. Revitalizing gender equality networks and efforts within the Canadian state is an essential part of that strategy. It is equally important to fund NGOs that embrace a transformative approach to gender, and support civil society coalitions campaigning for an end to neocolonial relationships in Canada and abroad. Regenerating Canada's links to transnational feminist networks and working with like-minded partners to move beyond the technocratic assumptions embedded in the project of gender mainstreaming is a key component of an intersectional, counter-hegemonic strategy. Taking a much more open approach to access to information would also enable researchers and activists to understand, and contribute to, creative policy and practice in this domain.

RESEARCH AND REFLECTION

In her work, Parpart (2014) suggests that theory and research have important roles to play in fostering "the ability to learn from others" that is central to the "more protracted, subtle efforts towards gender transformation" imagined by her and by many other engaged scholars. To borrow Stienstra's metaphor again, this volume offers "way-finders" to guide scholarly research in this regard. First, it reminds us that there is a need to continue carefully studying changing official discourses around gender, women, and girls. Particularly given the emergence of a new government since the 2015 federal election, critical discourse analysis should remain an essential terrain for policy and more theoretical research.

Second, the chapter by Swiss and Barry underscores the importance of tracking spending by Canada and other OECD governments on gender and on related priorities like the inclusion of persons with disabilities. It also underscores the importance of not accepting OECD DAC (or Canadian) coding practices at face value, but rather of probing those practices and interrogating the official data that flows from standard operating procedures.

Third, several chapters highlight the value of field-based research on how Canada's gendered practices play out in a variety of Southern societies and on a variety of global issues. Looking more carefully at the politics and outcomes of gender mainstreaming in a variety of cases and themes is also essential to generate a broader evidence base to inform practice. In this regard, it is encouraging to note the clear signal, in the mandate letter for the minister of international development, to ensure that "Canada's valuable development focus on Maternal, Newborn and Child Health is driven by evidence and outcomes, not ideology, including closing gaps in reproductive rights and health care for women" (Trudeau 2015b, 2).

Fourth, analysis of Canadian policy and practice is limited by the challenges in accessing information. Requests for information through access to information requests (ATIPs) has become increasingly challenging, and requests have taken longer and longer to acquire. ATIPs were used with some success by some contributors to this volume, notably by Butler. However, Hartviksen and Tiessen experienced greater difficulties in getting information. On several occasions they were asked to remove key words to help with searching for Canadian programs on gender, women, and mining in the DRC. The removal of the term "gender" became essential for getting any information, but even a search for "women" and "mining" in the DRC provided little information about Canada's program priorities and commitments in that context. Researchers should use their professional associations to demand movement towards much more open access to information practices by the new federal government.

It is vital to situate the evolution of Canada's approach to gender mainstreaming in a broader context, by updating comparisons to other OECD DAC donors – from their official policy frames to their spending and coding practices, to their gendered programming across the domains of aid, trade, and investment promotion (Paducel and Salahub 2011). Beyond these obvious reference points, it would be useful to compare Canada and other DAC donors' approaches to gender mainstreaming with those of emerging players in South–South cooperation, such as Brazil, China, and South Africa. To our knowledge, the literature on South–South cooperation has paid scant attention to the gender dimensions of those emerging relationships (Cooper and Flemes 2013; Richey and Ponte 2014); innovation on that aspect would be quite original.

Finally, looking at cases and issues through diverse theoretical lenses is also vital. This volume has showcased a variety of critical theoretical perspectives – from Keast's and Butler's discursively oriented postcolonial lens, to Abu-Zahra et al.'s greater emphasis on material forces and factors such as transnational class interests, to Baranyi and Binette's use of gender-sensitive Coxian theory and Stienstra's more explicit intersectional perspective. We have avoided holding any of these perspectives up as the best theoretical frame. Each one has their merits. We hope that their juxtaposition and their respective insights will inspire other researchers to experiment with different strands of critical theory in order to better reveal the many dimensions of changing gendered practices across borders – and above all to understand how those practices could be subtly transformed, over time, as suggested by Parpart.

A puzzle that merits deeper exploration, from diverse theoretical perspectives, is the issue of when incremental reform intersects with more transformative change. At what points could the renewed application of GBA+ by the Canadian government contribute significantly to intersectional transformation? What conditions would need to align in global campaigns or in particular partner countries for emancipatory changes to gel? Alternately, when might GBA+ be just the latest in a series of technocratic fixes that simply updates hegemonic forms of patriarchy and neocolonial domination?

REFERENCES

Cooper, Andrew, and Daniel Flemes. 2013. "Foreign Policy Strategies of Emerging Powers in a Multipolar World: An Introductory Review." *Third World Quarterly* 34, no. 6: 943–62.

Paducel, Anca, and Jennifer Salahub. 2011. "Gender Equality and Fragile States Policies and Programming: A Comparative Study of the OECD/DAC and Six OECD Donors." Working paper, North-South Institute, Ottawa, ON.

Parpart, Jane. 2014. "Exploring the Transformative Potential of Gender Mainstreaming in International Development Institutions." *Journal of International Development* 26, no. 3: 382–95.

Richey, Lisa Ann, and Stefano Ponte. 2014. "New Actors and Alliances in Development." *Third World Quarterly* 35, no. 1: 1–21.

Trudeau, Justin. 2015a. "Minister of Status of Women Mandate Letter." Office of the Prime Minister. Accessed 17 November 2015. http://pm.gc.ca/eng/minister-status-women-mandate-letter.

– 2015b. "Minister of International Development and La Francophonie Mandate Letter." Office of the Prime Minister. Accessed 17 November 2015. http://pm.gc.ca/eng/minister-international-development-and-la-francophonie-mandate-letter.

Turenne-Sjolander, Claire, and Kathryn Trevenen. 2010. "Constructing Canadian Foreign Policy: Myths of Good International Citizens, Protectors and the War in Afghanistan." In *Canadian Foreign Policy in Critical Perspective*, edited by J. Marshall Beier and Lana Wylie, 44–57. Toronto: Oxford University Press.

Contributors

NADIA ABU-ZAHRA is an associate professor at the University of Ottawa in the School of International Development and Global Studies. Her publications include the book *Unfree in Palestine: Registration, Documentation and Movement Restriction*, co-authored with Adah Kay.

STEPHEN BARANYI is an associate professor at the University of Ottawa. His recent works on the (gendered) challenges of international engagement in fragile and conflict-affected states have been published in *Conflict, Development and Security*, *Journal of Peacebuilding and Development*, *Canadian Journal of Development Studies*, and elsewhere.

JESSICA BARRY holds a BA in political science and sociology from Memorial University and an MA in sociology from McGill University. She is currently based in St John's, and her research interests include Canadian foreign aid policy, the non-profit sector, and gender and development.

SHANTELLE BINETTE holds a BA in international development and globalization from the University of Ottawa. She is currently working with the Mennonite Central Committee as a network capacity builder for MCC partner organizations in Rwanda. Her research interests focus on agriculture, gender, and development in Sub-Saharan Africa.

NICOLE BRANDT completed her MA in international development and gender studies at the University of Ottawa in 2016 and currently works in the development research division at Global Affairs Canada. In 2012, Nicole was an intern with Egypt's International Economic Forum in Cairo.

STEPHEN BROWN is a professor of political science at the University of Ottawa. He is the author of numerous publications on foreign aid, as well as editor of *Struggling for Effectiveness: CIDA and Canadian Foreign Aid* (2012) and co-editor of *Rethinking Canadian Aid* (2014). He has also published widely on democratization and political violence in Sub-Saharan Africa.

PAULA BUTLER is an assistant professor in the Canadian Studies Department at Trent University. She holds BA degrees in education and social science, as well as an MA from Carleton University. Her current research is on the gender dimensions of Canadian state, NGO, and private-sector involvement in Africa, particularly in extractive industries. Her recent publications include her book *Colonial Extractions: Race and Canadian Mining in Contemporary Africa.*

RUBY DAGHER is a PhD candidate at the School of Public Policy and Administration at Carleton University. She also teaches international development courses at Carleton University and the University of Ottawa. Prior to teaching, Ruby worked at the Canadian International Development Agency from 2006 until 2012.

MARC EPPRECHT is a professor and head of the Department of Global Development Studies at Queen's University. He has published extensively on the history of gender and sexuality in Africa including *Hungochani: The History of Dissident Sexuality in Southern Africa* (winner of the Joel Gregory prize for the best book on Africa published in Canada, 2004/2005).

KATE GRANTHAM is a post-doctoral fellow at the University of Ottawa. She completed her PhD in women's studies and feminist research at the University of Western Ontario in 2016. Her field of research includes gender equality and international development, exploring feminist and anti-colonial perspectives on global development, project management, and program evaluation.

JULIA HARTVIKSEN is a PhD candidate at the London School of Economics. She completed her MA degree at Queen's University in Kingston focusing on femicide in Guatemala.

JULIA KEAST holds an MA in globalization and international development, with a specialization in women's studies, from the University of Ottawa. Julia's research interests include gender and development, with a particular focus on maternal and child health.

HEATHER SMITH is a professor in the Department of International Studies, and the director of the Centre for Teaching, Learning and Technology at the University of Northern British Columbia. Her many publications on Canadian foreign policy, gender, climate changes, and diplomacy include the co-edited collection *Canada in the World: Internationalism in Canadian Foreign Policy*.

DEBORAH STIENSTRA is a professor in disability studies at the University of Manitoba, and the author of *About Canada: Disability Rights* (2012). Her areas of research are disability policy, gender, intersectionality, disability, and global development. She previously held the Nancy's Chair in Women's Studies at Mount Saint Vincent University (2013 to 2015).

KHALID SULIMAN is a postdoctoral fellow at the School of International Development and Global Studies at the University of Ottawa. He has a PhD in political sociology and a master's degree in women studies. Dr Suliman has extensive expertise in the Middle East; his research interests cover a wide spectrum of issues from women studies to democracy and human rights.

LIAM SWISS is associate professor in the Department of Sociology at Memorial University, where he teaches courses on development, gender, globalization, and research methods. His research includes the sociology of development and globalization, especially in relation to foreign aid. One of his most recent publications is "Gendered Leadership: The Effects of Female Development Agency Leaders on Foreign Aid Spending" in *Sociological Forum*.

REBECCA TIESSEN is associate professor in the School of International Development and Global Studies at the University of Ottawa. Her research is concerned with the role of Canada and Canadians in the world and her publications address Canadian foreign aid, particularly as it pertains to gender (in)equality, (in)security, and development.

SARAH TUCKEY is a PhD candidate in public administration at the University of Ottawa. She is completing her dissertation on the gendered whole-of-government approach in Afghanistan, under the direction of Dr Claire Turenne Sjolander. In May of 2014, she co-authored a report with Rebecca Tiessen for the Women, Peace and Security Network – Canada titled "Worth the Wait? Reflections on Canada's National Action Plan and Reports on Women, Peace and Security."

Index